By the Breath of Their Mouths

SUNY series in Italian/American Culture

Fred L. Gardaphe, editor

By the Breath of Their Mouths

NARRATIVES OF RESISTANCE
IN ITALIAN AMERICA

∽

Mary Jo Bona

April 22, 2010

To Maria —

*To the sisterhood of
all Italian American
women + men !*

yours gratefully,

Mary Jo Bona

SUNY PRESS

Cover art: "Basement Reverie" painting by Christine Perri.
Textured woodgrain background © Selahattin Bayram/iStockphoto.com

Published by State University of New York Press, Albany

© 2010 State University of New York

For information, contact State University of New York Press, Albany, NY
www.sunypress.edu

Production by Diane Ganeles
Marketing by Anne M. Valentine

Library of Congress Cataloging-in-Publication Data

Bona, Mary Jo.
    By the breath of their mouths : narratives of resistance in Italian America /
Mary Jo Bona.
         p. cm. — (Suny Press series in Italian/American culture)
    Includes bibliographical references and index.
    ISBN 978-1-4384-2995-3 (hardcover : alk. paper) —
    ISBN 978-1-4384-2996-0 (pbk. : alk. paper)
  1. American literature—Italian American authors—History and criticism.
2. Italian Americans in literature.   3. Italian Americans—Intellectual life.
I. Title.
    PS153.I8B65 2010
    810.9'851—dc22

                                                                    2009017905

10 9 8 7 6 5 4 3 2 1

To the memory of my beloved mother and twin brother

By the word of Yahweh the heavens were made,
Their whole array by the breath of his mouth.

—Psalms 33:6

Contents

꒜

Acknowledgments

In the mid-1980s when I began my foray into the literature of Italian America, it felt like walking into the barren spaces of the great Northwest, despite the fact that most of the narratives were urban-centered, cluttered, and noisy. Yet, as Gretel Ehrlich has so eloquently written of the solace of open spaces, I felt a peaceful coming-home among works that were largely unknown in the literary academy. Over the past twenty-five years, I and other scholars have attempted to make visible those writers of Italian America, traversing a literary terrain that is as wide ranging and complex as the villages, cities, and countries about which they write. This land is their land, too, inclusive of the literary landscape, *finalmente*.

Many colleagues have instrumentally shaped my thinking about the literature of Italian America, offering useful suggestions on organizational and theoretical approaches to interpret this body of work. I should like to thank Nancy Workman for discussions on the initial framework of the book, with especial emphasis on the function texts serve to create a public identity through a sustained and constantly evolving community of voices. Sandra M. Gilbert's early support of my work when the field was still in its infancy further provided invaluable scholarly validation. Scholars of Italian America have persuasively explored theoretical avenues that helped me think more deeply about the vernacular origins of written expression and from them I have drawn enormous sustenance throughout the writing process: William Boelhower, Dawn Esposito, Thomas Ferraro, Fred L. Gardaphe, Edvige Giunta, Josephine Gattuso Hendin, Mary Ann Mannino, Martino Marazzi, Chris Messenger, Louise Napolitano, Mimi Pipino, Roseanne Lucia Quinn, John Paul Russo, Anthony J. Tamburri, and Robert Viscusi. With deepest gratitude I thank in particular Josephine Gattuso Hendin—*la mia collega preferita*—for her careful and unstinting work as a reader of drafts of every chapter of this book. Josephine's contribution to this book is inestimable; however, any limitations in thought or deficiencies in execution are purely my own.

I would also like to thank my wonderful colleague at Stony Brook University, Andrea Fedi, for his useful advice on my translations of Italian proverbs and phrases and for reading the entire manuscript with a fine-tooth comb. Developing an academic field of Italian American literature also could not be sustained without a generation of graduate students whose work has both inspired and influenced my own. In particular, I thank those students, former and present, with whom I have worked closely: Patrizia Benolich, Kristin Girard, Jessica Maucione, Michele Fazio, Jennifer DiGregorio Kightlinger, and JoAnne Ruvoli Gruba. Chapter 4 of this book on Guido D'Agostino proved to be a joy to write collaboratively with JoAnne Ruvoli Gruba; together, we mined the archives of this largely unknown writer, and made connections with relatives still living in the rural Pennsylvania so ably memorialized in D'Agostino's final novel.

A much-needed and appreciated sabbatical at Stony Brook University enabled the completion of this book. And to those academic organizations that have allowed me to share largely untested ideas and arguments on literary Italian America I thank the following: the American Italian Historical Association, MELUS (the association of Multiethnic Literature of the United States), the Modern Language Association, the Center for Italian Studies at Stony Brook University, the Calandra Institute at City University of New York, the New York Council for the Humanities Speakers Program, and the National Italian American Foundation, which supported my work as a professor at Stony Brook University, enabling more penetrating analyses of Italian American culture.

A preliminary version of chapter 1 was published in *LIT: Literature, Interpretation, Theory* 13 (2002), 201–223. A portion of chapter 2 appeared in Joseph A. Varacalli et al. eds., *Models and Images of Catholicism in Italian Americana: Academy and Society* (Stony Brook: Forum Italicum, 2002), 162–174. Portions of chapter 6 first appeared in Elizabeth Messina, ed., *In Our Own Voices: Multidisciplinary Perspectives on Italian and Italian American Women* (Boca Raton: Bordighera, 2003), 145–160. In very different and condensed form, an earlier incarnation of my analyses of postmodern texts featured in chapter 7 first appeared in Philip V. Cannistraro and Gerald Meyer, eds., *The Lost World of Italian American Radicalism: Politics, Labor, and Culture* (Westport: Praeger, 2003), 287–299.

I heartily thank James Peltz at State University of New York Press, and Fred Gardaphe, SUNY series editor of Italian/American Culture, whose initial enthusiasm for and ongoing support of this project made its completion a joy to experience. For their professionalism during the shepherding process of this manuscript, I thank Diane Ganeles, my production editor at SUNY Press, A&B Typesetters and Editorial Services, and Carol Inskip, who compiled the index.

Finally, I thank my partner, Judith Pfenninger, whose support of my writing life has made all the difference.

Introduction

❧

In the beginning there are listeners and the storyteller; in the end there are the stories.

—Gioia Timpanelli, "Stories and Storytelling"

U.S. writers of Italian America give the lie to the idea represented by the code of *omertà*, with its injunction of silence, of keeping family matters and personal secrets private. Writers of Italian America cleverly employ that ancient rule of silence in their stories, refusing as their ancestors before them to comply with authorities represented by church and state. Translating into literature the orally transmitted tales of ancestral migrations to America, these writers tell and retell narratives of diaspora. Their immigrating forbears needn't have unloosed their tongues, for they carried with them to America verbal baggage much heavier than their trunks and valises. Perhaps in nineteenth-century villages Italians could abide a *proverbio* like this: "a buon intenditor poche parole," literally translated as "for one who understands few words suffice," wise words for those surrounded by family members to the fourth degree. But from the urban squalor of large industrialized cities to the bleak impoverishment of rural landscapes, Italian immigrants suffered both invisibility because they were not valued and hostility because they were considered an economic threat to native-born American workers. To fend off cultural annihilation, exacerbated by the xenophobia that met the second great migration, Italian immigrants managed to transmit their stories. This verbal act allowed old-world migrants to align themselves not only with their ancestors but also with their children, who inherited tales of wonder and *furbizia* (cunning).

1

Children of immigrants, caught between two languages, found creative ways to engage their parents' storytelling traditions with those tales they learned on American streets and in public schools. The literature that has emerged from over a century's worth of publications, from newspapers to novels, has revealed a culture in which verbal communication often exceeded frugal silence. The stories by U.S. writers of Italian America register the stress exerted by larger cultural forces that made few words a liability. Acts of writing ensured Italian Americans of at least two things: that they would not forget an ancestral heritage replete with communal and inclusive storytelling traditions; and that assimilation in America could be deflected by recording and establishing resistant voices in narratives expressive of folk practices and family cultures. Italian Americans continue in the millennium to create plots that resist the homogenizing influences of suburban culture, spurning regulating effects of assimilation in favor of cultural preservation and identification with other minority groups.

The stories produced by Italian Americans are acts of survival. They are also a gesture of homage bestowed on oral traditions that continue to exert literary influence on their works. Through narrative, Italian American storytellers have constructed another space to revise hierarchical discourse, to give voice to those without power to shape perception or invent alternative worlds. A folktale collected and retold by Italo Calvino (in *Italian Folktales*) paradigmatically exemplifies one of the kinds of stories to which Italian American writers have been attracted. In "Catherine, Sly Country Lass," Calvino retells the story of peasant victory over the nobility. Though I mean no disservice by condensing the tale, I offer only the briefest summary here. Catherine, the poor daughter of a farmer, manages through wit and perseverance to pass the outlandish tests devised by the king, who eventually makes her his wife. When she has the temerity to oppose her husband's poor judgment in his court of justice, the king decides to send her back to her father's farm, but tells her she may take the thing she likes most of all with her. At a farewell feast, Catherine gets her husband drunk and the king wakes up in her family's hovel. In a verbal sleight of hand, Catherine tells the king she took him home because she likes him best of all. They reconcile, return to the palace, and live happily ever after. Catherine's voice and judgment thereafter become central to the King's court of justice. As she is wiser than her husband, her acts of justice will predominate (261–266). The story's themes are fundamental to peasant morality: an insistence on equality and justice, despite arbitrary division of human beings; the desire to determine one's own fate, despite adversity; and, the belief that liberation can only be achieved, as Calvino relates, "if we liberate other people, for this is the sine qua non of one's own liberation" (xix).

From Rosa Cassettari's orally transmitted stories of nineteenth-century Italy to Toni Ardizzone's framed novel *In the Garden of Papa Santuzzu* told by another storytelling Rosa published at the end of the twentieth century, voices of community forge a literature through experiences of past oppression. A cursory peak at four narratives spanning the twentieth century reveals a representation of dominated peoples; the sound of their voices become standard cultural practice in resisting oppressions of poverty and silence within the narrative works of Italian America. Marie Hall Ets's *Rosa: The Life of an Italian Immigrant*, Jerre Mangione's *Mount Allegro*, Kenny Marotta's "Her Sister," and Tony Ardizzone's *In the Garden of Papa Santuzzu* are four such narratives that engage folkloric traditions in order to resist oppressions of class, gender, and ethnicity. These works represent only a small portion of the oeuvre of Italian American writings that incorporate folk wisdom and practice as measures of resistance.

An expert teller of tales, Rosa Cassettari achieves enough fluency in the powerful English tongue to transmit her life stories to Marie Hall Ets, an act of self-authorizing wholly unavailable to her in rural northern Italy. At the same time, Rosa performed her stories in front of Chicago audiences and gained local fame there as a wondrous teller of tales. She managed to turn the practice of verbal expression into a gesture of individuation but more importantly into an activity of community building with other immigrant women. In word and deed, Rosa embodies a folk ethos.

Within his memoir of Sicilian American life in the early twentieth century, second-generation writer Jerre Mangione explores the folk wisdom of his elders by giving them center stage in *Mount Allegro*. The stories they tell comprise the meat of the memoir. Told by the dramatic Uncle Nino, one such tale, a favorite of mine, is plucked from the fields of folklore, featuring the rich and handsome Baron Albertini and the peasant girl, Annichia, to whom he takes a fancy. Demonstrating all the qualities of the wily country lass, Annichia learns from her mother how to turn the tables on the nobility and maintain her self-respect (and her marriage) through cunning and resilience. Mangione humorously manages to couch a scathing commentary on the abuses of the noble class, his yarn spinning reversing the assumption about superiority based on social class and breeding. The weaver's daughter, Annichia, succeeds quite literally in tying the hands of the upper classes while teaching her husband a valuable lesson about the superiority of the lower classes. She spins a delectable yarn.

In the latter part of the twentieth century, Kenny Marotta and Tony Ardizzone further explore the uses of folk wisdom and individual voices that focus on the persuasive nature of storytelling in the service of assuring gender equality. Both writers employ features of folk practice in an effort to examine how female characters resist patriarchal behavior that would otherwise prevent them from liberating themselves from old-world ideology. Marotta's short story, "Her Sister," recapitulates Calvino's and Mangione's tales, but does so with a focus on feminism that deepens an understanding of how the female Italian protagonist plots her way to America. A tale that turns the Cinderella motif westward, "Her Sister" incorporates fairy-tale features (with a mother-in-law as the evil but furtive stepmother) along with religious customs, including the procession of the local Madonna, to reinforce women's determination to cast off allegiance to rigid caste restrictions. By the means available to her, the female protagonist ensnares her resistant husband, assuring her migration to America.

Giuseppe Pitrè, a Sicilian physician, was an indefatigable assembler of Italian folklore in the nineteenth century and Tony Ardizzone's *In the Garden of Papa Santuzzu* might be considered the twentieth-century fictional counterpart of Pitrè's collection. Laden with folklore, Ardizzone liberally sprinkles his multivoiced narrative with songs, rhymes, tests of faith and love, Giufà tales, medieval arguments, beast fables, stories of saints, cross-dressing escapades, and tales of family life in Sicily and America. In his desire to tell stories of nineteenth-century Italy after the Risorgimento, and twentieth-century stories about the lived experiences of Sicilian immigrants, Ardizzone engages the voices of the peasantry. Rosa, the storyteller of the frame and caesurae, weaves the thread and ties the knot as each Santuzzu family member spins his or her yarn. Addressed to a listening audience, and to her grandchildren, Rosa verbally and literally takes readers on a Sicilian pilgrimage:

> The rope is *la famigghia*, see? Each of us is a thread, wound up
>   in it. Before you were born, a rope connected me to you.
>   One still does, *figghiu miu*.
> *Stronger than twine or the truest of leather,*
> *Family binds us forever together.* (22)

Throughout his novel, Ardizzone engages voices from the subaltern to the scholarly. Demonstrating an abiding respect toward canonical Italian and Anglo literary traditions, Ardizzone fictionalizes Italian American history, making visible *la storia* of an island culture, Sicilia, kicked by the boot of peninsular Italy, whose thieving government made nationalism feel "like just another absentee landlord. . . . Since the beginning of time Sicilia has been dominated by many, conquered by none" (37). Published twenty years after Helen Barolini's 1979 triptych *Umbertina*, Ardizzone's *In the Garden of Papa Santuzzu* emulates Barolini's role of the *cantastorie* (folktale singer). Barolini's song of the Risorgimento spans eighty years, and two centuries and continents. From the socialist shoemaker Domenica Sacca to the goat girl Umbertina, whose status as an outsider in America sadly increases with time, Barolini embraces the vital importance of her actual grandmother's oral traditions by dedicating her novel to her mother, "the storyteller," who made the creation of *Umbertina* possible.

What these stories share is the continuous importance of voice— libratory, healing, resistant—within the mouths of ordinary folk whose thoughts and beliefs were neither heard nor respected much in the old or the new worlds. The storytellers briefly mentioned in this introduction value the importance of communal voices that, when read together, offer a compelling understanding of these writers' artistic focus on Italian America. Their works, like the others I discuss in individual chapters, participate in incorporating vernacular origins and multiple voices that, taken collectively, begin to form an artistic community that we might call Italian America. The maintenance of particular voices—those that focus on justice and faith, for example—into third and fourth generational writing, create a public, literary identity for Italian Americans. Such works continue to focus on the cleverness of a burdened people, whose cultural practices become verbal and behavioral markers that guide and define their lives and those following them. The voices of Italian America become a collectivity of sound, illuminating distinctive communities that offer reflections, for example, on loss and dispersal without succumbing to narratives of nostalgia. The writers regularly rely on voices of community emerging from folk, familial, neighborly, and spiritual sources. While the development of individual voices within these narratives is also demonstrated, writers of Italian America recognize many other determining factors that complicate subjectivity, including influences of region, class, gender, and personal history, to name just a few.

Grounded on the work of many scholars, my analysis aims to be faithful to the generous cross-referencing I have observed also in the primary works, with an especial nod to Tony Ardizzone, who paid handsome homage to all the writers and many of the scholars I reference in my own study. Cultural studies ranging from specific histories of migration and ethnographic interpretations of ethnic enclaves to surveys on broad topics as religion and death illuminate the ways Italian Americans thought and lived, informing my interpretations of how they are represented in narratives. Grounded also on recent theories of autobiography and narrative, the chapters that follow examine how dominated peoples through both oral and written storytelling traditions redefine marginality. Postcolonial and folk discourses have in common emancipative and appropriative uses of voice, and intersect throughout my discussion. David Palumbo-Liu's use of the term "critical multiculturalism" also helps me to examine how the literature of Italian America resists dominant literary and historical expression, creating and inventing alternative meanings and spaces. Profoundly important are also those scholars of Italian American culture who have instrumentally shaped an academic discourse and discipline on Italian America to which I am gratefully indebted.

Chapter 1 relates folklore, storytelling, and the subaltern status of the population through a discussion of the voice of justice that is central to several narratives of Italian America. As such, this chapter lays much of the theoretical and historical groundwork that supports the subsequent chapters. The voices of law and the supposed institutions of justice in the public sphere fail dramatically to support immigrant Italians, thus inviting a careful reinterpretation of Italian American noncompliance with public authorities.

Closely intertwined with the voice of justice is the voice of faith, the topic of chapter 2. The role of Catholicism in relation to folk tradition for Italian Americans remains essential to an understanding of devotional practices considered aberrant to the Catholic hierarchy, especially in America. Women writers in particular have recorded with ambivalence their resistance to an institutionalized Catholicism that defines them as inherently inferior and requires their subordination. From Catholic girl stories to full-length travel narratives such as Susan Caperna Lloyd's *No Pictures in My Grave*, women authors confess plenty about their resistance to formal Catholicism alongside their emphatic attraction to the folk religious beliefs of their ancestors.

Chapters 3 and 4 examine individual authors and how the voices of the storyteller(s) complicate ideas about subjectivity, authorship, and community. From transcription through publication, Rosa Cassettari's life story is mediated by the hand of Marie Hall Ets, a social worker turned successful children's book author. Rosa's role as an expert story-teller and Marie Hall Ets's recognition of the narrative potential of such an awe-inspiring tale affected its construction, but did not underesti-mate the vitality of oral cultural features that informed Rosa's voice. A voice that is both libratory and performative, Rosa tells stories with a purpose: to liberate and heal others, including Marie Hall Ets, who was grieving the death of her husband when Rosa first met her.

The novels of Guido D'Agostino are the focus of chapter 4, intro-ducing the voice of land and, in particular, the village ancestor who speaks for the people about establishing a vital relationship in rural America for immigrant Italians. The voice of the village ancestor, pragmatic and liber-ating, is expressed by various representatives in each of his four novels. The title of D'Agostino's first novel, *Olives on the Apple Tree*, encapsulates the author's artistic vision in its activity of grafting, uniting homeland Italy with American soil. A potent agricultural metaphor, the procedure of grafting unites a detached bud or shoot with a growing plant. For D'Agostino such a metaphor also projects his belief in fruitful transplan-tation of immigrant Italians through assimilation. Through the voices of his cultural spokesmen, D'Agostino portrays the necessity to assimilate to an idea of America that has as its core the sanctification of nature in the Emersonian sense as a symbol of the divine. Like Willa Cather before him, D'Agostino portrays hardworking immigrants who embrace nature's severity and bounty. Through the voice of nature, D'Agostino manages throughout his works to join Italian rural antecedents with American land-scapes. In his farmer's hands, early twentieth-century Greenwich Village never looked so green, and Italian transplants in urban settings also form part of the ongoing dialectic D'Agostino establishes between rural and urban settings.

Linked by their focus on female individuation, chapters 5 and 6 ex-plore in fiction, memoir, and poetry those voices of ancestry, genealogical and literary, to which several writers of Italian America make thematic and stylistic connections. Comparative literary methodology invites cross-cultural conversation, initiating a dialogue in chapter 5 between two historically segregated groups: Italian Americans and African Americans. The vernacular voices heard in the debut novels of Tina De Rosa and Paule Marshall illuminate the folkloric voices of female ancestors, whose storytelling traditions direct the artistic trajectories of young protagonists. Because of the voices of their history-singing guides, these aspiring women recognize that the language they inherit is not only a refuge, but also a requirement of their collective identities, which they offer as testimonials of their ethnic cultures to American readers.

Chapter 6 extends the conversation discussed in the previous chapter on powerful female precursors, but in the genres of memoir and poetry, examining recognizable links between older and younger generations of writers. Through autobiographical writing, memoirists Louise DeSalvo and Mary Cappello and poets Maria Mazziotti Gillan and Rose Romano give cultural visibility to Italian American histories regarding social justice, cultural loss, and familial conflict. Their voices, at times colloquial and deliberately nonliterary, recall Rosa Cassettari's orally told stories, and allow these women writers to create habitable spaces for their voices to breathe within reconstituted Italian American households.

In the epigraph to this introduction, Gioia Timpanelli explains that in the end there are the stories, which function as gestures of continuity after the storytellers are long gone. The voice of mortality merges with the voice of continuity in chapter 7 as I examine how stories of death are told from the mouths of many Italian American writers, from Garibaldi Lapolla's *The Grand Gennaro* to Carole Maso's *The Art Lover*. Deathbed scenes, widows' lamentations, and textual endings illuminate some of the operative ways in which U.S. writers of Italian America explore bereavement. Writing beyond a conventional belief in a Catholic afterlife, these writers incorporate oral traditions that merge with illness narratives, offering culturally elaborate stories about lessons in survival and moral value.

Continuity also marks the focus of chapter 8 with a discussion of the processes involved in shaping a body of U.S. Italian American writing. In this concluding chapter, the voice of revival is paramount. A case study from the 1930s in particular exemplifies the processes set in place by the academy and by other forces that both increased the value of Italian American writers and also continued to obscure their presence on American literary soil. I then explore the intersection between poststructural methodologies and critical pedagogical theories, which open up Italian American texts to counterreadings that reinstate the value of ethnic realism vis-à-vis experimentalism. Italian American writing, like other ethnic writing, uses linguistic codes that reveal their resistance toward a dominant culture that would keep them quiet. Scholars of Italian America have been largely instrumental in analyzing the ways in which writers have maintained textual and linguistic resistance through stylistic technique and coded language. Through their inventive use of vernacular expressions, U.S. writers of Italian America continue to express the importance of voice in an effort to preserve the authenticity of their culture, to insist that nothing goes away if we continue to talk our truths.

The voices of Italian America run deeply along my pulse. So in a final introductory comment, I express profound gratitude toward those writers from the past and present, whose narratives made my words possible. My *de profundis* thankfulness is a psalm of joy not sorrow, recognizing the potential of words to liberate, heal, transform, and teach. To the writers of Italian America I dedicate this book.

1

Justice/Giustizia

჻

Private Justice and the Folkloric Community in the World of Italian Americans

Genuinely just, she gave audiences to everyone, listening to the rich with her right ear (the ear of intellect) and to the poor with her left ear (the ear of the heart).

—Lucia Chiavola Birnbaum, *Black Madonnas*

In marked contrast to mainstream conceptions of justice, Italian American writers have conceptualized justice in their works through a folkloric view of the world, which includes storytelling, ritualized gatherings, and proverbial beliefs. Institutions of business, official forms of Catholicism, the legal system represented by the police force, and the public school are modified in distinct ways by the cultural behaviors enacted in Italian American families. Writers such as Jerre Mangione, Mari Tomasi, and Pietro di Donato—early practitioners of Italian American themes—engage plots that *silence* official discourses of power, replacing institutional forms of the law with behavioral rules distinct to the ethnic communities they create. Within the fictionalized enclaves of later writers such as Mario Puzo's Hell's Kitchen in New York City

11

and Tina De Rosa's Little Italy on the West Side of Chicago, adult characters transmit codes of honor and loyalty reflective of an enclosed world that is often antithetical to the established customs and laws of the majority culture. When Italian American writers return to the world of their ancestors—as Tony Ardizzone does in his portrayal of Sicilian migration, for example, the yearning to tell the characters' stories is linked to a folkloric worldview that challenges official power and replaces it with subaltern forms of resistance.

Each of the works I consider in this chapter develops plots that revolve around Italians' vexed adjustment in America. Stories of justice and equality emerge from experiences of oppression in the country of descent: Italy. Disenfranchised as they were in their homeland villages, Italian immigrants continued to experience firsthand the sting of oppression in the American public sphere. Despite their poverty and powerlessness, the Italian American characters portrayed by such authors as di Donato, Tomasi, Mangione, Puzo, De Rosa, and Ardizzone do not relinquish their cultural ethos but instead obscure institutional forms of control and authority represented in their works to varying degrees by economic, religious, and legal institutions. While less didactic in tone than Guido D'Agostino's *Olives on the Apple Tree*, the works echo in sentiment the voice of the village ancestor, Marco, who laments the "end of life for the free man with his own ideas in Italy" (162). Unlike D'Agostino's Marco, who longs for rural life unencumbered by long hours spent working in factories, the characters portrayed by the authors listed above remain rooted to urban settings. Former peasants from the *Mezzogiorno*, areas south and east of Rome, the lion's share of immigrant Italians were tied to industrial wage labor.

The cultural world of Italian Americans portrayed by the aforementioned authors requires a brief examination of the historical reasons underlying their exodus *and* the reasons informing their retention of conceptions of private justice in America. Factors such as family economy, the phenomenon of *campanilismo*, anticlericalism, concepts of honor and justice and the oral traditions that exemplified them, contributed to a communal ethos that Italian immigrants at times fiercely maintained in America. Not only had the children of immigrant parents, but also successive generations, absorbed such Italian beliefs. For example, Pietro di Donato, the eldest son of Abruzzese parents, published *Christ in Concrete* in 1939, but it bears a striking resemblance in cultural perspective to the grandchild of Neapolitan immigrants, Tina De Rosa, whose novel *Paper Fish* was published forty-one years later in

1980. Both authors write autobiographical novels set in ethnic enclaves in which a southern Italian view of the world is transmitted through ritual and storytelling. In doing so, each author also approaches mainstream conceptions of justice with a wary eye.

The violent history of invasion and foreign rule of southern Italy and Sicily necessitated the heightened value Italians placed on private justice and the institution of the family. While the authors under consideration descended from families that migrated from both northern and southern Italy, and Sicily, each area nurtured a sense of family cohesion that was intensified by centuries of misrule and exploitation by landowners. Despite rebellion from the landless classes in southern Italy, most *contadini* (peasants) or *campagnoli* (country folk) had to develop their own sense of culture based on family solidarity. Intense family cohesion in southern Italy parallels the family dynamic portrayed by the six authors whose works exemplify self-protective family reliance: "Family solidarity was the basic code of such family life and defiance of it was something akin to a cardinal sin. . . . The family solidarity was manifested by uniformity of behavior, adherence to family tradition, and, also, a community of economic interests" (Covello 150–151).

Those Italians of the Mezzogiorno suffered for centuries from foreign despots including Greeks, Romans, Arabs, Normans, Spanish, and various northern Italian powers. Influenced by four hundred years of Spanish and Bourbon domination, the nineteenth-century inhabitants of south Italy and Sicily remained rooted to a medieval world. As Jerre Mangione and Ben Morreale relate in their five-century history of Italian American experience, in 1860 "only 2.5 percent of the population could speak Italian; the rest spoke the dialects of their regions. There was no unifying language" (*La Storia* 34). By 1861, however, Italy became a nation and Victor Emmanuel II was proclaimed king of Italy. To complete the Risorgimento (the years between 1815 and 1870 in which Italy achieved nationhood and became modernized), the Papal States were annexed by Italy in 1870.

The south suffered the most from the northern Italian government's exorbitant taxing. Combined with extreme poverty, widespread malaria, and outbreaks of cholera, southern inhabitants began a mass exodus after the unification. If conditions proved insufferable enough, southern Italians and Sicilians gave the lie to the notion that they were harnessed by a heritage of fatalism. A single malediction was said to have ranged from the Alps to Sicily, encapsulating the people's attitude toward the northern Italian government: *governo ladro* (thief of a government): "But it was in the *Mezzogiorno*, where poverty and misgovernment were most deeply experienced, that the government was most despised and defied. By the time the southerners began leaving their native provinces in great numbers, their distrust of all politicians had festered into a deep-seated conviction, which they carried with them wherever they settled" (Mangione and Morreale 57).

Tony Ardizzone echoes the very lines of Mangione and Morreale's history in the voice of the firstborn son, Gaetanu, who avoids conscription by the northern Italian government by emigrating, understanding that the domination of his Sicilian homeland is symbolized by the north's ubiquitous taxing: "The thief of a government was stealing everything. . . . I didn't think I owed this Italia seven years of my life. Italia seemed like just another absentee landlord to me, the soldiers her uniformed *gabellotti* [overseers]" (*In the Garden of Papa Santuzzu* 37). Feelings of distrust toward outsiders inform the responses of immigrants *and* their children in the authors' works discussed below. In particular, an abiding distrust of American mainstream institutions such as the public school and the Catholic Church served to strengthen Italians' belief in social justice as a private matter best negotiated within families.

The very topography of Italy reinforced an emphasis on settling matters privately. Isolationism between regions further exacerbated lack of trust not only between landless peasants and their landlords, but also between people from different villages. One of the most important features of Italy's geographical identity has been its regionalism. Identified with their villages and with the cultural mores and dialects specific to them, nineteenth-century Italians felt intense regional loyalty. As one Italian immigrant says, "'I say Italy; but for me, as for the others, Italy is the little village where I was raised'" (qtd. in Williams 17). Turn-of-the-century Italian immigrants all felt this way regarding their regional identities in their various villages. Certainly this phenomenon of campanilismo (village-mindedness) increased the Italians' tendency to depend solely on the institution of the extended family to promulgate the rules distinct to their codes of behavior. Literally translated from the Italian, campanilismo means parochialism, but this definition does not offer a picture of the isolating topography and lack of mobility that made Italy a country of regions. Campanilismo is a figure of speech that describes the unity of those who live within the sound of the church tower, *il campanile*. In the Mezzogiorno, the sound of the bell "was a physical fact defining the perceptible social boundary of a southern Italian's world" (Alba 23). And those boundaries, albeit precise and protective, both narrowed and stabilized the Italian's perceptions of family and outsiders, localizing the core value of trust within families only.

When Italians were forced to emigrate from their small villages to American towns and cities, they tended to settle as other ethnic groups did in neighborhoods near immigrants from the same region or village. Perhaps as an attempt to recapture the small-town clustering of their native villages, Italians managed to recreate in their enclaves old-world customs in a new-world setting—often in urban settings driven by the forces of capitalism. Early in immigrant history, Neapolitans, Sicilians, Apulians, and Calabrians initially settled on separate streets from each other, maintaining their regional distinctions in urban America.[1] While such distinctions remained fervent in the immigrants' minds, native-born Americans had a tendency of "lumping together . . . all Italians," regardless of their regional affiliations (Williams 13).

Oblivious to the old-world geography of Italians, the host country characterized southern Italian and Sicilian immigrants in virulently negative ways, associating them with mendicancy and crime. Two fin de siècle writers, the urban photographer Jacob Riis, and the highly educated adult émigré, Luigi Donato Ventura, present nineteenth-century Italian immigrants on the Lower East Side in antipodal ways, with Riis's interpretation of the Italian immigrant in *How the Other Half Lives* as "lighthearted and, if his fur is not stroked in the wrong way, inoffensive as a child" (47), possessing much more cultural visibility than Ventura's avuncular treatment of a twelve-year-old boot black in the 1885 *Peppino*, originally published in French. Needless to say, the phenomenon of campanilismo survived the transatlantic crossing, providing the immigrants with buffer zones called "Little Italys" that sprung up across America. Each of the works under consideration is set in a neighborhood in which distinct regional customs rather than institutional structures such as the Catholic Church and the public school form an integral part of the community's daily life.

A high percentage of Italian immigrants came from a nonreading, poorly educated background, which was further intensified by their distrust of those literate authorities who ruled their lives—the landowners and priests.[2] Helen Barolini reiterated in her introduction to *The Dream Book* the ignoble fact that most southern Italian immigrants were "not wanted or valued in their land of origin," and immigrated to America "without a literary tradition" (4). Oral storytelling traditions, proverbs, and aphorisms were nonetheless part and parcel of a verbal art at the disposal of immigrant Italians, often guiding their thoughts and influencing their responses to foreign and frightening American traditions. For example, many immigrant parents treated the American institution of public schooling with intense suspicion, believing that *la legge è fatta contro la famiglia* (the law is made against the family). Describing the literary heritage of those impoverished peasants who made their way to the new world, Barolini further explains that the Italian immigrants' deep distrust of education stems from their awareness that such knowledge is a fundamental attribute "of the very classes who have exploited you and your kind for as long as memory carries" (*The Dream Book* 4).

Sensing the magical power of books, the illiterate mother of Puzo's *The Fortunate Pilgrim* nevertheless believes that her children are numbing their brains with foolishness by reading (206). Yet Puzo's matriarch, Lucia Santa, does not forbid her daughter's activity of devouring books "long into the night," and sanctions her marriage to a Jew, Norman Bergeron, whose only vice is related to his literacy and not the cultural stereotype of materiality commonly attributed to his ethnicity: With no judgment except deadpan realism, Lucia Santa thinks: "'And she, my most intelligent child, picked for a husband the only Jew who does not know how to make money'" (*The Fortunate Pilgrim* 206, 208). In contrast, Lucia Santa characterizes Norman's activity of carrying a book under his arm wherever he goes, and writing poetry in Yiddish as a "stigma," the singular form of "stigmata." Norman's intermarriage is anathema to his family, rendering him a wounded outcast who is nonetheless accepted, books in tow, by the Christian, albeit anticlerical, Italian immigrant mother, Lucia Santa.[3]

Italian immigrants during the second Great Migration may have come from a nonreading environment, but they arrived in America with their oral traditions, their proverbial culture, and their sense of private justice intact. Additionally, many children of immigrants attended public school, learned English, and were often compelled by American culture to reconsider their family's traditions and conventions. In an effort to guard the family from continuing encroachments from the outside world, immigrant Italians could be vigilant about maintaining their cultural authority. As in Italy, Italians in America continued to regard the family institution as *sopra a tutto*, "above all."[4] Each of the narratives under consideration depicts an Italian worldview that highlights an alternative form of justice in a complicated and at times failed effort to sustain family cohesion.

The southern Italians' subscription to omertà, the cultural injunction to be silent, may have originated in the Sicilian countryside where bands of brigands fought against unjust governmental authorities. Such conditions gave rise to a "morality in which justice was regarded as a private matter, not a public one. This . . . is the real meaning of the code of *omertà*, the so-called code of silence" (Alba 37). Ensuring that the family institution remained impenetrable to strangers outside the family, southern Italians adopted a kind of furberia (shrewdness) as a cultural response in a society that had to develop its own means of social control in the absence of state support. In a preindustrial, land-based economy in which resources were scarce and the concept of honor was "thought of as the ideology of a property holding group which struggles to define, enlarge, and protect its patrimony in a competitive arena," Italians knew that only the institution of the family could maintain its integrity (Schneider 3).

Each of the authors portray characters who adopt strategies of furberia in order to reinforce an Italian worldview for the next generation and to survive a hostile reception in America. Each narrative examines in various ways how institutional laws and customs of the majority culture are muted in favor of portraying an autonomous world of Italian Americans, who maintain a folkloric, anticlerical, and often communal view of their world. To be sure, the children of immigrants experience a duality of consciousness emerging from their positions as second-generation Italian Americans. Their ethnic identities are at times experienced as vexatious and unresolved. Nonetheless, the authors of these narratives ultimately reinforce the necessity of a sense of selfhood, that is, as Michael M. J. Fischer wisely explained, "a deeply rooted component of identity, . . . something reinvented and reinterpreted in each generation" (195).[5]

Though certainly not the earliest narrative of immigrant life, Pietro di Donato's 1939 *Christ in Concrete* has been considered prototypical because "the signs of *Italianità* are foregrounded in this novel as in no other writing yet produced by an Italian American" (Gardaphé, *Italian Signs* 68).[6] Fred Gardaphé in fact understates the case since di Donato's incorporation of italianità is hyberbolic, producing a kind of manic linguistic style that by turns beguiles and overwhelms with its excess. *Christ in Concrete* at the same time emphasizes the necessity of maintaining a folkloric worldview comprised of ritualized gatherings and a protective immigrant community in order to guard against the inhospitable American institutions of business and religion. After the untimely death of his immigrant father, Pietro di Donato went to work as a bricklayer at the age of twelve. As di Donato explained in an interview, "A twelve year old boy that weighs 72 pounds begins to compete with men whose fingers are thicker than his wrists. But I did it because of this incredible faith, this absolutely unilateral faith" (von Huene-Greenberg 43).

In 1937 di Donato published an autobiographical short story in *Esquire* magazine, which was expanded into the best-selling novel *Christ in Concrete*.[7] This novel depicts the lives of Italian immigrants who worked in the construction trades on the Lower East Side of New York City before the Great Depression. The immigrant father, Geremio, is a master bricklayer who is killed at a construction site on Good Friday at the age of thirty-six, leaving a wife and eight children to fend for themselves in a heartless world uninterested in this family's plight. Literally buried in concrete, this father dies as a result of shoddy construction materials and a greedy company that reduces immigrant workers to disposable tools. The State Bureaucracy agrees with the thieving construction company, which lies about the cause of Geremio's death, thus relieving themselves of any responsibility for the conditions under which immigrants work. The construction boss portrays Italian workers as childlike and unable to control themselves without constant supervision, echoing the negative stereotypes pervasive in the early twentieth century about several immigrant groups and blacks in America. The protagonist and eldest child, Paul, is prematurely catapulted out of his boy's world and forced into the male world of bricklaying.

The mother in *Christ in Concrete*, Annunziata, is unable to protect her son from his growing realization that his family is being destroyed in America.[8] Despite Geremio's wholesale adoption of the American dream—"all my kids must be boys so that they someday will be big American builders"—his twenty years on the job as a "nation builder" is shattered in a matter of seconds (*Christ in Concrete* 7). Annunziata's unwavering devotion to the Christian belief in the sacrifice of Jesus cannot shield her son from his ultimate realization that Christ saves neither his father nor his godfather, who are victims of gruesome and horrifying deaths from construction accidents. *Christ in Concrete* details Paul's quest to find justice and salvation in a world that destroys immigrant workers. By rejecting both his mother's religious convictions—which would keep him passive in the face of injustice—and his father's American dream of accruing wealth and position—Paul manages to survive but not without overwhelming turmoil and burdensome adult responsibility.

Di Donato may describe his final novel, *American Gospels*, as his "revenge on society," his "answer to all the nonsense of authority and of Church" (von Huene-Greenberg 33),[9] but he began his career by jettisoning traditional authorities through his narrative style and his depiction of Paul's encounter with the Catholic Church in *Christ in Concrete*. Di Donato proffers an alternative view of justice throughout his first novel by critiquing American capitalism and Catholicism as ruinous institutions for the poor and uneducated classes. When asked how he arrived at the style of *Christ in Concrete*, di Donato answered "by virtue of not having an education, I can be direct and literal and translate literally" (von Huene-Greenberg 36). The first part of di Donato's response, however, belies his youthful bookishness. In fact, di Donato earlier boasted that he was "'probably the only apprentice-bricklayer in the United States who [came] to the job site with *The Divine Comedy*, *The Golden Bough* and Lampriere's classical dictionary'" under his arm (qtd. in Viscusi, "*De Vulgari*" 37). Notwithstanding, di Donato refused to adopt "the prescribed literary posture of the day in which the writer would efface his or her own class or ethnic identity in order to speak in the sonorous voice of 'the people'" (Casciato 70). Instead, di Donato created a novel that resounds like a "ventriloquial voice" (Orsini 192), incorporating the sounds of several linguistic registers.

One example of di Donato's translation of the Italian into English occurs when Paul's Uncle Luigi is preparing to leave the hospital where he was taken after a construction accident left him an amputee:

Luigi dressed himself carefully. He sat on the bed, and nurse helped him. In his breast was a newness and a sublimation. Today Annunziata and Paul were coming for him. Home would he go now. . . . There is motion without. God's Christians are ever in the streets. . . . But where belong I rightfully? . . . I man disjoined? Air of Job will no longer nourish me. (*Christ in Concrete* 144, 146)

In this passage, di Donato relinquishes his tendency to fracture conventional grammar, elide diction, and shift anarchically from broken English to Italian epithets. This passage instead highlights Luigi's chastened interior reflections, translated literally from Italian to English. As Robert Viscusi reminds us, the word "Christians" is a standard synecdoche for "human beings" in Italian, not in English ("*De Vulgari*" 26), and thus must be kept as such in Luigi's thoughts. As he does throughout the novel, di Donato deletes the definite article before "Job," reinforcing both its ubiquitous presence in the lives of laborers—"Job loomed up damp, shivery gray. Its giant members waiting"—and its predatory and coercive history (8).[10] Back in the tenements, Luigi describes to his *paesani* the phantom pain he feels in his amputated leg: "'Pins and needles—needles and pins. I am now a Christian thermometer of meat and bone'" (149).

Luigi does not allegorize his condition; rather, he literally describes the grotesque consequences of his labor.

Throughout the novel, di Donato makes a parallel between Christ and the immigrant laborer, reinforcing their connection through the use of literal and metaphorical crucifixion scenes. In an unedited version of his speech to the Third American Writers' Congress, di Donato explains that he did not write *Christ in Concrete* to "be mystic and revel in self-mortification. I was trying to use this idea of Christianity, to get an 'in' there, using the idea of Christ" (qtd. in Casciato 70). But just as capitalism destroys workers' lives, Christianity paralyzes the poor. After his father dies, Paul tries to sustain his mother's fervent piety, and like the allegorical Christian, he attempts to take a journey toward salvation through a belief in Christ's intercession. Ultimately Paul abandons his quest, insisting on justice and salvation in his present world.

Pietro di Donato reinforces the ethnocentrism of those authorities to which Paul initially goes in order to relieve his family's suffering. While it is true that di Donato's narrative is filled with dreamscapes and nightmare visions, none is more frightening than when Paul walks the streets of New York City in broad daylight. Paul has not yet imbibed the fundamental distrust of authorities that his Italian community harbors and thus approaches the public world represented by the police station and the Catholic Church as a naïve initiate. Both places diminish him. Trying to locate the whereabouts of his father whose body has not yet been retrieved from the accident, Paul hears the cruel words of a police officer who affirms his father's death: "'the wop is under the wrappin' paper out in the courtyard!'" (*Christ in Concrete* 26)

Paul's encounter with the Catholic Church is equally crushing. It will compel him to adopt a belief in private justice alongside American self-reliance, which will be his salvation. In this way, Paul will develop the same skepticism and lack of reverence that southern Italians held for the institution of the Catholic Church.[11] On his quest to seek help for his starving family, Paul enters Saint Prisca's where he observes the sexton snuff out the candles near the altar. The symbolic significance of that gesture anticipates Paul's disappointment. Yet, he continues his quest by seeking help at the rectory. On his way there, he meets the local midwife, Dame Katarina, whose guidance proves immeasurable. Scolding the domestic who initially refuses Paul's entry, the Italian midwife acts as an intercessor, pushing open the door of the rectory. The linguistic registers Katarina uses comprise literal translation into English, broken English, and Italian epithet: "She shook a violent finger . . . and yelled, 'Whattsa matta you! Whattsa matta you bestia! Animale vecchia [*sic*] catch Padre John subito! . . . Antique rotted son of a whore! His decayed stomach is full!'" (57). Father John refuses to support or guide Paul—he revealingly utters "'I have nothing to do with the Charities'" (*Christ in Concrete* 59).

Taking leave of the rectory with strawberry shortcake to bring home to his starving mother and seven siblings, Paul asks a question to which he inchoately knows the answer: "Will they ever protect me and mine?" Anticipating that Paul will be cruelly rejected by the Church, Katarina gives him her only loaf of bread after his meeting with Father John. Her advice to Paul is salvific: rely solely on the self in service to the family: "'From the sweat of our blood comes the bread in the mouth'" (60). Through the language of aphorism, Dame Katerina offers bread to Paul's family and yeast to his soul.

In time, Paul realizes that he must adopt a philosophy of self-reliance in order to find justice in his present life, even if it necessitates rejecting the old-world piety of his mother, Annunziata, who becomes both the quintessential *mater dolorosa* and a Christ figure by the novel's end. Her death at the novel's conclusion, as Gardaphé has explained, "frees her son from the burden of his Catholic past" (*Italian Signs* 72). Di Donato's *Christ in Concrete* establishes in writing a behavioral tradition already ensconced in Italian culture of wariness toward outside authorities. The justice that the novel's protagonist seeks stems from recognition that shrewdness and independence will save his family. Throughout *Christ in Concrete*, di Donato emphasizes the egregious failure of mainstream authorities, represented by majority bureaucracies, including official Catholicism. Moral fineness is linked to the impoverished immigrants themselves, who, though starving, give bread to their suffering neighbors.

Localization of trust and a critique of business practices and traditional Catholicism also appear in Mari Tomasi's 1949 novel *Like Lesser Gods*. This novel capitalizes on the importance of furbizia to the daily lives of northern Italian immigrants in the stonecutting industry of Granitetown, a fictionalized Barre, Vermont. Like di Donato, Tomasi began her novel with a short story called "Stone," first published in the Spring 1942 issue of *Common Ground*.[12] Tomasi memorializes the Italian story in Barre, Vermont, by portraying the painful and premature deaths of immigrant stoneworkers. Calling it the tragedy of "dusty lungs, or stonecutter's T.B.," Tomasi explains that before the installation of dust-removing equipment (made a law in 1937), the death toll from tuberculo-silicosis was extremely high ("The Italian Story in Vermont" 82). Killed by their art, an entire generation of immigrant stoneworkers, Rudolph Vecoli explains, "fell victim to the insidious dust in the sheds," and thereby broke with the tradition of handing down the skills of stonework to their sons ("Finding, and Losing" 8). Like the precarious work sites where construction workers toiled in di Donato's urban world, the stonecutters of small-town Vermont in Tomasi's novel create "their own figurative and literal tombstones" by working in closed sheds and inhaling the noxious dust particles from the granite they work (Rosa 73).[13]

Like Lesser Gods silences official discourses of power inventively. Implicitly, Tomasi critiques mainstream justice by portraying young immigrant men dying prematurely as a result of indifferent business practices. Working the granite is the sole source of income for several ethnic groups in Granitetown (Irish, Welsh, Scottish, French, Spanish, and Italian), but Tomasi recreates this world by giving it a distinctively Italian appearance through her subscription to campanilismo. In her detailing the ways in which an ethnic group can reorient itself to a hostile culture, Tomasi submerges conflict in order to maximize the lyrical quality of the folkloric Italian community she portrays.

Tomasi suppresses tensions between employers and immigrant workers in order to accommodate a view of Italians who maintain old-world customs *and* assimilate American ways. Tomasi explains in her nonfiction essay on Italian stonecutters in Vermont that at the beginning of the twentieth century the city of Barre was one of America's "hotbeds of anarchism," but she suppresses this history in her fictional work *Like Lesser Gods* ("The Italian Story in Vermont" 81). Helen Barolini earlier found such an omission a problem, along with other curtailments distinct to the stonecutters' stories: "the bitter strikes; the antagonism between Scotch and the Italian settlers in Barre; . . . the sense of discrimination experienced by Italian immigrants, . . . the reasons for their shame and guilt during the Second World War when Italy was an enemy ("The Case of Mari Tomasi" 181).

Tomasi's suppression of radical politics is also deliberate. Twenty-four years after Tomasi's death in 1965 (she was born in 1907), Rudolph Vecoli interviewed various octogenarians of Barre about Luigi Galleani, the leading anarchist in their city at the beginning of the century.[14] Not one old-time resident of Barre claimed to have heard of him! Attributing the erasure of a socially significant personality to "historical amnesia," Vecoli offers an interpretation of such silence that sheds light on Tomasi's avoidance of controversy in her creative work. With respect to the radical antecedents of many Italian immigrant families, Vecoli explains, "the second generation [of which Tomasi is a member] had the difficult task of reconciling its Old World traditions with the new ways of America. That task was made more difficult if one's parents were identified as 'reds' as well as foreigners" ("Finding, and Losing" 8). Leftist ideologies, including socialism and anarchism, were labeled un-American during the Red scares at the beginning of the twentieth century and were further punished through incarceration, beatings, ostracism, and deportation. Such episodes punctuating the history of Barre, Vermont, "inspired feelings of pain, fear, and shame," in its adult residents, who sheltered their children from their "painful and shameful parental memories" (Vecoli, "Finding, and Losing" 8).

An expert on the quarrying industry in Barre, Tomasi was no stranger to the influences of radicalism, including her mention of Emma Goldman's lecture appearance in Barre in 1906 ("The Italian Story" 81). Tomasi's deliberate suppression results from her refusal to reinforce a stereotype of Italians as inherently violent, already in currency by 1880. Thus, while historically it is true that some northern Italian stonecutters fought and died for their politics, the granite industry by far outdid that number by killing an entire generation of young men. Tomasi's *Like Lesser Gods* therefore functions as her version of a corrective palimpsest: she writes over the historical reality of Luigi Galleani (who lived and worked at 29 Pleasant Street with his wife and children) by setting her story of the history of one northern Italian stonecutting family, the Dallis, on the same street— Pastinetti Place, which makes its nomenclatural shift to Pleasant Street in the second part of the novel. Setting her novel in two phases of stonecutting social history, 1924 and 1941, Tomasi avoids having to treat the anarchist movement, which died out after Galleani's departure in 1909, *and* World War II, when fascist Italy was an enemy.

Old-world Italian culture pervades instead in this Vermont setting, thus contributing to Tomasi's lyrical style. Gardens are covered with grapevines, dandelion greens make up a salad, men search the Vermont fields for mushrooms, homemade wine and grappa appear on kitchen tables, and women make ravioli and homemade sauce for spaghetti. The Italian enclave enjoys festive picnics (with polenta and homemade wine) and accordion music fills the air. Italians play briscola and bocce, reside on streets with Italian names, subscribe to two or three Italian newspapers, and sing Italian folk songs. The enclosed world Tomasi creates neither excludes other ethnic groups (particularly the Irish and the Scottish), nor avoids the painful suffering of stoneworkers, including Pietro Dalli, who dies from the stone dust, but manages to live to see each of his children grown. Tomasi memorializes the lives of stonecutters, who are "like lesser gods," taking up where God left off. As Pietro explains to Gino, his doctor, and the son of a stonecutter who died young from tuberculo-silicosis, "'We take up the chisel, we carve the name, we make a memory of that life'" (*Like Lesser Gods* 166).

Another strategy Tomasi uses to cope with the fact that an entire generation of immigrant stoneworkers died at the height of their artisanal powers is to create a character in the community who functions as a kind of cantastorie, a teller of stories. This character, Michele Tiffone, or Mister Tiff as he is popularly called by the children, comes to America already having established his life in northern Italy as a schoolteacher. At fifty-five, Tiffone has no illusions about his role in America; he immediately resumes his function as a storyteller by becoming the expert voice on quarrying in Vermont.[15] In this way, Tiffone also has a hand in memorializing the stoneworkers' artistry by connecting their history back to the "ragged bondmen in Egypt" and the great Carrara quarries of Italy (*Like Lesser Gods* 48, 30). Not surprisingly, Tomasi's creation of Michele Tiffone parallels Guido D'Agostino's portrayal of the hobo-philosopher, Marco, in *Olives on the Apple Tree*; both men lament the fascist ideology epitomized by Mussolini and migrate to America in protest against Italian politics. In their respective communities in America, both men continue to resist rule-mongers, employing a combination of inherent shrewdness and advanced education to guide other characters less fortunate.

Michele Tiffone's storytelling buttresses the Dalli children by extending the genealogy of their father's craft and by creating a mythical Italy, which is powerful and good. That the maestro teaches stories of the saints to all children of the community, including the Protestant Scottish son of the quarry owners, reinforces the necessity Tomasi feels for maintaining and transmitting Italian cultural heritage. Mari Tomasi's brand of Catholicism is anticlerical but with a gentler tone than Pietro di Donato's. The town's Catholic priest is neither cruel nor insensitive, but like Father John of *Christ in Concrete*, he is ineffectual. In contrast, Michele Tiffone functions as a spiritual agent for each member of the Dalli family; like his namesake, St. Michael, he brandishes a sword on behalf of the family and the community with a sensible and shrewd understanding of good. Tiffone's intercession on behalf of the Dalli's eldest daughter, Petra, enables her to make the right decision about a marriage partner. Named after her father, Petra demonstrates her strength in adulthood by aiding her father during his illness. Perplexed about her feelings toward Denny Douglas, her childhood friend and the Scottish son of the quarry owners, Petra represses her passional feelings, aware of their differences in religion and class. In the meantime, Petra incurs the ire of her mother when she resorts to accepting drives from the town bootlegger, Tip Gioffi. Demonstrating wiliness as always, Tiffone manages to intercede on Petra's behalf in a brilliant though subtle way when he casually mentions to Petra a fatal bootlegging road trip involving Gioffi to Canada, in which one of the passengers was thrown from the speeding car and later died from untreated wounds. After relating the story, Tiffone observes "a quiet thoughtfulness . . . graven on Petra's face" (*Like Lesser Gods* 215). Toward the conclusion of the novel, Petra makes the decision to marry Denny Douglas, who agrees to convert to Catholicism on behalf of their relationship.

Michele Tiffone mediates between old and new worlds, functioning to alleviate conflict between distinct social groups: the bosses and the workers; immigrant parents and rebellious second-generation children; Anglo-Americans and immigrant Italians. He achieves the status of community adviser through his allegiance to furberia and his recognition that justice is achieved through private means. Throughout the narrative, in fact, Tiffone is unafraid to use benevolent bribery to effect change for the good of his community. He succeeds in resolving the political chief's illicit love affair through bribery. As a result, he ensures that the chief's illegitimate daughter is supported fiscally, thus allowing Amerigo Dalli, the youngest of the Dalli children, to establish a relationship with her that is acceptable to his Italian family. While di Donato outright rejects the American dream in *Christ in Concrete*, Tomasi redefines it by believing that the strength of Italian culture will indelibly affect core Anglo-American values. Tomasi supports her contention by developing a mythical figure like Michele Tiffone, who reinforces the necessity of using private means to achieve personal justice. A fighting angel on earth, Tiffone models the capacity of finding joy in small things and applauding the capacity of his people to endure hardship.

Like Mari Tomasi, Jerre Mangione portrays American values through the lens of italianità in his memoir, *Mount Allegro*. Portraying an enclosed world of Sicilian Americans, Mangione examines how his community manages to use stories to understand concepts of justice in Italy and America. In a 1983 interview, Mangione admitted that, forty years later, he could not write about his hometown in Rochester the same way after having done extensive research: "I was shocked by what had happened to Italian-Americans, by the kind of hostility they had to endure" (Mulas 74). In fact, when Mangione's memoir was published in 1942, "aliens of enemy nationality in the country," including Italians, were being gathered and put in internment camps (Mangione, *An Ethnic* 320). Sheltered like Tomasi was by relatives who did not discuss outside antagonisms with children, Mangione only later discovered that his "relatives' insistence on being themselves . . . was their way of coping with an alien world that was generally hostile" (*An Ethnic* 15). Mangione's father was so sensitive about the honor of Sicilians that when he learned "that Boy Scouts carry knives, the weapon that was commonly associated with Sicilian homicide, he forbade his sons to become Scouts" (*An Ethnic* 16).[16]

According to William Boelhower, *Mount Allegro* achieves classic status because of Mangione's "detailed presentation of the Sicilian Way as an alternative model of man and society, . . . a combative response to the American Way and an overturning of it" (182). Like Mari Tomasi's fictional portrayal of Barre, Vermont, Mangione's Rochester neighborhood comprises several ethnic groups, but he primarily focuses on his large extended family in Mount Allegro, celebrating the spirit of campanilismo. Boelhower's description of the tripartite structural tempo of the work reveals one of the principal strategies Mangione employs to attenuate official voices of power and capitalize on the multiplicity of voices emanating from his many relatives. The first chapter focuses on the school-aged narrator, who wonders whether he is American or Sicilian. Chapters 2 through 10 offer a response to the young boy's perplexity. As the learning subject, the narrator's voice is silenced; his developing self is subservient to the multiple voices of his loquacious, storytelling family members. In chapters 11 though 14, "sharp focus [returns] once again on the now mature protagonist," who prepares to take leave of Mount Allegro by attending college and traveling to Sicily (187).[17]

Firmly ensconced inside the world of his Sicilian relatives, the narrator silently listens and learns. While he is from the second-generation and educated in English, Mangione's intimate recollection of his ancestors' Sicilian folktales nonetheless is as detailed and finely tuned as Rosa Cassettari's stories told to Marie Hall Ets, which I further examine in chapter 3. Prominently informing Mangione's home life in America is the relationship established between storytelling and issues of social justice. Many stories that his relatives tell revolve around the peasant's search for justice in an unjust world. They spin yarns about nineteenth-century Sicily and the lives of immigrants in early twentieth-century America; the stories in both settings demonstrate the wit and shrewdness of peasants, a frequently highlighted theme in folk stories (Birnbaum 47).[18] The narrator's relatives tell stories of peasant victories over the wealthy and powerful, emphasizing the fact that the poor were traditionally treated unfairly by the law and were led historically to consider justice a private matter.

The sundry tales told by Mangione's extended family function to teach the younger generation an ethic based on the importance of unwritten over written laws: "ahead of written laws they placed the unwritten laws that had been passed down to them for centuries" (*Mount Allegro* 191). Boelhower notes that "*Mount Allegro* is [the narrator's] school," introducing the youthful Mangione to the "'un-American culture' of his family and relatives" (187). Sensitive to the stereotypical connection native-born Americans persistently made between Sicilians and crime, Mangione tackles that issue in his chapter entitled "Uncle Nino and the Underworld," wryly noting that, "in the sphere of crime, my relatives were a distinct disappointment" (*Mount Allegro* 181). Overturning such a connection, Mangione focuses on the theme of justice, including several stories about the triumph of personal justice by the peasant class in Sicily despite the odds against them receiving fair treatment. His Uncle Nino relates more than one tale of a crime avenged through personal means, telling the story, for example, of Giovanni, the son of poor caretakers—Salvatore and Grazia—who learns that his father was murdered by the lascivious wealthy landowner, who vainly tried to seduce his resistant mother.

With a bread knife, Giovanni kills Don Alfonso Cavallo, the murderous landlord. An old woman witnesses the attack. Giovanni is arrested for the crime. The peasant community sympathizes with him: "Giovanni had done the honorable thing in avenging the murder of his father. Law or no law, they declared that any Sicilian worth his salt would have done the same under the circumstances" (*Mount Allegro* 199). With the help of his mother, a wily old judge, a clever lawyer, and a brilliant plan (Giovanni sneaks out of prison and brandishes a knife in front of the old woman), Giovanni is freed at "one of the briefest murder trials on record in Caltanissetta" (*Mount Allegro* 203). As opposed to what happens to immigrant Italians in America, in this story and several like it, "the peasants win and are thus able to achieve dignity, or at least a status in which they are respected" (Boelhower 211). Throughout the memoir, Mangione submerges his narrative self in deference to the folkloric voices of his extended family, who teach the young boy through example how to become a storyteller and to insist on the dignity of humble origins. Through his amiable use of humor, Mangione also distances himself from family origins, but maintains a belief in the efficacy of folk wisdom to resist oppressions of poverty and silence. *Mount Allegro* remains the most loquacious of memoirs in Italian America.

Family cohesion also takes precedence over the legal system represented by civil authorities in both Mario Puzo's *The Fortunate Pilgrim* (1964) and Tina De Rosa's *Paper Fish* (1980). Puzo and De Rosa create narratives that reinforce the phenomenon of private justice within urban enclaves of Italian Americans. While both novels offer an implicit critique of the ineffectiveness of outside authorities, their focus remains unwaveringly on the Little Italys that inform the development of second-generation children of Italian Americans. Puzo establishes a parallel between the Neapolitan ghetto of Hell's Kitchen and the village squares of the old country: "each tenement was a village square; each had its group of women, all in black, . . . recall[ing] ancient history, argu[ing] morals and social law" (6). One of these women from the mountain village of southern Italy is Lucia Santa Angeluzzi-Corbo. She is the undisputed matriarch and immigrant heroine of Puzo's novel *The Fortunate Pilgrim*.[19]

Burying her first husband and institutionalizing the second, Lucia Santa's primary goal is to bring her six children into "adulthood and freedom" (*The Fortunate Pilgrim* 8). Illiterate and poor, as were so many women of her station, Lucia Santa bravely manages to sustain the family during the Depression of the 1930s, using her instinct for survival to guide her. Lucia Santa's only weakness is her "lack of natural cunning and shrewdness which does so much more for people than virtue," but her strength lay in her wariness toward life and in her recognition, after her second marriage to a mentally unstable man, that she would "never let the world deceive her again" (*The Fortunate Pilgrim* 8, 11). Her word is the only official power that the children heed. Lucia Santa recognizes that defiance against family solidarity is akin to a cardinal sin and will not be borne.

Lucia Santa maintains the honor of her family through her Italian understanding of private justice. Her eldest son has dared to besmirch the family's honor by his absence at Sunday dinner, by his consorting with neighborhood bootleggers, and by his bedding the wife of the bootlegging couple. When he takes to sleeping away from his mother's house, Lucia Santa, "her word of decision," says *basta*. Like an Italian woman warrior, Lucia Santa dresses in her Sunday best—black dress, black hat, and black veil—and walks to the bootleggers' residence to do battle, hoping to catch "the enemy, the Le Cinglatas, unaware" (*The Fortunate Pilgrim* 64). Finding her son at their place, Lucia Santa issues a series of Italian maledictions at him—"*Animale! Bestia! Sfachim!* [sfaccim] *Figlio di puttana!*" In contrast to the harangue delivered to her son, Lucia Santa politely and cleverly threatens the bootleggers with the law—"selling wine and whiskey is one thing, but here in America they protect children" (*The Fortunate Pilgrim* 71). Feeling only contempt for these people, Lucia Santa manages to maintain *bella figura* throughout the uncomfortable encounter. She reestablishes her matriarchal authority by regaining control of her son. He returns to sleep at the family home.

Toward the end of the novel, Lucia Santa knows but does not accept the fact that her firstborn son, Lorenzo, has finally succumbed to the lures of criminality, the only one of her six children to do so. Unlike Puzo's romanticizing of the mafia don in *The Godfather, The Fortunate Pilgrim* is seen through the eyes of the pragmatist, Lucia Santa. This immigrant mother has succeeded virtuously in building a world for her family; "she had been its monolith" (*The Fortunate Pilgrim* 201). Reflecting on her forty-year struggle in the tenements of Hell's Kitchen, Lucia Santa realizes that Lorenzo's life of criminality does not represent Italian manhood or reflect justice, despite the fact that his ill-gotten money partly allows the family to move to Long Island: "No. Lorenzo would never be a real man as the peasant fathers on Tenth Avenue were real men, as her father in Italy was a real man: husbands, protectors of children, makers of bread, creators of their own world, accepters of life and fate who let themselves be turned into stones to provide the rock on which their family stood" (*The Fortunate Pilgrim* 225–226). Lucia Santa distinguishes between private justice in which the family controls values and establishes laws and a parasitic existence, in which thievery and extortion are employed by despoiling others. Lucia Santa's dismissal of her firstborn is also a dismissal of an unofficial form of authority that she finds morally repugnant.

Creating a rather hermetically sealed setting in *Paper Fish*, Tina De Rosa quietly though determinedly dismisses culturally anemic mainstream mores through a wholesale submerging of institutional forms of control and authority. A folkloric worldview is contained in the stories told by the paternal grandmother, whose interpretation of her extended family's suffering controls the movement of the novel and influences the development of her granddaughter, Carmolina. Despite De Rosa's fulsome efforts to protect the virtues of italianità from outside hostilities, she nonetheless represents the father figure working in a job not unusual for second-generation white ethnics, as a police officer, a role traditionally perceived by Italians as antithetical to their understanding of private justice. De Rosa yet manages to maintain a strict adherence to an Italian view of private justice and family honor by continuing to focus her novel on the enclosed enclave of immigrant Italians, shrewdly setting the novel during the summer months, when American children have vacation from public school.

De Rosa also rejects a straightforward chronological ordering of her material in an effort to represent the inward states of consciousness of four generations of one family both in Italy and America. Doing this allows De Rosa to close off the Bellacasa family and the surrounding neighborhood from harmful voices of prejudice in much the same manner as Mangione's memoir. At the same time, De Rosa's choice of style affords her the opportunity to tell several intersecting stories: about terrible suffering, about wholesale dismantling of an Italian American community, about the development of a young girl, Carmolina Bellacasa, into an adulthood marked by the stories of her paternal grandmother and, finally, about the silence of her older sister, whose illness represents the painful lives of De Rosa's wounded characters.

Just as Mari Tomasi created a godparent figure to function as the local cantastorie and as a mediator for second-generation Italian Americans, Tina De Rosa created Grandma Doria to succor her granddaughter and to guide her into an artistic future. Doria's final injunction to Carmolina—"'Now it you turn. You keep the fire inside you'"— reveals the importance De Rosa places on elders who function as guides for future generations (*Paper Fish* 116). Through stories and proverbs, Grandma Doria directs and strengthens the development of the third generation represented by Carmolina, who will choose not fully to Americanize, despite her public schooling and the American emphasis on autonomy and accrual of possessions.

A lesson in artistry that De Rosa personally received was from her police officer father, fictionalized as Marco Bellacasa in *Paper Fish*. Admitting that writers receive their inheritances unexpectedly, De Rosa has written that "this man taught his daughter to be an artist. . . . This lesson was nothing that my father said; it was hidden in who he was. . . . His attitude toward work has eventually, slowly become mine" ("My Father's Lesson" 15). Like Puzo's ideal of manhood voiced by Lucia Santa, De Rosa espouses an Italian-descended model of manhood in *Paper Fish*. Marco Bellacasa is cut from the same peasant cloth as the men of Puzo's Hell's Kitchen: he'll turn himself to stone to provide the rock on which his family stands. Such a model of manhood, however, does not translate well on city soil. When his eight-year-old daughter, Carmolina, runs away from home, Marco does not alert his own police department of her absence even though he is a beat cop in Chicago and she's been missing for three days.

Traditionally for Italians, the police officer threatened to take away the authority of the family, imposing laws from outside the bounds of the family home. For three days, Marco silently shoulders the burden of finding his lost daughter. As paterfamilias, Marco's role is to protect and control the family. Mistakenly assuming callousness on Marco's part, Sergeant Cooper rhetorically asks himself "what the *shit* kind of guy waits three days to report his own damn kid missing?" (*Paper Fish* 82) That he fails to locate his daughter by himself illustrates the loss of control many second-generation fathers felt in America as they lost their children to the urban streets and the schoolroom. His voice "made of glass," Marco's vulnerability parallels that of the Italian community at large, whose men dig their hands into the dirt beside the curbstones to find "no olives, only chips of glass" (*Paper Fish* 30, 40).

Throughout *Paper Fish* De Rosa silences the increasingly looming powers of outside authority represented by the police force, the classroom (which is never mentioned in this book), and the Catholic Church. In doing so, De Rosa lays special claim to the necessity of the family to create and maintain Italian-descended values such as storytelling, family honor, and private justice. Like each of the narratives earlier discussed, De Rosa's Little Italy—at least for a time—is self-contained, the spirit of campanilismo fully intact and Italian values maintained.

No author has more fully celebrated the folkloric community in the world of Italian Americans than has Tony Ardizzone in his most important novel to date, *In the Garden of Papa Santuzzu* (1999). Borrowing generously from canonical literary traditions of storytelling, including Boccaccio and Chaucer, Ardizzone unites Italian and Anglo narrative traditions in an effort to simulate the increasingly dual traditions from which Italians in America partake. Paying homage as well to many writers of Italian America—including those represented in this chapter—Ardizzone functions much like a verbal ventriloquist, donning several literary hats, including that of historian, folklorist, magical realist, and contemporary author. Like Jerre Mangione's Sicilian ancestors from Agrigento, Tony Ardizzone investigated his paternal Sicilian background, learning that his grandfather was also from Agrigento, "the north African side, Arab side of the island" ("Interview with Tony Ardizzone" 209). Riffing on Mangione's description of himself as an admixture of Roman, Arab, and Saracen (*Mount Allegro* 18), Ardizzone's Sicilian characters are as different as the variegated colors and background of their island nation. Yet they share a tradition, Ardizzone explains, based on "the fact that the characters don't read, that they *tell* the stories they have heard before and will tell again" ("Interview with Tony Ardizzone" 209), echoing professional storyteller Gioia Timpanelli's explanation of narrative time informed by storytelling "in which the story is '*cunta e s'arricunta*' (is told and retold)" (140).

Many of the stories told (and retold from the perspective of another character, whose version of said story is equally right) treat the topic of justice and the ancient conflict between disenfranchised peasants and figures in power such as landowners and clergy. Ardizzone explains that employing the lens of folktales validates for his characters "a way to talk about frightening and awful things" ("Interview with Tony Ardizzone" 211). Resistance demonstrated by the downtrodden is traditional fare in folktales. Compelled to use their mature sense of wit and furberia in order to sustain their families and maintain a sense of justice in cruelly unjust environments—in Sicily and America—each of Ardizzone's twelve storytellers is involved in the issue of justice in one way or another. At the heart of each of their stories lay a conceptualization of justice based on a folkloric worldview and the community of Sicilians who shares and transmits a cultural acceptance of familial rules supportive of an anticlerical and antigovernmental ethos.

Ardizzone structures his novel around the stories told by twelve voices, all relatives/in-laws of Papa Santuzzu, the Sicilian patriarch who initiates the migration of each of his seven children, justifying their leaving out of a sense of paternal compassion for their impoverishment and furious anger at an indecent God: "'No decent father would allow his children to suffer as we do here'" (*In the Garden of Papa Santuzzu* 132). Refusing to accept the *miseria* of rural areas as a sign of God's will and the Sicilian's *destinu*, Papa Santuzzu utters maledictions at a system of belief that would require more sacrifice from poor peasants than from God's only son, Jesus Christ: "'I sent them away! I did! All seven! God sent away only one! . . . Seven against one! . . . I guess we both know which is more. . . . [T]here are some things here on earth, here in the ground that we walk, in this air that we breathe, in the lives that we live, that are more sacred!'" (*In the Garden* 134). Only a closeness of a son to a father would allow Papa Santuzzu to utter what seems to be a blasphemous criticism at a God he pities for not understanding the centuries of "newer—nearer Crucifixion" (as Emily Dickinson put it earlier) suffered by the chronically malnourished and brutally exploited Sicilians. Ardizzone prefaced his novel with several epigraphs, including one by Booker T. Washington, who observed that the American Negro is in an "incomparably better" condition "than the condition and opportunities of the agricultural population in Sicily"; and, Karl Marx, whose dire pronouncement is, alas, no exaggeration: "In all human history no country and no people have suffered such terrible slavery, conquest and foreign oppression, and no country and no people have struggled so strenuously for their emancipation as Sicily and the Sicilians."

Sicilians responded differently to perpetual deprivation, but one form of resistance included banditry, demonstrated by second son Luigi's struggle for emancipation before he migrates to America. Hearing the alluring voices of what he calls the "wolves . . . up in the hills, deep in the forest," Luigi's seduction occurs because of his deprivation—because of his literal hunger for food and his desire for social justice denied him as a peasant (*In the Garden* 73). Luigi only applies the appellation "wolf" to himself, never "bandit," as Ardizzone explains in his interview with Cristina Bevilacqua: "Nobody has to tell the whole truth, only pieces of the truth" (210). In a subsequent chapter another truth emerges from his eventual betrothed, Ciccina Agneddina: violence is executed in order to protect peasant honor and to defend peasant women from the detested droit du seigneur.

Out of the tradition of folklore, the fabulous occurs in Luigi's tale: with risqué humor, he describes his sudden transformation into a wolf after he eats the stolen food of the *baruni* (barons): "A streak of lightning shot up from a fissure in the ground, right through the crack of my *culu*" (*In the Garden* 76). Like the other young men who took to the hills to defend their family's honor, Luigi justifies their actions—which included stealing, killing, and kidnapping—and addresses an audience he assumes will dare to judge him: "Tell me, how can a man do nothing while his brothers and sisters starve? How can he remain a man?" (*In the Garden* 79). Ardizzone clearly uses the beast fable explicitly in Luigi's story in order to reinforce how rural Sicilians were methodically dehumanized by the northern government's exploitation after the Risorgimento. In effect, Ardizzone's *In the Garden of Papa Santuzzu* echoes in sentiment Carlo Levi's description of the poor peasants of a remote, impossibly impoverished southern Italian village after Levi was banished from northern Italy for his opposition to fascism. Quoting directly from the villagers, Levi writes: "'We're not Christians,' they say. 'Christ stopped short of here, at Eboli.' . . . We're not Christians, we're not human beings; we're not thought of as men but simply as beasts, beasts of burden, even less than beasts, mere creatures of the wild" (3).

Luigi recognizes that exploitation by the treacherous landowners and the complicit clergy reduce and deprive him more than his adventures do as a brigand, which teach him that "some force on the people's part was necessary to correct the unjust forces working against them. The wolf packs were only fitting. They were only natural and just." Defending his right to take back "a small portion of what was rightfully ours," Luigi characterizes his brief time as a bandit as an honorable existence (*In the Garden* 79). In this explanation, Luigi supports what Lucia Chiavola Birnbaum describes as a "vernacular view of justice, those who steal from the poor can expect no mercy, but the poor person who steals out of hunger has not committed a sin: this is a *'diritto alla vita,'* a right to life, of the poor, a right guaranteed by the lord" (60).

That Luigi also assumes the role of cook among his fellow bandits is no small irony on Ardizzone's part. Luigi's dual position as a cook and a wolf is Ardizzone's nod to the ubiquitous figure of the Italian American gangster, whose cooking and killing are skills held in high regard.[20] As Gardaphé explains, "wolves are often used to symbolize characteristics associated with the gangster: success, perseverance, intuition, independence, thought [and] intelligence . . . [t]hese . . . local men . . . fight for the honor of their existence" (*From Wise Guys to Wise Men* 165). Unlike traditionally represented parasitic gangster figures who bully and intimidate their own neighbors (as we see Larry do in Puzo's *The Fortunate Pilgrim*), Luigi characterizes his purpose as purely honorable though he recognizes that his outlaw status inevitably requires him to "walk the path in between light and darkness" (*In the Garden* 85).

After he returns from his forest adventures, Luigi migrates to America with Ciccina, whose honor he defended by killing the lascivious baruni. Refusing to tolerate injustice in his homeland—from landowners or priests—Luigi's migration is another form of resistance, but his life in America is filled with deprivation and, early widowed, he is alienated from his original family. Ardizzone extends his focus on themes of justice, equality, and rights of the poor through Anna Girgenti's story, the daughter of Luigi and Ciccina, whose tale entitled "The Black Madonna," constitutes the longest and arguably the most radical chapter in *The Garden of Papa Santuzzu*. Luigi Girgenti's submission to violence as a justified form of retaliation against injustice is challenged by the indigenous goddess figure of the black Madonna, whose autonomy liberates her from vengeance, but whose insistence on equality liberates Anna from patriarchal traditions represented by Church authorities. For Ardizzone, Anna's form of resistance through nonviolent activities—including prayer and verbal protest—supersedes the narrative of her father's early life as a bandit.

After suffering a primal wound from her mother's death in birthing a stillborn boy child, Anna is sent by her father to an orphanage run by nuns. Anna's departure is prefaced by the knife wound she inflicts on her father in order to protect herself from his crazed reaction to seeing what in actuality is menstrual blood not the residuum of first sex. Neither his fight against the heartless aristocracy nor his battle experiences during World War I caused Luigi to bleed, but this wound inflicted by his own daughter opens the floodgates of confession. Having been refused absolution by the priest in Sicily, Luigi's confession to his daughter—after he nearly kills her—catapults Anna into her own conversion from defense through violence to a love of peace through a belief in equality, prayer, and nonviolence. The figure of the black Madonna, appearing to Anna in seven visitations in the chapel of the orphanage, enables the young girl—despite *violent* protestation by the white church fathers—to become the revolutionary spirit informing Ardizzone's novel. The ongoing conflict between the religion espoused by traditional Church doctrine and the spiritual experiences of subaltern peoples is encapsulated by the apparition of the shift-changing Madonna, who denies hierarchy and insists on her equal position as the Holy Ghost of the Trinity: "'J[G]esù and I are twin souls, and one with God the Father'" (*In the Garden of Papa Santuzzu* 256). Constitutionally unable to tolerate equality, the priests parrot the received wisdom, spouting racist, sexist, and xenophobic comments unfounded in history. They are countered by an enormously gifted and intellectually savvy "dark young priest," who, "for the sake of argument," challenges each insupportable assumption, reminding the men that Anna's experience of seeing a dark-skinned apparition is perfectly in line with her native Sicily, "closer to Africa than it is to Rome" (*In the Garden* 259).

Despite the Vatican's refusal to acknowledge the miraculous powers executed by what the people in the neighborhood call *la Madonna Nera*, her shrine continues to hold sway over scores of pregnant women and sick and invalid children. Not surprisingly, after Anna Girgenti takes her vows, she spends years in east Africa doing missionary work, and rewitnessing the miraculous apparition of the black Madonna in the faces of "the beautiful Eritrean people for whom it was my blessing to care" (*In the Garden* 269). As Birnbaum has explained in her book on black Madonnas, the "veneration of the indigenous goddess of Old Europe merged with African, Middle Eastern, and Asian dark goddesses and persisted in the Christian era in vernacular beliefs and rituals associated with black madonnas [*sic*]" (4). Throughout Anna's chapter, Ardizzone reinforces the idea of what Birnbaum explains is central to the role of the Madonna figure: hope for "liberation of the poor, the marginal and the suppressed on earth" (12). Dismantling hierarchical and patriarchal institutions, Ardizzone, through his creation of Anna Girgenti, insists on a fundamental vernacular belief in equality with difference, concluding with the words: "That day [of transformation from veneration of the crucified male to adoration of the living female] will mark the beginning of God's third order, two thousand years of rule by the black Madonna, the Holy Ghost and third face of God" (*In the Garden* 270). Birnbaum reminds us that "justice is the central value that emerges from studying the earth mother" (23) and the appearance of the black Madonna to Anna Girgenti is indeed the not so concealed figure of Giustizia, or the goddess of Justice.

Not coincidently, the Church's refusal to acknowledge the efficacy of la Madonna Nera, renaming her instead "Our Lady of the Orphanage" (*In the Garden* 269), invites Ardizzone's sleight of hand when, toward the novel's conclusion, he offers tribute to "the great and holy woman known more simply as Mother Cabrini, founder of the Missionary Sisters of the Sacred Heart as well as countless orphanages and schools, convents and clinics and hospitals, each devoted to the care of the poor and needy, and particularly the immigrants from Italy" (*In the Garden* 306). It is she— Mother Cabrini in one of her clinics who saves Luigi from dying after being struck ill working as a day laborer out West and breathing in the poisonous powders sprayed in the fields to guarantee high crop production. Despite the fact that Mother Cabrini was later recognized as a saint *by* the institution of the Catholic Church, she continued a life of unencumbered service to the impoverished and was known by the weak and disempowered to have supernatural powers.[21] The ongoing conflict between powerful institutions of Church and government and the folkloric beliefs of subaltern peoples—represented by Sicilian Americans here—is encapsulated by a folk story in which the mother figure of Francesca Xavier Cabrini holds the higher power of moral law against the robber barons of American industry—Andrew Carnegie, John Jacob Astor and John D. Rockefeller. Ardizzone embraces the figure of justice through a folkloric vignette on Mother Cabrini, who is a revolutionary sister of the Madonna, with a "glowing face circled by a bright halo of stars" (*In the Garden* 313).

In their silencing of official discourses of power, writers of Italian America illuminate the folkloric world of storytelling and ritual, and support values of cooperation *and* individualism within protective and albeit poor communities. In a 1909 editorial from *Harper's Weekly* focusing on the problems of those clannish southern Italians, the writer explains that these immigrants "imperfectly . . . appreciate *our* institutions. [The Italian] believes to excess in self-defense and personal reprisals, and is distrustful of law and legal methods" (qtd. in La Gumina 126–127). Emphasizing only the criminal element of Italian Americans, articles like this one so popular at the end of the nineteenth century and into the twentieth failed to account for the majority of Italian families in America, who neither broke laws nor praised them. In a culture that largely devalued them, Italians in America retained their understanding of social justice, which enabled them to maintain family honor and function in society.

Italian American writers continue to portray and honor the world of their ancestors. Recent works such as Louisa Ermelino's *The Sisters Mallone*, Joseph Bathanti's *East Liberty*, Christopher Castellani's *The Saint of Lost Things*, and Billy Lombardo's *The Logic of a Rose: Chicago Stories* recreate Italian American spaces and, within them, characters who subscribe to a folkloric view of the world, which offers them redemption from the sometimes tragic, and often sad, elements in their lives. The Italian American writers presented here—di Donato, Tomasi, Mangione, Puzo, De Rosa, and Ardizzone—offer historically viable reasons for a belief in private justice and their recognition that, at times, only shrewdness and loyalty to family would save their lives. An equally pervasive voice within these works and others that follow has been the voice of faith, inflected by folk traditions and familial customs, which is the focus of chapter 2.

2

Faith/Fede

❧

Plenty to Confess

WOMEN AND (ITALIAN) AMERICAN CATHOLICISM

All saints are not buried.

—Sister Blandina Segale, *At the End of the Santa Fe Trail*

You were always irish, god,/in a church where I confessed to being Italian. . . ./O god,/god, I confess nothing.

—Elaine Romaine, "you were always irish, god"

Capitalizing only two words in her entire poem, "Italian" and "St. Anthony," Elaine Romaine semantically diminishes the power of Irish domination and the conventional ritual of the Catholic sacrament of communion in her poem "you were always irish, god." Romaine's description of the annual *festa* also illustrates its association with patriarchy as only male figures (most likely Italian)—priest, father, uncles, and brother—are involved in the sacred outdoor procession. By the end of the poem, in an apostrophe of exhausted resistance, Romaine makes her own confession: "O god,/god, I confess nothing." Overtly distancing herself from Church hierarchy, Elaine Romaine voices a loyal dissension from a distinctly *American* incarnation of Catholicism, maintaining ties with an Italian cultural heritage that recognizes the sacred in the everyday: "And all the sights of you god,/were wine-filled." Writers of Italian America regularly explore folk traditions and voices of faith as countervailing discourses vis-à-vis institutional practices of American Catholicism. As discussed in chapter 1, issues of justice often intersected with those of faith, rendering those most impoverished and silenced ripe for exploitation, but producing in them a worldview conditioned by ongoing experiences of oppression.

Women writers of Italian heritage in particular respond with ambivalence and resistance to the institution of Catholicism, particularly in its belief in the subordination of women. While she admired the religious structures of the Catholic Church, including the liturgy of the Mass, Sandra M. Gilbert recognized that those structures "for so long and so nakedly embodied—and perpetuated—the assumptions and oppressions of a patriarchal culture that defines those of us who are women as secondary and inferior, indeed as basically vessels for the transmission of physical life" ("Foreword" xi). Women writers of Italian America capitalize on the fact that the American Catholic Church at times misunderstood and delegitimized Italian Catholicism, thereby underemphasizing the preeminent role of women to influence entire families. The Church's scornful attitude hardly dissuaded Italian women from practicing their religion, even if they were not welcomed in the doors. As Linda Ardito points out, Italian immigrant women represented the link between home and Church. Unlike the men, who did not regularly attend Mass or abide by the doctrines or the liturgy of the Church, the women "represented the family in fulfilling such religious duties as hearing Mass on Sundays and holy days of obligation, going to confession, receiving communion, and seeing that children received the sacraments and religious education. An Italian American woman's position in this regard was so influential that Protestant denominations would appeal to her if they were to secure a possible conversion by other members of the family" (139).[1] John Paul Russo, citing Robert Orsi's *The Madonna of 115th Street*, identifies one of the central features of Italian Catholicism brought to American shores as the religion of the home, a concept tracing "to the Romans for whom religion begins in the home. . . . Centered on family relations and the casa . . . the religion of the family extends in concentric circles outward from the home to the neighborhood, city and country, ultimately to the natural universe" ("DeLillo" 13).[2]

A confluence of factors accounts for the difficult situation for Italian Catholics who came to America with their spiritual beliefs in tact.

These include an Italian Catholic popular religion practiced in Italy; the migration to America of Italian Catholics, making it second only to that from Ireland (Vecoli, "Prelates and Peasants" 220); and the response of the hierarchical Church in America to Italian immigrants. Make no mistake about it: Italian immigrants were deeply Catholic. Yet their devotional practices—*in America*—were perceived as unacceptable to the official Church. In his analysis of Italian Catholicism, Rudolph Vecoli explains that "the peasants [of the Mezzogiorno] were intensely parochial and traditional. While nominally Roman Catholic, theirs was a folk religion, a fusion of Christian and pre-Christian elements, of animism, polytheism, and sorcery with the sacraments of the Church" ("Prelates and Peasants" 228).

Rudolph Vecoli echoes the sentiments of Carlo Levi, whose antifascist stance as mentioned in chapter 1 caused his banishment in 1935 to a small province in southern Italy where he movingly described the pagan rites imbued in southern Italian Catholicism: "Even the ceremonies of the Church become pagan rites celebrating the existence of inanimate things, which the peasants endow with a soul and the innumerable earthly divinities of the village" (*Christ Stopped at Eboli* 163). Likewise, both Phyllis Williams in *South Italian Folkways* and Leonard Covello in *The Social Background of the Italo-American School Child* also express a "two monads model" originally examined by Gabriele De Rosa, a paradigm which suggested "that Italy was divided into two camps. On the one side stood the Church, which worked to promote 'official' Catholicism, and on the other side were a variety of economically subordinate groups, mainly peasants, who clung to beliefs and practices inherited from dim pagan pasts" (Carroll 177). Michael P. Carroll suggests that popular Catholicism in Italy indeed was shaped by priests in local churches—*chiese ricettizie*—challenging the assumptions made in the scholarly literature on immigrants of an unnecessary binary between official forms of Catholicism and local traditions.[3]

Agreeing with Michael P. Carroll, John Paul Russo further explains that *American* scholars of Italian immigration have traditionally erred "in minimizing the role and significance of the Church," creating a "false dichotomy" between local practices and the role of the Church ("DeLillo" 10). Offering a transnational perspective on the relationship between Rome and U.S. Catholics between the years of the Risorgimento to the rise of Fascism, Peter R. D'Agostino, in contrast to earlier disclaimers made against perceiving a dialectical relationship between the institution and the faithful, explains that "modern Catholics within states forged an 'imagined community' with myths, shared symbols, and a calendar of prescribed rituals. The Holy See in the Eternal City was the center of this community" (7). Migration to America brought Italians in conflict with their religious practices in an entirely new way, increasing the tendency of scholars and writers of Italian America to separate official Catholicism from the popular brand of religion practiced by subaltern peasants from the Mezzogiorno.

Needless to say, ritualistic Italian Catholicism met with dogmatic Irish American Catholicism, making for decades of strained relations between the two groups. Due to the less than welcoming greeting from Irish Catholics, Italian immigrants were wont to express anticlericalism, distancing themselves from the austerity of a doctrinal form of Catholicism at odds with an emotionalism derived from popular Catholic practices such as the festa and its accompanying processional rituals.[4] Yet no other group relationship profoundly affected the Italian immigrants in the early decades of their migration than that of the Irish. In his analysis of Irish and Italian interaction, Richard N. Juliani cites an Irish Catholic writer in 1888 who correctly assessed the religious situation for Italians in the new country: "'The fact is that the Catholic Church in America is to the mass of Italians almost like a new religion'" (28). Examining ethnic hostility between the two groups, the first represented by hegemonic Catholicism and symbolized by the papacy and the second by the majority of whom were self-identified Catholic Italian immigrants, Juliani attributes Italian Catholic defection from the Church to "the conflict between the Italian unification movement in the homeland and the Papal States [which] had already aggravated this problem for many Italians in the United States" (28).[5] Despite tensions and overt hostilities between Italian immigrants and the Church hierarchy, Italians did not convert to Protestantism in great percentages; nor did they relinquish their religious practices. Successive generations of Italian Americans were highly affected by the influences of the official Church, embracing what Mary Gordon calls the "excluding fence" of Catholicism as a form of protection and reification of neighborhood cohesiveness, but refusing its anti-intellectualism and conservative positions on women (*Good Boys and Dead Girls* 164).

HELEN BAROLINI'S AND MARY GORDON'S CATHOLIC GIRL NARRATIVES

For many writers of Italian America, American Catholicism is treated with an old-world skepticism and distrust held by peasants toward the wealthy landowners and northern rulers whose misgovernment triggered the widespread diaspora of southern and Sicilian Italians to new lands. Women writers in particular have achieved independence from the conventional, Hibernian version of American Catholicism, but Italian Catholic iconography pervades their work as they negotiate, challenge, and recreate religious rituals and folkloric beliefs. Despite their decision at times to minimize outward forms of piety in their writing, many Italian American women have responded through direct confrontation with what they have observed are the limitations of the traditional Catholic Church, especially for its women. Mary Gordon and Helen Barolini are two such writers. Their voices—pithy and intellectual—examine the reasons underlying their decision to leave the Church.

Barolini's girlhood Catholic experience occurred during a particularly inauspicious time for Italian Americans—World War II, when Italy was an enemy.[6] Born in 1925, Barolini was entering high school during the war years. That she transferred from an elite high school with affluent Anglo- and Jewish Americans (except for, glaringly, her Italian self) to the Convent School run by Irish-descended Franciscan nuns, suggests her need for sanctuary rather than spiritual instruction (*Chiaroscuro* 11). Included in her book of essays, *Chiaroscuro: Essays of Identity*, "Another Convent Story" focuses on the intersecting threads of ethnicity, Catholicism, self-loathing, and class consciousness. Her expulsion from the Convent School just before graduation is no mere symbolic occurrence; it gestures toward Barolini's refusal to be docile in her decision to be intellectual. In this way, she deliberately follows in the footsteps of Irish American Catholic writer, Mary McCarthy, whose fiction revealed the kind of nun absent in Barolini's school: "the clever, witty women of Mary McCarthy's Catholic girlhood, the skilled adversaries of sin who meet it on equal terms and make each encounter a thrilling intellectual skirmish" (*Chiaroscuro* 17).

Barolini's reference to Mary McCarthy is telling. Like Barolini, McCarthy is neither Anglo-American nor Protestant. Yet, her Irish heritage does not alienate her from her Catholicism as it does Barolini who admits to feeling out of place "because I *was* out of place. . . . Without the right name I could be neither Wasp nor Jew; I wasn't Irish Catholic; and I didn't want to be Italian" (*Chiaroscuro* 13). Deeply aware of the fact "the test of one's Americanization was how well one compared to the anglicized model" (*Chiaroscuro* 12), Barolini left Nottingham High to attend the Convent School for sanctuary away from the anxiety of not belonging, though she continued to admire everything Anglo and to detest everything Italian. Unable to identify with the moneyed children of the professional class (represented by Nottingham), Barolini simultaneously distances herself from others in her social class—Catholic, identifiably ethnic, Italian or otherwise. Her rejection has less to do with religious disbelief or personal disdain for her schoolmates than an insidious form of discrimination seeping down the social hierarchy from Anglo-American Protestantism to Irish Catholicism. Barolini both highlights and complicates the generalization made of the American Catholic Church that its dual mission was to maintain the immigrant's faith while promoting good American citizenship (Vecoli, "Prelates and Peasants" 217). As an Italian American she finds herself at odds with both her ethnicity and her religion *within* the confines of a parochial Catholic high school. She is a good citizen of neither.

Unlike her Irish American schoolmate, MaryAnn Sheed, Barolini entered parochial school with her anticlerical tendencies—learned from her father—unimpaired: "I was much looser than strict interpretation permitted, and certainly more irreverent toward the clergy. . . . I wasn't the kind of Catholic the Irish were; I was skeptical, questioning, detached from ritual except in its aesthetic function. And, paradoxically, I was too spiritually ambitious for the Convent. I was interested in the search and skirmish for faith, not in being an unthinking follower of set dogma (*Chiaroscuro* 12). Mary Gordon complains similarly in her analysis of conservative Catholics who thoughtlessly accept a "tradition that provided them with answers before they thought of the questions" (*Good Boys and Dead Girls* 190).

Much more inclined to question tradition than mindlessly to conform to religious observances, Barolini used the Convent School as her stomping ground for intellectual—and adolescent—protest. Refusing to keep quiet on such matters as female chastity, Barolini asserts in class that a girl might find something more than faith to keep from getting pregnant. She is summarily expelled. Only years later does Barolini learn that her intellect rather than her parents' intervention gets her reinstated for she is the Convent School's first Regents award winner. The Catholic Church can overlook youthful ingenuousness—in Barolini's mind—or egregious apostasy—in its own—when honor is bestowed on the institution.

Barolini's most appalling infraction in hindsight is not her pious refusals and outlandish comments, but her ethnic shame. Made to feel alien because of an Italianness so in contrast to the Irish tone of the Convent School, Barolini not only abjures a heritage that was "at that time and place, too painful" for her to accept, but also shuns a potential ally—

Mary Ciccio—"a heavy-browed classmate" whose ethnicity, to Barolini's prejudiced mind, marks her as *more* Italian than she (*Chiaroscuro* 19). Mary Ciccio is Barolini's courageous doppelgänger, and perhaps a not so shadowy figure, but rather an example of having done everything right according to rules written against you from the start. Unjustly losing the coveted French prize to a lesser but distinctly Irish American opponent, Mary Ciccio's superior pronunciation falls on prejudiced ears. Only in retrospect does Barolini recognize her own complicity—a form of self-hatred—in Mary's defeat: "The fact that her French was so good was held against her. I hadn't yet identified the ugliness of a discrimination so subtle and so generally accepted that even the very strengths of a person could be turned to a disadvantage, into cause for shame. Stupidly, with no understanding that the prejudice used against Mary could, in other ways, be used against me or anyone, I basked in her defeat" (*Chiaroscuro* 20). The shame that Barolini feels is also tied to her inchoate sense that her Italian American classmate has been "made to seem alien," that is, less American and thereby less of a citizen, even though "Mary [is] as American born as Ann [O'Fallon]" (*Chiaroscuro* 20).

Internalizing a hatred based on her cultural heritage, Barolini only later—and thankfully—recognizes the psychic damage inflicted by those who wield cultural power. In this way, Barolini echoes the realization expressed by Maria Mazziotti Gillan, who wrote in a similar vein: "Without words, they tell me/to be ashamed./I am./I deny that booted country/even from myself,/want to be still/and untouchable/as these women/who teach me to hate myself" ("Public School No. 18"). Once in college, however, Barolini is awakened to a love for her ancestors' homeland and thereafter makes many trips to her grandparents' Mediterranean world. Barolini's shame gives way to fascination with what becomes a bicultural identity—as a Sicilian Calabrian American married to a Venetian Italian, and raising children, who are Italian American and native Italian. For Barolini, the visible symbol of her double consciousness is the view of Lake Como, its two arms spreading east and west: "It was emblematic: a pattern of life and work was made strikingly clear as I saw in the lakes both the main body of who I am, American, and the Italian tributary. From these two confluences am I and my writing formed. My straddling position could be none other than that of the Italian American" (*Chiaroscuro* 128). Barolini is not alone among Italian American writers in claiming American citizenship *and* an ethnic heritage through reaffiliation with the Italian homeland of her ancestors. As early as Pascal D'Angelo's 1924 autobiography *Son of Italy*, writers of Italian America have felt it necessary to return to the booted country in order to reinforce their sense of American identity in a country that for so long did not value them.

Like Helen Barolini, Mary Gordon has little patience with thoughtless devotees of American Catholicism. While Barolini's tone reveals at times a contemptuous annoyance for the treatment she received as Catholic *Italian* during the war years, Gordon's tone rather reveals the luxury of having grown up a generation later (she was born in 1949) to parents of mixed ancestry, with an Irish and Italian mother and a Lithuanian Jewish father, a father whose married life was shaped by his wife's Catholicism. Gordon's autobiographical essays and articles collected in *Good Boys and Dead Girls* reflect an unconflicted annoyance with the Irish cast of the American Catholic Church, having been raised in that tradition herself and having benefited from the religious hegemony of the institution. Despite their intellectualism, both Barolini and Gordon enjoyed their experiences in the parochial school and the parish, respectively, recognizing the constricted landscape of Catholicism as paradoxically liberating them from the exclusionary reality of Protestant America.

For both Helen Barolini and Mary Gordon, Catholicism provided a visual landscape of religious homogeneity. Whether they were performers or spectators within it, both Catholic girls found solace in what Gordon spatially terms the "sectarian compound" of Catholic institutions (*Good Boys* 164), their imaginations inflamed by the Puritanism of the nuns, the "fascist regimentation" of the rules (*Chiaroscuro* 15), and the "systematic theology" of Catholicism, but "like modern architecture," they like it to be there though they do not want to live in it (*Good Boys* 161). As children, however, Barolini and Gordon were shielded from anyone non-Catholic until each went on to college. Gordon notes a kinship between the enclosed world of Catholicism to that of the novelist, both building a fence and calling it "his or her subject" (164). Only in adulthood does Gordon recognize the tendencies toward separatism and cultism in the Catholic world: "Real life, the friendships, the feuds, the passions of proximate existence, took place in the sectarian compound, a compound, like any other, with its secrets—a secret language, secret customs, rites, which I now understand must have been very menacing at worst or at the best puzzling to the outside world" (*Good Boys* 164). Gordon might very well be describing the ethnic enclaves that surrounded the Catholic parish world of the early and mid-decades of the twentieth century. For Italian Americans, the neighborhood provided a neutral zone to the outside world while at the same time reinforcing territorial space, reflecting the protective and parochial nature of campanilismo in United States cities.

In her autobiographical essay, "Getting Here from There: A Writer's Reflections on a Religious Past," Mary Gordon examines the twin dangers of religious life—abstraction—"the error that results from refusing to admit that one has a body" and its cousin, dualism, which "admits there is a physical world but calls it evil" (*Good Boys* 160), which bequeathed her "a kind of poetry of accumulation" such as those catalogues of sin she memorized as a child (*Good Boys* 161). Absorbing unconsciously the language of the Mass through the body, Gordon implicitly challenges the principle of male asexuality that historically governs Church hierarchy with celibate males excluding "women from the center of their official and their personal lives," and evincing a "history of hatred and fear of the body" (*Good Boys* 161). Because her parents' marriage was entirely shaped by Catholicism—it was, according to Gordon, "literally the only thing they had in common" (*Good Boys* 165), regular devotion informed her earliest childhood memories. Despite Gordon's childhood attraction to the incorporeity of religious experience in early-morning Masses with "inexplicable, untraceable noises of the priest and the altar boy" in a cold church (*Good Boys* 162), Gordon's religious experience is deeply embodied: "Whatever religious instincts I have bring their messages to me through the senses—the images of my religious life, its sounds, its odors, the kind of kinesthetic sense I have of prayerfulness" (*Good Boys* 161). Early in childhood, Mary Gordon absorbs the "varied and supple use of language" represented by the Mass itself, realizing that regular attendance at Mass is "excellent training ground for the novelist" (*Good Boys* 163, 162).

That Mary Gordon manifests a secular response to a sacred event anticipates her eventual departure from the closed world of Catholicism. Explaining to her readers—presumably many of whom are non-Catholic—the meaning of transubstantiation (the miraculous transformation of substance from bread and wine to body and blood), Gordon remarkably uses the central event of the Mass—the consecration—as her own transformative experience: from aspirations to being a nun (semicloisered of course!) to becoming a writer. Like Barolini, Gordon invokes the literary memories of Catholic writers Mary McCarthy and Flannery O'Connor, solidifying a kinship with them based on two central markers of her identity as a writer—religion and ethnicity. The conversation she imagines her predecessors having reflects less anticlericalism (so evident in Italian

American writing) and more acceptance of Catholic sacraments tinged with humorous skepticism:

> Somewhere there's a conversation I like between Mary McCarthy and Flannery O'Connor in which McCarthy tries to get O'Connor to admit that she really believes that transubstantiation is only a symbolic act. And Flannery O'Connor is reported to have said, "If I thought it were just a symbol I'd say the hell with it." (*Good Boys* 162)[7]

For Mary Gordon, being brought up Catholic and female—despite the subordinate status of women—was a boon because of the heroic images of women, beginning with the Virgin Mary. Helen Barolini's Catholic school experience of Marian theology is unhappily imbued with examples of visible piety. The Irish nuns use the irreproachable status of the Virgin Mary as a measuring rod of decorum against which female students are found wanting. Mary Gordon's Catholic experience of women is less punitive and more rhetorical. Neither the Church's view of female instrumentality—the subordinate status of women represented by her material rather than spiritual reality—nor the Italian cultural belief in the inviolate stature of the Madonna deflect Gordon from the transcendence of Mary as a heroic figure. In this way, Gordon's brand of Catholicism is more in keeping with American Protestantism, with its emphasis on instruction and Bible study. That Gordon refers to the Magnificat—Mary's canticle in Luke I:46–65—as a poem that "points out her place in the divine order," places the Virgin Mary squarely within the hierarchy of Catholicism, acknowledging the importance of "a woman's speech, . . . which at least in some subliminal way a girl got to hold on to" (*Good Boys* 169). Likewise, rather than petitioning the saints (and scolding them when they failed to deliver as is the wont of Italian Catholics), Gordon read narratives of autonomy in their lives. They were:

> examples of women who defined themselves not in terms of men but in terms of each other. You had the founders of orders. You had women who defied the Pope, defied the bishops, to go off and do things that women were not supposed to do. You had "doctors of the church"—women saints who were given that title. Did I know at age five what that meant—"doctor of the church"? Not exactly. But there was something there. You had an image of an alternative female world that often had to trick the

male world. . . . It wasn't a bad arrow to have in your quiver.
(*Good Boys* 169–170)[8]

A pivotal year in the life of adolescent Mary Gordon—age fourteen—
occurred simultaneously with the beginning of the Second Vatican Council, ushering in new changes in the Catholic Mass, including replacing the
use of the Latin Mass with modern languages.[9] During this period,
Gordon clarifies her role as an aspiring poet, as an artist, by discerning the
difference between her departure from the Catholic Church and the conservative reaction from many furious Catholics deeply dissatisfied with
the new liturgy. Having passively accepted their institution as unchanging
and parochial, American Catholics "felt that the rug had been taken out
from under them, particularly if they grew up, as [Gordon] did, in a working-class neighborhood" (*Good Boys* 174). Like those ethnically enclosed
neighborhoods that were also eventually dismantled, scores of American
Catholics "resented change in what they believed was an unchanging
institution" (Dolan 195). For Gordon, the Church of her childhood,
"which was so important for my formation as an artist, is now gone" (*Good
Boys* 175) but this fact did not eventuate in a nostalgic pining for pre-
Vatican II days or support for the reintroduction of the Gregorian chant
into the liturgy. Rather, Gordon developed an appreciation for the extraordinary church women such as the nuns killed in El Salvador and those
courageous enough to stand up to the Pope on their different positions on
abortion—these are the very living heroic women whom Gordon admires
as she concludes her autobiographical essay on Catholic girlhood (*Good
Boys* 175).[10]
    The voices emerging from Helen Barolini's and Mary Gordon's au-
tobiographical essays reveal little sentimentality regarding the American
Catholic Church. Having enlarged and deepened their understanding of
the ways in which American Catholicism intersected with such factors as
ethnic background, class status, and gender insubordination, both writers engage Catholicism on intellectual grounds, shunning the practice of
religious piety not moderated by thoughtful reasoning. These writers are
less interested in discussing or partaking in the mysterious elements of
Catholicism—particularly of Italian Catholicism—than in examining the
practical effects an enclosed world had on their development as women
and as aspiring artists. Other writers of Italian America imagine the effects of immanence—a religious theory postulating the inherence of a
deity or spirit in the world and in the individual—within those enclosed
Catholic worlds that made sectarianism a gift to be cherished.

POPULAR CATHOLICISM IN WALDO, DE ROSA, AND LLOYD

It is no exaggeration to say, as Robert A. Orsi explains in his important work on the traditional festa of the Madonna of 115th Street that "Italian popular faith in both Italy and America sought the streets to express itself" (*The Madonna* 2). For Italian immigrants in particular, processional activities that included the festa reinforced homeland regional affiliations while simultaneously engendering a "heightened sense of belonging," especially for those readjusting to city streets not completely their own (Sciorra 319). Despite the fact that most areas in the United States designated as Little Italys were indeed multiethnic in composition, Italians continued their ceremonies in the streets, constructing a geographical idea about their space that reinforced Italian Catholic subjectivity.[11] Italian popular Catholicism enacted in the festa not only served to reinforce southern Italian devotional practices, so opposed by the official Church, but also to assert "ethnic hegemony of the area as well as extending popular notions of a religious moral imperative to the city streets" (Sciorra 330). Italian Americans, like other city folk, "create a sense of moral order for themselves," mapping onto the landscape of their city streets a narrative that makes sense: "it is safe here, our kind of people live here, we understand the codes in force here but not there. Conversation becomes cartography" (Orsi, "The Religious Boundaries" 336).

One of the most important and sustaining stories Italians told about themselves occurred during the annual processions and *feste* after their migration from southern Italy and Sicily beginning in the 1880s. Observing a feast day of Italians in the Mulberry District in 1899, Jacob Riis wrote, "The religious fervor of our Italians is not to be pent up within brick walls" ("Feast-Days" 494). The Italian procession, rather, is a story about movement outdoors and the sacredness of home. Kay Turner describes a religiously motivated procession as a "ceremony of movement designed to fulfill certain symbolic and metaphysical aims"[,] . . . primarily "to affirm sacred membership in community" (6). The traditional festa in Italy was an annual celebration of a town's patron saint or Madonna. During the procession, the image of the statue is removed from the church and carried on worshippers' shoulders through the streets. As Phyllis Williams wrote in 1938, "The feast-day celebrations of the patron saints . . . are conducted [in America] in much the same fashion as they were in Italy, with church services followed by processions through the streets of the district. . . . Practically every American town with an Italian community of any size and wealth observes one or more occasions of this nature" (149). Often accompanied by a carnival-like celebration that includes fireworks, music, food, and dancing, the festa dismantled boundaries between sacred and secular spaces. As Joseph Sciorra writes, "The paraded image of a saint of the Madonna encapsulates a sacred narrative of heavenly intervention or a Marian apparition and superimposes this mytho-historic time onto the everyday world of sidewalks and street corners" (317).

Accepting the immanence of the divine in daily life, Italians in America maintained a fluid consanguinity between religion and magic, epitomized by their engagement in processions and feste. While many Italian immigrants may have been turned away from the Church and denounced as "Dagos" from the pulpit (Vecoli, "Prelates and Peasants" 230), they continued to engage in feast days, despite the fact that— pre-Vatican II—such expressions did not accord with the standards of re-ligious conduct prescribed by the ecclesiastical hierarchy in America. As Kay Turner explains, the "unorthodox desire to bring the sacred into the streets . . . thereby collap[ses] the rigid boundaries between sacred and secular realms" (7), and restores the cleavage between the divine and the ordinary. By incorporating processional ceremonies in their narratives, Octavia Waldo, Tina De Rosa, and Susan Caperna Lloyd not only un-settle the idea of sacred membership in community, but also construct contested landscapes that are fragile if not doomed.

Octavia Waldo's 1961 novel, *A Cup of the Sun*, explores the limita-tions of conventional Catholicism on one of its central characters, Niobe Bartoli. Set in the outskirts of Philadelphia during World War II, Waldo's novel revolves around a neighborhood of Italian immigrant fam-ilies who struggle to maintain old-world customs in a rapidly changing environment. Waldo focuses on the painful lives of second-generation Italian American characters, whose adulthood is constricted by internal family codes of responsibility and outward influences, such as the for-midable presence of the Catholic Church. Waldo inserts a description of a neighborhood procession in this Philadelphia Little Italy, but her char-acters remain remote from its charms. As a plaster statue of the Madonna is paraded through the streets on the day of the Assumption (the bodily taking up of Mary into heaven after her death), Niobe pri-vately rejects the mother figure, disallowing any connection to shared humanity or pain. As a way of discounting (and at the same time blam-ing) her own mother for not protecting her from the sexual advances of her brother, Niobe rejects the entire procession not out of an anticleri-calism boisterously displayed by her father, but out of a recognition that she cannot depend on the Church—or her home, which is its sacred representation—for her protection.

Throughout the procession scene, Niobe is haunted by memories of religious confession, at first by her memory of the priest's excoriation of her refusal to confess and, later, by her memory of confessing the fact that she had illicit sex with her brother. Fourteen years old when this one-time incident occurs, initiated by the older brother, Niobe's family situation and traditional Catholicism prevent her from understanding what happened to her. Struggling to achieve autonomy outside the rigid strictures of home and church, Niobe nonetheless remains loyal to the imperative of the confessional: the obligation to utter the truth about having committed incest with her brother. Waldo suggests that Niobe has lost her faith in the power of doctrinal Catholicism to heal its practitioners: "The Church offered confession for comfort and nothing to grasp hold of afterwards except fear" (69). The physical space of the confessional dictates against spiritual wholeness. One kneels in a dark, small, enclosed stall with a screen separating the discloser from the confessor who confers absolution. In her anger and frustration at the priest's complete misunderstanding of her suffering, Niobe wants to "scream out, to break down the partition between them, and beat her hands against his black-robed chest" (71).

Niobe remains silent during and after sex with her brother, fearing her father's wrath and, later, her brother's threat of self-emasculation. Enforced silence in the home prevents Niobe from coming forth later in the church, which is its patriarchal equivalent. For remaining silent in the confessional, Niobe suffers the vitriolic response of a censorious priest: "It is a grievous sin to withhold your sins in the confessional. . . . You must not receive communion after a confession of lies. If you should die afterwards, God will abandon you to the rodents of the soil. . . . His disgust will be worse than any torment you can now imagine. Worse than having your eyes gouged from their sockets to roll their blood over the driest sand" (64). Sounding more like a Calvinist than a Catholic, the priest's condemnation of Niobe does not move her to confess any quicker. Her Philomela-like status is both imposed from the outside and chosen as a form of self-protection. Aware of the influence of a more doctrinal-based ideology in the American Catholic Church, Waldo's confessional scenes focus on reverence and fear of the Godhead in contrast to the intimate association Italian Catholics felt toward the divine.

During the second confession scene, which will precipitate Niobe's leaving the church, the priest engages the young girl in what Michel

Foucault has described as the meticulous rules governing "confession of the flesh," including "insinuations of the flesh, thoughts, desires, combined movements of body and soul" (19). Effectually, the priest encourages Niobe to engage in a question–answer format that details her sexual encounter, intensifying her memories of the act. Concluding with another oratory of condemnation, the priest, having first exacted from Niobe intimate details of her sexual encounter, paradoxically reinforces a hatred of the body. The confession of Catholicism parallels what Foucault describes as an institutional "incitement to speak about [sex] . . . a determination on the part of agencies of power to hear it spoken about" (18). Niobe's experience of incest is far less obscene than the priest's refusal to stop the sexual line of questioning after Niobe has properly confessed.

Leaving the church requires that Niobe confess her decision to her mother, whose Catholicism—both popular and doctrinal—is unswerving. Asserting to her mother out loud—"'I have nothing to confess'"—Niobe begins to reconcile the conflict she experiences at home and church. After Niobe leaves the church, she clarifies to her mother that neither the American nor the Italian church suits her, and, despite her mother's cajoling, she maintains her stance: "'I have thought it out, and I just don't believe any more [sic]'" (159). Notably, Niobe rejects both the Italian and American churches in her community, recognizing that she will enter adulthood without the limited ministrations of Catholicism. The town's local sculptor, whom Niobe loves, ultimately confers upon her healing absolution, but he requires no confession when he intuits her secret suffering and reassuringly says: "'It doesn't matter—not to anyway who loves you'" (203). That the plaster statue of the Madonna used in the procession is modeled after the sculptor's mistress is no small irony. While the primary purpose of processions is to release the holy, as Turner explains, it remains unclear in Waldo's procession scene if community members affirm sacred membership (7). Perhaps also due to the uncertainty of the war years and the Americanization of second-generation Italian children, the families on which Waldo concentrates are neither healed nor united by popular Catholic rituals.

Tina De Rosa sets *Paper Fish* on Chicago's West Side, a novel of Little Italy, spanning the years after World War II (1949–1958), but the neighborhood De Rosa portrays could be taken from the archives of early twentieth century as enclaves served as buffer zones for displaced immigrants. Unlike Waldo who directly addresses anticlerical tendencies of Italians alongside their interest in popular religion, De Rosa mostly elides direct representation of *American* Catholic traditions in order to focus on

Italian female power. De Rosa highlights the possession of authority of a young woman's identity with help from a female mentor. The uncontested female individual in *Paper Fish* is the paternal grandmother, Doria, the matriarch of the Bellacasa family. She is as much the voice of justice (from an Italian worldview) as she is a coercive presence for her daughter-in-law, whose Lithuanian background is entirely muted by the looming ubiquity of her mother-in-law. Like Rosa Cassettari, the focus of chapter 3, Grandma Doria is a natural storyteller, and through storytelling, she extends her granddaughter's lineage by connecting her to Neapolitan great-grandparents and to healing memories of the booted country. Such stories save Carmolina emotionally, succored by her grandmother's allegiance to oral traditions, to stories that explain as they heal.

To celebrate and honor Grandma Doria's singularity as a sacred figure and as an artist of oral traditions, De Rosa concludes *Paper Fish* with a procession. Unlike the Italian festa, culminating with a High Mass and procession of the statue of the saint or Madonna through the streets, De Rosa's reinterpretation of the procession is understated and ostensibly unorthodox, making the folk ceremonies of immigrant contadini commonplace by comparison. Aware that she is dying and must pass on the torch of inspiration to her artistic granddaughter, Grandma Doria requests to see Carmolina dressed in bridal garb. The ensuing ceremony between grandmother and granddaughter poignantly depicts Carmolina's painful acceptance of her grandmother's imminent death and her own vocation as a storyteller turned literary artist.

Seventeen-year-old Carmolina initially resists partaking in the ceremony. Her denial of her grandmother's death *and* her refusal to appear in public dressed in wedding clothes begins the crucial inversion that will take place between Carmolina and Doria. Unable to walk well, Grandma Doria must be carried in her mahogany chair up three flights of stairs by her two sons to Carmolina, who awaits her grandmother in her parents' apartment. In this scene, De Rosa reverses the traditional processional movement from indoors to outdoors in order to accomplish several aims. The author portrays each woman's preparations in front of the mirror—a central metaphor used throughout *Paper Fish*—crosscutting between grandmother and granddaughter. Because Grandma Doria needs to present una bella figura not only to her granddaughter, but to the entire neighborhood gathered in the streets awaiting her presence, De Rosa focuses on the meticulous preparations Doria makes in front of the mirror. Emphasizing through reiteration of the color blue—the Madonna's color—De Rosa equates Grandma Doria with the preeminent figure of Italian Catholicism.[12] Rhetorically, De Rosa makes an excess of reiteration, as extravagant as a procession:

> She wore her *blue* dress. . . . She pulled a tortoise shell comb through [her hair] . . . she asked the *blue* Virgin Mary on the dresser to help her comb her hair. . . . Grandma Doria looked at her *blue* body in the mirror. . . . She looked into the mirror and behind her *blue* eyes with stars in them, and her mouth with the lines of her mother, she saw the reflections of the women dressed in black, standing in a long line behind her. . . . That night, Doria prayed to God. . . . She lay on the white pillow with her *blue* eyes seeing clearly into the night. . . . She closed her *blue* eyes a moment, whispered something, opened them into the ancient mirror. . . . She walked slowly into her daughter Katerina's bedroom, opened the top drawer. There . . . in a *blue* velvet box were three coins. . . . Doria sat with her hands in her lap, over the *blue* purse precisely. The long sleeves of her dress were edged in *blue* lace. (emphasis added; *Paper Fish* 109, 110, 111, 112, 113)

Emphatically, Grandma Doria is represented as the figure of the Madonna, as she is paraded through the neighborhood by her stalwart sons who carry her in her chair because of the pain in her feet. De Rosa does not offer her imagined community or her readers an iota of breath in this emotionally charged scene, where unsurprisingly neighborhood men kill their cigarettes out of respect. The sons' carrying the mother is represented not only as sacred procession—a "form of public religious ritual . . . performed by members of a community" (Turner 6), but also as a *Via Dolorosa*. In this scene, Grandma Doria's route is not to Calvary. Rather, as she prepares for death, she makes a final entrance into community to confirm her membership within it and to ease the transition from life to death. She is the living voice of death. De Rosa's referencing the fact that the sons accidentally bump their mother's foot as they twist and turn up the three flights of stairs (the spiral staircase?), causing pain that "made itself a snake in her leg," reinforces her iconic status as a holy figure.[13] Throughout the ritualized movement outdoors, De Rosa affirms that Grandma Doria is the sacred icon, the word made flesh, and her movement through the neighborhood is an old-world reminder of the transformative potential of making secular into sacred territory.

In privatizing the meeting between grandmother and granddaughter, De Rosa is also able to enforce the individual nature of Carmolina's entrance into an adulthood marked by features of Americanization, including autonomy and eventual distance from the family. In an effort to heighten (if that's possible) Doria's singularity, De Rosa also equates her with the village priest. Unlike the young priest in *Paper Fish* whose ineffectuality is underscored by the fact that he is dying, the elderly Doria functions like a priest who has the power of transubstantiation: she is able to convert secular into sacred. She does this through the procession itself, of course, sanctifying the community through her spiritual presence—as she passes them, she takes into her withered hands the hands of men and women neighbors—and also through her capacity to ignite the flame of creative inspiration for her disciple granddaughter. Like the father in a wedding ceremony, Grandma Doria gives Carmolina away, not to someone else, but to herself. Bestowing sacred status upon the storytelling Grandma Doria encapsulates De Rosa's belief that art is sacred, handed down from above.[14] That Grandma Doria is functionally illiterate (like her historical counterpart Rosa Cassettari) gains fuller resonance in light of De Rosa's belief that art is the sacred word made flesh. Carmolina Bellacasa is the recipient of such knowledge; it will be her responsibility to convert the sacred stories of ancestry into literary art— received from the most sacred spaces of all: the Italian American *casa*.

De Rosa's privatization of Italian American popular customs reflects an awareness of the changing demography of a post–World War II America, where Italian American enclaves were being dismantled one by one. The unorthodox description of the procession is less radical than it is a valediction—espousing mourning. In a final effort to commemorate a lost world, De Rosa takes sectarianism to a different realm. The "sectarian compound" of Mary Gordon's Catholic world is a proximate existence in De Rosa's world of one block, two houses, and one family. De Rosa's "excluding fence" is campanilismo in extremis, literally meaning, at the point of death, which is the state of the Italian American Little Italy at the conclusion of *Paper Fish*.

As part of the enterprise of reconnecting with one's ancestral faith, many writers of Italian America return to Italy.[15] For Susan Caperna Lloyd, whose 1992 memoir, *No Pictures in My Grave: A Spiritual Journey in Sicily*, the Easter time procession in Trapani, becomes the locus of her renewal. Born in California and raised in Oregon, Lloyd's connection to Italian identity did not emerge from an Italian American enclave so present in the autobiographical novels of Waldo and De Rosa. Rather, through her grandmother Carolina, who immigrated alone with children to America in 1922, Lloyd develops a yearning to reunite with the world her grandmother forever left. Unable to return to Italy to visit with her much-beloved mother, Carolina mourns this loss in ways that simulate the Madonna's infinite sorrow. Lloyd compares an old photograph taken of her grandmother with children in 1920s Rome to an "immigrant Madonna, surrounded by her *portatori*" (carriers, bearers; 9). Carolina's son, who witnesses firsthand his mother's holding her husband in her arms after a fatal heart attack, compares her to a "damn *Pietà*. She was like some great Virgin . . . holding her son, Jesus" (n.p.).

Susan Caperna Lloyd makes several trips to Trapani, Sicily, to partake in the Easter season Procession of the Mysteries. These pilgrimages allow Lloyd to connect with her grandmother's seemingly inexhaustible strength and to revise the mater dolorosa role written into the script of an Italian woman's life. Lloyd organizes her memoir spatially, beginning and ending with descriptions of her participation in Trapani's Holy Week rite, in which twenty statues, the *Misteri*, depicting scenes from the Passion story, are paraded for twenty-four hours through the streets. Throughout the subsequent chapters of the memoir, Lloyd travels to archeological sites, tracing ancient female roots such as on the cave walls of Levanzo, and at the shrine of the Black Madonna of Tindari. In the faces of the bread ladies of San Biagio, Lloyd is reminded of her grandmother, and in their *pane*, she sees "a priestess in an ancient fertility rite. [The] bread offering was like the ritual cakes the women had brought to the old sanctuaries of Demeter and Persephone" (*No Pictures in My Grave* 170). Unlike the procession in Trapani, predominantly a male-sponsored and male-controlled event, the women of San Biagio literally shape (baking hundreds of bread ornaments) the Easter tradition. Witnessing this community of women inspires Lloyd when she returns to Trapani for the Procession of the Mysteries.

Throughout her memoir, Lloyd reinforces a viable connection between Roman Catholic tradition and ancient fertility rituals. She discovers through a female scholar turned restaurateur that Trapani's original place name—Drepanum—is a Latin word meaning "scythe" and alludes to the story of Demeter, who "dropped her sickle here when she went to look for Persephone, and the distinctive shape of Trapani was formed" (83). Lloyd shares company with other anthropological scholars like Kay Turner, who explains that "Mary is historically and prehistorically related to fertility cults and worship of the old earth goddesses" (7). The choice to begin and conclude her memoir with the procession, therefore, parallels the circular movement that is distinctly female. According to Turner, "in a model procession dedicated to Mary, the movement must inevitably take place in a circular, if winding, route because such processions are based in that type of agricultural-fertility ceremony which simultaneously imitates the circular patterned movement of the heavens, the progress of sowing to reaping to sowing again, and the cyclic process of women's menstrual-fertile period" (7).

Despite her Italian antecedents, Lloyd partakes in the Italian *processione* clearly as a spectator, an *americana*, whose husband and son are conferred the honor of participating integrally in the processional movement because of their gender not culture. Thus, in the first chapter, Lloyd functions as an investigatory agent, connecting the invisibility of the Sicilian women to the long-suffering *Madonna Addolorata* (one of the statues taken out on a platform), who leaves the confines of the church to search for her crucified son. Observing the procession from the sidelines, Lloyd reinforces the connection between Christian and pagan traditions, supported by the townspeople, who rank Mary in stature above the Christ figure. As Lloyd examines the platform of the statue of Christ crouched under a cross, and of Veronica, the woman who offered Christ a handkerchief on his road to Calvary, she highlights the Marian worship of the Trapanesi:

> As I looked up at this apparition, the story of Demeter and Persephone came alive. . . . Was it Christ's flowing, feminine robes, which billowed out underneath the cross, that reminded me of Persephone? His silver jewelry, his fine-featured face? The bed of flowers he stood upon, as Persephone had on Lake Pergusa's shore? I glanced over at the Demeter-Madonna in her sweeping black cape as the porter jumped off the [platform] and came over to me. . . . "You know," he said, "the *processione* is not really the story of Christ's death. It is about his mother, Mary, and the terrible thing he did to her by dying. Some people even think that Christ was irresponsible to get himself crucified like that." (*No Pictures in My Grave* 10)

The Trapanesi women follow the Madonna's platform, grieving for lost husbands and children. While Lloyd empathizes with their loss, which reminds her of her grandmother's mother loss, she ultimately chooses not to join the band of grieving mothers, disconnecting from the mater dolorosa story further when she lets her young son walk in the procession without her guidance. Instead, Lloyd refuses to stay in her place as a woman in Sicily and realizes, belatedly, and to her dismay, that she needs an escort to be out alone so late. Crowded the next day with others at the Church doors, Lloyd recounts her surprise at her tears as she watches the men pausing at the ramp, resisting their final movement inside, not wanting "the procession and their twenty-four hours together to end. Clutching each other in tears, they expressed a collective sorrow intermixed with joy. The men went in and out of the door three or four times, to the dismay of church officials who thought this dramatic 'penetration' a bit too pagan. It was a sensual love act. They were entering the womb: mother, home, the church" (26).

When Lloyd returns to Trapani and the processione in the final chapter of her memoir, she returns, as she says, "on her own terms," without family or male support (28). That only men participate fully in the procession, a gender privilege that imitates the Church-sanctioned subordination of women, does not deter Lloyd's will to power, or, as her scholar friend reminds her, to *potenza*, a feminine word (175). In order to liberate herself from an image that has informed and limited the lives of Italian women, Lloyd inserts herself in the procession, following beside the *Ceto dei Salinai*, which bears the figure of the Madonna holding the dead Christ in her arms. This figure of the pietà reminds Lloyd of her grandmother as she walks alone beside the procession the entire night. However, she is not satisfied to be a spectator or a handmaiden to the men's privilege. Through dogged willfulness, she manages to get invited to shoulder the platform, performing the foot movements with grace and power, equaling the men.

Lloyd remains a carrier for the most important honor: bringing the platform back into the church: "The *entrata*, the culmination of the procession, was a sacred act that thousands of people watched. The waltz had to be performed exactly right, the platform turned, the timing perfect" (185). During this scene, Lloyd's presence blurs gender boundaries and overturns the hierarchical theology of the official church that subordinates ordinary women, rendering them inferior. She also reinforces the inversion that takes place between mother and child—as Mary is given preeminent power during her nighttime retrieval of her dead son. Kay Turner's description of another procession in which Mary and Jesus are principal characters, the Virgin of Sorrows procession, sheds light on the Trapani procession: "Verticality, generally associated with the male principle (upward thrust, infinity, heavenly), becomes a feminine force while horizontality, usually thought of as feminine (earthly, limited, etc.) is identified with masculinity" (23). The horizontal casket of the crucified Christ follows directly after the platform that Lloyd helps shoulder.

Rather than describing the carriers' stalled entrance into the Church as a penetration (as she did in the first chapter), Lloyd focuses on the community united by this spectacle, transforming their environment into sacred space. During her experience as a platform bearer, Lloyd celebrates the necessity of community, yes, but americana that she is, Whitman-like she celebrates herself, too. The focus on the Madonna's power cannot be underemphasized, however. As Turner explains, "At this time of liminal chaos and fear brought on by the death of the Saviour . . . the limitlessly fertile and inclusive power of the Mother is relied on to rethread the tattered, ripped cloth of community. . . . The essential aim of the Mary-Jesus status inversion, then, is to effectively reestablish the primary root metaphor of mother and child: the Southern Italian paradigm of union (family and community) and generation" (15). As an American of Italian descent alone in Trapani, Sicily, for Lloyd the processione also has deeply personal meaning, coextensive with her recognition of the relationship between pagan and Christian imagery. She ends her memoir, *No Pictures in My Grave*, with this encomium to the Trapanesi community and to herself:

> I had become the Goddess I had sought. And it seemed right and proper that she had rejoined the world of men. By joining these men, I felt I had given them, too, a new strength. With the *portatori*, I cried. I could hear their sobs around me, so beautiful, in the discovery of our newfound strength. . . . I, too, had found the lost part of myself. Together with the dancing men, I gladly waltzed up the ramp. We paused one last time. Then, unafraid of what I would find inside, I entered the doors and came home. (188)

Belief in the immanence of the divine in the streets of America and Italy continues to inspire its writers. The ritual of procession itself—inherently transformative—is rescripted by writers such as Octavia Waldo, Tina De Rosa and Susan Caperna Lloyd to meet the needs of women who will and do partake in a world utterly in contrast to their ancestral homelands, imagined and realized. Because of their admiration for popular Catholicism, these writers give themselves permission to steer away from a strict rendering of Italian rituals—however unorthodox to American Catholics—and toward a more inclusive embrace of women's worldly power and their capacity for transcendence—through the Catholic Church—or not. The stories they tell are of faith in women's power to transform and heal through the art of storytelling and ritual.

RADICAL RUPTURES FROM ITALIAN AMERICAN CATHOLICISM

The ambivalence toward the institution of Catholicism and an ultimate refusal to abide by the strictures of orthodoxy marks the works of Nancy Savoca, Mary Cappello, and Susan Leonardi. Each author demonstrates a form of resistance that liberates women from patriarchal structures that would otherwise render them voiceless and invisible: without stories, disembodied. Resistance compels women to redefine their community's coercive construction of femininity, exacerbated to varying degrees by the marker of ethnicity or cultural identity. The women in Savoca's, Cappello's, and Leonardi's works succeed in different ways in wresting from control male effort to regulate their identities within familial and religious arenas.

Teresa Santangelo of Nancy Savoca's film *Household Saints* achieves singularity—and therefore a sui generis distance from her family— through a mystical piety that recalls her deceased grandmother's religious devotions. Based on Francine Prose's 1981 novel of the same name, *Household Saints* portrays the lives of three generations of women in New York's diminishing Little Italy of the 1950s through the 1970s. All three generations of Italian American women in *Household Saints* do not abide by religious conventions, either rejecting formal liturgical precepts outright or refusing to adopt the formalities of an Irish-dominated Catholic hierarchy. Carmela Santangelo, the widowed matriarch and first-generation Italian woman (and as commanding a presence as the grandmother of De Rosa's novel), is old-world Catholic, a hearty blend of superstition, including spells and incantations, and direct access to celestials in the upper firmament. Carmela is considered by formal Catholicism to be unorthodox because she directly worships the saints and maintains a mystical relationship with her triad of sacred supporters: patron saint, Madonna, and dead husband. Defining the "Romance of the Wild Woman" as an ideological construct that distinguishes the good from the bad woman in cinema, Dawn Esposito explains that Italian women have been represented as passively accepting their "inscription into patriarchy" and thereby contributing to their own inferiority (32). The woman who remains unconquered (not yet controlled by men or speedily ushered into the positions of wife and mother) is represented as dangerous, primitive, and in need of control. That Carmela, according to Esposito, remains the "quintessential Wild Woman," despite her serving the interests of the Italian family in her role as sausage maker for her son's butcher shop, has everything to do with her unconventional mode of worship (43).

Relying solely on an intimate relationship with the heavenly sphere, Carmela manages to maintain a maternal subjectivity within the boundaries of what Esposito calls the "cult of domesticity," the underpinning of "contemporary western discourse and gender representation" without relinquishing her mystical practices (42). As a widow, she manages to have the best of both worlds: matriarchal control of her home *and* her son's butcher business outside of the strict containment of marriage. As Aaron Baker and Juliann Vitullo explain, "Like her mysticism, the sausage allows Carmela to assert an important role within the family, but also to submit [ostensibly] to the authority of her son Joseph in a masculinist Italian/American culture" (56). Carmela's connection to mysticism is underscored by Savoca's subscription in *Household Saints* to a form of cinematic magical realism in which the conventionally realistic portrayal of an Italian American community is juxtaposed to the insertion of fantasies and the use of animation. Baker and Vitullo underscore the parallels inferred between Carmela and the Madonna, though Savoca never directly portrays these in the film. According to Caroline Bynum, the hagiographic paradigm for female mystics of the late medieval period was understood as "an extension of their traditional everyday roles as mother and wife in the service of others" (qtd. in Baker and Vitullo 56). It is merely a step in the right direction to suggest the relationship between a figure like Carmela and the street procession of the Madonna (most famously displayed during the first half of the twentieth century in Italian Harlem): "This ritual honored not only the Madonna, but also the women's own domestic work" (Orsi; qtd. in Baker and Vitullo 56).

Remaining firmly tied to her brand of mysticism and motherhood, Carmela Santangelo manages to maintain an uncompromising relationship to her spirituality. At the same time, she, like the nuclear family patriarch, effects the gradual control of her daughter-in-law, Catherine, who surrenders to the cult of domesticity as exuberantly as she recites her husband's surname on their wedding night. Second-generation Italian American Catherine eventually assumes the role of making the Santangelo "Miracle Sausages," and, even though she has rejected her mother-in-law's access to the divine (for which she is punished), she supports her husband's butcher business through this activity. When Savoca films the scene of Catherine's sausage making, she uses an overhead shot, obscuring the actor's face by focusing only on the movement of hands. The voice-over incantation is that of the dead Carmela, and yet Catherine, new-world cook, seems unaware of what Esposito calls the "deep intonation of a mother tongue recal[ling] more primitive rituals" (44). Submitting to a faux position of authority in the household after Carmela's death, Catherine entirely severs a connection to female power through a complete acceptance of a domestic, nonreligious, and consumerist 1950s lifestyle. Her potential to resist patriarchy and maintain authority of her power as a woman has utterly vanished as she soundly rejects her mother-in-law's "feminized, Old World legacy" (Baker and Vitullo 58). It remains the role of the third-generation child to recover that legacy.

Seen through the lens of generational enumeration, *Household Saints* works typologically, with the grandchild—Teresa—functioning as the antitype of the foundational character, Carmela. As such, Teresa fulfills individually the role that her grandmother fulfilled through marriage under the role of female domestic worker within the household. Resuming her deceased grandmother's mystical piety in an excessive display of saintliness, Teresa models herself on her namesake, Teresa of Lisieux, the young French saint who served God by performing routine chores, seeking divinity in the ordinary. She begins her journey to transcendence through material means, resurrecting the religious icons that were her grandmother's and that her mother assiduously stowed away before performing a decorator's "exorcism" on her mother-in-law's apartment (Makarushka 86). By early adulthood, Teresa Santangelo's spiritual excessiveness consumes her entire identity. In a narcissistic effort to maintain her singularity within an Italian American enclave devoted to marriage and motherhood, Teresa spurns the traditional roles open to women of her culture, but not in an effort to explore the relaxation of those roles afforded her by the counterculture of the 1960s and 1970s. Her transgression, if it may be called that, is deeply paradoxical. Teresa *chooses* sainthood as a role she feels fated to fill, but within the domestic space traditionally reserved for wives and mothers: the home. Like nuns and other cloistered religious, Teresa is able to free herself from the bodily constraints of motherhood, but preserve the sanctity of domestic space by residing there and spending entire days intensively focused on the minutia of household duties.

Savoca's musical choices in the film, including the iconic Janis Joplin, offer a counternarrative of Teresa's trajectory. Growing up during the turbulent 1960s, Teresa's tunnel vision on all things Jesus gives one pause for thought. Unlike her ancestors, she's not a Marian worshipper whatsoever.

Nor does she develop a relationship, like many Italians before her, to American Catholicism that challenges received wisdom or emulates, Italian style, the incarnation of the Madonna and saints. Teresa, rather, pines for Jesus love so much that during her obsessive ironing of her boyfriend's checkerboard shirt, Jesus appears in bloodied robes, crown, and thorns, blond and green eyed (with a British accent to boot) to keep her company! Never does Savoca (or Francine Prose) interpret Teresa's behavior as either solely reflective of the girl's changing gender position in a post-World War II culture or as primarily a reactive form of resistance to her father's objection that she join the Carmelite order (of nuns). Becoming the ultimate antinomian allows Teresa to kill two birds with one stone—the Catholic Church and her Italian American father. But she is soon exiled (after the ironing-board vision) and committed to a Catholic psychiatric institution where she dies shortly thereafter of unknown causes. She is nineteen. Brilliant strategist or deranged lunatic? Teresa seems a subversive combination of both. In reality, Teresa has no intellectual awareness of her behavior; she's more a manufactured product of the two institutions vying for her attention.

Teresa's religious extremism is enabled by the church and the home. Despite the virulent anticlericalism of Joseph Santangelo, he sends his only child to parochial school. Such schools in America espoused traditional Catholic beliefs and were oriented toward the memorization of dogmatic religious principles and strict adherence to rules. Esposito notes that "the uniforms clue the spectator into what the grandmother's spirit is up against, patriarchal religion, man's image of himself raised up to the heavens that eliminates the woman as fertile mother and condemns her to the state of virgin bride" (45). Clearly, this description is not in alliance with Italian forms of Catholicism practiced by the immigrants in the early decades in America. No Madonna/Christ inversion exists inside the parochial schools; rather, emphasis is placed on doctrinal features of Catholicism reflecting a Hibernian inflection. It is not an exaggeration to suggest, as John Paul Russo does, that the official Church in America, "shared certain features with northern European and American Protestantism: an emphasis on transcendence, juridical formalism, neo-puritanism, a concentration on instruction" ("DeLillo" 6). As such, Irish Catholicism has been called "Jansenistic," that is, a "'milder version of Calvinism', but with the 'severity of the Calvinist mentality'; 'the believer suffers from extreme scrupulosity' and 'rejects all the popular traditional forms of devotion'" (Reinhardt; qtd. in Russo, "DeLillo" 6).

Teresa's scrupulous devotion to Christ bears similarity to a neo-puritanism that makes her an able foe for her recalcitrant father, who refuses to allow his daughter to become a nun. In an effort to combat his objection, Teresa works within a system of orthodoxy that bears more resemblance to the Puritan era than to 1960s Catholic America. As Amy Lang said of prophetic women of seventeenth-century America, visible sainthood offered them a "perfectionist theology wherein election is witnessed and sealed by the spirit and cannot be tested by outward means" (7). Thus Teresa's devotion to the labors of domesticity, the mundane activities no one notices, allows her to concentrate passively on awaiting Christ as her bride. While her father's refusal to let her join the Carmelites initially puts a crimp in her holy plans, Teresa aligns herself ironically with the mystical part of her heritage in order to wrest control—without seeming to—from her Italian American father. In this way she parallels the devotion of female mystics to Christ as a way of "resisting patriarchal control" and proving "her connection to the divine" (Baker and Vitullo 62). Joseph Santangelo's anger with his daughter's behavior has as much to do with his distrust of the Catholic Church as it does with his inability to control his daughter's placement within the patriarchal system of marriage and motherhood. Not only does Joseph lose his daughter to Jesus, but he loses future economic support in a system that requires women to maintain and uphold the work of men.

Becoming the ultimate antinomian, Teresa manages to avoid the notion of "visible sainthood," that is, the idea of grace emanating from good works in the community, and instead believes in an individual identity subsumed in divinity—and which cannot be tested by outward means. Thus the confusion at her death. Teresa Santangelo comes to mean different things to different people in her Italian American neighborhood. Like a saint, she is prayed to and revered *after* her death. Her otherworldliness frees her from patriarchal family control but also functions as her ticket to immortality. Like a good Puritan, Teresa's brand of mystical Catholicism quenches all endeavor. She is free to indulge the furthest extremes of self-assertion, but only under the auspices of liturgical belief in sainthood. And she gets away with it, but not without losing her mind and her life. No Hester Prynne she, Teresa's unconventionality is neither intellectually nor spiritually challenging. Unlike the literary Hester Prynne and her historical precursor, Anne Hutchinson, whose female empowerment and possession of authority over their own identity forced them to defy established religious laws, Teresa's death reinstates her passivity within the Italian American family—as a household saint.

Mary Cappello describes Nancy Savoca's *Household Saints* as an "antidote in the form of a critique of Catholicism as a woefully inept medium for the incongruities of these people's lives—which I will insist on calling their queerness" ("Nothing to Confess" 107). When gay sexuality intersects with Catholicism, writers such as Mary Cappello and Susan Leonardi have much to confess. The metaphor of coming out of the closet does double duty in their works: as an assertion of their sexual difference and as a final confession each woman makes as she distances herself permanently from the official Church. As Cappello writes in her memoir, *Night Bloom*, "The Catholic coming out story is equivalent to a sharing of stigmata: 'Here's my wound, my battle scar, my badge,' we seem to say, 'Can you imagine that? Can you imagine I survived to tell the tale?'" (147).

The tales told by Cappello and Leonardi take gay sexuality as a fundamental determinant of one's identity, thereby complicating one's relationship to the Church. Mary Cappello's autobiographical essay "Nothing to Confess: A Lesbian in Italian America"[16] and Susan Leonardi's novel *And Then They Were Nuns* offer shrewd interpretations of the intersection between sexual and religious identity, discovering as their literary foremothers before them that the Church as an institution is incapable of responding to difference with genuine acceptance. The subordination of gay women is double-edged: the hierarchical structure of the Catholic Church already defines women as secondary. The patriarchal and misogynist bent of the Catholic tradition has accepted only asexual male superiority as worthy of exercising power and, indeed, has cast a centuries-long blind eye to those male clergy who dissented from that position. For Mary Cappello and Susan Leonardi, loyal opposition to the Church's precepts is simply not acceptable. They tell stories of alternative desire and love, but they are unwilling—and unable—to attribute such difference to aberration.

Cappello begins her essay with the invocatory formula the penitent utters in the confessional after the priest opens the metal grate: "bless me Father" (89). An inauspicious entrance into the confessional life of Catholicism occurs when Cappello recites the entire confession before the priest has opened the partition to hear it. Associating her initial confusion with a wrongness drummed into her by her Catholic training, Cappello reiterates an observation made by writers of Italian America about how the official Church's sanctioning of desire affects cultural rituals: "the disciplinary structure . . . may have converted the pleasures of my Italian American family (especially food and music, dance and a good deal of hugging) into signs of old country, peasant, non-capitalist depravity" ("Nothing to Confess" 94). That Cappello willingly employs the word "depravity" in connection to Catholicism's strictures reinforces her awareness of a Calvinist ethos within the institution.

The fear, discomfort, and disciplinary structure that Cappello experiences in the confessional box parallel her parochial school experience, which is developed in more detail in *Night Bloom*. Cappello's descriptions of the corporeal punishment of the nuns and the focus on memorization of the rules rather than development of the mind echo the complaints of her predecessor, Helen Barolini. Unlike Barolini, and Gordon before her, Cappello grew up after Vatican II (she was born in 1960), but the punitive nature of parochial schools continued to dominate the classroom. As Cappello writes, "I never forgave the nuns their belief in redemption through, not only self-inflicted, but other directed, pain. Or the way they made us feel the unprotected nature of our bodies" ("Nothing to Confess" 101). The next generation—of which Cappello is part—followed in the footsteps of literary mothers like Barolini and Gordon, both of whom refused to partake in an institutional structure that denied their intellectual appetites. As a theoretically oriented writer, Mary Cappello's most forceful denunciation of the official Church occurs when she describes the institution as a "world increasingly devoid of language capable of expressing a new idea" ("Nothing to Confess" 101).

Aware of the fact that her marginalization as a gay woman compels her into a nonsacred, (anti)confession, Cappello chooses to share a secular disclosure with her readers regarding the intertwining phenomena of ethnicity and sexuality. Articulating a specifically Italian American Catholicity in which the sacred and profane uneasily coexist in American culture, Cappello senses "some unmet desire" that she observed on both sides of her original family, and that was "maybe even violently forced into religious or materialist forms" ("Nothing to Confess" 96). In an effort to express a "more appropriate medium" for her family's love of opera, affinity for kitsch, and, for third-generation female cousins, an incredulous movement into religious cloisters, Cappello names "queerness in its broader sense" as the form of expression denied them by Anglo-American standards, middle-class aspirations, and the official Catholic Church. In a dramatic gesture, Cappello literally "outs" her Italian American family, asking the provocative question, "Is the lesbian in an Italian American family the *embodiment* of the family secret?" ("Nothing to Confess" 93) To which Cappello would reply, "Indeed, yes!" Cappello insists on the fluidity and inclusiveness of the terms "lesbian" and "Italian American," dismantling the binary construction that would render such a dyad antagonistic and mutually exclusive. Instead of confessing a sin that needs absolution, Cappello embraces a family that—despite its limitations—gave her the keys to a gay kingdom that has fulfilled her life:

> However well I try to place it, "my lesbianism" insists on returning to the unarticulated space between my maternal and paternal legacies. . . . [M]y willingness to inhabit a space of transgressive pleasure found its impetus in the unresolved area of desire/lack that was the space between Anglo ideals and Italian realities. In "becoming queer," I was becoming what my Italian American forbears denied about themselves even as they provided the example. In becoming queer, I see myself as having made something wonderful out of an Italian American fabric, the Italian American weavers of which were too ready and willing to discard. ("Nothing to Confess" 96–97)

Without overtly referring to Italian American popular Catholicism, Mary Cappello's description of her family's behavior suggests a tendency toward the *carnevalesco*, or, applying Bakhtin's theory, as Lucia Chiavola Birnbaum does, "spontaneous explosions of vernacular culture that defy the powers that be" (75). For Birnbaum as for Bakhtin, carnivals are "utopian projections of how people would like to live in a community of freedom, equality, and abundance, . . . [t]he ultimate egalitarian festival, . . . carnival turns everything inside out, bottom to top, front to rear, and unveils, unmasks and uncrowns" (77). One such utopian projection from Italian America is Susan Leonardi's *And Then They Were Nuns*, a novel of female community that turns assumptions about identity, sexuality, and womanhood on their head.

The narrative hybridity of *And Then They Were Nuns* reflects Leonardi's desire to overturn hierarchical assumptions about cloistered religious women living in community. The novel traces the thirty-five-year-old fictional history of one such community, Julian Pines, named after the medieval female mystic, Julian of Norwich, whose experience of God's revelations demonstrated divine love for all humans. Through the use of multiple voices and genres, Leonardi decentralizes authorial control in her novel in order to accomplish several aims:

1. To explore the thought, care and struggle required for any group to live imaginatively in a religious community.
2. To dismantle stifling structures of hierarchy traditionally represented by the Catholic Church.

3. To examine the attributes and differences between the contemplative and the active life.
4. To enlarge an understanding of how subversive Catholic women use the monastery setting to protect, shelter, and heal needy women.
5. To celebrate the importance of creativity in work and love.

Leonardi is no polemicist; rather, she uses humor, parody, and narrative play to explore the serious problems inhering in Catholicism and the ways religious women go about revising them. And they are religious, these women. But they refuse to abide by destructive habits of being that many of them learned in other religious orders. Living frugally with limited resources, they manage to maintain an independent existence in the foothills of a rural California monastery.

While Leonardi focuses her novel primarily on women's relationships, her placement of them within a religious community takes center stage. Catholicism thus is interrogated on these premises, found lacking, and accordingly revised—with grace, generosity, and creativity. Making such a community effective is hard work, requiring regular negotiation among its members. Despite a desire to topple unwieldy forms of hierarchy—that mimic the institutional church—the women at Julian Pines assume titles that carry status. Beatrice, one of the founders of the monastery, has assumed the title of "Abbess," which, quite literally, makes her the superior of her convent. Aware of the fact that she has "conspired with language and tradition" in donning such a title, Beatrice discharges her role as a "reverend Mother" with equanimity, intelligence, and kindness, demonstrating an ability to render sound judgment of others and to manage her own desires and needs without misapplying her power (153).

One such demonstration of Beatrice's wisdom is her ability to concede to the judgments of others. Beatrice loses the argument against calling one of the nuns at Julian Pines, the "priest," "so concretely did it conjure up a male human being, a hierarchy, a corrupt church" though Karen does function as confessor and consecrator of her community (111). The counterargument, offered by Anne, one of the nuns central to the spirit and pace of Leonardi's novel, cogently insists that "the very contrast between those expectations and the reality of *their* priest—a woman who conceived her priest part as just that, a part, no more or less important than other parts she could play in the group—was itself salutary both for themselves and for their many visitors and correspondents" (111). Beatrice relents. Because she promotes an egalitarian atmosphere that is supported by her even-keeled nature, Beatrice is beloved by each woman in the monastery. With her flair for employing a kind of coded language, Leonardi avoids overt description of Beatrice as a voice of *giustizia* (justice), but the author implicitly associates the Abbess of Julian Pines with an earth mother figure. Like Demeter, Beatrice's daughters are devoted to her, but rarely make seasonal returns to the underworld. Like the black Madonna who appears as a goddess of justice to Anna Girgenti in Ardizzone's novel *In the Garden of Papa Santuzzu*, Beatrice is *the* figure of justice in *And Then They Were Nuns*. As such, Beatrice dismantles hierarchical institutions that destroy, an undertaking that is coextensive with her desire and ability to liberate marginal people.

Observing religious rituals is another salutary recursion to Catholic traditions at Julian Pines. Leonardi restores features of the Latin Mass, pre-Vatican II, in which days are organized prayerfully around Matins and Lauds, Vespers and the Compline.[17] Meditational practices and the choice to lead a contemplative life in no way prevent these women from embracing visitors (nuns from other orders, former members, women needing sanctuary), whose work in the world as human rights activists, psychiatric social workers, and gay ministers require retreat and prayerful support a monastery such as Julian Pines provides. One such visitor is Bernadette Palermo, whose story reveals the limitations of traditional American Catholicism to nurture its women, a theme recurring in much Italian American literature. "Bernie Becomes a Nun" tells the story of an Italian American girl whose route toward independence is limited in the 1950s to entering a convent. Class status and gender circumscribe and determine Bernadette's life: the oldest of ten, Bernadette may very well love God, but she becomes a nun "to get out of the house" (94).

By the age of eleven, Bernadette Frances Palermo inchoately realizes that she does not want to repeat her mother's life of multiple pregnancies and bad health. An exemplary student, Bernadette's first avenue of independence is through education. Leonardi introduces sixth-grader Bernadette as class librarian appointed by Sister Mary Ascension, which reinforces Bernadette's desire to be distinguished outside her role of the firstborn caregiver to her mother's many children. The initial setting in which Leonardi places Bernadette is the cloakroom (where the books are stacked), positioning her as closeted. Bernadette's desire to control the checkout of one of the books in the 154-book collection reveals her recognition that her life's script may already be written for her. *Bernie Becomes a Nun* is the book that becomes the very "Hound of Heaven" barking at Bernadette's heals (85). A children's book about a privileged girl who becomes a Maryknoll nun, Bernie, the storybook girl, takes the name "Sister Joseph Marie," the very name Bernadette cynically takes years later when she enters the novitiate herself. However, the order Bernadette enters, the Sisters of Saint Clare, recalls the first Franciscan order of nuns, the Poor Clares, whose vows of impoverishment and seclusion do not initially improve Bernadette's life.

In time, however, Bernadette receives a room of her own. Never before had she private time for personal reflection to cry, to keep a diary, to "sleep for eight hours straight without listening for a waking babe or hearing a sister toss and turn" (98). Leonardi establishes a parallel between sixth-grade cloakroom and private room because both are spaces for Bernadette to experience independence. The private room is Bernadette's second avenue of independence because she is able to ponder, albeit tentatively, her own lesbian sexuality. Throughout the story, only fleeting references are made to Bernadette's sexual feelings for women, which began in grammar school. Leonardi limits the omniscience to Bernadette's point of view in order to suggest how familial and religious rearing severely proscribed Bernadette's thoughts. Thus a full telling of the sexual desire fueling her decision to enter a nunnery remains incipient at best.

During the climax of the story, after twenty-four years of service as a nun and, having become a psychiatric social worker (with a medical degree), Bernadette visits Julian Pines as a novitiate. With Beatrice's help as a mother confessor, Bernadette begins to reexamine the limitations set by her social class, gender, and religious upbringing. In her forties now and reassessing her limited life choices, Bernadette offers Beatrice a humorous turned serious exegesis of the sixth-grade book, *Bernie Becomes a Nun*:

> "Pure propaganda. And of the worst sort. White, thin, Anglo-Saxon, pretty, popular Bernie—the kind of girl God likes best. That's the message, isn't it?" Beatrice didn't answer the question; it was, after all, a rhetorical question, so Bernie kept talking. "That's always been the message. And I was brown and fat and poor and ugly and there didn't seem to be many alternatives. I've been a nun for twenty-four years because I found that fucking book in the sixth grade library." (103)

Refusing any longer to deny either the socioeconomic or the sexual forces that informed her choice to enter the convent, Bernadette requests an extended leave of absence from the order. Eventually, Bernadette leaves her order and moves to Julian Pines permanently. Leonardi implicitly reiterates the concerns of so many Italian American writers: women cannot be healed by their family of origin or the traditional Catholic Church. Bernadette's medical degree in psychiatry may have unlocked her desire for self-analysis, but a nontraditional nun her mother's age becomes the key to Bernadette's emotional healing. Retreating to the monastery called Julian Pines allows Bernadette to observe doctrinal church work performed by other women, including Karen, who says Mass and hears confessions. By excluding the voices and precepts of traditional Catholic ideology, Leonardi strips away institutional structures and rules of the Church that disallow women's active participation. Limited autonomy and marginal status are not countenanced at Julian Pines; communal participation in the sacraments is invited, though not required.

Italian American women have confessed plenty. Breaking away from the official Church becomes essential for these women to assert themselves outside a structure that inherently diminishes them. Italian American authors have regularly developed characters whose brand of Catholicism—unorthodox at best—requires them to function in a doubly marginalized way—as *Italian* American Catholics and as *Italian* American citizens. During the lion's share of the twentieth century, official Catholicism spurned Italian American devotion to popular ritual. Italians continued their devotional practices, despite struggles to be accepted as good Catholics and good Americans. The writers tell us their secrets in fiction and memoir. Coming out of the confessional box is an act of liberation. Refusing to return to that suffocating space is an act of American independence. Still, casting aside conventional Catholicism does not prevent writers from recreating it in their works, employing a distinctively Italian-based Catholic iconography. What these writers continue to confess outside the box reminds us that spiritual belief transcends institutional authority.

Stories of faith and justice deeply inform the voices of Italian America, ensuring a continued resistance against silence and subordination. One of the earliest and most vibrant voices in the Italian American canon is Rosa Cassettari, whose expert storytelling provided a means not only of her own liberation, but also, like all good tale-tellers in the folk tradition, a means to liberate others. Through sundry tales told to Marie Hall Ets and her various listening communities, Rosa performed an inestimable service that was both libratory and community building. Rosa's individual life story and the ways in which the genre of as-told-to autobiography achieves authority ultimately become indistinguishable from the tales she tells to eager audiences throughout Chicago. Her story and stories are the focus of the next chapter.

3

Story/Racconto

☙

Una chiacchierata nel passato

ROSA AND MARIE OF
ROSA: THE LIFE OF AN ITALIAN IMMIGRANT

The story is not beautiful if nothing is added to it.

—Tuscan proverb

A long time ago, two women met and talked for thirteen years. From 1918 to 1931, a middle-aged Italian woman named Rosa Cassettari shared stories with a young widow named Marie Hall Ets. A cleaning lady for over forty years at the Chicago Commons Settlement House, Rosa's status as a custodian did not prevent her from pursuing her art of storytelling, though she would not have perceived herself as an artist in a traditional Western sense, which places a high premium on individualism and originality. Rosa, in contrast, used her storytelling voice in relation to others, a voice emerging out of the folk traditions of her northern Italian roots. Rosa's storytelling voice always served libratory and performative functions, as she intuitively recognized the joy and relief she brought not only Marie who was crying when Rosa first spoke to her, but also the largely female communities of listeners in rural Lombardy and Depression-poor Chicago.

73

Guided by verbal markers that defined her life, Rosa's prowess as a teller of tales emerged from the communal and spiritual traditions of her rural, peasant culture, which she absorbed in her childhood and adolescence. Several voices inform the tales Rosa tells to Marie Hall Ets, her interlocutor and initial connection to audiences outside their dyad. Chicago listeners heard Rosa's old-world tale-telling traditions of the stables, where such stories took place in her Italian community, and which were influenced by conservative religious principles and a rigid caste system. Rosa's personal stories told to Marie include narratives, among others, about justice with prolific illustrations of the inequality between classes, and about divinity, influenced by folk religious beliefs in the supernatural and immanence of the divine, especially the Madonna, who becomes Rosa's most treasured audience. Once Rosa is encouraged by Marie to tell personal experience stories—which include a powerful migration narrative—she becomes not only the narrator and heroine of her own life, but simultaneously the voice of justice and faith as she merges her own life story with features of folktales in which triumph is victorious over adversity. I offer below the complex publication history of *Rosa* as a modern equivalent of the adversity involved in publishing the words of an unknown and undervalued woman whose verbal art reveals a brilliant and vibrant voice.

Twenty-seven years after Rosa Cassettari's death in 1943, the University of Minnesota Press published Marie Hall Ets's *Rosa: The Life of an Italian Immigrant*. Before she became an award-winning author of children's books, Marie Hall Ets did social work and resided at the Chicago Commons Settlement House following the untimely death of her first husband from pneumonia in basic training camp in the armed forces during World War I.[1] Located on the corner of Grand Avenue and Morgan Street, the Chicago Commons was a smaller settlement house than the more famous Hull House on Halsted Street. At the Commons, Marie met Rosa, or "Mrs. C., as she liked to tell everyone," inaugurating a thirteen-year daily connection between the two women.[2] As Marie Hall Ets writes in the introduction to *Rosa*, even after Marie left the settlement house in 1931, the two women visited each other until Rosa's death in 1943 (4). Marie clearly describes the relationship with Rosa as one of friendship. Before the advent of the tape recorder, Marie painstakingly transcribed Rosa's stories, which includes a still unpublished manuscript of several dozen folktales and the later published narrative of Rosa's pre- and postmigration life told in *Rosa: The Life of an Italian Immigrant*.

The publication history of this as-told-to autobiography with Marie Hall Ets featured as its sole author reflects the complexity of its construction, the collective identity of it voices, and the coercive influence of publication houses. Despite Marie's abiding recognition of Rosa's contribution to the book—practically speaking, Rosa gave Marie her stories—Marie Hall Ets was unable to persuade the University of Minnesota Press to recognize the literary collaboration between the two women. This failure to feature both women as coauthors should not be solely attributed to the press, who took a risk in publishing an autobiography about an Italian immigrant woman, well before the study of women's immigration and women's history became commonplace in academic and literary circles. In fact, such a failure is also a reflection of individualistic paradigms that, as Susan Stanford Friedman explains, "ignore the role of collective and relational identities in the individuation process of women and minorities" ("Women's Autobiogaphical Selves," *Women* 72).

Marie Hall Ets herself was not always certain about how best to tell Rosa Cassettari's story. Unsuccessful in publishing Rosa's folktales earlier in the 1930s, Ets seemed to have changed her mind in the years that followed about what she thought she was writing: oral history, autobiography, or fiction.[3] In fact, as Barbara Ciccarelli discovered after doing extensive research on the Ets manuscripts, "from the late 1920s to 1970, Ets would write several versions of Rosa's life story, employing different points of view. Her first attempt was the outline of a novel in the first person . . . focusing on Rosa's life, from her birth in northern Italy to her divorce from her first husband and remarriage in Chicago" (39). Three versions followed, in which Rosa narrates her story in first person with Ets modifying orthography and punctuation to reflect Rosa's heavily accented English, but eventually, dialect was dispensed with and proper names and places were fictionalized (Ciccarelli 40).

In her introduction to *Rosa*, Marie Hall Ets explains that because Mrs. C. was illiterate in English (and minimally literate in Italian), she wrote down the stories as they were told (and retold) by Rosa and only later "put them in order," explaining also that Rosa's heavy dialect "proved too difficult for the reader" (7). Frequent use of dialect in American works—for example, Mark Twain's *Huckleberry Finn*, George Washington Cable's *Old Creole Days*, and William Faulkner's *The Sound and the Fury*—was fairly commonplace in the latter part of the nineteenth century and the early part of the twentieth century, and was surely not unfamiliar to Marie. Nonetheless, the pronounced dialectical speaking voice of an unlettered Italian immigrant, despite her northern provenience, was simply not acceptable in written form and Marie Hall Ets no doubt also knew this. Mimi Pipino explains that shaping the progression of Rosa's narrative, Ets also acquired "the difficulties of transcribing oral performance," managing nonetheless to maintain elements of orature within Rosa's stories (21).

After Rudolph Vecoli successfully approached an editor at the University of Minnesota Press in 1968 regarding the publication of *Rosa*, Marie Hall Ets was compelled to compromise in two other ways that fundamentally changed her relation to the manuscript and to Rosa. First, Marie was required to remove all parenthetical comments between herself and Rosa transcribed in the earlier manuscript, eliminating a secondary discourse that reveals the close friendship between the two women.[4] In doing so, Ets's authorial relation to the book, *Rosa*, became individualized, preventing Rosa's subjectivity a fuller flowering *and* simultaneously decreasing Rosa's narrative authority. Second, Ets lost the battle of seeing Rosa Cassettari's name next to hers on the book contract (and cover), for which she fought. Lest she lose the interest of the publisher altogether, Marie Hall Ets "relented for the sake of getting her friend's story published" (Ciccarelli 57).

Marie Hall Ets's various mediations (often required by her editors), her role as an indefatigable researcher on northern Italian customs, and, finally, her own aspirations as a writer of children's books certainly influenced the final outcome of this autobiography. Questions yet remain: How does Rosa still function as a narrating subject of this as-told-to autobiography, despite the fact that she remained unlettered in English and excluded contractually as a coauthor? How did Rosa's role as a skilled storyteller of traditional Italian folklore influence how Ets transcribed the stories? How were Rosa's own stories subject to the influences of nineteenth-century ideologies on religion, gender, and class? Finally, how does the autobiographical "I" affect an understanding of the complex condition of Rosa's subjectivity? In effect, is the foundling Rosa (born Ines/z) Cassettari (changed to Cavellari in *Rosa*) so colonized as a subject that her speech must be seen through the lens of a wounded migratory and minoritized voice (Ciccarelli 8)?

In order to classify *Rosa* carefully, attending to its complex structure, the role of Marie Hall Ets as strictly that of an amanuensis must be challenged. That is precisely the role to which Rudolph Vecoli ascribes Ets when he writes in the foreword to the 1970 publication "with great patience, Mrs. Ets meticulously wrote down these accounts [of Rosa's life]" (xi). Vecoli's sponsorship of the book cannot be overlooked, since he was instrumental in seeing that the work was published after finding the typescripts of the manuscript at the Chicago Commons in 1960, while doing research on Italian immigrants in Chicago (Ciccarelli 9, 35).

Between 1918 and 1929, Ets transcribed Rosa Cassettari's many stories, which included folktales and personal stories of her pre-American past and her postmigration life. The story of their first encounter (recalled in Ets's introduction to *Rosa*) not only foreshadows the collaborative nature of their future literary relationship but also illuminates the central, defining feature of Rosa Cassettari's life: storytelling. Finding the newly widowed Marie Hall Ets alone in her settlement room weeping, Rosa Cassettari "just sat down and started telling [Marie] one of the folk tales she knew from her childhood in Italy" (3). Like a reconstituted version of the cantastorie, the history singer of local traditions, Rosa remained strongly tied to the oral traditions of Lombardy.

In an effort to learn more about storytelling traditions in northern Italy, Ets recorded Cassettari's folktales and anecdotes for a book-length manuscript entitled "These Stories I Know from Italia." In publishing a couple of these tales recently in the journal *Italian Americana*, the editors recall Ets's belief that such stories would hold little interest to "moderns" (*Rosa* 7). "Perhaps they were omitted as being tangential to Rosa's dramatic life story," the editors write ("Folk Tale" 107), but perhaps also Ets was sobered by her inability to get the stories published earlier in the century. In addition, Ets was writing during a time when the female autobiographer was invisible and for the most part unpublished. Her recognition that Rosa Cassettari's life story was "amazing," places the autobiographical "Rosa" squarely into the traditional masculine genre of autobiography in which the life represented is seen as exemplary.

Nonetheless, the editors of *Italian Americana* correctly explain that Rosa's folktales, in contrast to being peripheral to her amazing life story, "reflect the communal myths and fantasies of the poor and downtrodden" and appeal to a sense of justice denied the subaltern ("Folk Tale" 107). Recognizing the importance of the communal narrative in Rosa's life adds texture to the autobiography, *Rosa*, giving it the features of many women's life stories in its historical specificity and its oral cultural forms.[5] Rosa Cassettari's folktales and anecdotes are at times given in direct response to questions asked by her interlocutor, Marie Hall Ets. For example, Marie obviously wanted to hear more information about the setting for storytelling in northern rural villages. Rosa's response, "Stories in the Barn," begins with "So you want me to tell about the barn?" Rosa's knowledge reflects the poverty of rural inhabitants of Lombardy and basic efforts made to stay warm in the winter: "They were poor—

awful poor, in my time in those villages in Lombardia—no wood, no coal. . . . Oh, it was nice in the barn. . . . All those animals make it nice and warm in the little room" ("Folk Tale" 108).

Carefully detailing the activities in the barn, Rosa distinguishes between women's work—embroidering, knitting, and spinning—and men's playing *murra* (more commonly spelled *morra*), a game of extending the fingers of one hand and guessing the total number.[6] In the piece entitled "These Stories I Know from Italia," Rosa continues to explain that the men in the barn were the storytellers (from whom she learned the art), even though "they never went to school to read and write, but they were smart" ("Folk Tale" 109). One of the defining features of good story-telling is the ability to enhance the tale. Learning from the men in the barn how to "put more on to make it more interesting" ("Folk Tale" 109), Rosa clearly fits into the tradition of gifted tale-telling, handed down orally and modified by the talents of the teller. As the Tuscan proverb goes, "'the tale is not beautiful if nothing is added to it' . . . its value consists in what is woven and rewoven into it" (Calvino, *Italian Folktales* xxi).

All of what Rosa tells Marie accords with the folktales that emerge from a village economy of scarce resources. In his foreword to *Italian Folktales in America: The Verbal Art of an Immigrant Woman*, Roger D. Abrahams explains that the stable was "the warmest place of domesticity . . . readily accessible to both family and people from outside the household as well, and was the place where most of the important community exchanges took place, including the telling of old stories. . . . The central activity of the stable was the *filo* [*filatura*], the spinning of hemp on a spindle or spinning wheel . . . and it was here, too, that stories were spun and woven: the trope is not a conceit, for it is the traditional way in which storytelling is described in most of the world in which weaving is done" (xi).

In Rosa's illustrative story "The Little Chapel in the Black Woods," a young man named Corrado is reunited with his long-lost sister after the death of both parents. Before their serendipitous meeting, Corrado worked as a traveling peddler, selling threads, strings, and needles, basic parapher-nalia of women's work. While the story ends happily, with the children re-united and taken in by a wealthy woman with land, themes central to poor communities persist: the loss of one or both parents; the effects of poverty and powerlessness on children; the demonstration of *furberia* (wiliness) tempered by *deferenza* (observance, deference), and "a willingness to live within the traditional code of family and community obligations" (Abrahams xiii). In impoverished villages, "everyone is expected to do his own task in good spirit" (Abrahams xii), and in Italian folktales in general, humans struggle to free themselves from difficult and complex circumstances. As Calvino summarizes, "This complexity pervades one's entire existence and forces one to struggle to free oneself, to determine one's own fate; at the same time we can liberate ourselves only if we liberate other people, for this is a sine qua non of one's own liberation" (*Italian Folktales* xix). Rosa's verbal art is fundamentally emancipatory in nature: as a child laborer in the silk mills and at the work camp to which she's indentured, Rosa tells stories to liberate herself and the other girls from the drudgery of ceaseless labor and the cruelty of the factory owners and the nuns at the *istituto*, the convent which houses orphan girls where Rosa's adoptive mother sends her for three years. One of the most trenchant personal stories Rosa shares recalls the unjust treatment one of the inmates received from the nuns. Punished for wetting her bed, Filomena is forced to sit up in a rickety campanile all night. Unable to tolerate such mistreatment, Rosa recalls how she personally attended to Filomena by dint of stealth and empathy. "Quiet, quiet," Rosa recalls sneaking out at night and sitting with Filomena until dawn, *l'aurora*, or, as Rosa describes it, *l'alba*—"that first false light before morning came"—in effect dampening the effects of cruelty and powerlessness through a stealthy defiance of those unjust figures in authority (100).

Rosa's devotion to telling folk stories is indeed central to the story she tells Marie of her life in Italy and America. Rosa's sense of herself as a person is coterminous with the Italian oral traditions that she learned as a child. They cannot be separated. The story Ets ultimately published of Rosa's life sounds much like the folktales Ets also transcribed. It is no exaggeration to reiterate the fact that "Rosa's life is a complex folktale in its own right" (Hendin, "Social Constructions" 15). Rosa's connection with storytelling began early in her difficult life, perhaps in utero. Orphaned at birth in 1866–1867, Rosa, whose birth name was "Ines," is left at a baby depository by her biological mother, whom Rosa believed was an actress in Milan, though recent archival research has unearthed the fact that she was rather a needlewoman who worked for the Fossati Theatre in Milan (Milani 232). That her birth mother might also have performed on stage or possessed such aspirations thereto might account for Rosa's seemingly natural inclination toward performance through storytelling, often in settings that require improvisational talent. Not uncommon, infant abandonment in Italy by the mid-nineteenth century included a high percentage of newborns, many of them dying in their first year (Kertzer 3, 143). Illegitimate children were stigmatized by Church and civil authorities, referred to as *"figli [della] colpa,"* "children of guilt" (Kertzer, 27). Placed in a *torno* or *ruota* (a kind of turnstile), the abandoned infant could be left anonymously. Nonetheless, some mothers left on their children signs of recognition—"*segni di riconoscimento*"—should they wish to reclaim their child in the future (Kertzer 113).[7] For Rosa, a square piece of cloth was put on a card around her neck which "meant that the mother intended sometime to come back and get her baby" (*Rosa* 9). Even before Rosa is adopted by foster parents in rural Cuggiono (renamed as Bugiarno in *Rosa*) and learns the art of storytelling, she already has within her the makings of a triumphant story.[8]

As David I. Kertzer discusses, Western literature is replete with stories of abandoned babies: "a thousand versions of the same story of abandonment and ultimate redemption are told . . . ranging from sacred texts to fairy tales. From the founders of Rome—two foundlings taken in by an unlikely wetnurse—to the man who let the Israelites out of Egypt, . . . stories of abandonment are legion" (11). When ordering Rosa's stories into a chronological narrative, Marie Hall Ets quite literally begins with Rosa's abandonment at the Milan foundling hospital, perhaps to suggest that, unlike the untold thousands that died under this mass system, Rosa survived. She was provided with a wet nurse and, when that woman could no longer feed her, Rosa was lucky again and given a bottle (*Rosa* 9–10). Before Rosa is even conscious of herself, she has managed to beat the system that thwarted so many others. Recognizing her fortune, Rosa reiterates the fact that her day of birth is the same as the *Purificazione di Maria*, aligning herself spiritually to a Marianist sensibility (*Rosa* 10, 11). This identification allows Rosa to confer upon herself a magical relationship with the Holy Mother, who, as Marina Warner explains, "occupies the principal mediating position as a creature belonging both to earth and heaven" (xxii).

While David Kertzer believes that the southern city of Naples was unique in conferring supernatural benefits to those children who went through the foundling wheel, making them "*figli della madonna*," children of the Madonna (107), Rosa from the northern region of Lombardy equally benefits from the Madonna's guidance and protection throughout her life. One of Rosa's earliest childhood memories recalls the processione of the local village's patron saint, the Madonna, whose corporality Rosa describes as spiritually benefiting her: "Oh, how beautiful She looked with the sun shining on Her blue robe! . . . She came nearer and nearer. Just opposite me She stopped. And then, as I watched, She turned Her head just a little and looked right at me! I couldn't breathe. . . . Then the Madonna looked down again to the Baby in Her arms" (19). Rosa's allegiance to the Marianist tradition of Catholicism is fully established by the age of four or five. Rosa believes the Madonna to be incarnate, affording her concrete proof of a loving mother figure, which neither her birth nor adoptive mother provided. Throughout the many difficult events of her life, the Madonna becomes the confidante of Rosa, responding to her prayers and pleas in practical ways, giving her the means to effect an escape not only from her biological mother, but also, later in Missouri, from an abusive husband. For Rosa, the Madonna is a paragon of liberation and justice, which Rosa emulates in her own altruism toward others.

Despite the special powers derived from her status as the daughter of the Madonna, Rosa was forcefully subject to the proscriptive ideologies of religious and civil authorities. The system that regulated infant abandonment in Italy was fundamentally a "system of control over women," in which Church and state authorities attempted to "regulate families, reproduction, and sexuality" (Kertzer 3, 6). Applying Michel Foucault's work on sexual behavior in the late eighteenth and early nineteenth centuries to the story of forced abandonment, Kertzer explains how the topic of sex became the concern of the state as well as the Church: "'Sex became a matter that required the social body as a whole, and virtually all of its individuals, to place themselves under surveillance'" (qtd. in Kertzer 6). Rosa's treatment by her adoptive mother—Mamma Lena—reflects in extremis how Rosa's behavior was brutally monitored. Punished by Mamma Lena for being the daughter of a "*diavola*" because her biological mother bore her illegitimately, Rosa's early years before and after legal adoption are literally spent in various prisons.

From the enclosed confines of the torno (or ruota) to the literal jail she was placed in after her biological mother comes to claim her as her rightful daughter, Rosa's body was unceasingly subject to confinement. Through a combination of ingenuity and verbal skill, Rosa manages at age six to escape a dire situation when her biological mother, Diodata, briefly returns to reclaim her. In breathtaking detail, Rosa retells the story of her triumphant escape *from* her birth mother, using the practical realism of the peasant to accept the fact that her birth family "didn't love me" (71). Rosa subsequently tells of another equally inspiring escape from Missouri to Chicago after she migrates to America, making this escape narrative comparable not only to other immigrant stories (such as Mary Antin's *The Promised Land*), but also to female slave narratives, demonstrating a coextensive relation between transcendence *and* communalism, which I further discuss in the final chapter.

When Rosa is legally adopted by the fiercely authoritative Mamma Lena, whose ownership of her body is highlighted at the conclusion of the first stage of Rosa's life, Rosa accepts a fundamental fact of her existence. Winifred Bevilacqua's description of Rosa's social reality is apt here: it includes "the acceptance of deprivation and fatigue and accommodation to the restrictions her society places on individuals of her class and gender. For, although set apart from the other members of her community by her greater intelligence and vitality, as a child in Italy she has scant opportunity to control her own life" (548). Rosa reflects this understanding when she says: "So then I was no longer the daughter of the hospital and I was no longer a daughter of Diodata. I belonged to Mamma Lena entirely. Mamma Lena could do what she wanted with me now" (74).

Sent to work in the silk factory—the *filatoio*—at age six, Rosa manages to endure harsh conditions and exploitation, working long hours and paid little money. Unlike several young girls in Rosa's childhood who collapsed on the job or died from infectious diseases, Rosa manages to maintain good health in the face of overwhelming odds. Coupled with a strong body, Rosa's attitude about suffering evinces an acceptance of her situation without self-pity. Bevilacqua does not exaggerate when she says "Somehow, the young Rosa never loses a sense of her own worth or retreats into an attitude of victimization, but instead seeks to transcend her limited and limiting circumstances and to assert her individual self" (548). Rosa's sense of individuation is further reinforced when she was later encouraged to tell the story of her *self* to Marie Hall Ets. What made this ultimately possible was Rosa's early developed skill as a teller of folk stories—fundamentally communal—earning her "the attention and pleasure of others, giv[ing] her an identity that is related to her community and expressive of her individuality" (Bevilacqua 549).

Harnessed by poverty, beholden to the constraints of a European class system with fixed demarcations between classes and sexes, taught to fear the nobility and prohibited from speaking to males, Rosa's social indoctrination makes her, by turns, obedient and rebellious. Beaten into submission by her adoptive mother, Rosa nonetheless continues verbally to rebel against these divisions, in effect, questioning their authority and recognizing inherent injustice. To keep her subservient, Mamma Lena sends Rosa at around age ten to a convent for orphan girls, albeit assuring her protection from unscrupulous boys, yet reinforcing her status as an abandoned child. Run by nuns, this istituto is, in effect, a boardinghouse for poor girls without families who fatten the pockets of the silk-making bosses, for whom they work. Nonetheless, Rosa's skills as a silk maker and a storyteller—cementing the relationship between work and speech—are refined during her three-year servitude at the istituto, perfecting her performances in both arenas.

When Rosa relates the story of Beata (whose name in Italian means blissfully happy and, in the religious sense, blessed) to Marie, it is not one of the folktales she shares with the girls in the convent. Rather, it emerges from lived experience as a subordinate whose class and gender prohibit mobility and prevent change. As expected, the story Rosa tells of her orphan friend comprises features of the fairy tale, along with a cautionary if not bitter conclusion. Chosen to be married to the nephew of the mill boss, Beata's tale retains the sharpest edge of criticism for Italy's social hierarchy and its concomitant treatment of the poor. Separated from the other girls at the istituto, Beata is whisked away by the nuns in order to prepare her for the wedding. Told breathlessly like a fairy tale, Rosa's retelling of this incident includes the girls' invitation to the church wedding, but their physical separation from Beata, who remains with the owners of the mill, signals the rigid demarcation between classes and undercuts the fairy-tale atmosphere of the wedding.

Rosa's story of Beata does not conclude with the church wedding. Listener, Rosa seems to say, she did marry him. Rosa's addendum on the marriage is strictly cautionary when she recalls making a visit to Beata a year later after Rosa's three-year term ends at the istituto. Ets places Rosa's visit to Beata at the conclusion of chapter 12, effectively making a sober comment on the ongoing and irreparable divisions between gender and class in nineteenth-century Italy. Dressed in black from the death of her first child and ignoring the suggestive viciousness of her husband, Beata has not been blessed by patriarchal protection or class mobility. Her separation from the community of women from her social class makes her an anomaly, susceptible to the crueler machinations of a domineering spouse. As Rosa concludes, "the jolly, lively Beata I had loved so much was gone" (110). A doppelgänger figure for Rosa, Beata's conjugal experience is a disaster, a Cinderella tale gone wrong. Ets places this story directly before the chapters leading up to Rosa's arranged marriage, foreshadowing an equally dangerous situation for the narrator.

Developing into womanhood early in her life, Rosa Cassettari was subject to the policing of her body by many. From the early beatings she sustained from Mamma Lena for disobeying her command to the nun who faulted her for having large breasts, Rosa's culture surveyed and controlled all aspects of her sexual life. Arranged marriages were not uncommon in nineteenth-century Italy, so Mamma Lena's decision to arrange a marriage for Rosa is part and parcel of her duties as a responsible mother. Nonetheless, her choice to arrange a marriage to a much older man outside her village, who is a stranger, is unusual. Unwilling to lose Rosa to her husband's family, Mamma Lena arranges this marriage to a *forestiero* (foreigner) so that she can continue to control Rosa's sexual life, which includes controlling her children: "'But with Santino for a husband you can stay here with me and I will take care of the babies'" (153). After beating and starving Rosa for three days until she submitted to her wishes, Mamma Lena's rationalization for her behavior reflects the prevailing sexual ideology of nineteenth-century Italy: "'You need someone to control you. You need an older man to make you meek and save you for heaven in the end'" (152).

While it would be unlikely for Rosa overtly to criticize the institution of the family or the Church for enforced surveillance of her every move, Rosa manages to voice her discontent, paradoxically, in quiet ways. On her wedding day, Rosa recalls to Marie that she physically could not utter "yes" to her marriage vows, refusing at least symbolically to agree to marry a man she loathed. Not coincident is the fact that the priest to whom Rosa earlier made confession and who later marries Rosa is literally deaf, further reinforcing the Church's suppression of opposing points of view. Mistreating her immediately, Santino's abuse escalates to the point—later in America—where he nearly kills her. Significantly, Rosa utters repeatedly throughout the narrative that she must leave reference to her first husband out of her story, "'I can't stand to tell about that marriage and about Santino. I have to leave them out of my story, that's all. I can't tell about them!'" (155).

Rosa's self-censorship deserves commentary. Refusing fully to disclose Santino's abuse, Rosa nonetheless informs readers about the precarious childbearing events she experienced in Italy and America. Only fourteen or so when bearing her first child, Rosa does not understand the connection between sex and pregnancy. Neither, it seems, does Mamma Lena, unable to bear children of her own and hoping for a miracle from the Madonna to deliver her daughter's baby. Nearly dying during parturition, Rosa suffers from a fever, loses her hair, her singing voice, and cannot walk for a while: "'So I was around fifteen years old and I had to be like an old woman'" (159). This precarious narrative is repeated, unfortunately, again in America, throughout Rosa's childbearing years, well after she divorces Santino in Chicago and remarries.

Quite willing to share with Marie the perilous conditions surrounding giving birth, maternity expected of all good Italian married women, Rosa nonetheless continues to censor herself when she speaks of her abusive first husband. Rosa's autobiographical voice dictates against a confession of sexual abuse because that voice is also integrally connected to a communal identity. Rosa's communal identity has been inculcated by "social mechanisms which prevent the poor from realizing their full potential by keeping them ignorant, servile, and fearful" (Bevilacqua 548). Betty Bergland states that "ideology secures certain subjectivities within the prevailing social order" (104) and nineteenth-century ideology on sexuality in Italy enforces silence on the topic of sex between men and women. Rosa also subscribes to the cultural phenomenon of bella figura (maintaining proper social behavior in public), a code that has especial relevance for her role as a storyteller who performs stories to eager audiences in rural Italy and urban America.

Yet Rosa's migration to America unsettled and reconfigured her status as a traditional storyteller. As Fred Gardaphé explains, "[I]n the Italian oral tradition, the self is suppressed; it was not used as a source for storytelling in the communal settings of Italy," as supported by Rosa's transcribed folktales (*Italian Signs* 29). Rosa's folktales as we know emerge from oral traditions passed on by the men in the stables, but in America, Rosa's old-world space cannot be perfectly replicated in a new-world urban setting.[9] Marie Hall Ets's decision to focus on Rosa's stories about her past encourages a shift from a communal identity to an identity based on one's *self*, and the self "became a new and, for the first time, safe subject for public discourse" (Gardaphé, *Italian Signs* 36). But the self Rosa becomes in telling Marie her personal stories is, indeed, an "autobiographical self," and as such, is as much a construction as is her role as an esteemed storyteller at the Chicago Commons.

The two roles—traditional storyteller and American autobiographer—are linked in Rosa's tale-telling, preventing her, for example, from confessing details about Santino's treatment of her. As Elizabeth Mathias and Richard Raspa explain, "while legends and märchen [fairy tales] uphold the peasant social and political order and its accompanying ideology, personal experience stories are generally a response to conditions and events outside the village and tend to undermine village boundaries and beliefs" (18). Thus, when Gardaphé argues that Ets transformed Rosa "from a singer of a people's history, the traditional role of the *cantastorie*, into a singer/sayer of an individual's history" (*Italian Signs* 37), we must keep in mind that such personal experience stories are generically instructive too. Like another artful northern Italian storyteller, Clementina Todesco, Rosa Cassettari's personal stories are told like a folktale, in which "she becomes the folk hero, repeatedly confronting adversity and triumphing over hardships. . . . [T]here is no final resolution of life's dilemma. To be human means to be willing to confront the totality of human experience. [Like Rosa] Clementina['s] . . . childhood and adolescence of rugged adversity prepared her to confront the immensity of life with resilience, compassion, and endless creative energy" (Mathias and Raspa 19). Folktales firmly remain in Rosa's repertoire, and, even though Ets the editor separates the actual tales from Rosa's personal history, Rosa's tale-telling ingenuity lends folktale qualities to the personal stories she shares with Marie Hall Ets.

Rosa Cassettari's personal stories are primarily set in her northern Italian village, which comprise more than two-thirds of the book *Rosa: The Life of an Italian Immigrant*. It must be said that Rosa lived in America for fifty-nine years, immigrating as a young mother around the age of twenty. But her as-told-to autobiography *Rosa*, like many immigrant autobiographies, is devoted to her pre-American life in Italy.[10] Eventually migrating to America in 1887, where her husband was working in the iron mills of Missouri, Rosa Cassettari bore a second child alone, withstood continued beatings by her husband, and managed to escape his threats to kill her by fleeing to Chicago. Obtaining a divorce in the courts of America, Rosa later remarries Gionin [*sic*], a former ironworker of Missouri who aided in her escape. One of the coping strategies Rosa adopts to survive her husband's brutality and the extreme isolation of rural Missouri is her acceptance of "the friendship of another male immigrant, Gionin from Tuscany" (Bevilacqua 550). Rosa's defiance of the normative separation between the sexes reflects her covert rebellion and parallels her earlier refusal in Italy to utter aloud her marriage vows to Santino in Church. Rosa describes to Marie her developing friendship with Gionin as utterly virtuous, as the two come together on Sundays to walk a long distance to Church together. Her friendship with Gionin allows Rosa to achieve the justice denied her in a violent marriage, and she capitalizes on their allegiance to each other through the voice of faith as they are both devotedly religious and abide by Catholic precepts, despite having to walk miles to attend Sunday Mass.

Recognizing the linkages in Italy between gender, class, and region— "Girls were not allowed to speak to boys. The boy and the girl, they were like the rich and the poor together, like the man and the woman, like the North Italian and the South Italian"—Rosa demonstrates a combination of wiliness and obedience as she severs ties with social proscriptions that are not as pronounced in America (86). Santino's desire to force her into running a bordello in the backwoods for him gives Rosa moral permission to rebel against degrading her womanhood. Rosa applies her belief in the supernatural intervention of God and the Madonna to assert herself vocally:

"'I said, "Never! Never! I belong to God and the Madonna! You can't give me to the Devil!"'" (199) Rosa has managed to show piety in the face of a moral *infamia*, reinforcing her religious *osservanza* while showing *furbizia* by developing a friendship for a man whom she later marries in Chicago.

The Chicago Commons Settlement House becomes the primary locus for Rosa's genial memories of a painful Italian past and significantly the pivotal space where she gains local fame in America as a storyteller. Founding director of the Chicago Commons, Graham Taylor, influenced by "the spirit and ideals exemplified by Jane Addams at Hull-House [*sic*]," opened the doors to the Commons the year after the Columbian Exposition in 1894 (Taylor 5). In his *Chicago Commons through Forty Years*, Graham Taylor describes the plans for moving in 1901 into a better building, which he says "proved to be very available for neighborhood use. And yet for such a large building, its characteristic features are far more homelike than institutional. . . . The settlement house is really an addition to every little tenement home. Its books and pictures, the nursery and play spaces, the lobby and living room, the music and flowers, the cheery fireplaces and lamps, . . . are an extension of the all too scant home equipment of most of the neighbors" (41–42). Graham Taylor's reference to the quadricentennial of the voyage of Columbus and his later description of the new building are given fuller resonance when Rosa Cassettari offers her testimony of the Depression of 1893, the worst the nation had known up until that time.

Throughout her autobiography, Rosa uses the cadences of Italian for emphatic purposes as when she inserts double adjectives (functioning adverbially too) to describe her early years in Chicago as "a terrible, terrible poor time!" (210). Rosa's husband is forced to go to Wisconsin to find work, while she and her children "were home there and starving" (210). Experiencing no improvement in her living conditions at that time, Rosa courageously ekes out an existence, drawing on the reserves she developed in rural Italy: persistence, good will, and vitality. With regularity, Rosa petitions the Madonna to intervene on her behalf, considering it a miracle when she finds a quarter in the snow, which allows her to buy her starving children day-old pieces of bread (212). Bevilacqua describes the filth and congestion of the Chicago tenements and Rosa's painful struggle to survive as the "arduous but largely uncelebrated battle waged by immigrant women to keep their families alive, healthy, fit for work in the midst of these abominable and alienating conditions" (551). Describing in vivid detail the swill boxes in the alleys where garbage collects and white worms proliferate, Rosa hardly exaggerates when she exclaims, "I don't know why everybody in Chicago didn't die" (222).

After finding decent living quarters "in the big house with the Norwegian families," Rosa and the other tenants are forced to vacate because "one day a high-educated man came there, Dr. Taylor, and he wanted to rent the whole building to make something" (*Rosa* 219). It is in this first building that the Chicago Commons Settlement House is lodged and where Taylor rationalized that the rooms were "wholly unfit for family use," and where "eight very poor Italian families dwelt" (*Chicago Commons* 11). Despite undervaluing the very people he aimed to serve, Graham Taylor built a settlement house located in the middle of one of Chicago's poorest neighborhoods and manned it with middle-class volunteers, providing tenement dwellers a "haven from hostility" (Batinich 165).

Here begins Rosa's long-standing relationship with the Chicago Commons. Furious from having to clean out flooded rooms in another dilapidated apartment, Rosa returns to her old residence crying, but using the power of her words to express her rancor: "'It's you people—on account of you people I had to get out from this home! And now come and see where I live!'" (220) On that day, Rosa meets settlement house tenants of the Chicago Commons who help her locate better housing and hire her as a cleaning woman: "Forty or fifty years I've been scrubbing the floors, cleaning the rooms, doing the cooking, and telling the stories in the Commons. I grew old with that building. I love it like another home. I know every board in the floors" (221). Rosa's intimate relationship with the Commons bears little resemblance to Graham Taylor's homelike atmosphere. Domestic service was considered a "highly undesirable occupation many immigrant women considered too heavy" (Bevilacqua 552). Yet, Rosa's sturdy constitution and accommodation to suffering made such work acceptable, and represented another triumph over hardship as seen in folktales with heroic protagonists.

The settlement house, despite its limitations, helped Rosa learn English and provided her enough remuneration to keep her family out of poverty.[11] Rosa's relationship with the Italian Mother's Club in particular provided her, among other things, access to other Italian women (many southern Italian), Columbus Day celebrations, and most importantly a forum for her storytelling. As Mary Ellen Batinich explains, "The Chicago Commons was not unique in its program to provide activities to help Italian women in the assimilation process, but like Hull House, its model, forerunner, and neighbor to the south, the Commons provided activities intended solely for Italian women" (165). The settlement house as a space for the demonstration of Rosa Cassettari's verbal dexterity cannot be underrated. During her difficult early years in rural Missouri, Rosa did not have an audience for her storytelling, so she was unable to express herself or the communal values reflective of her northern Italian origins. The Missouri years might be described as Rosa's speakerly nadir. In her isolation, Rosa was disconnected from the fundamental activity that gave her life its texture, helping her and her listeners cope with extreme adversity. The Chicago Commons reignites Rosa's passion for tale-telling again, giving her access to an audience, which grows larger over time. That Rosa must unite the activities of work and storytelling—as she did in the silk factories in Italy—reinforces the fact that telling stories is as basic to her survival as work. Perhaps more importantly, Rosa Cassettari's position as an immigrant Italian woman and mother is not centered in the family home with Gionin and her children.[12] In the family home, she would not have piqued the ear of Marie Hall Ets, who recognized the brilliance of Rosa Cassettari's verbal art. Rather, in the final chapters, Rosa's focus remains mostly on her relationship to the settlement house, enlarging her discursive power as her audience grew. Rosa's own description of this verbal process bears full citation:

> Me, I was always the one that liked to entertain the people. So every noon I used to tell a story to the other cleaning women in the Commons when we were eating our lunch in the kitchen. In that time I didn't talk much English but I acted out those stories so good that they understood anyway. I made those women bust out laughing when I told some of those funny stories from the barn in Bugiarno. One day Mis' Hill, the housekeeper, came and heard me telling. She was so crazy for the way I told the story, she went and told Dr. Taylor. Then Dr. Taylor found me one night and said, "Come in the parlor, Mis' Cavellari, and tell the story to the residents."
>
> Me, I felt like one penny the first time I went in before all those high-up, educated people, and I had to talk half in Italian. But I was so reverent and acted the story so good that when I was the sister seeing the Madonna come alive all those residents raised up from their chairs with me. . . . After then I all the time had to tell the stories to everybody—to the Woman's Club, to the man's meeting, to the boys' party, to the girls' party, to everybody. Sometimes when they had big meetings in Hull House they would tell me to come there. One time that university in

Evanston [Northwestern] made me come there and tell stories
to those teachers going to school to learn the storytelling. I went
everywhere. (234–235)

Rosa's description of her storytelling aptly reinforces her effective-
ness as a performer in front of audiences large and small, including those
middle-class tenants who, like the poor cleaning women in the kitchen,
are transformed by listening to Rosa. That Rosa shares a story of the immanence of the Madonna is no small accomplishment for a minoritized
person in early twentieth-century America who is an Italian, an immigrant, a Roman Catholic, a working-class domestic, and not fully fluent
in English. But she shares that story with a receptive audience, demonstrating her verbal power to liberate both working- and middle-class listeners. The Madonna "comes alive" for them, and Rosa describes the
middle-class tenants literalizing their transformation by standing up during Rosa's performance. Like the Italians' engagement in procession discussed in chapter 2, Rosa transfers her religious fervor onto non-Catholic
audiences, who respond to her performance as though observing the paraded statue coming to life themselves. Rosa, through storytelling, fulfills
the function of ceremonial processions, as she affirms the listeners' sacred
membership in *her* community of faith. Like Rosa, they are not seeing
the Lord, but the preeminent figure of Italian Catholicism, the Madonna,
whose ministrations on behalf of Rosa empowered her throughout her
life. Rosa's storytelling reflects the continued importance of her voice that
is at once libratory and performative as she builds community with various audiences, diluting class and cultural distinctions, and, like bringing
the sacred statue into the streets, collapsing boundaries between sacred
and secular realms. All this because of her vocal agility.

The autobiographical voice heard in the above-quoted citation—
and, in effect, throughout the narrative—is the locally famous and
much-appreciated storyteller. No longer severed from community, Rosa
manages to replace the stable with the settlement house, both spaces
providing access for built-in audiences and gatherings of groups. Rosa
feels diminished at first in the presence of English-speaking listeners
from a more socially advantaged class, reflecting her abiding awareness
of linguistic and class barriers—even in America. However talented storytellers were deemed in the old country, the activity was "primarily an
activity for the very poor. . . . [S]torytelling was class linked. Enjoyed by
the socially underprivileged, it was shunned by those economically better off" (Mathias and Raspa 9).

Not fully fluent in English at the time she recalls first speaking to a middle-class audience, Rosa's inspired versions of Italian folktales originate from the great tradition of commedia dell'arte, employing improvisational comedy and the performative art of gesturing and voice inflection. Without referencing Rosa's own feelings of diminishment in front of the residents, Marie Hall Ets remarks in her introduction to *Rosa* on how founder and head resident, Graham Taylor, insisted on taking Rosa into the residents' parlor one evening after vespers to tell a story to those gathered (4–5). After Rosa's initial feeling of insignificance, she quickly gains vocal and dramatic stature once she ensconces herself inside the house of storytelling, successfully replacing the stable of yore with the settlement house of new.

Rosa is never remunerated for her sundry tale-telling activities. Graham Taylor's insistence that Rosa speak to the staff is a gesture of paternalism, not uncommon to the ideals of Progressive Era reformers. Yet Rosa's response is tempered by her class and gender identities, early formulated by social controls that policed the behavior of the peasantry and women. Despite new-world freedoms—as Rosa reiterates, America taught her "not to be afraid"—throughout the narrative, Rosa continues to be subject to the indignities of being a poor immigrant Italian woman with little social status and limited upward mobility. Perhaps for some in her middle-class listening public, Rosa's performances might be described as "spectacle-based entertainment," exercised in philanthropy toward immigrants, thus maintaining a distinct social hierarchy (Jirousek 35) and securing a subjectivity harnessed by old-world social codes. But for many of her audiences, especially with the other cleaning women, Rosa met listeners entirely receptive to her enthralling tales of magical relations with the divine and equally amazing tales of triumph over unjust divisions between poor and rich.

For Rosa, the settlement house always remained the place where she derived her greatest pleasure. A primary locus for Rosa's astonishingly genial memories of an adverse and often abusive past, the Chicago Commons is the place where she gains fame as storyteller, and, posthumously, as coauthor of her personal life experiences. Marie Hall Ets's concluding chapter focuses on Rosa's later status as a widow, which Rosa describes in liberating terms: "no man to scold me and make me do this and stop me to do that" (253). But the central focus of the final chapter of *Rosa: The Life of an Italian Immigrant* is firmly rooted to Rosa's class identity as a domestic laborer, whose migratory experience did not elevate her status or provide her with the means to become educated or moneyed. Marie's description of Rosa's stature in the introduction to *Rosa* emphasizes the physical toll that grueling labor had on her body: "Her shoulders were somewhat narrow and stooped from so many years of hard labor, but her hips and legs were so heavy that she found it hard to stand and walk. As she grew older she sat on a chair on the platform when telling her stories and used a cane when walking" (*Rosa* 6). In a final story about present-day suffering, Rosa tells the tale of her friend Ollie, another cleaning woman at the Commons. This story serves as Rosa's most incisive criticism of the social hierarchy at the settlement house. For Rosa and Ollie, meeting the housekeeper, Mis' Bliss, downtown after another punishing day of scrubbing—"Poor Ollie, so tired with her sore feet aching"—exemplifies the unbridgeable distance between the classes.[13] Self-absorbed and applauding her own generosity for taking the women out to a good restaurant, Mis' Bliss is blithely unaware of their exhaustion. Rosa trenchantly recognizes the class distinction that permits a social worker like Mis' Bliss to use her status to perform an act of Americanization, showing the working class what they might aspire to.

Not surprisingly, Rosa's final wish is to return to Italia before she dies. The reason Rosa gives for her desire is intimately connected to her keen awareness of social status. Empowered by her fluency in English, the new-world language, Rosa demands from those civil and religious authorities—the "high people"—answers to her candid question about their cruelty toward the underclass. To the convent sisters, especially the authoritative *Superiora*, Rosa questions and warns: "'Why were you so mean?—you threw out that poor girl whose heart was so kind toward you? You think you'll go to heaven like that?'" (254). Recognizing the power she would wield as an American, Rosa wears U.S. status like a badge of honor that protects her from further violation: "They wouldn't dare hurt me now I come from America" (254). Rosa's final words echo the act of civil disobedience she performed when she first returned to Italy on Santino's behest. Like an Italian Rosa Parks, Rosa Cassettari claims equal status with the upper classes at the bank she visits, refusing to abide by restrictive measures as she opens up the gate that encloses chairs reserved for only the "high people" (190). Responding to the chastising janitor that she authorized herself to sit in those chairs, she later speaks English to the Italian bank teller, who does not understand that the sparse vocabulary she has thus far acquired—"If you please. How do you do? Thank-you. Good-bye"—makes no grammatical sense, but clearly empowers her as an *americana*, despite her peasant origins (191).

Rosa's autobiographical voice is borne of her migratory status. No doubt she was a wounded storyteller, who faced adversity with enormous strength during her formative years in Italy. Later, in America, Rosa used the confidence she gained as a speaker of English, sharing her own personal stories to fight against that feeling of injury. That "she clings so strongly to her memories of her Italian past" as Bevilacqua observes, may very well indicate a compensatory measure she used to escape her "psychologically uncongenial present reality" (553). Indeed, in one of the passages deleted from the final manuscript that becomes *Rosa*, but that is included in the archives of the Marie Hall Ets collection at the Immigration History Research Center, the speaking voice reveals Rosa's sadness as poor woman in America not the locally cherished storyteller at the Commons. Compare the citation that follows from the one quoted in full above in which Rosa warmly states "I grew old with that building. I love it like another home" (221).

> I keep on and think and think w'at I can tell you, Mis' Mary. A lot of little things c-ome in my mind in the night, but they run away before I can catch them. I sorry I can't tell you more goo-d story—true story—from Chicago, but you don' write them because you say 'is not me. Me, I grow old with the settlement house, that's all. I was all the time working there. Thirty, thirty-five year scrubbing the floor and cleaning the room of the resident in Neighbor House, how I going to tell you a goo-d story about that? (qtd. in Bevilacqua 554)

Marie Hall Ets instrumentally encouraged Rosa Cassettari to authorize herself as a speaking voice in command of her stories, but she preferred a voice that was upbeat not beaten down. Clearly, Rosa Cassettari comprised both women, both voices. Marie noted the difference she saw in Rosa's affect when she was sitting alone, her "beautiful eyes often look[ing] sad," in contrast to those eyes that "sparkled with life when she was with anyone, and changed from one expression to another when she was acting out her stories" (*Rosa* 6). The ease, vivid detail, and breathless telling of these stories are a testimonial to Rosa Cassettari's tale-telling expertise, in the house of storytelling where she felt most alive, most at home. Both women contributed to the production of *Rosa: The Life of an Italian Immigrant*. That Marie Hall Ets's name is featured as sole author does an injustice to the construction and understanding of this immigrant autobiography. Rosa Cassettari knew all about injustice. Her stories exemplify that liberty cannot come at the price of confining another. But Rosa managed to liberate herself and others through storytelling and her speaking voice breaks through the literary confines of standardized English, strict adherence to chronology, and elimination of the dialogical relationship established between storyteller and storywriter.

In an earlier unpublished introduction, Marie includes a story of Rosa's disagreement with her husband's belief that one day the two of them would be able to afford "a little piece of land way out on Grand Avenue." Believing in the American dream of land purchase through dint of hard work and careful savings, Gionin meets a resistant Rosa, who subscribes to an old-world fatalism: "And I said 'No! We will never be rich—we will always be poor—and better we keep our money, so if hard times come again we will have something to eat! We can't eat the land!'" (qtd. in Ciccarelli 33–34). Despite her fear-borne protest, Gionin buys property, and Rosa ultimately defers to her husband's forward-thinking optimism: "(And he was right, too. I wouldn't have this house and yard now if he didn't do like he did)" (qtd. in Ciccarelli 34).

Both gainfully employed in 1920, Gionin and Rosa Cassettari owned a home at 3716 West Grand Avenue with a mortgage (Ciccarelli 33). Despite the tremendous detail packed into the final chapters of *Rosa*, this important fact is left out. While she was neither highly upwardly mobile nor educated, Rosa Cassettari's economic circumstances improved in middle age and owning a home supported this fact and certainly proved an important milestone for both Gionin and Rosa. The settlement home, however, continued to be the locus of Rosa's storytelling inspiration—and Marie's storywriting focus. Yet the belief that owning a piece of land be it ever so humble reflected the desires of a diasporic people, who were no longer allowed or able literally to *lavorare la terra* or *vivere dei prodotti della terra*: to work and to live off the land. The voice of land is not only a contrast to metropolitan culture but also a testament to an abiding Italian connection to the rural and rugged in America. The voice of land is the focus of chapter 4 and the thematic inspiration of Guido D'Agostino's novels.

4

Land/Terra

୬

Village People in Guido D'Agostino's Novels

WITH JOANNE RUVOLI

Like their stories, storytellers are also rooted with love and knowledge of the land.

—Gioia Timpanelli, "Stories and Storytelling"

Guido D'Agostino believes in the land. The four novels he published within a twelve-year period (1940–1952) reflect an agrarian idealism nurtured in homeland Italy but sewn in new-world America. D'Agostino seems to be implicitly remarking on the U.S. industrial marketplace that hired and exploited immigrant Italians, who lived in cities and putatively extinguished any desire in them to remain connected to their rural antecedents. Even in his most urban of novels, *My Enemy, The World*, D'Agostino positions his protagonist as living interminably between two worlds, the agrarian Sardinia of his youth and, as the Popular Library edition stated on its back cover, the "teeming jungle" of Greenwich Village, where the author sets much of the action.

95

In each of D'Agostino's four novels, the author establishes uneasy relations between rural and urban sensibilities, locating his Italians in both worlds, but giving the edge to the agrarian. Respect and desire for land were firmly established in the Mezzogiorno by the contadini themselves, who coveted but were denied access to land. As unjust as feudalism was in a preunified Italy, *burgisi* (peasants) were afforded access to baronial lands for hunting, fishing, and foraging (Diner 23). Once the new social order imposed itself during the Risorgimento, peasants found themselves land-poor sharecroppers, seeking food, and, due to the punitive measures of a northern government, disallowed the privileges of using common lands that supplemented their diets (Diner 22–23).

Guido D'Agostino responds to land-poor peasants by juxtaposing the Italian desire for land with the American sanctification of nature refracted through an Emersonian sense of nature as a symbol of the divine. To assure readers of Italians' participation in the project of industrial America, that is, of literally making the United States by building its roads and laying its railways, D'Agostino assimilates his immigrant Italians to an America that sanctifies nature *and* recognizes the dignity of manual labor *on the land.* Within each novel, D'Agostino incorporates a wise voice of the land as a reminder and hope to Italian Americans of the bounty that can be found on U.S. soil when workers transplant their agrarian passions and increase their expertise in cultivation on *terra firma America.*

Unlike his contemporaries, Pietro di Donato, Jerre Mangione, and John Fante—each of whose works have been resurrected in the late twentieth century through subsequent reprintings—Guido D'Agostino has had few recent advocates in either the academic or the publishing world. While his first and arguably most famous novel, *Olives on the Apple Tree,* was republished in 1975 under the Arno Press imprimatur,[1] his subsequent novels remain virtually unknown, though they received some fine contemporary reviews. Two early scholars of Italian America, Olga Peragallo and Rose Basile Green, included critical assessments on D'Agostino's novels, in particular on *Olives on the Apple Tree,* examining the recurring theme of social dislocation for Italian immigrants and their progeny in America.[2]

Descended from Sicilian immigrant parents, Guido D'Agostino was born in 1910 in New York City's Little Italy, and educated in its public schools. Unlike his contemporary, Pietro di Donato, whose father's untimely death forced his son prematurely into the laborious world of construction, D'Agostino's boyhood included bicycle racing and amateur boxing (Peragallo 62). In adulthood, D'Agostino demonstrated his tie to the skilled labor of his ancestors through the activity of masonry, building "an ideal country gentleman's home" in Westchester County, further testifying to his "love of the land and of the outdoors" (Peragallo 63). In her reference to the land, Olga Peragallo early captures one of the most salient voices of D'Agostino's literary work. Unlike the novels of di Donato and Fante—whose focus on work in urban settings preclude encomia to nature[3]—D'Agostino's novels are often structured around the conflict between those committed to the land and the increasingly mechanized world of the city.

An early reviewer of D'Agostino's first novel presciently observes an important distinction between *Olives on the Apple Tree* and that of di Donato's and Fante's first books: "You compare Guido D'Agostino, inevitably, with Pietro di Donato and John Fante, two other Italian Americans who wrote remarkable first novels. I suspect he is older than they, and more at home in America. His writing has, perhaps, less individuality; his outlook on life is richer and mellower" (Gannett 219). Pietro di Donato and John Fante were both born in 1911, one year after D'Agostino, making the age disparity moot. Nonetheless, their autobiographical first novels, Fante's 1938 *Wait Until Spring, Bandini* and di Donato's 1939 *Christ in Concrete*, focus intensively on ethnic prejudice toward Italian American families, whose poverty and powerlessness awaken second-generation boy protagonists to the injustice of American civil and religious institutions. In contrast to the more somber tone of di Donato and Fante, another contemporary of D'Agostino's, Jerre Mangione, writes about his Sicilian family's seeming indifference to American customs, using humorous folktales to explore the rich heritage of his descendants in his 1942 *Mount Allegro*.[4] In each of these works, the narrative is driven by the developing sensibilities of a second-generation young male narrator or protagonist, who becomes a spokesperson for his culturally distinctive Italian family.

Guido D'Agostino is similar to his contemporaries in his attempt to elucidate the fragile situation of Italian immigrants in early twentieth-century America. But, unlike them, D'Agostino's narratives tend to be more idea driven than protagonist driven. Like a romanticist, D'Agostino likes to create characters that represent important truths— about the country, about the city, and about cultural heritage. Speech events punctuate the pages of *Olives on the Apple Tree* through the eloquent voice of Marco. Soliloquizing, Marco delivers his tributes to the land as though in solitude, for his words are meant to stir the emotions of readers outside the world of Italian America. In an early speakerly event in the novel, Marco explains to his *compagni* that his frustration with America lies in his position as an immigrant whose work over the past seven years has led to sickness, which only his cultural community can cure: "Always I have looked for people like me—Italians. I have looked for the love of the things that I love because I am me and my father was my father. Is something inside goes 'way back. The love of work and what you do. The love of the ground and the good crops. The love of the grapes and the good wine. The love of the food and the table and the conversation" (*Olives* 26–27). For Marco, whose speeches resonate with images of privation and plenitude, fulfillment as an immigrant in America comprises reconnection with land and with fellow Italians, reinforcing a communitarian ethic, which will contribute to a higher and happier standard of living for first-generation Italian Americans.

Guido D'Agostino's portrayal of smaller communities of Italian immigrants (as opposed to those living in large cities) might be more fruitfully compared to another of his contemporaries, Mari Tomasi, whose second novel, *Like Lesser Gods*, explores the development of Italians into Americans while creating a character outside the immediate family to voice important ancestral beliefs. Like Tomasi, D'Agostino does not fully jettison Italian cultural values in an effort to Americanize his characters. Rather, he examines the complex interplay between Italian values (primarily represented by his fictional personae's relationship to the land) and an American emphasis on individualism and marketplace struggle in an industrialized society. Refusing to submit to the prescriptions of literary naturalism, D'Agostino creates characters driven by certain ideals, but not ultimately destroyed by hereditary or environmental forces. Nor does D'Agostino's brand of realism emerge from social protest fiction or proletarian novels of the 1920s, which may have put his work more solidly on the American literary terrain during the time period in which he wrote. D'Agostino's representations alone of Italian Americans are worth the price of entry wherever he places them—in rural Pennsylvania or in Greenwich Village. He examines their struggle to maintain a sense of cultural integrity while adjusting to changing economies—on the land and in the city.

Guido D'Agostino's works have not had the sustaining help of secondary discourse to explore more faithfully his contribution to Italian American literature and U.S. literature more largely. The reason for this has much to do with D'Agostino's attempts in subsequent novels—especially in *Hills Beyond Manhattan* and *The Barking of a Lonely Fox*—to write mainstream "American" literature, attempting perhaps to achieve canonicity by aligning himself with such nineteenth-century luminaries as Emerson and Thoreau, and to twentieth-century novelists as Hemingway and Fitzgerald. As such, D'Agostino distances himself from the documentary-style fiction of a Dreiser or a Norris, and also from the raw realism of a di Donato or a Fante. Guido D'Agostino shapes his subsequent narratives around the *idea* of the struggle for American badges of success, featuring characters already having achieved some upward social mobility. Like mainstream Anglo-American writers of both the nineteenth and twentieth centuries, D'Agostino also expresses in his works an ambivalent relationship to an increasingly industrialized country of factories and, in their wake, urban blight. This type of urban critique is more complex than an immutable bias against or a deep distrust of "the city." Leo Marx best describes the puzzle of what he calls antiurbanism in the fiction of canonical American writers this way: "anti-urbanism is better understood as an expression of something else: a far more inclusive, if indirect and often equivocal, attitude toward the transformation of society and culture of which the emerging industrial city is but one manifestation" (64).

Guido D'Agostino's novels register such an equivocal attitude toward urban America, beginning with his first novel, *Olives on the Apple Tree*. In his debut novel, the featured Italian immigrant family has separated itself from the Italian colony, having achieved financial success in America. The effects of their isolation cause conflict. The successful Gardella family—moneyed, propertied, rearing college-educated children—resides in town in contrast to their paesani who live from hand to mouth in a crudely sheltered hilltop community derisively called "Wop Roost." The author's second novel, *Hills Beyond Manhattan* (1942), effectually reiterates this conflict between working Italians and the nouveau riche townspeople, whose consumerist mentality will deprive the laborers of hunting ground, echoing the class system of a modernizing Italy, whose landowners, through the gabellotti (overseers), prevented poor people from owning small plots of land. By creating a protagonist in this second novel who is French, D'Agostino might be said to distance himself from the importance of maintaining Italian heritage in America.[5] Uttering land aspirations through the voice of a rather dispassionate French protagonist, D'Agostino loses the idealism that distinguishes his first novel. The creative tendency in *Olives*, however, was to place too much responsibility on his spokesman for promoting an agrarian community, for which the author was criticized in a contemporary review: "The characterization is good except in the case of the hero-hobo, Marco, who is just too fine, too noble. . . " (Sylvester220). Without Marco, there is no *Olives on the Apple Tree*—it's the equivalent of expunging Vito Corleone from *The Godfather*. For good reason, Puzo has Vito functioning like a demigod, a feudal king whose protection and power are out of this world. The same can be said for D'Agostino's creation of Marco in *Olives on the Apple Tree*.

Returning to Italian American themes in his third novel, D'Agostino's 1947 *My Enemy, The World* examines the conflict between Italian and American ideas about class mobility and social justice. His most urban of novels, *My Enemy* comes closest to the gritty realism of a di Donato novel and ultimately anticipates that most popular Italian American novel mentioned above, Mario Puzo's *The Godfather*. In its emphasis on private justice over institutional forms of social control, *My Enemy* paves the way for *The Godfather*, in which the criminal family solely determines matters of justice. D'Agostino's most urban novel yet continues to recall the Italian peasant's love of land, inserting a folk narrative that examines the eternal conflict between landed gentry and the pauper peasant whose sense of justice and higher level of intelligence make living in post-Risorgimento Italy increasingly impossible. *The Barking of a Lonely Fox* (1952), D'Agostino's fourth novel, seems rather like a narrative retreat from the pressures produced by urban living. Returning to the village atmosphere of his first novel, D'Agostino reiterates in a more mainstream manner his major themes: the land as an important indicator of Italian American identity; the ancestral voice who embodies truths about the land to be honored and transmitted; and the ethnic culture that is increasingly diluted by values antithetical to a harmonious community identity.

By this final novel, however, D'Agostino has carefully submerged Italian American voices by producing a text that reflects some ambivalence toward cultural identity as a major focus for his fiction, a deliberative move to produce books that might appeal to more mainstream, middle-brow readers. D'Agostino focuses on a theme central to our national literature: the ongoing conflict and range of diverse emotions demonstrated in U.S. writing between the country and the city. As Joyce Carol Oates explains, the image of nature, "the *idea* of Nature" is "the dramatic background against which fictional persons enact their representative struggles with those values the City embodies, which are frequently internalized" (11, 12). D'Agostino's fictional contribution to this struggle gains resonance when he employs Italian American characters whose ideas about the land have a history as long as their oral traditions. Narratives from immigrant Italians about scarcity of land and food often revolve around personal experience stories of peasants and small farm owners whose love of the land has little to do with idealism and much to do with the effects of hunger. D'Agostino manages in his novels to bring into play both idealistic and practical reasons for working the land in America, effectually grafting Italian land consciousness with American internalization of nature's offerings.

American literature is replete with examples of the contrast between pastoral idealism embodied in nature and the industrial capitalism represented by the city. Memorable characters in American literature—from Hester Prynne's Massachusetts forest to Ántonia Shimerda's Nebraskan soil and Per Hansa's (of O. E. Rölvaag's *Giants in the Earth*) Dakota prairie—are aligned in both environmental and mystical ways to the land. Whether a writer of romance like Nathaniel Hawthorne uses the land as a means of temporary escape for a trenchantly isolated figure like Hester or a transplanted southerner like Willa Cather explores the immigrant's desire to earn a living from the land, a remarkable similarity is shown by the authors' acceptance of the inherent possibility of freedom and creativity emerging from one's relationship to an American landscape. Leo Marx examines mainstream American writing that boasts a

> familiar roster of pastoral figures: Natty Bumppo, the "I" of Emerson's *Nature* and Thoreau's *Walden*, Ishmael, Christopher Newman, Huckleberry Finn, Jay Gatsby, Nick Adams, and Ike McCaslin. All of these [male] characters enact the ideal life of the American self journeying away from the established order of things into an unexplored territory we tend to think of as Nature. The object of the journey, implied or avowed, is the nearest possible approximation to the situation of the autonomous unencumbered self. (74)

The Thoreauvian character in D'Agostino's oeuvre, Marco of *Olives on the Apple Tree*, is the pastoral figure *willing* to be encumbered. Without the crankiness of a Thoreau, Marco critically evaluates the miserable lives of the immigrant Italians living in Wop Roost, calling them in one breath "good people" and "fools." His desire to become a farmer will positively influence the futures of those Italians who presently live like "animals . . . satisfied today and never think[ing] of tomorrow." In contrast, Marco maintains the idealism of his Italian father, who became land-poor after the unification of Italy. He will plant his heritage in American soil, thereby becoming a loyal, pastoral citizen: "the man who

plants a field and is careful what he plants because he loves the ground
and he knows there are others who will love and care for it when he is
gone. That is happiness—if out of yourself you give something that will
last when you, the man, will be no more. That is the real work of the
Italian in America" (164).

On the other side of the literary spectrum is the ever-increasing ubiquity of the city, which is often represented in U.S. literature by "various
embodiments of the dominant culture of industrial capitalism. (These are
likely to be negative images like the scaffold or the valley of ashes)" (Marx
78). Guido D'Agostino was born at the beginning of the twentieth century, at the same time that the American city "became more materialistic [which then] engendered a hostility in the literary imagination. . . .
From Ralph Waldo Emerson to Ralph Waldo Ellison, writers have de-
picted the material city cut off from spiritual energy" (Lehan 5). Like
other writers of the early twentieth century—Eliot and Fitzgerald, for
example—Guido D'Agostino was aware of pointed attitudes—often antipodal—about the county-city dichotomy, exploring in his own writing
the oppositional feelings produced by contrasting environments. As
Richard Lehan explains, "The urban drama played itself out against a
Europe transformed by the Enlightenment; by an America that offered
a New Jerusalem, and by a wilderness and a frontier against which the city
assumed its meaning" (6). For Guido D'Agostino, fictionalizing a New
Jerusalem in novels about Italian Americans served as an assimilative
measure, protecting his ancestral culture from the prevailing nativist discourses and scientific racism current in contemporary thought. At the
same time, the author preserves the voice of the land as a celebration of
the rootedness of Italian immigrants on American soil.

Pertinent to this discussion, then, is the fact that southern Italian
immigration—the heaviest occurring between 1880 and 1920—coincided
with virulent protests by native-born Americans and policy makers against
"unlimited immigration" (Friedman-Kasaba 95). As part of the ideology
of racial nativism current in early twentieth-century America, immigrants
from southern and eastern Europe were perceived to be racially different
from white Americans.[6] Quoting John Higham's seminal work on American nativism, Kathie Friedman-Kasaba explains that in manufacturing
"'sharp physical differences between native-[born] Americans and European immigrants,'" recent immigrants, such as southern Italians "could
seem to be 'a fundamentally different order' of people" (95). This nativist
ideology reinforced the "social vulnerability of eastern and southern
European immigrants. The more central immigrant labor became to

economic expansion, the more racial nativism became incorporated into particular labor force structures and the more it regulated immigrants' lives outside of employment" (Friedman-Kasaba 95). In the first decade of the twentieth century—when D'Agostino was born—"the strictly foreign born comprised nearly 45 percent of New York City's population" (Friedman-Kasaba 97). In an effort to restrict immigration—selectively— the U.S. Immigration Commission produced a report in 1911 that placed southern Italians—in contrast to northern Italians—in the category of the unassimilable immigrant: "[T]he South Italian [is] excitable, impulsive . . . an individualist having little adaptability to highly organized society" (qtd. in Friedman-Kasaba 100). Guido D'Agostino was most likely aware of such racial nativist discourse. His fictional creation of a self-hating Italian American in *Olives* indeed reflects one of the self-immolating responses to being perceived racially and culturally inferior to the host society.[7]

Guido D'Agostino's *Olives on the Apple Tree* best encapsulates the author's feelings toward the American land and the immigrant Italians who came to inhabit it. Perhaps because this novel is D'Agostino's most didactic, it also emphatically reveals his desire to fuse Italian American identity with love of the land. The author's first novel met with primarily positive reviews, though the aforementioned review by one Harry Sylvester in *The Commonweal* negatively compared D'Agostino to Fante, and described D'Agostino's characters as "two-dimensional and without vitality." Offensive to this reviewer was D'Agostino's creation of Marco, whose role in the novel is profoundly misjudged by Sylvester, who aligns him with a "type that occurred frequently in the more poorly-written proletarian novels of a few years ago.".

D'Agostino's dedication to the land and to Italian ancestry in *Olives on the Apple Tree* is embodied in his creation of the stranger figure that gives voice to the yearnings of his countrymen. Refusing to be diminished because of his status as an outsider, Marco is slowly absorbed into the world of the Wop-Roost inhabitants and the upwardly mobile Gardella family, whose material well being has allowed them to live in town, separated from their impoverished compatriots. Marco represents the figure of the stranger in the sociological sense that Georg Simmel early identified: "he is the freer man, practically and theoretically; he examines conditions with less prejudice; he assesses them against standards that are more general and more objective; and his actions are not confused by custom, piety, or precedent" (146).

Marco quickly assesses the two contrasting environments—that of the Italian enclave disparagingly labeled "Wop Roost," peopled with the sounds of dialectical speech, and that of the New York town, representing business and commerce, in short, urban interests. The Gardella family in fact features elements of both the Italian enclave they have escaped and the new-world desire to accumulate money and assimilate American ways. Contractor, Federico Gardello, propelled by an excessively ambitious wife (ironically named Giustina) to attain money and power, remains insistently first-generation in his respect for the Italian laborers and in his impatience with his son, Emile (born Emilio) Gardella, M.D., whose own ambitions to enter Anglo-American society are thwarted by his naïveté and self-loathing. Emile's life is regulated by the nativism in hering in mainstream American culture, which contributes to the shame and hatred he feels toward his ancestry.

D'Agostino's introduction of an outsider figure, who stays with the "hill-top community of his own people" (37), is the author's attempt to give voice to disenfranchised immigrant Italians. Marco's speechifying events are sprinkled liberally throughout the novel, forming a running commentary on country over city values, emerging from an Italian peasantry denied land and respect in their country of origin. Marco's ongoing conflict with Emile represents in extremis the conflict between ethnic resilience and ethnic hatred.[8] In *Olives on the Apple Tree*, retention of some Italian values remains paramount. Unafraid of change, Marco also recognizes the need to relinquish old-world customs that are no longer applicable in America, disconnected from historical and social practices of nineteenth-century rural Italy.

D'Agostino creates Marco in order to build a bridge between Italian and American dedication to working the land. In several speech events, Marco laments the shift in America from country living toward urban commerce. As an Italian peasant who worked in vineyards as a child, Marco ruefully migrated to America in order to escape Mussolini's fascism—and the subsequent loss of land for peasants.[9] Fired by the idea of America, Marco sails from Naples, a trip which he nonetheless describes as "like dying," in order to experience the freedom of working the land without the custom of primogeniture (163). Forced initially in America into boot blacking and factory work—work associated with the city—Marco recoils from the kinds of labor in which the majority of Italian immigrants were compelled to engage.[10] Conferring upon himself instead the American prerogative of initially wandering around the country—à la Natty Bumppo or Huck Finn—Marco's observations position him squarely within the tradition of American pastoral literature. Placing him in this tradition also allows D'Agostino to claim assimilation for the Italian in America through a reconstituted relationship to the land. Marco explains that through a long-term connection with American land the Italian "becomes the true citizen" (164). Marco clearly wants to establish permanent relations with the Italian immigrants of Wop Roost, ensuring their revitalization through land labor. While Marco is not per se a storyteller in the traditional narrative sense of a Rosa in Ardizzone's *In The Garden of Papa Santuzzu,* he has nonetheless imbibed a fundamental feature of the folktale: the liberation of other people. In this way, he shares the same concerns as those historical storytellers Rosa Cassettari and Jerre Mangione.

Variously called a vagrant, a hobo, a Wop, and a greenhorn, Marco, in the style of an American wanderer, evinces no shame and maintains an assured sense of his identity as an Italian immigrant who regularly vocalizes his refusal to be diminished by American ethnocentrism. Marco's various encomia to the land reflect both idealism and practicality. Echoing the thoughts of the earlier Swedish immigrant character, Alexandra Bergson, of Willa Cather's *O Pioneers!,* Marco believes that "the land always pays. The land will always support the man who works it" (95).[11] In one of his many speeches to his immigrant paesani, Marco carefully subscribes to a work ethic that raises laborers from the status of mules to men: "Many of the things we remember from the old life we must forget. They have no place here. No more the long hours of work from when it gets light in the morning to the night when it is dark. Work is good but it can kill a man too. Here you do your work and you have time to think and the time to enjoy other things too. There is more balance to the life" (139).

Guido D'Agostino's inclusion of Marco as the voice of the village people achieves important aims for Italian American literature. Throughout the narrative, Marco exemplifies the self-respecting voice of conscience for the entire Italian community. He teaches the immigrant laborers the value of self-respect and recognizes the debilitating nature of ethnic shame for an upwardly mobile second-generation character like Emile Gardella. The desire to erase all traces of ethnic identity is deemed by D'Agostino a form of cultural suicide, but that tendency should not be confused with the author's assimilative gesture of aligning Italian rural antecedents with American farming and dedication to the land.

Marco, wandering vagrant turned farmer, remains the stranger in the Simmelian sense of being the "freer man," able to "examine conditions with less prejudice" (Simmel 146). (D'Agostino's second novel, *Hills Beyond Manhattan,* makes a fleeting reference to the marriage of Marco to

Federico's daughter, Elena. As a wedding gift, the couple receives what Federico believes is one of his bad investments—a farm!) When Elena, Federico's daughter, first meets Marco, she hears him humming an aria from Pietro Mascagni's *Cavalleria rusticana*, an opera set in Sicily and based on Verga's play (which was based on his story). Literally translated as "rustic chivalry," the opera illuminates Marco's passionate devotion to working the land, and, eventually, to his love for Elena. Unlike the tragic ending of the opera, however, this couple remains faithful, and, like the opera's first scene, they remain devoted to the Sicilian peasants of Wop Roost.

D'Agostino's inclusion of a voice of the land whose deeper understanding of the conditions under which his people live is similar to Toni Morrison's description of the Black ancestor, whose presence in the city allows the characters to remain connected to their history: "the ancestor is not only wise; he or she values racial connection, racial memory over individual fulfillment" (43). Responding to Elena's suggestion that America might not be the place for him, Marco's belief in *fare l'America* has nothing to do with the values associated with industry, but rather, with working the land: "There is no more a place for me over there, or the men like me. It is here I belong. . . . It is here I will stay and stay like I am—Italian. And I will grow" (116). D'Agostino's creation of the Italian ancestor also pays respect to the political intellectual, Antonio Gramsci, whose writings "developed out of [an] organic engagement with his own society and times" (Hall 5). D'Agostino's recursions to this wise voice, an organic intellectual, become fainter as he mainstreams his themes in an effort to insert himself into canonical American literature. Yet the voice of the land remains paramount in his subsequent novel.

Hills Beyond Manhattan received good reviews, including one from the *New York Times*, which praised the novel for "both a graceful and re-assuring" conclusion and for moving beyond "the bulk of light fiction" in its emphasis on immigrant adjustment, fascism during World War II, and tensions between laborers and landowners (Hauser BR7). Nonetheless, the French protagonist, Gustave Chambord, is a diminished version of Marco in *Olives*. An established architect supervising work for the town's wealthy shoe manufacturer, Chambord remains disengaged from the struggles of the village laborers who fear the loss of their hunting grounds to the construction of an exclusive club. Only when the opportunity arises to date an American girl does Chambord show interest in the laborers' concern. As one contemporary reviewer explains, Chambord's decision to assimilate American ways has more to do with his romantic interest than with the villagers' struggle to maintain access to hunting and fishing grounds: "Because he is on the side of the villagers Chambord sees more of Sheila Stewart and eventually his Americanization is complete" (Rev. of *Hills Beyond Manhattan* 180).

Relinquishing the heavy-handed didacticism of his first novel, D'Agostino's *Hills* suffers by not developing further the anxious backdrop of World War II and Chambord's response to the ideology of racial superiority espoused by Hitler. While one contemporary reviewer praises D'Agostino for burying his "'message' skillfully in a story that runs along easily" (Rev. of *Hills Beyond Manhattan* 180), another reviewer wishes the writing were "less accommodating" (Hauser BR7). It is this accommodation that gives *Hills Beyond Manhattan* its dispassionate tone. While subordinated to the romantic plot, the laborers' struggles continue to reflect D'Agostino's commitment to village cooperation over urban competition. City values—acquiring land and badges of material success—threaten to overtake the values associated with the countryside—access to the land and cooperative sharing. In order to quell an increasing urgency to acquire land and increase class divisions in small-town America, D'Agostino incorporates an American-born character of social and monetary means to reassert the values of country living.

Sam Marvin is the recuperating figure in *Hills Beyond Manhattan*. As D'Agostino has one character say, "If anybody knows what's going on in the village, Sam must" (*Hills* 139). Though a minor character, it is he, not the French immigrant, Chambord, who voices the values associated with living close to nature. Ultimately withdrawing his property from the plans for a private country club, Marvin restates values associated with the American countryside: "It'll lay there open, in the way that's always been tradition in my family, in the American way, friendly to anyone who wants to enjoy it. No signs, no fences, no barriers—just neighborly land. And it'll stay that way, too!" (235) This profoundly optimistic statement occurs toward the end of *Hills*, and functions to reinforce D'Agostino's insertion of himself into the American literary tradition that equates land with American democracy, mobility, and, what Leo Marx calls "the autonomous unencumbered self," a species of "transcendental pastoralism" (74, 73).

Ambivalence about the efficacy of agrarian idealism occurs midway through the novel when Chambord visits Sam Marvin. Recalling his past as a boy in the country, Marvin remembers his father reading from Charles Dickens, an author who well realized, what Lehan calls the "lure and trap" of city living: "a lure to those who called to it as if by a magnet, because the city offers the means of realizing a heightened conception of self; a trap in its workings, which lead to human destruction" (40–41). As if anticipating the eventual futility of Marvin's generous gesture at the end of *Hills*, D'Agostino describes his recuperative character as a "scarecrow dragged out of storage," suggesting a well-meaning, but ineffective agent of country values (115). Married to a wife fiercely associated with city values (an Anglo-American equivalent to Giustina of *Olives*), Sam Marvin's outmoded longing for the old days is more nostalgic than practical. *Hills Beyond Manhattan* reads much less like one of Willa Cather's immigrant novels that sustains its tribute to the land and more like a John Cheever story of suburban ennui. Readers must wait until D'Agostino's fourth novel for a more positive and practical portrayal of farm work.

The lure of the city continues to loom beyond the pages of *Hills Beyond Manhattan*, however. Perhaps that is why D'Agostino next published his most urban novel, *My Enemy, The World*—which might be better titled "My Enemy, The City." Placing his Italian American characters in the first decade of the twentieth century in New York's Greenwich Village, D'Agostino explores the unsettling ramifications of city life on a young Italian man whose old-world cultural beliefs in private justice and land ownership threaten to destroy his life in America.

My Enemy, The World departs from his previous novels by portraying an earlier historical period, and like *Olives on the Apple Tree*, argues almost exclusively about the future place of Italians in America. Written after Guido D'Agostino returned from World War II where, stationed in Sardinia, he served in the U.S. Office of War Information, the novel was not as widely reviewed as his previous books. The suspenseful revenge plot appealed to reviewers from newspapers in Oklahoma City and Indianapolis, and the book was eventually reprinted as a pulp novel. One reviewer from the *Honolulu Star Bulletin*, however, recognized the pensive immigrant dilemma at the core of the novel, and wrote: "The well-contrived climax allows the central figure to make a choice between two cultures which is both satisfying to the reader and consistent with the character development employed by the author" (qtd. from the dust jacket of the first Australian edition of *My Enemy, The World*).

D'Agostino uses a dispute at a farming estate in Sardinia to trigger the main character's return to the American city and to reflect his ongoing alienation from both the Italian and American way of life. Philip Brancatti struggles with what Jerre Mangione terms the "double life" of the "urban ethnic." In the opening pages of the novel, the twenty-four-year old Philip returns to New York after twelve privileged years of studying in Sardinia. He has imbibed ideas about an old-world class structure with its landed aristocracy that makes social mobility a dream permanently deferred for laborers. American born, Philip has spent equal time in Italy and America and is an extreme example of "the children of immigrants [who] were truly victims of circumstances, born to live a double life, caught between two sharply differing cultures" (Mangione, "A Double Life" 171). In place of the old-world class structure of Italy, Greenwich Village functions in early twentieth-century America as a hybridization of urban capitalistic values and the values of the village brought by Italian immigrants with rural antecedents. Transplanting their localized form of regionalism, campanilismo, Italian immigrants continued to embrace the life-sustaining institution of the family, "where the unity of the family was secured by custom and common rights in the land[;] the family was the regulating principle of immigrant experience" (Tricarico 5, 8). Philip ultimately experiences neither the privileges associated with the landed aristocracy nor the localized sense of *la famiglia* typical of early twentieth-century Greenwich Village.

Sent to Sardinia to live with his dead mother's relatives, Philip has been educated as a member of Sardinian's landed society.[12] His father, Silvio, is a first-generation immigrant who owns a successful importing business in New York. Over the years, Silvio has been buying up piece by piece the Sardinian estate of Villaflores owned by a Count Alivesi whose focus on maintaining his own social status caused him to mismanage the farm. In the underlying dispute between the landed aristocracy and the landless peasantry, D'Agostino returns to the preoccupation with land reflected in the first two novels, but instead of an argument for a specific treatment of the land, *My Enemy* turns into an antiurban cautionary tale. Like *Olive*'s Marco, Silvio in *My Enemy* has no access to any land until he leaves Sardinia and succeeds in America. In Sardinia, he was a "tinker" who roamed from village to village and repaired tin pots (105). If Giustina Gardella in *Olives* pushes Emile to be too American, then Silvio Brancatti in *My Enemy* has educated Philip to be too Italian. Philip is just as alienated from the land as the upper class Italian society, who employed gabellotti and servants to run their estates while they often resided in luxurious urban villas. Like Silvio, Philip views the estate primarily as a way to seek justice and revenge against the Count and secondarily as an investment to increase his financial and social status. Functioning as an absentee landlord, Philip hires relatives and friends to farm it and when he hears news of "a drought which had killed the wheat crop" he is amused and excited because it means the Count will have to sell off more land to his own gain (84). Because Philip does not value the work of the farm and in fact rejects these values when the other characters try to teach him,

D'Agostino will leave Philip in devastated discontent; there is no hope for redemption while he espouses only the capitalistic values of the city.

In honor-bound Sardinian society, the Count recognizes Philip, the just-graduated engineer, as Silvio's son, spits on him, throws him out and effectively shames him in upper class society (106–107). Returning home to Greenwich Village specifically to ask his father to explain the history behind the public dishonor, Philip arrives at the hour of Silvio's "suicide" and hears rumors that a rival importing company may have been blackmailing his father. The mystery then that Philip has to solve is twofold; the New York murder-suicide and the bad blood between Silvio and the Italian Count are appropriately located on two continents. Given the freedom of the Simmelian stranger figure to move freely through American and Italian space, characters such as Marco and Gustave maintain personal integrity; in contrast, D'Agostino denies Philip the integrity or objectivity of *Olive*'s Marco or *Hills'* Gustave. D'Agostino writes Philip as completely confused by customs, emotions and prejudices, prevented from knowing basic life-sustaining information about his lineage that, rather than liberating him, enslaves him like the contadini, who had no more control over the means of information than they did their own consumption.

In New York's Greenwich Village, Philip seeks private justice as the honor bound Italian community dictates. As he starts investigating his father's death, he disregards advice to go to the authorities, and explains, "there was a code about such things" (64). D'Agostino's descriptions of the city's decay and poverty early in the novel emotionally move Philip (11). At first Philip shows interest in egalitarian justice when he employs friendship and furbizia to free a group of immigrant laborers from the indentured servitude of a self-profiting "travel agent" named Gamba, a padrone whose sole purpose was to profit from the ignorance and desperation of immigrants. In exchange for passage to America, Gamba kept the laborers under employment obligation while "squeezing" them out of their wages (21). Instead of helping the laborers file complaints with the immigration authorities and take advantage of the labor laws already in place, Philip uses his friend Ben Riordan's engineering firm to hire the laborers away from Gamba and cleverly leverages information about Gamba's shady business dealings with Silvio to guarantee omertà.

Gamba is a partner in the competing importing company with Philip's childhood rival, a man named Tony Cribbo. Against Cribbo, whom he suspects has murdered his father, Philip also seeks private justice. Instead of turning to the police, he hides evidence from the authorities, and tries to bury Cribbo through both "legitimately" putting him out of business by outselling and outmarketing him and by "illegitimately" interfering with his smuggling and swindling. In addition to avenging his father, seeking this private justice through the specific use of American capitalism becomes the means by which Philip hopes to earn his fortune in America and to return to Sardinia and triumph over the Count. D'Agostino links Philip's use of private justice to both his American and Italian ambitions, but as Philip loses his egalitarian motives, like *Olive*'s Emile or Sam Marvin's wife from *Hills*, he increasingly alienates himself from everyone including Jacqueline his Anglo-American wife.

Unlike Mario Puzo's Kay Adams of *The Godfather*, Jacqueline fights against Philip's insistence on old-world Italian codes of behavior, and through their lengthy arguments about installing their infant son on the Villaflores estate, D'Agostino interrogates the dilemma of the successful Italian immigrant in America. D'Agostino organizes the discussions in part around the question of place: Jacqueline sees Philip and her American-born son as *Americans* in New York while Philip wants to return to Italy to claim justice through land acquisition now that he has the financial means, not because he feels bicultural. Jacqueline repeatedly—and, perhaps insensitively—asks her husband what Italy has to do with their son (146); then after reminding her husband that Philip is the son of a peasant and no money or education could ever make him into a nobleman, she pleads, "You belong here with the vitality of things that are new and things that grow. You can become really great here. Your son can become great. In Europe you'll both stagnate and die" (146). In this important passage, Jacqueline's pleas echo Marco's of *Olives*, insisting on the vibrancy of the village within urban America, such as the Italian South Village, which housed Italian immigrants from Venice to Sicily, offering them jobs and opportunities unknown and unavailable to them in their ancestral lands.[13]

Husband and wife cannot agree because Philip is not interested in growing anything but more money. D'Agostino contrasts Philip's middle-man importing business where nothing is produced, only "bought and sold" with Jacqueline's involvement in Ben Riordan's engineering business that specializes in building cement foundations that are solid and lasting (83).[14] In rejecting the engineering career he trained for, Philip will make the cash he desires to put Tony Cribbo out of business, and when he looks at the immigration maps of the lands beyond New York he sees only new markets (76) to sell the Italian grown products, which until now no one has thought to exploit as he has (96). Philip's urban capitalistic values combined with his motivation for private justice reduce his view of everything to how he can profit from it. Even his marriage becomes part of the assimilation plan: by marrying Jacqueline with her "Anglo-Saxon allure" (121) he thinks he will achieve quicker access to capitalistic ventures; and the old money he receives allows him to gain the social status he craves and was denied by the Count because of his father's low-grade artisanal status.

D'Agostino provides Philip with three advisors to fulfill Toni Morrison's ancestral function but Philip rejects each: Dr. Carter his father-in-law and the neighborhood physician, Anselmo—Silvio's trusted accountant, and Cesar Winwar—a special investigator for the insurance company. Philip rejects or ignores all three, ensuring, as Morrison predicts, his own devastation (Morrison, "City Limits, Village Values" 43). Again, D'Agostino creates representational characters. Dr. Carter is an inverted Emile Gardella; an American doctor, he has devoted his practice to helping the poor Italian immigrants usually for bartered compensation. He advises Philip on the American humanist way of doing things and consistently reminds Philip of his personal obligations to individuals. Anselmo explains how things were done in Italy with emphasis on what went wrong. He includes healthy criticism and earnest warnings about the negative consequences Philip's vendetta will bring. Cesar Winwar, as fully assimilated second-generation American, represents a negotiated Italian and American way of acting in the world. An insurance investigator, Winwar is not quite the law and he's not quite private justice, but a mediated justice of combined business and litigation. Despite Philip's intrusive use of omertà, Winwar brings Cribbo and the importing rivals to justice for their swindles, smuggling, and the murder before Philip can fully execute his punitive plans. In comparison to Philip, Winwar has Americanized his name from the Italian, Vinciguerra; he speaks both Italian and English, and worships President Theodore Roosevelt and "Detective Joseph Petrosino of the famous New York Italian squad" (179).[15] In every aspect, he serves to contrast Philip—Winwar is the cool headed, pedantic reasoner who patiently seeks out evidence and folly. Paralleling the long discussions between Jacqueline and Philip about where Philip belongs in the world, D'Agostino includes conversations between Philip and Winwar (180, 243) and Philip and Anselmo (159, 250) about work and justice that again argue for and against the place of Italian codes of behavior in America. The resolution represented by Winwar may anticipate D'Agostino's last novel *The Barking of the Lonely Fox* and Julian as its central assimilated character.

Unlike Mario Puzo's Corleones who get away with their vengeance, Philip is destroyed by his quest for private personal justice and his rejection of the (Greenwich) Village wisdom offered by his mentors. As Donald Tricarico explains of the immigrant community of Greenwich Village, "the cultural shelter comprised by paesani made it possible to live with strangeness, anonymity and impersonality of the city" (14). Village enclaves within urban neighborhoods not only symbolized a collective identity for Italians, but also made the American environment hospitable to growth via the humanistic values of Italian transplants. In contrast, Philip has angered and alienated all the people who mattered to him, and Jacqueline vows she will fight him officially in the American courts should he try to take his son back to Villaflores. Though he has a wife, a son, a beautiful house (outside the Italian enclave) and a successful business, at the end, D'Agostino grants him only anger and loneliness as he grieves for the loss of justice on his own terms.

The Barking of a Lonely Fox reasserts D'Agostino's belief in maintaining through the generations an abiding connection with the land. Reprising the themes in *Olives* and *Hills*, the author creates fictional personae to reflect an increasingly diverse population of European-descended immigrant groups, including Irish, Italian and Polish. Intermarriage, class mobility, and city aspirations characterize this 1952 novel, but dedication to the land remains preeminent. In fact, D'Agostino all but elides description of the protagonist's experience in the army during World War II, in effect avoiding commentary about the fall of Mussolini and the American Allied force's invasion of Sicily and Italy in 1943. That Julian, the protagonist, returns to America seemingly unscathed by the experience of war abroad both surprises and disturbs. More telling is the fact that D'Agostino's protagonist is the foster son of Mike and Mary Baretto, the owners of a flagging Pennsylvania dairy farm. Although beloved and fathered by Mike Baretto, Julian's status as an orphan figure is a distancing gesture on D'Agostino's part. The son of a Polish American father who died in a coal mining accident, Julian may be affectionately referred to as "Juliano" [Giuliano] by the patriarch of the Baretto family, first-generation Alessandro Baretto, but his status as an outsider remains prominent.

In his guidance and intelligence, Julian is like Marco of *Olives*, but without the accent. Just as Rosa Cassettari's status as an abandoned infant conferred upon her a magical relationship with the Holy Mother, so Julian's status as an orphan gives him extraordinary ability with the land. Unlike the historical Rosa and the fictional Marco, however, Julian is third-generation and fully Americanized. Of the Baretto household, but not blood-related, Julian, like the Simmelian stranger, is freer and thereby better able to make sound assessments regarding the farm.[16] Not coincidentally, D'Agostino's Italian American characters cannot succeed without Julian's talent. The patriarch, Alessandro, is doddering from old age and his son, Mike Baretto, is an amputee, having as a young man mangled his arm in the belt of a threshing machine. In his attempt to align himself with pastoral traditions fundamental to many works by mainstream, Anglo-American writers, Guido D'Agostino removes Italian cultural identity from the primary focus. One contemporary reviewer, in fact, noted that D'Agostino's "sound book" forms part of an "established, and recently much neglected, tradition" (qtd. in *Book Review Digest* 222), perhaps suggesting that novels about the land were increasingly scarce in post–World War II America. Reiterating this idea from a different perspective, a contemporary *New York Times* reviewer rather condescendingly explains that the daughter of the wealthiest farmer-in-absentia, Timothy O'Malley, is forced to "conform to the author's theme that virtue lives on the farm, evil in the big city streets" (Teller BR 14).

The Barking of a Lonely Fox revolves around the Baretto's decades-long struggle to become debt-free and earn a good living from the land. Their eventual acquisition of the opulent Timothy O'Malley farm—called Fox Ledge—is D'Agostino's celebration of a communal over an individual ethic. D'Agostino's depiction of the tyrannical lawyer, Timothy O'Malley's absenteeism on the farm, may be a parodic reference to the absentee landlords on large estates in nineteenth-century Italy and Sicily: "By 1900, 65 percent of all the acreage in Italy was the property of land barons. . . . The largest of these estates were in the *Mezzogiorno* (lands south and east of Rome). The overseers were generally ignorant of farming techniques and either indifferent to the welfare of the soil or knew nothing of crop rotation and soil conservation" (Mangione and Morreale 51). Despite their arguments, pessimism, and loss of faith in the land, the Baretto family, with the guidance of Julian, maintains their property and improves their farm. Unlike the O'Malley's farmstead, in which all work is performed by hired hands, family members only using Fox Ledge as a retreat from the city, the Baretto's farm is family run, even though Mike Baretto's biological son (Alf) and daughter (Gloria) reject the exhaustion and ingenuity unavoidable in farming.

Eventually, however, each sibling returns to the Baretto farm, renewed by a belief in its potential to ennoble their lives. The citified Gloria divorces her milquetoast husband, returns to the farm, and takes over the books, in effect preparing herself for what the author perceives as her destiny: "Her strength and drive came from within and was as enduring as the land itself, as unyielding" (215). Gloria eventually marries Julian. D'Agostino's description of Gloria's inherent strength echoes Cather's of Alexandra Bergson and Ántonia Shimerda. However, unlike Willa Cather's belief in the autonomy of women, Guido D'Agostino seems to agree with Gloria's comment when she protests to Julian: "I'm not a man and I can't run this farm" (211). In good patriarchal fashion, D'Agostino focuses primarily on the trajectory of Julian's life as a farmer who wrestles not only the land but also his own desire to marry O'Malley's daughter, Lucille, who remains upper-crust and ultimately unavailable.

Throughout the novel, Julian refuses the lures of quick wealth, power, or the dictatorial behavior of a Timothy O'Malley, whose career as a New York lawyer makes him at best distasteful from the author's point of view. The auction scene best epitomizes opposing value systems, one based on fidelity to family and hands-on farming, the other reflecting an urban sensibility of individualism and acquisition. Julian attends an auction in Harrisburg of purebred Holsteins, having carefully researched the pedigreed quality of two first-calf heifers, which Julian thinks of as "beautiful creatures," with "well-slung udders showing the promise of their ancestry" (62).

In an act of competitive one-upmanship, O'Malley twice outbids Julian. Only later does Julian realize O'Malley's covert surveying of Julian's examination of the heifers, but Julian nonetheless shows moderation and maturity during the bidding process.[17] Refusing to compete foolishly a second time, Julian allows the second heifer to be sold to O'Malley, whose self-congratulations on his shrewd business maneuver is equaled only by his utter disregard for the Baretto family. During their ensuing conversation, Julian has the last word. Refusing O'Malley's proposition that he manage Fox Ledge, Julian reiterates D'Agostino's belief in the family over the individual, firsthand knowledge of husbandry over accumulation of land for profit. The subsequent movement of the narrative supports the Baretto's difficult struggle to maintain the family economy of the farm, despite temptations "to sell out, to give up, to move to the city" (178).

The conclusion of *The Barking of a Lonely Fox* reiterates D'Agostino's major themes about the land and the voices embodying its ideals. The family celebration in the concluding chapter is also marked by sadness, perhaps a reflection of D'Agostino's own ambivalence toward inevitable changes in mid-twentieth-century rural America. After assuming possession of Fox Ledge, the Baretto family organizes a community party for

Alessandro to let him know that "all his back-breaking work came to something in the end, something big" (268). The family dinner is initially a private affair for close family members, deliberately mimicking the powerful localism described by first-generation campanilismo. The private dinner occurs before the whole community—"the whole countryside as well and all the people in it"—attend the celebration (269). Having achieved all the comforts, the family now has gained enough distance from their post-Risorgimento past to partake in Italian cuisine immune from the limited and precarious diet of their poor ancestors. Before D'Agostino offers a list of Italian delectables *only* the Baretto family eats, he regales the reader with an Irvingesque description of home-cooked *American* cuisine, "huge platters of food, chicken salad, roast pork, roast beef, cakes, and pies and the kegs of cider and beer" (269) in which the community partakes. Demonstrating ethnic resilience *and* a will to Americanize, D'Agostino ultimately builds a Pennsylvania bridge between landowners and laborers. The very ubiquity of both Italian and American cuisine is the author's comment on an old-world culture of scarcity that has now been replaced by nature's bounty and an invocation of Italian immigrants in rural America.

The *Barking of a Lonely Fox* is D'Agostino's most deliberate attempt to write an American novel with inflections of italianità throughout the narrative. In doing so, the author may lose the earthy voice of the Italian ancestor, best embodied by Marco of *Olives on the Apple Tree*, but he gains a whole multiethnic community in mid-twentieth-century rural America. From the beginning of *The Barking of a Lonely Fox* the Italian patriarch, Alessandro, is aged and can no longer voice the aspirations of his people. In his effort to maintain a connection to a Gramscian organic intellectual, however, D'Agostino creates Julian, the orphan child of Polish Americans, who best voices the agrarian aspirations of the Baretto family. Aware of the increasingly diverse inhabitants of America, Guido D'Agostino does not idealize a hermetically sealed version of Italian ethnicity the way Mario Puzo will try to do seventeen years later with *The Godfather*. In this way, D'Agostino avoids falsifying Italian American history and, as Micaela di Leonardo explains, creating a "misconceived nostalgia for worlds we have never lost" (135).

Mike Baretto is married to the Irish American, Mary, whose relatives "went away back to the early days of settlement" (269). Their children are Irish/Italian and each is married to a partner of another ethnicity. That Gloria cannot bear children due to a botched abortion from her first marriage is perhaps D'Agostino's way of punishing her for desiring to control her own reproduction—and seeking the city to procure the procedure.

More likely is the author's squeamishness regarding the marriage between Gloria and her foster *brother*, Julian. Infertility guarantees the end of a line, progeny impossible. In the final lines of the book, Julian cannot assure Gloria that their inability to reproduce does not matter: "The words would not come" (274). Knowing something about their tenacity and mutual dedication suggests that words may very well come with time. The two strongest and most capable characters in *Barking* cannot however establish a lineage that will be reproduced generationally. Their sadness concludes the novel.

The Barking of a Lonely Fox assuredly establishes another ancestral line to the Pennsylvania Dutch and to the English Quaker colonizer, William Penn, who founded Pennsylvania in 1681. In his attempt to write a novel about America and subsequent immigrants' relation to a "new land and bad land" (1), D'Agostino places Italian ancestral voices side-by-side with Anglo voices of early America. D'Agostino reaches even further back in his creation of the farmstead, Fox Ledge. Standing out like a "glistening, miniature hilltop community" (3), the description of Fox Ledge is in fact the author's own rural version of a "city upon a hill," a decisive recursion to John Winthrop's Puritan colony.[18] Thus, D'Agostino succeeds in locating a New Jerusalem for Italian immigrants in rural America. For Winthrop and the Englishmen burghers who migrated to America, "their aim was to set up villages, towns and *potential cities* in the wilderness" (emphasis added; Marx 65). D'Agostino's ambivalence toward industrial cities (epitomized by New York City) does not prevent him from recognizing the "vital institutions of mental production" that make possible the scientific methods applied by Julian in animal husbandry (Marx 65). Unlike their predecessor, Timothy O'Malley, the Barettos of Fox Ledge maintain a city in the wilderness, embracing the best of rural and urban sensibilities.

D'Agostino's final novel ultimately celebrates and invokes some of the rural families like the Gallos who brought expertise in winemaking to America and built great fortunes by transplanting that expertise in producing and processing grapes.[19] Like the characters in a D'Agostino novel, rural Italian immigrants in history were in tune with both the harshness and bounty of nature and form a chorale with the nineteenth-century pontificators of nature such as Emerson and Thoreau who believed that nature sanctifies those who work it with industry and respect. For Guido D'Agostino, embracing the literature of his homeland—America—allowed him to discover echoes of his own soul, which also remained tied to his parents' ancestral homeland—Sicily. Guido D'Agostino's works are

worthy of remembrance. Unlike his Italian American contemporaries—
di Donato, Fante, and Mangione—D'Agostino penned a group of novels
that moved him toward the heart of American mainstream literature. In
his allegiance to rural antecedents, D'Agostino ably embraced both his Sicilian peasant origins and the American landscape, which he claims as his
own. Refusing to submit to the nativist ideology that would prevent Italians from upward social mobility, D'Agostino gives the lie to the stereotype of his cultural group as "amoral familists," emerging from an
"ambitionless, self-reproducing, urban working class" (di Leonardo 95).[20]
In placing his Italian characters on American soil, the author enlarges their
patrimony, guaranteeing them security perhaps for the first time in their
long history.

5

History Singer/Cantastorie

❧

Vernacular Voices in Paule Marshall's and Tina De Rosa's *Kunstlerromane*

Language is the only homeland.

—Czeslaw Milosz, "Language Is the Only Homeland"

For writers who locate their characters in urban enclaves, guaranteeing them long-term security is undercut by rapid changes in the marketplace and the mobility that allows some to move away from old neighborhoods. Urban working-class families, subject to assimilative desires, sometimes managed to purchase a home, further testimonial to American-borne values of acquisition and individualism. When projects for urban renewal (as they were called in the 1960s) destroyed entire neighborhoods in ethnic colonies within the large cities of Brooklyn and Chicago, for example, represented characters did not uniformly embrace that change, perceiving it as opportunity to achieve American dreams. Resisting change was a reflection neither of obdurateness nor lack of ambition, but rather a continued intervention on the part of ethnic Americans. In an effort to create a cultural space that subverted the dominant discourse of upward social mobility and the commodification of everyday life, authors imagined characters who managed the contradictory demands of dual cultures through the creation of folkloric ancestral voices which function as guides for young, urban protagonists.

119

When Paule Marshall cited the émigré Polish writer Czeslaw Milosz, who wrote "Language is the only homeland," she could have been describing the principle feature of her 1959 novel, *Brown Girl, Brownstones*, whose pages are filled with the folkloric voices of the Caribbean ("From Poets in the Kitchen" 630). Equally laden with the sounds of ancestral folklore, Tina De Rosa's 1980 novel, *Paper Fish*, explores the intersection between oral traditions of southern Italy and the literary expression that gives them modern form. Both writers created novels in which the presence (or absence) of voices informs the development of their female protagonists entering adulthood and accepting a difficult creative legacy from their maternal forbears. For each young woman, language itself becomes the cultural space that is preserved and protected while actual geographical locales that housed ethnic neighborhoods were systematically bulldozed throughout the country.

Though ostensibly separated by culture and race, and published twenty-one years apart, Paule Marshall's *Brown Girl, Brownstones* and Tina De Rosa's *Paper Fish* experienced parallel publication histories and explored similar topics, making them invitingly comparative. Debut novels for each writer, *Brown Girl, Brownstones* and *Paper Fish* explore vibrant cultural communities within urban landscapes. In *Brown Girl*, Marshall portrays first-generation Barbadian immigrants living in a Brooklyn neighborhood during the 1940s. Once dominated by European immigrants—Jews and Italians—the neighborhood then called Stuyvesant Heights (now Bedford-Stuyvesant) "takes on a colorful, distinctively African-Caribbean dimension" by 1939, the year the novel begins (Denniston 10). Like Marshall before her, De Rosa similarly emphasizes the importance of the neighborhood within the city in *Paper Fish*. De Rosa locates her novel in Chicago's near West Side, the Taylor Street area, focusing on the village atmosphere of the Italian colony, the city's largest Italian enclave in the first decades of the twentieth century (Nelli 14).

Despite direct forms of hostility from the dominant culture, both authors recreate in their novels spaces of protection, sheltering for a time their female artist figures from outside forces. In this way, such tightly knit communities "in the urban centers of America allowed the bonds of custom, kinship, religion and language to be transmitted and maintained" (Mathias and Raspa 55). Recognizing the dense population of immigrant urban enclaves, both Marshall and De Rosa nonetheless depict their neighborhoods as functioning as shock absorbers for first-generation immigrants and their children. Maintaining a village atmosphere within congested areas and apartment living is no small feat. Both writers yet manage to maintain a cultural space for their characters, recognizing that "the village is the fixed point by which the villager knows his position in the world; it is the principle of order and structure in the universe" (Mathias and Raspa 55). Reinforcing this structure is the presence of the village ancestor. As Toni Morrison points out, "The city is wholesome, loved when such an ancestor is on the scene, when neighborhood links are secure" ("City Limits, Village Values" 39). For Selina Boyce of *Brown Girl, Brownstones* and Carmolina Bellacasa of *Paper Fish*, such links are secure, but they are also fragile and ephemeral.

Related to their urban settings is the context of migration that informs the lives of the characters and the trajectory of the plots in Marshall's and De Rosa's novels. Caribbean and Italian migration to the United States primarily occurred between 1880 and 1930. According to Dorothy Denniston, like other immigrants, including Italians, Barbadians "chose to leave their homeland to escape poverty and exploitation. But, unlike other immigrants, they also left their native land to escape the historical effects of slavery and colonialism" (10–11). Despite clear-cut distinctions between Caribbean and Italian migration experiences due to racial discrimination and the tendency by the host American culture to erase ethnic background in favor of inscribing monolithic racial identifications, both Marshall and De Rosa write within contexts of migration narratives and generational schemes.[1] While *Brown Girl, Brownstones* and *Paper Fish* might be considered autobiographical because Marshall and De Rosa explore their lineage and draw deeply upon their childhood experiences, at the same time they are highly crafted fictional responses to the experiences of migration and vexed adjustment to American culture.

Those fictionalized characters populating Marshall's West Indian enclave of Brooklyn and De Rosa's Italian enclave of Chicago, despite a simulation of village spirit, often suffer from poverty, hopelessness, and illness. The first-generation's migration to urban America from Barbados and Italy caused for some what Joyce Pettis says of Marshall's characters, a fracturing that "disorients perceptions of the world and complicates the manner of survival" (12). Both authors examine how migration from a rural homeland to an industrialized milieu affects not only the first-generation pioneers, but also their children. Alongside the portrayal of cultural retention from the homeland through language, cuisine, and religion, *Brown Girl* and *Paper Fish* present fundamental shifts in mindset required by an industrial economy. As Pettis explains, "black people [must] contend with Western constructions of culture that are antithetical to African sensibility," a sensibility at odds with "the cold conceptual logic of European civilization" (13). De Rosa's Italian immigrants descend from a nineteenth-century rural economy of Neapolitan Italy, producing a sensibility equally antithetical to the rational logic Pettis ascribes to European culture. In an interview with Lisa Meyer, De Rosa says of her grandmother figure: "She's coming from another language and religion—Roman Catholicism, which helps form the Mediterranean impulse toward sharing, loving, sacrifice, and beauty. It's a totally different space. And she doesn't find that space in America" ("Breaking the Silence" 229).

Those characters least equipped with the physical, psychological, or spiritual means to adjust to America suffer enormously in Marshall's and De Rosa's novels, often at the hands—inadvertently or not—of their own people. In Marshall's *Brown Girl, Brownstones*, the first-generation father, Deighton Boyce, is a case in point. Unlike many in the West Indian community who conform to the American dream of upward mobility through land acquisition, Deighton's dream remains firmly rooted in Barbados, "the one buffer he created to protect himself from a hostile world—his fantasy of building a house in his homeland" with land bequeathed him from his family (Hathaway 109). Determined to purchase her rented brownstone—"even if I got to see my soul fall howling into hell"—a grimly pragmatic Silla punctures her husband's dream through a devious scheme that wrests the land away from him (*Brown Girl* 75). Thereafter, the West Indian community persecutes Deighton, literally ostracizing him from their circle, unable to accommodate a personality that refuses to sacrifice homeland dreams for economic security in the new world.[2]

Marshall and De Rosa explore the costs involved in transplantation for first-generation immigrants and their forbears. In their focus also on both second and third-generational characters, Marshall and De Rosa upset the traditional scheme of generations, famously promulgated by Marcus Lee Hansen and referred to as "Hansen's Law."[3] In his posthumously published essay, Hansen attributed a negative behavioral response toward immigrant parents by the second-generational children in their desire to assimilate American ways. A second-generation son, Hansen did not reflect his own paradigm, but his emphasis on declension for the second generation has influenced the field of ethnic studies for decades.[4] Marshall and De Rosa complicate popular generational imagery in their creation of girl protagonists who come from different generations, but function similarly in their struggle to "solve the mystery" as De Rosa states in her epigraph of their role in family history. In both novels, second-generation characters in general neither reject ancestral mores nor easily embrace American values. Aware of equally influential factors of race and gender informing the construction of one's identity, Marshall and De Rosa complicate generational schemes in their migration narratives.

The portrayal of young artist figures whose legacies catapult them out of the narrative worlds created by Marshall and De Rosa is enriched by each author's focus on racial and ethnic hybridity within a seemingly homogenous cultural community. Both authors examine how tightly knit communities maintain cultural control in the midst of misunderstanding and hostility by native-born Americans. Italians traditionally use the term "campanilismo" to describe intense provincial and linguistic solidarity and mistrust of outsiders. For Carmolina of *Paper Fish* and Selina of *Brown Girl, Brownstones*, such communities exist as a collective character, providing the girls with vital information about their roles as ethnic women who live in a racist or xenophobic culture.[5]

Provided with several guides, Selina's initial rejection of her mother's Barbadian community is forcefully challenged by the local hairdresser, Miss Thompson, an African American, whose own damaging experience of racism in the American South helps to prepare Selina for the world outside her neighborhood.[6] While differently motivated, Carmolina's rejection of her family reflected in her running away at age eight, affects the entire Italian colony. From the priest who breaks the holy silence of confession by calling out Carmolina's name to another child in the confessional to the seedman who blows his horn and yells "pistachios" in the same breath as he calls the name of Carmolina, the village wills their little girl's return home. As in traditional African societies, rural Italian villages also possessed the concept of "communal parentage" (Denniston xx), which survived the transatlantic crossing in the ethnic enclaves that emerged liberally in urban America.

Both Selina of *Brown Girl, Brownstones* and Carmolina of *Paper Fish*, while ultimately honoring their communities, recognize the tendency of their respective Barbadian and Italian cultures to enforce what Martin Japtok describes as "coercive ethnic solidarity" (309). Japtok explains that Paule Marshall's novel, *Brown Girl, Brownstones*, explores "the potential of coercion behind the notion of ethnic solidarity" (305). Identifying her community with a materialism she loathes, Selina, in a fit of anger at the Barbadian Association meeting she attends, rejects it outright, calling the people in it "Clannish. Narrow-minded. Selfish" (227).

Nonetheless, before she can truly appreciate the reasons underlying her community's forms of self-protection, and their need for *ethnic* identification, Selina must enter mainstream America, which confers upon her a monolithic *racial* identity based on reductive and damaging racist ideology. Carmolina escapes from her Italian enclave less out of rejection than confusion over the unnamed illness from which her older sister, Doriana, suffers, and which paralyzes her entire family. Her trip away from the family, like Selina's experience of racism by white America, utterly changes her life. Carmolina returns with an awareness of differentiated identities: her difference from the community outside her enclave, which reduces her solely to the one-word epithet, "dago," and her difference within her family symbolized by the burdensome role to which she has been assigned.[7]

Both Selina and Carmolina initially resist the tendency of their communities to define their future roles. *Brown Girl, Brownstones* and *Paper Fish* offer counternarratives of their female artist figures, whose identification with their communities is complicated by their cultural hybridity *and* the American individualism they will necessarily embrace as adults. Selina's second-generation status as a Barbadian American and a black woman, and third-generational Carmolina, an Italian American whose mother's Lithuanian ethnicity has been erased from the family topography, enter adulthood with complex legacies resulting from the migration experiences of their respective families. As Japtok says of Marshall's novel, which is equally true of De Rosa's, the narrative resists "the idea that ethnicity is destiny and embraces individualism as an important value. However, its protagonist still feels that responsibility toward her ethnic group or ethnic heritage is one of the duties and that ethnicity is inescapable after all" (306). When Carmolina says to herself at the conclusion of *Paper Fish*, "They won't ever let us go, will they?" she comprehends her role of reclaiming the stories of beauty and pain reflective of her cultural past (111).

Gioia Timpanelli explains that the storyteller is the "intermediary between listener and story, between past and present" (131). Artist figures both, Selina and Carmolina will assume the oral mantle of their communities. From their maternal forbears, they learn to listen to the stories that will help to preserve the cultural past and enrich future generations. Transmitting the cultural heritage orally, female storytellers in Marshall's and De Rosa's novels give voice to the silences imposed on them by outside forces that would otherwise overwhelm or deny their voices. Both authors explore the intersection between voice and silence, between collective voices and voices of the dispossessed and colonized, between oppressive hierarchies (including the nuclear family) that silence the voice and the recuperating strategies to reclaim the voice. These are the sounds that emerge from *Brown Girl, Brownstones* and *Paper Fish* and both authors attribute to their female ancestors their earliest lessons in storytelling.

Youthful recipients of stories from their ancestors' country of origin, Paule Marshall and Tina De Rosa were apprenticed by immigrant women in the art of storytelling. Marshall refers to her mother and her friends in the Brooklyn basement kitchen as the "unknown bards," whose "exuberant talk" was an "art form that—in keeping with the African tradition in which art and life are one—was an integral part of their lives" ("From the Poets in the Kitchen" 628, 629). Marshall credits the group of women around the kitchen table for providing her with her "first lessons in the narrative art. They trained my ear. They set a standard of excellence. This is why the best of my work must be attributed to them; it stands as testimony to the rich legacy of language and culture they so freely passed on to me in the wordshop of the kitchen" ("From Poets in the Kitchen" 633).

Exposed to the Neapolitan folk traditions of her paternal grandmother, Tina De Rosa also learned the art of narrative by listening to her grandmother's stories, feeling no need to do research for her novel. Unlike Marshall who had visited her ancestral homeland, Barbados, De Rosa had never visited Italy, but had no trouble imagining a land when she "heard so many stories about it from my grandmother and from the people in the old neighborhood" ("An Interview" 23). Both writers expressed a profound desire to capture the stories of their childhood, retrieving memories of communities now lost. As De Rosa says of the Taylor-Halsted Little Italy of her youth, "I wanted the neighborhood to live again, to recreate it. . . . I wanted to make those people and that neighborhood alive again. I wanted the readers of the book to care about it, to realize that something beautiful had existed and that it was gone" ("An Interview" 23).[8] In writing their debut novels, Marshall and De Rosa determined whether or not they had, as Marshall says in an interview with Joyce Pettis, "the same power with language that I sense the mothers possessed" ("A *MELUS* Interview" 120). Both early recognized that the conversion of oral art into literary expression occurs through the writing process. As Marshall explains, "It's in the process of writing that things get illuminated" ("Paule Marshall" 2).[9]

Both novels were originally published to good reviews but were not commercially successful and soon went out of print. Eventually resurrected by the Feminist Press, *Brown Girl, Brownstones* in 1981 and *Paper Fish* in 1996, the scholarly afterwords provided a literary and cultural context by which to read the books.[10] First published in 1959, *Brown Girl, Brownstones* was considered a literary anomaly, and, along with Zora Neale Hurston's *Their Eyes Were Watching God* and Gwendolyn Brooks's *Maud Martha*, as Barbara Christian relates, "not at all in tune with the published works of their respective periods" (104).[11] In Marshall's case, *Brown Girl, Brownstones* "issued in a new period of female characters in Afro-American literature, for it merged together qualities of earlier black women's fiction with major elements of black women's novels that were to emerge in the 1970s" (Christian 103). Despite its lyrical and thematic sophistication, *Brown Girl, Brownstones* was initially slotted in libraries "as a book for juveniles," a gross injustice and misrepresentation of Marshall's focus on black women's development (Christian 107).[12]

Heralded by fellow Italian American writer, Jerre Mangione, as "an outstanding literary event," Tina De Rosa's 1980 *Paper Fish*, met with a similar fate to Marshall's *Brown Girl, Brownstones*: publication, and then silence.[13] Despite its literary obscurity, *Paper Fish* was not the anomaly that *Brown Girl* was since it was during this period that multiethnic literature was introduced in the academy, making the study of noncanonical authors part of its objective. Nonetheless, De Rosa's narrative style compels a reconsideration of conventional migration narratives, reflecting an innovative approach to traditional themes. Like *Brown Girl*, *Paper Fish* also recalled elements of earlier writing, such as Henry Roth's novel of immigration, *Call it Sleep*, and qualities of modernism of the post–World War I era in its experimental examination of the inner self.

For both Marshall and De Rosa, publishing their first novels made them *feel* like writers, made writing their vocation, whether or not they were commercially successful (Christian 107; De Rosa, "Breaking the Silence" 223). Despite the silences pervading the publication histories of both works, both authors paid homage to their ancestors in their incorporation of oral traditions passed down to them by female kin. Like ancient storytellers, Marshall and De Rosa retell "vividly the stories in their keeping. [They are] important guardians of the history of the place where they lived as well as keepers of their people's literature" (Timpanelli 132). Two instrumental guardians of history are the mother Silla of *Brown Girl, Brownstones* and the grandmother Doria of *Paper Fish*. The folk voices they transmit to their daughter and granddaughter respectively are intended, as is the nature of storytelling, to be communal and inclusive (Timpanelli 131). They reflect folk narratives that developed in an atmosphere of communal work (Mathias and Raspa 3) and are transmitted in America in an effort to maintain and reclaim a cultural past necessarily subject to change, dispersal, and loss.[14] Both novels convert spoken words into written language, connecting oral traditions to literature, commemorating the sounds of their respective homelands, and reconstructing vernacular voices into literary expression exemplified by Selina and Carmolina as they develop their art.

Dorothy Denniston identifies several features of the folk voice incorporated in Marshall's *Brown Girl, Brownstones*, including the use of proverbs, double adjectives, hyperbole and metaphor, and Biblical allusions (10–11). These oral traditions are reflective of the Barbadian vernacular that Marshall generously incorporates in *Brown Girl*, "the rhythmic, lilting, colorful West Indian dialect [which captures] the essence of black language as a forceful tool of communication [and a demonstration of] how speech itself can be a form of art" (Denniston xvii). For Selina and the neighborhood mothers who flock to the kitchen brownstone on Saturdays to make and sell Barbadian delicacies, it is the voice of Silla that rings loudest. Overwhelmed and seduced by that voice, Selina feels powerless to resist her mother's verbal dexterity, recognizing at a tender age that her mother "became the collective voice of all the Bajan women, the vehicle through which their former suffering found utterance" (*Brown Girl* 45).

Like traditional storytellers of yore, Silla and her friends combine the activities of work and talk in the kitchen, reflecting the working-class realities of unabated labor, more fully evidenced in the economic and racist exploitation they experience in the work force outside their homes. Employing an oft-used image of the sea, Marshall describes Selina's reaction to her mother's voice as a "net flung wide, ensnaring all within its reach. She swayed helpless now within its hold, loving its rich color, loving and hating the mother for the pain of her childhood" (46).[15] Unable as a ten year old fully to understand what Marshall describes as the "triple invisibility" of Silla and her friends—"black, female, and foreigners"—and how those markers affect Selina's second-generational status, Selina remains "out of the mother's way yet near her," inchoately acknowledging her mother's defining power (*Brown Girl* 67).[16]

For Selina must learn how to interpret the voices of the immigrant generation in order to survive psychically in a world outside the confines of her Bajan community. Perhaps because she is second generation, a Barbadian *American*, Selina dis-identifies with her mother and her mother's increasingly obsessive focus on buying the brownstone, which is both an assimilative gesture and, according to Eugenia DeLamotte, the "primary means by which an oppressive economic system exploits . . . and appropriates [the oppressed] . . . through materialism, which the novel depicts as a displacement or corruption of erotic desire" (11). In order to achieve her goal, Silla quite advertently destroys her marriage with Deighton, whose wholesale resistance to American values makes Silla's quest all the more exhausting, stripping her of a complexity that reveals itself during the kitchen table talk with her women friends. Using the standard Caribbean fare of antonymic adjectives, hyperbole and Biblical allusion, Silla responds to her daughter's silent resistance by saying, "'Oh I know. I know I isn't to do a thing against your beautiful-ugly father. He's Christ to you. But wait. Wait till I finish with him. He gon be Christ crucified'" (*Brown Girl* 77).

No area of conversation is off-limits to Silla, whose topics range from cultural differences in child-rearing to the colonization of her homeland. When discussing the effects of cultural hegemony on a colonized Barbados, Silla implicitly recognizes the life-saving reasons she left her homeland while at the same time sympathizing with those who remained to be exploited by poverty and colonialism: "The white people treating we like slaves still and we taking it. The rum shop and the church join together to keep we pacify and in ignorance. . . . It's a terrible thing to know that you gon be poor all yuh life, no matter how hard you work. You does stop trying after a time. People does see you so and call you lazy. But it ain laziness. It just that you does give up. You does kind of die inside" (*Brown Girl* 70).

Marshall describes Silla's friends as listening raptly and with respect, applauding her refusal to be minimized by racial or gender discrimination. As one of her friends, Florrie Trotman responds, "'Talk yuh talk, Silla! Be-Jees, in this white-man world you got to take yuh mouth and make a gun'" (*Brown Girl* 70). Finding herself equal to the task of taking on the world's problems, Silla functions as "the avatar of the community's deepest values and needs" (Washington, "Afterword" 313). As Denniston explains, the women in Marshall's novel "refuse to be made powerless by their condition of being black, female, and foreign; they use language as one means of exercising some measure of control over their lives and the events that shape them" (12). Selina's resistance to her mother's behavior cannot be sustained when in the presence of Silla's powerful use of language. Learning about her mother's migration experience and the struggle to achieve material well-being, Selina is both edified and awed by her mother's strength, abetted by the "collective force" of "power and literacy and community strength" epitomized by the Barbadian community (Washington, "Afterword" 312). Selina's position as a second-generation American-born child of native West Indians will compel her to make personal and artistic decisions that reflect her differentiated identity from that of her warring parents. In order to maintain psychic stability, in fact, Selina must come to recognize that her parents' migration experience and the assimilative forcefulness of the Barbadian community destroyed their relationship. While Selina's later selection of Clive as her lover ostensibly appears unsettling evidence of her having imitated her mother's romantic choice of Deighton, Selina will ultimately make a different decision regarding him. As second generation, Selina has been given more latitude, more mobility and education than her mother could ever know. Balancing her individualism with her roles as a second-generation Barbadian American and a black woman, Selina will finally learn to accept her role as an artist figure, interpreting the ancestral legacy bequeathed her.

Perhaps because she is third generation, Carmolina of *Paper Fish* has less a problem identifying with her paternal grandmother, whose Neapolitan dialect and nineteenth-century worldview are in one sense utterly in contrast to the English speaking urban world in which she's been raised. In another sense, De Rosa has constructed a narrative wholly in keeping with an old-world Italian village. Maintaining a fierce regional distinction, De Rosa recreates the Taylor-street neighborhood in accordance with the phenomenon of campanilismo, a village spirit in which the neighborhood is self-contained and wary of outsiders.[17] Throughout *Paper Fish* De Rosa reinforces the enclosed space in which the Bellacasa family lives, describing a family meeting ambivalently in the metaphor: "the family together, tight like a fist" (67). When Carmolina snatches her mother's earrings, she unclips one of the hoops and holds it to her eye, spying through "the golden hoop" her mother and grandmother talking across the street on a bench (59). In both instances, the family is beset by discussions of the elder sister, Doriana, whose illness enforces further concealment, especially for the mother Sarah, who does not know how to heal her daughter.

In order to mourn and commemorate the Italian family of her childhood, De Rosa, like Marshall before her, embraces the storytelling traditions of her forbears, paying special attention in particular to the grandmother figure. The very structure of the book—framed by a prologue and an epilogue—attests to De Rosa's recognition of the intimate relation between oral and literary traditions. Using such a framing device recalls one of the "most influential books of fiction ever written," Giovanni Boccaccio's *The Decameron* (Timpanelli 137), allowing De Rosa to defy linearity and manipulate time, conflating events and valuing a sensibility informed by storytelling in which the story is told and retold and the audience is inside the frame, *illo tempore* (at that time, mythic time, story time) (Timpanelli 140, 145).[18] Incorporating a *cornice* (frame) also allows De Rosa to simulate the values inhering in village-mindedness, including protective family relations and linguistic solidarity among Italians.

For Carmolina Bellacasa, the world of her Neapolitan grandmother initiates her into an appreciation of the duality that occurs as a result of migration and permanent dislocation from the homeland. Like the historical Rosa Cassettari, the fictional Grandma Doria engages her granddaughter in the art of tale-telling while doing daily work such as crushing red peppers into Mason jars to use in making sausage. Learning about her grandmother's voyage from Italy, "the land that got lost across the sea," Carmolina interprets the transatlantic crossing precociously, accepting literally a dual location and psychologically a subjective reality that embraces a double perspective: "Sitting on Grandma's porch . . . Carmolina would laugh, . . . because that's where *she* was sometimes, on the other side, in the kitchen [of her mother], watching Grandma on the porch, only now she was on this side and she was lucky, because she could see both sides" (15).

Emotionally nurtured by Doria, Carmolina is sustained by her grandmother's storytelling after she runs away from home. Perceiving "what she is about to do [as] a sin" (71) that is, misuse the grocery money Grandma Doria drops down in a handkerchief to her, Carmolina instead uses her grandmother's stories about running off to a circus to give her courage to leave her neighborhood. Despite the seemingly unchanging nature of the tightly knit enclave De Rosa has constructed in *Paper Fish*, Carmolina resists its self-containment by escaping for three days, eluding even her policeman father, trained in night-time surveillance.[19] Carmolina misinterprets her parents' anguished reactions to her sister's illness because she is unable at eight years old to discern the difference between her older sister and herself. As De Rosa explains, "She is terrified because she doesn't know what is wrong with Doriana. And Carmolina is afraid that whatever it is, Carmolina might have it too" ("Breaking the Silence" 229). Only through physical separation from her family and community does Carmolina achieve what De Rosa calls "some kind of epiphany" that allows her to distinguish herself from her ill sister while simultaneously maintaining her fierce devotion to Doriana and her family (De Rosa, "Breaking the

Silence" 229). Invoking memories of Grandma Doria during her absence allows Carmolina to recognize the edifying nature of her grandmother's storytelling, which becomes instrumental in Carmolina's development into an artist who will "keep the fire inside" her (116).

Away from home, Carmolina struggles to comprehend the suffering that has riven her family, but by invoking her grandmother's wisdom, told as a story while Grandma Doria works, Carmolina achieves clarification (99). Steeped in the folklore of her ancestors, Grandma Doria places Doriana in the land of the forest, dissociating her eldest grandchild from the city, which she identifies as the source of the child's sickness: "The buildings of the city were bones crushing against little Doriana, giving her pain" (64). Believing that Doriana would gain health in her homeland country, Grandma Doria earlier in *Paper Fish* imagines an Italy undisturbed by poverty and magically untouched by the ravages of a dying economy in the Mezzogiorno, impelling a mass exodus that included Doria and her husband, Dominic. When Carmolina recalls the story her grandmother tells her to explain her sister's illness, it is not about Italy, but further removed, entering the mythic time of traditional tales.

> "Doriana," Grandma said in the quiet, 'Doriana she get lost in the forest.
> Carmolina's hands stopped.
> "Where, Grandma?"
> Grandma held her white head high like a proud horse; she would not look at Carmolina. "We no know where. We try to find her. We still try to find her. We look. We never stop looking."
> . . .
> 'She try to come home. From the forest. She no find her way.'
> . . .
> "Where is the forest, Grandma?"
> "Behind her eyes," Grandma whispered. . . . "Her face, why you think it so beautiful?"
> Something squeezed tight inside Carmolina. It was made of glass; it could break.
> "I don't know, Grandma. Why?"
> "Her face, she so beautiful," Grandma swiped at the tears, she was angry at them, "because Doriana fight so hard to come home. She look out her eyes every day and try to come home. When you fight to come home, you beautiful." (99)

Using the forest to explain Doriana's illness allows Grandma Doria to offer her perplexed second grandchild both a concrete image and a mystery, since the forest in folklore and legend as Robert Pogue Harrison explains, "came to be viewed as having genetic as well as symbolic connections to memory, custom, national character" (*Forests* 165). The etymological meaning of the word "forest" from the Latin *foris*, means "outside," and in Italian, the derivative word, *forestiero*(a), means foreigner, stranger, *proveniente dall'estero*, from the outside. Unlettered, Grandma Doria is nonetheless no stranger to language, intuitively understanding the alienation from which her first grandchild suffers. Impulsive and mute, Doriana is unable to function behaviorally according to social norms and tends toward self-injury. That De Rosa uses the trope of the forest is telling, for it recalls her ancestral homeland and its Neapolitan philosopher, Giambattista Vico, whose theory of origins in the *New Science* led him, according to Harrison, "deep into the forests of prehistory" (*Forests* 3). Those solitary creatures of the forest, it might be added, achieved a reckless freedom, which Vico called "bestial freedom," "a freedom from terror and authority, a freedom from fathers" (Harrison, *Forests* 3). Not surprisingly, the forests of antiquity—of story time, I might add—"stand opposed to the city" (Harrison, *Forests* 2), and Grandma Doria's story attests to her dual recognition of the hostility of the city and the anarchy of the forest. Grandma Doria's story in this scene is also nostalgic, presenting the forest as an "imaginary, inaccessible, or unreal" "lost paradise," but such nostalgia, we are reminded "keeps open the expectation of grace" (Harrison, *Forests* 156), and Doria fundamentally believes that her granddaughter is not a forest creature, but a heavenly one, blessed by God, "her eyelids seemed carved by the hands of a saint-maker" (63).

The stories told by Silla Boyce and Doria Bellacasa to their most cherished listeners—Selina and Carmolina, respectively—prepare each child to enter adulthood armed with knowledge about migration, poverty, powerlessness, and continuing struggle. The pain of their childhoods, however, is directly linked with their mother's suffering, which compels both girls to dissociate from their mothers in order to survive emotionally. For Selina who does not possess the luxury of generational "space" from her storytelling mother, this separation is particularly vexatious and countered by Silla with regularity. In contrast, because Carmolina's storytelling mentor is her grandmother, *not* her mother, her third-generational status cushions her from the old-world *miseria* of her grandmother's life in Italy *and* offers shelter from her mother's unabated sadness. Silla and Sarah fight against their voices being silenced and colonized by coercive discourses both economic and cultural, but both are thwarted in heart-rending ways (DeLamotte 1–9). Selina and Carmolina feel the loss of their mothers well before either daughter leaves her community.

The question that De Rosa poses of her character, Sarah—"What is the problem with the mother?"—can be applied to both mothers in *Brown Girl, Brownstones* and *Paper Fish* ("Breaking the Silence" 239). Seeking answers to this question lies at the heart of both girls' pain and their early estrangement from their mothers remains a preeminent grief in their lives. Both Silla and Sarah are the "monumental tragic figure[s]" in their respective novels (Washington, "Afterword" 313). Both women are disempowered by particular acts of silencing: Silla by the hegemonic culture that discounts her existence as a Black immigrant woman altogether, utilizing her as manual labor only; Sarah by the impoverishment of tenement life and the life-altering results of exogamy, marrying into an Italian family whose language becomes coercive to Sarah, a form of linguistic exclusion. Both Silla and Sarah futilely try to control family dynamics, functioning further to estrange themselves from their daughters. Marshall and De Rosa explore what Adrienne Rich calls "this cathexis between mother and daughter—essential, distorted, misused"—in order to foreground and foreshadow each daughter's necessary movement away from home (*Of Woman Born* 225).

In *Brown Girl, Brownstones*, when Silla hatches her plan to wrest Deighton's property in Barbados, her obsession takes precedence over all else. She embodies an idée fixe, utterly consumed by her sleight of hand, that is, by clandestinely forging letters to Deighton's sister in Barbados in order to sell his property. In her "illicit act of self-empowerment," De-Lamotte explains, Silla subversively appropriates power and becomes "a kind of madwoman in the basement," using the pen in the manner of Gilbert and Gubar's thesis, "as an act of rebellion" (23). Guaranteeing the destruction of her marriage, Silla's ruinous act and subsequent retribution—she has Deighton, an illegal immigrant, deported to Barbados—not only leaves her a widow, but also causes her daughter to equate her mother with the quintessential figure of hegemonic domination—Adolph Hitler. During the "Hitler" scene which follows Deighton's deportation, Selina's screaming iteration of this name ushers in a poignant scene in the novel. Marshall's employment of one of the most resonant images of Western iconography—the mater dolorosa—not only solidifies the mother-daughter dyad, but also captures, mirror-like, their equally painful positions: the image of the wounded child draped over her grieving mother's knees. As Marshall writes, Silla "carried her [Selina] out of the room . . . she sat holding her on the sofa . . . Then, almost reverently, she touched the tears that had dried white on her dark skin . . ." (185). Denniston explains that Marshall's portrayal of the mother-daughter conflict in *Brown Girl, Brownstones* "really camouflages deep-seated frustrations over the costs to the spirit in a racist, sexist, and materialistic society" (25). Succumbing to her compulsion to advance materially, Silla loses the respect of her daughter, but she remains the imposing figure of autonomy that Selina will emulate.

Carmolina's estrangement from her mother also occurs early and irrevocably in *Paper Fish*. While the handling of time is fluid in this modernist text, De Rosa clarifies early that Carmolina loses her mother well before her mother actually dies, "and oh how the little girl would miss her all of her life" (18). Leaving the backyard world of single-family homes in her working-class Lithuanian neighborhood on the other side of the city, Sarah's exogamy alienates her both from her family of origin—her linguistic autonomy is "stilled," De Rosa writes—and from the family into which she marries (40). Despite her working-class background—her family owns and operates a greasy spoon—Sarah's move to the cold-water flat in the Taylor Street neighborhood is a downwardly mobile gesture, giving lie to the assumption that second-generational ethnics slowly but surely made economic strides.[20] In addition, Sarah's English-speaking voice is denied access, overpowered linguistically by the Italian dialect spoken by everyone in the Bellacasa family, Marco's sisters, brother, and mother. But it is the dominant voice of the matriarch, Grandma Doria, that snaps Sarah's "words in two," not only silencing her tongue, but mutilating it, too (50). While her voice and body are colonized by the family's Italian language and their ubiquitous presence in her life, Sarah silently refuses to relinquish her personal views, especially concerning the reasons underlying her first daughter's illness.

Like a modern-day Philomela, when Sarah is alone, she covertly communicates with Doriana, sharing stories about her life before she married and then attempting, albeit futilely, to heal her daughter. During a particularly resonant kitchen scene, De Rosa employs as Marshall did earlier the iconographic image of the pietà to reflect the parallel pain of mother and daughter.[21] Dragging her nine-year old daughter into the kitchen—the space regularly dominated by the extended Bellacasa family—Sarah attempts to suckle her silent daughter who is presently suffering from a high fever: "In her sleep, Doriana suckled the dry breast" (96). While it might seem irrational and senseless to perform such an activity—Sarah the Lithuanian madwoman in the Italian kitchen—such a gesture reinforces the "something wrong in the house," a kind of emotional autism that has paralyzed this family (12).

Sarah's hopeless gesture to cure her daughter occurs during Carmolina's absence from the family. When Carmolina is returned and delirious with a fever herself—paralleling Doriana's illness—Carmolina's ostensibly irrational thought makes perfect sense in light of her burgeoning awareness that she will have to tell the story of her suffering family: "They weren't really her family at all. Her family went away and left all these strangers. . . . She would have to live with them and no one would ever tell her where her real family was" (106). After this scene, De Rosa advances the narrative nine years, preparing the way for Carmolina's eventual leave taking, which will forever separate her from her family of origin.

Paule Marshall and Tina De Rosa devote the final sections of their novels to the coming-of-age stories of Selina and Carmolina, who are on the brink of adulthood and difficult acceptance of their roles in the family dynamic. Mary Helen Washington explains that Selina functions as "the witness and record keeper," of her mother's and her community's pain (315); similarly, Carmolina develops into an adulthood that requires her to find words where there is only speechlessness on the part of her family. As *künstlerromane*, *Brown Girl, Brownstones* and *Paper Fish* clarify the positions of their artist protagonists as they wend their ways to worlds outside the protective spaces of their respective communities. As De Rosa pointed out in an interview, children and grandchildren of immigrants struggled to find acceptance in a world that excoriated foreigners: "It has to do with the whole psychology of wanting to be accepted by the very thing that rejects you. . . . Did I want to be part of this other culture that hurt them so badly and where I felt like a total stranger?" ("Breaking the Silence" 231). For both Selina of *Brown Girl* and Carmolina of *Paper Fish* becoming part of American life is fraught with the recognition of their cultural roles as ethnic women who live in a racist culture. Their artistry will enable them to cope with and express the beauty and pain of their respective backgrounds.

Marshall dedicates book 4 of *Brown Girl, Brownstones* to Selina's development into an artist and a black woman. The racist episode that follows Selina's superb dance recital at her college—she's given thunderous applause and achieves artistic autonomy—powerfully demonstrates the depths of American hostility toward blacks. The postperformance cast party directly following Selina's dance debut takes place at the apartment of one of the cast members, Margaret Benton, described by Marshall in a distinctly racially coded manner: "her hair catching each passing light, a full-blown Wagnerian heroine" (283). As Hathaway points out, Marshall associates "Margaret with Wagner, a composer used throughout the German Third Reich to epitomize Aryan ideals," as preparatory to what ensues between Selina and Margaret's mother (114).

Mrs. Benton proceeds to insult and reduce Selina, subjecting her to ruthlessly condescending comments about "Negroes from the West Indies" and her "race's natural talent for dancing and music" (287, 288). Physically and vocally overpowered—"held down by her [Mrs. Benton's] hand, drowning in the deluge of her voice"—Selina achieves a shattering clarity when she realizes that her black skin is the sine qua non of her existence to the Mrs. Bentons of the world. Selina thinks, "And knowing was like dying" (289). But as Hathaway tellingly comments, "Selina rejects this figurative murder of her identity" (115) and wordlessly flees the scene.

Like De Rosa, Marshall regularly employs mirror imagery to explore her protagonist's regular negotiations with herself vis-à-vis the impingements of the cultural world outside her community. The pivotal mirror scene at the end of *Brown Girl* takes place outside through a reflection in a window and compels Selina to recognize how her image has been reduced and distorted by racism, which, as Denniston reminds us, "makes no distinctions in culture" (24–25). Exhausted by the emotional confrontation with a representative of American racist culture, Selina painfully realizes that "their idea of her was only an illusion, yet so powerful that it would stalk her down the years, confront her in each mirror. . . She cried because, like all her kinsmen, she must somehow prevent it from destroying her inside and find a way for her real face to emerge" (291). Clearly, for Marshall, Selina must embrace her Barbadian community to reinforce cultural cohesion before she proceeds further into American society. Only then can she look in the mirror and see a multidimensional self, also nurtured by cultural values distinctive to her Bajan ancestry.

As Susan Stanford Friedman explains of the scene of the "false self in the window," Selina "tries to shatter the alienating image in the cultural mirror" but cannot do so "until she can learn to respect the Bajan community she despised. . . . The illusion that she was a single individual who could make her way alone in the white world nearly destroyed Selina. The lesson of the mirror is the lesson of collective identity, in both its alienating and transformative aspects" ("Women's Autobiographical Selves," *The Private Self* 51). After a long, harrowing day, Selina returns to Brooklyn, recognizing the ineluctable tie she has to her community, further secured by her new power to empathize: "And she was one with them: the mother and the Bajan women, who had lived each day what she had come to know. How had the mother endured, she who had not chosen death by water?" (292–293).

In *Paper Fish*, De Rosa also incorporates a lesson in the mirror for Carmolina before her grandmother dies. Unlike Selina, however, whose second-generational status ultimately aligns her more closely to the Barbadian immigrants she had earlier rejected (overturning Marcus Hansen's generational schema), Carmolina's status as third generation buffers her from the direct impact of immigration, ultimately alienating her more from both grandparental and parental generations even though she is not fully able to partake in American culture.[22] That De Rosa chooses to portray Carmolina and Grandma Doria *separately* in front of their mirrors preparing for a private ritual suggests their imminent separation *and* their similarity. Due to the illness suffered by Doriana throughout Carmolina's developmental years, she has not been afforded the space or time to be a child as her second-generational parents were unable to cope with the family's suffering.[23] Like Selina, Carmolina's artistic role becomes more apparent toward the end of the novel.

Because she can no longer walk, Grandma Doria is carried in a chair by her sons up three flights of wooden stairs to visit Carmolina privately in the Bellacasa flat. As discussed in chapter 2, De Rosa recuperates a long-standing tradition among Catholic Italians, the procession of the Madonna in public, merging sacred and secular. While the neighborhood people witness and honor this event—"the men killed their cigars and cigarettes out of respect"—in De Rosa's scenario, the processional movement is reversed because the sacred event takes place privately with Carmolina, who is given the artistic legacy (112). In keeping with the sacred nature of the event, Carmolina, though initially resistant, dons a wedding dress "just so Grandma could see her dressed as a bride," though the marriage that takes place is paradoxically singular and solitary for Carmolina (114). At the sight of her beloved Grandmother, Carmolina "could find no words" but just feels "a weight in her chest like gold" (114). The mirror event that concludes the scene compels Carmolina to accept a legacy that will unite her to her Italian ancestry and the artistic legacy her grandmother bestows upon her, with the injunction " 'Now it you turn. You keep the fire inside you.' Carmolina looked into the mirror's silver face. It gave back to her her own face" (116). Doubling the possessive pronoun while Carmolina is mirror gazing illuminates the duality of her position required of the artist—to be able to "see both sides," as De Rosa earlier described her protagonist's dual perspective

(15). This "*achieved* doubleness of which she is creator rather than victim" describes both Selina and Carmolina who will absorb the oral traditions of their respective cultures as they negotiate their way in American culture without the community ties that nurtured them in childhood (DeLamotte 4).

Marshall and De Rosa conclude their novels with a focus on their neighborhoods in Brooklyn and Chicago, respectively. Both protagonists are witness to the destruction of the very communities in which they were raised and wanted to escape. In order to reinforce the vital necessity of the village within the city, Marshall and De Rosa portray their protagonists returning to their enclaves at the conclusions of each novel, their cultural roles clarified. Both young women assume the role of preserver of their cultural communities. Selina, Washington explains, "is the *griot* of this [Barbadian] community, the preserver of its near and ancient past" (emphasis added; "Afterword" 318). Likewise, Carmolina develops into the cantastorie of the Italian community, the history singer, who parallels the storytellers of Italy, "the keepers, creators, and repositories of the popular literature of Europe" (Timpanelli 135).

Selina and Carmolina have difficult roads ahead of them, for their communities are being dismantled before their eyes. As Rudolph Vecoli writes of Italians in Chicago, their neighborhoods "were literally reduced to heaps of rubble" ("Are Italian Americans Just White Folks?" 4). When Selina takes a final walk through Fulton Park, she bears witness to the unfortunate changes in her neighborhood: "Before, on a spring night, the mothers would have been sitting there, their ample thighs spread easy under their housedresses, gossiping, while around them spring rose from the pyre of winter" (309). Observing in contrast a "ruined park" and "ravaged brownstones," Selina is led to a "vast waste—an area where blocks of brownstones had been blasted to make way for a city project. A solitary wall stood perversely amid the rubble, a stoop still imposed its massive grandeur, a carved oak staircase led only to the night sky" (309).

Marshall presents this scene as an example of terrible loss for the community, exposing the fragility of their lives in the city as blatantly as she portrays the naked staircase in the night sky. At the end of *Brown Girl, Brownstones*, Selina walks through the ruins of her neighborhood, hearing and seeing the "bodies of all the people she had ever known broken . . . all the pieces piled into this giant cairn of stone and silence" (310). Feeling like "the sole survivor amid the wreckage," Selina becomes "the figure of redemption, the Ishmael left alone at the end to tell the story" (Washington, "Afterword" 313).[24] Selina, like her creator, Paule

Marshall, will have to tell about her Bajan community before it's lost, the compulsion never more irresistible than when the neighborhood is being destroyed.

Carmolina's solitary role at the conclusion of *Paper Fish* is equally redemptive. Shifting out of the personal story of Carmolina, De Rosa incorporates an epilogue, which functions as snapshots of people forced to leave the neighborhood. In the role of the witness-bearer, the narrator inserts brief vignettes of the Italians responding to the city's decision to raze their neighborhood: "'The city, you think she do it?' the seedman asked. 'You think she come tear us down like we a rotten building?' He spat in the street. 'I think she do it. I think she make us all move'" (117). Giving voice to poor and invisible Italians, De Rosa legitimizes their concerns, trumping the dominant narrative spouting urban renewal and changing demography. Nonetheless, the death of this Chicago Little Italy occurred amid confusion and despite verbal protest: "The city said the Italian ghetto should go, and before the people could drop their forks and say, pardon me? the streets were cleared" (120). Describing the desolation in terms similar to Marshall, De Rosa suggests that a second enforced migration was required of Chicago Italians from their transplanted village in the Midwest. An equally powerful loss that comes with displacement by the mainstream culture, the destruction of the old neighborhood "marked the end of the first chapter of the history of the Italians in America" (Vecoli, "Are Italian Americans Just White Folks?" 4).

In terms similar to Marshall, De Rosa describes the demolition of the neighborhood by recalling images of destruction during World War II,[25] including the bombings that ravaged southern Italy and Sicily:

> Giovanni went to sit alone on the concrete stoop of his house. Berrywood Street had disappeared as though it were a picture someone wiped away.... Next to Giovanni's house, where the little wooden home of Mrs. Consuelo had been, a dark wooden fence made a perfect square around nothing. The sunflowers still grew in Doria's garden, behind the house that wasn't there. Across the street, all the buildings were gone, so that Giovanni could sit on his stoop, and look into Quincy Street a block away. Augie's grocery store was an empty frame, like a stage prop someone forgot to move. The butcher shop stood empty of its chickens. Mrs. Schiavone's butcher block shone under the sun in the alley, the blood congealed on the wood like skin. (120)

Selina of *Brown Girl, Brownstones* and Carmolina of *Paper Fish* leave their communities out of necessity, but they each memorialize their ethnic locales at the conclusions of each novel through important gestures: Selina hurls one of her two silver bangles into the desolation that is becoming her neighborhood, promising reconnection through memory and imagination (310). Carmolina assures her grandmother that "nothing goes away," in the final vignette, reversing the adult-child role and assuming the position of protector though language (121). In writing about their families, both authors commemorate and grieve. Paule Marshall quotes directly from Grace Paley, whose words encapsulate a paramount feature of both Marshall's and De Rosa's novels: "If you say what's on your mind in the language that comes to you from your parents and your street and friends you'll probably say something beautiful" (qtd. in "From The Poets in the Kitchen" 627). Paule Marshall and Tina De Rosa knew from childhood experience that language would ultimately be their only homeland. *Brown Girl, Brownstones* and *Paper Fish* are the expressive fictional responses to that knowledge.

Writers of memoir and poetry in Italian America have also been steadily engaged in saying what's on their mind, often employing accessible language to embrace and inform readers. In the past twenty-five years, the Italian American literary terrain has been populated with autobiographical voices which reveal vital connections not only with familial forbears, but with literary precursors of Italian America, who legitimate the autobiographical acts of those who follow them. The next chapter examines how such a literary lineage mutually affects women writers of memoir and poetry, as they write out of an awareness of existing literary traditions in Italian America.

6

Precursor/Precursore

ॐ

Mother's Tongue

ITALIAN AMERICAN DAUGHTERS AND FEMALE PRECURSORS

It is as if we could, by looking at another's fever, catch it.

—Alicia Ostriker, *Stealing the Language*

While Italian American male and female authors share many of the same cultural and literary concerns, including their incorporation of oral, folk, and family traditions within literary writing that reveals hard-core skepticism toward institutional authorities and reverence toward nontraditional forms of worship, a gulf often separates them in their responses to genealogical and literary precursors. Male and female writers have explored how family affects individual identity within Italian American cultural worlds. Yet male writers in general differ in their approach to forging a literary identity distinct from a familial culture that traditionally raised a wary eye toward the private activity of writing. Aspiring Italian American men and women writers alike signaled a disconnection from family origins in their audacious acts of literary autonomy, but they did so in different ways.

For second-generational male writers of the early twentieth century, disconnecting from the Italian father allowed such writers as Pietro di Donato, Guido D'Agostino, Louis Forgione, John Fante, and Jerre Mangione to explore the damaging effects of Italian migration to the United States through an avowal of the father's destruction within a capitalistic system of indifference and greed. Becoming the writer son was as much a response to the hostility the father endured as it was a refusal to achieve the father's American dream of upward mobility through a specific kind of hard work and determination. Writing careers were not dreams deferred by Italian immigrant fathers; they were aberrant American ways peripheral to men's work in stonemasonry and bricklaying, or, in professional fields such as pharmacy and law. Sons who became writers, especially in the first decades of the twentieth century, reenacted another form of uprooting, and through a literary act of opposition, forged separate identities that allowed them to forsake and commemorate their fathers who were already lost to them.

The father–son dyad, a familiar coupling in Western literature, serves as a prototypical archetype in Italian American literature by men. Two of the most lauded novels by U.S. writers of Italian American background focus obsessively on the father-son bond: Pietro di Donato's *Christ in Concrete* and Don DeLillo's *Underworld*. Quite early in the literature of Italian America the concern over fathers and sons took precedence on the fictional stage. Luigi Donato Ventura's 1885 novella, *Peppino*, appearing just a year after Mark Twain's complex portrayal of father-son dynamics in *Huckleberry Finn*, might be said to pave the way for extended treatments of father-son plots featured in Louis Forgione's 1928 *The River Between* and, ten years later, in John Fante's *Wait Until Spring, Bandini*. While the critical conversation on Mario Puzo's *The Godfather* has focused on Sicilian family dynamics, the novel pays sustained attention to the father-son relationship between Don Vito and his son, Michael Corleone. In each of these novels, the son is presented in opposition to the father due to a variety of social factors, most of them unfortunate. Bereft of paternal protection, boys like Ventura's Peppino and di Donato's Paul, must ultimately reject the father, whose absence forecasts an equally negative destiny for the son. As Fred Gardaphé explains of Paul's limited future in construction work, where his father meets an awful death, "There is no redemption through the father" ("Italian American Novelists" 169).

Pietro di Donato emphatically explores how a second-generation Italian son must oppose the father's dreams in order to survive. For di

Donato, the father's tongue must be excised, so that the son may live beyond physical survival. However, to achieve what Emerson called "'the splendor of [the father's] renown'" (qtd. in Bloom 27) di Donato competes linguistically with the skilled laborers of his father's generation and thereby writes arguably the most dazzling work of Italian America in the first half of the twentieth century. *Christ in Concrete* may be described as di Donato's war of words—in English, Italian dialect, and hybridized forms of both languages. Di Donato fights against God the Father, American literary traditions, and an Italian father who has forsaken him through death, producing ventriloquial voices in *Christ in Concrete*.[1]

Di Donato speaks in tongues—using an Abruzzese dialectal speech translated literally into English alongside invented words that are neither Italian—Tuscan or southern dialect—nor English, idiomatic or otherwise. Forsaking the Christian God, di Donato writes a fictional allegory of a young boy's progress from staunch Catholic belief in the "newer—nearer" Crucifixion of his Olympian father who dies a gruesome death—to a denial of Jesus love to develop the anger necessary to write beyond the father. As Robert Viscusi explains, removing the father's power to speak is *the* primal scene of writing, "the son stealing the power of words from the father" (*Buried Caesars* 103). The father's tongue is not only broken—literally in the sense of speaking Italian-inflected English—but he suffers literal castration and suffocation at the hands of his interpreter son, who imagines the sounds associated with live burial. In appropriating his father's tongue, di Donato achieves a literary authenticity valued in Anglophone letters, a validity espoused theoretically by Harold Bloom in his well-known *The Anxiety of Influence.*

For many Italian American women writers, spiritual and literary redemption occurs through collaboration with rather than opposition to a parental guide, sometimes familial, often literary, but in an effort explicitly to establish oral connections with precursors. Not until the inception of the women's movement in the 1970s and its ancillary, women's history in the academy, did the study of immigration and women's participation in it become central to a more balanced approach to women's experience. Rather than lamenting a paucity of primary sources, scholars discovered a rich harvest of works by Italian American women, including immigrant letters, newspaper articles, autobiographies and novels. As the nation's libraries built research centers that collected materials on immigrant life, scholarly inquiry likewise burgeoned in areas of women's history and immigrant writers. Women writers of literary Italian America have reaped the benefits of such rediscoveries, inserting the voices of their precursors within autobiographical works that reinforce ethnic visibility.

Fundamental to the emergence of a *visible* presence of Italian American women writers is the phenomenon of literary precursors. For several writers of Italian America anxiety-laden conflict between literary and genealogical forbears expressed in the prototypical immigrant novel, *Christ in Concrete*, is absent between literary mothers and their writing daughters. Early twentieth-century storytellers such as Rosa Cassettari and writers such as Frances Winwar and Mari Tomasi were publishing evocative works during the same period that second-generation male writers were flourishing. Mari Tomasi is as much an exemplar of the literary realism produced in the first half of the twentieth century as are John Fante and Guido D'Agostino. Even during this early period, however, women writers like Mari Tomasi portrayed fictionally her relationship to her original family as complementary to her desire to write, not as embattled as we see in the characterization of Italian American fathers and sons in Fante's and D'Agostino's autobiographical novels, *Wait Until Spring, Bandini* and *Olives on the Apple Tree*, respectively.[2] Instead of portraying lashing or mutilation to excise the biological or literary mother's tongue, female writers of the second-half of the twentieth century emphasize attraction more than anxiety, allure rather than struggle with precursors. In contrast to contestation, mutuality enables women writers to seek connection *and* independence from literary forbears whose voices are not quelled but extended in innovative ways.

According to Harold Bloom's paradigm on creativity, mutuality signals weaker writing. Bloom applies Freud's psychosexual model of relationships to literary genealogies, interpreting poetic influence as a filial relationship. The anxiety that the poet son feels is intensified by a post-Enlightenment realization that artistic genius transcended effort (*The Anxiety of Influence* 28). The nineteenth-century Romantic poet's emphasis on Genius and the Sublime intimidated the son. If the son were a strong, authentic poet, he would proceed by misreading the prior poet, an act of creative correction that is necessarily a misinterpretation (30).

In their inventive reinterpretation of Bloom's paradigm, Sandra M. Gilbert and Susan Gubar in *The Madwoman in the Attic* reiterate Bloom's premise that the strong poet "must engage in heroic warfare with his 'precursor,' for, involved as he is in a literary Oedipal struggle, a man can only become a poet by somehow invalidating his poetic father" (47). Bloom's male-oriented theory, Gilbert and Gubar insist, cannot be "simply reversed or inverted in order to account for the situation of the woman writer" (48).

Unlike their literary brothers, nineteenth-century women writers from the Anglophone tradition participated in a very different literary subculture. These writers substitute an 'anxiety of influence' with "an 'anxiety of authorship,'" "an anxiety built from complex and only barely conscious fear of that authority which seems to the female artist to be by definition inappropriate to her sex" (Gilbert and Gubar 50, 51).

Both Bloom and Gilbert and Gubar focus their analyses on nineteenth-century writers and the larger occurrence of intellectual revisionism. Bloom's paradigm and Gilbert and Gubar's revision of it are especially useful for a reading of twentieth-century ethnic writers whose marginality has circumscribed their literary visibility and at times limited their output. Bloom's emphasis on the artist's struggle against his precursor (which he calls *clinamen*, or revisionary swerves, or misreadings) *and* Gilbert and Gubar's examination of the female artist's struggle to seek a female precursor (who does not represent a threat to be removed) illuminate the strategic movements of several female writers of Italian America since the inception of Helen Barolini's *The Dream Book*. Writers emerging from this period (post-1980) comprise what I describe as second wave, reflecting the influence of feminism *and* ethnicity, and exploring the intersections of gender, ethnicity, and social class in a synergistic manner that complicates and enhances a multifarious conception of identity. Writers who once thought of themselves as "unique" in the sense of being without a culturally identifiable literary tradition—specifically Italian American—became visible to each other for the first time in U.S. literary history. Such visibility has encouraged Italian American women to learn stylistic cadence, thematic focus, and generic strategies from writers sharing similar cultural terrain.

Gilbert and Gubar's assertion that female writers seek models to "legitimize [their] own rebellious endeavors" (50) applies well to the creative acts of women writers of Italian America, who have made visible the cultural practices of the traditionally silent family and the fears attendant within nuclear and patriarchal family structures. Unlike many of the male writers, female writers have often remained within the Italian American family for a longer period of time and within the house during formative years, returning years later in adulthood in the well-trod role of caretaker.

Second-wave Italian American writing by women reflects the development of a visible presence of writers working in genres particularly welcoming to self-revelation: memoir and poetry. Many writers have thus established rich connections with familial and literary forbears. Two memoirists—Louise DeSalvo in *Vertigo* and Mary Cappello in *Night Bloom* and two poets—Maria Mazziotti Gillan in *Where I Come From* and Rose Romano in *Vendetta* and *The Wop Factor* demonstrably exemplify the activity of creative revisionism essential to imaginative production, but they do so more as lovers than as foes. Easing the anxiety of authorship, Italian American literary mothers such as Louise DeSalvo and Maria Gillan have been instrumental in supporting literary daughters.[3] Refusing to interpret their strong literary mothers as attenuating their own subjectivity, writers such as Mary Cappello and Rose Romano have embraced Italian American precursors, an imperative strategy for legitimating an ongoing tradition of U.S. writers of Italian America.

That Mary Cappello and Rose Romano—unlike their literary foremothers—identify themselves as lesbians is no small matter. Feminist revisions of psychoanalytic theories early promulgated by Nancy Chodorow in her analysis of the feminine oedipal complex were useful in establishing the fact that girls traditionally come to define themselves more in relation to others, "having more permeable ego boundaries" (93). While this "relational complexity in feminine self-definition" (Chodorow 93) in object-relations theory maintains heterosexuality as the norm for girls, feminist literary theorists have further explored how alternate women-centered stories such as the story of Demeter and Persephone rather than the Oedipus story—"subvert the constraint of dominant patterns by means of various 'emancipatory strategies'—the revision of endings, beginnings, patterns of progression" (Hirsch 8). Concerning their lesbianism, Mary Cappello and Rose Romano subvert what Biddy Martin describes as "homogenous conceptions of identity," and also employ stylistic forms that further unsettle a "totalizing self-identification" as either lesbian or Italian American (Martin 82).

Unlike heterosexual daughters, writers or not, Mary Cappello and Rose Romano as lesbians resist many forms of male domination in their lives, establishing primary relationships with women. Their critique of heterosexual paradigms has the potential to increase the magic and intensity of the bond they share with their biological and/or literary female forbears. Mary Cappello's *Night Bloom* is a case in point. Her bond with her biological mother is reinforced textually with her literary mother, Louise DeSalvo, to whom she directly pays homage in *Night Bloom*. From a strictly psychoanalytic perspective (which is traditionally male-centric), Cappello overidentifies with her biological mother in *Night Bloom*, but this gesture reflects a continued desire for women, suggesting "other possible subjective economies based in women's relationships" as Marianne

Hirsch explains in her examination of literary mother-daughter plots (10). Despite conflicts emerging from a patriarchal family situation in which, as Adrienne Rich observed, "the relationship between mother and daughter has been profoundly threatening to men," Cappello's level of commitment to understanding her Italian American mother never diminishes but only grows stronger as she enters adulthood (*Of Woman Born* 226).

Further enhancing the mother-daughter dyad, Mary Cappello complicates the idea of "dis-identification," in which the daughter refuses heterosexual romance and marriage to achieve a singularity from the fate of the mother, thus making the mother "the primary negative model for the daughter" (Hirsch 10–11). Cappello in contrast focuses on her mother's own disconnection from Italian American family life—first through depression and agoraphobia, and later, through divorce and creativity. In effect, Cappello's mother, Rosemary, becomes more like her author/daughter than an unhappily married mother. In an effort to establish an equally evocative connection to her literary foremother, Cappello signals her relationship to Louise DeSalvo through the textual strategy of reiteration, rejecting like her foremother the submissive role reserved for her by a patriarchal Italian American family in both the choices she makes in her life and the stylistic ways she chooses to write about them, dismantling traditional ideas about authority and layering a text that honors and enhances DeSalvo's *Vertigo*.

Published in 1996, Louise DeSalvo's *Vertigo* spans the years of her early childhood in Hoboken, New Jersey, to her later development as a scholar of Virginia Woolf and a professor of English. With the debatable exception of Diane di Prima's 1969 *Memoirs of a Beatnik*, for the first time in Italian American autobiographical history, DeSalvo offers readers an inside look of an "unlikely narrative of how a working-class Italian girl became a critic and writer" (xvii), paving a path for subsequent writers who quickly followed her lead.[4] Placed in the context of feminist autobiography, *Vertigo* also falls within a subgenre of prominence in recent years: the feminist confession.

Rita Felski relates this particular species of confession to "the exemplary model of consciousness-raising," describing this form of writing as signaling "its intention to foreground the most personal and intimate details of the author's life" (83).[5] DeSalvo's confession is divorced from religion in the orthodox sense of admitting sin and transgression. Though DeSalvo does devote a chapter to Catholic grammar school, her work differs markedly from the school girl narratives of Helen Barolini and Mary Gordon examined in chapter 2 and which focused on the influences—good and bad—of institutionalized Catholicism. While the genre of autobiography emerges from religious confession, Felski reminds readers that since the eighteenth century, literary confession has been "primarily concerned with not the admission of guilt and the appeal to a higher authority, but rather with the affirmation and exploration of free subjectivity" (87). For DeSalvo, as for many feminist autobiographers, this exploration is often motivated by "a personal crisis which acts as a catalyst" (Felski 83).

Two other characteristics of feminist confession underscore the deliberate way DeSalvo chose to write *Vertigo*. First, in her decision to render the most authentic—uncensored—self-expression, DeSalvo distances herself from the aesthetic criteria of literature—obvious literary features such as poetic language and elaborate narrative structures—in order to persuade "readers that they are reading an intimate communication addressed to them personally by the author" (Felski 86). While *Vertigo* is written with the care of a writer who values words and clearly knows how to construct a text, revealing DeSalvo's intellectual acumen as a literary critic, it simultaneously encodes an audience through gruff honesty and intimate detail (Felski 86). Related to DeSalvo's decision to write in an accessible unselfconscious manner, is the second feature of feminist confession: an implicit invitation to the reader to examine conflicted identity through the lens of proscriptive ideologies on gender and class. DeSalvo thus seeks to affirm "a female experience which has often been repressed and rendered invisible by speaking about it, by writing it into existence. The act of writing promises power and control, endowing subjective experience with authority and meaning" (Felski 90).[6]

DeSalvo examines her Italian American family of origin as fundamental to her emotional development and to her personal turmoil. The author's direct style and unabashed portrayal of her rebellion against her parents makes *Vertigo* generically one of the first autobiographical works in Italian American literature to reveal the unabated frustration and anger that she felt inside the traditionally venerated Italian American home.[7] Typical of the nonlinear and fragmented structures of feminist confession, throughout *Vertigo*, DeSalvo moves back and forth between past and present, interweaving memories and reflections with seeming ease, aware that such movement parallels her ongoing fascination with the terms "vertigo" and "verse," as she seeks "to turn a phrase in the midst of my instability" (9). Two traumatizing events—her sister's suicide in 1984 and her mother's death in 1990—compel Louise to reevaluate her status as a sister and daughter, as an Italian American woman, and as a critic turned sleuth, that is, trained to analyze the relationship between writers' lives and their works.

Framing her memoir with an early chapter called "My Sister's Suicide" and a final chapter dedicated to her mother called "Personal Effects," De-Salvo's memoir functions elegiacally as she struggles to accept the instability of both her sister and mother, who suffered from clinical depression all their lives. That Louise comes out of the closet on the topic of mental illness is a heroic gesture of affirmation. Women's autobiographies are not averse to raising the specter of madness, mental imbalance, and illness, but Italian American literature has traditionally shied away from or fictionalized such experiences. Through the process of writing about her family's suffering, in particular her mother's anguish, DeSalvo creates herself as the family member cured by literary activity. Through the process of academic writing on Virginia Woolf's literary life and suicide, DeSalvo recognizes her own struggle for independence as a woman writer. Through the process of confessional discourse, DeSalvo saves herself from a similar familial trajectory, identifying the activity of writing as both sacred and curative.[8]

During the 1940s and 1950s, a young Louise DeSalvo responds to the conflicts with her parents in two key ways: through intellectualism and through sexuality. Unable to separate the life/work binary, which has been the traditional prerogative of male writers, DeSalvo struggles to divorce herself from a destructive dialectic which would entirely prevent her from becoming a writer. Early in her memoir, DeSalvo announces that "the ivory tower doesn't exist for me" (12), positioning herself as a writer and academic who does not assume the aloofness—and disdain—for practical affairs such as having children, taking vacations, and trying to clean her basement. Throughout her youth, Louise is fortunate to observe female mentors whose work is integrated into their lives as married women and mothers, providing a contrast to her Italian American mother, whose life is circumscribed by family duty and depression. Women like her boyfriend Carmine's mother and her neighbor, Mrs. Neil, an English teacher, provide DeSalvo with models of female fortitude, despite difficult lives. Both of these women are from the same generation as DeSalvo's mother, but achieve independence from male expectations through financial autonomy and an abiding passion for the work they do.

Even though Louise is having sex with Carmine Carrero, she seems to be more in love with his mother: "She never wears makeup and her hands and nails are filthy, but I think she is the most beautiful woman I have ever seen because she can pick up a hundred-pound bag of mulch and fling it over her shoulder and take it out to the customer's car as if it were as light and easy to carry as a newborn baby" (152). Recognizing that gender is socially constructed, DeSalvo observes a family dynamic that succeeds when traditional roles are reversed as they are in the case of Carmine's parents.

Likewise is the case for Mrs. Neil, a capable woman who performs all manner of laborious tasks without giving a second thought to gender roles. Observing Louise's love of books, Mrs. Neil hires her to organize her vast library, during which she gently guides Louise's reading choices and helps her develop critical insight into the often spurious divisions made between high literature and popular novels. Alongside enlarging her reading interests, Louise learns an invaluable—and unlovely—fact of life, stimulating her decision not to behave according to constraining patterns of heterosexual relationships that subordinate women in marriage. As DeSalvo relates, Mrs. Neil is a

> terrific woman, who becomes very important to me. She tries very hard to please her husband. She works a full-time job, she cooks, she gardens, she mows the lawn, she does the laundry, she shovels the snow, she changes her flat tires, she's caring, she's an interesting conversationalist, and her husband leaves her anyway. When I ask my mother why, she tells me something, something I remember: "There is no justice in this world." (133)

While Louise's mother implicitly recognizes a fundamental lack of fairness "in this world," it will be Louise's job to unpack the gendered implications of Mrs. Neil's and her mother's life, defining her autobiographical self by her dissension from and adherence to culturally normative heterosexuality.[9]

DeSalvo's open discussion of her sexuality—from her one-time same-sex relationship to her frantic sexual desire for boys, expands the parameters of allowable discourse in her Italian American family. DeSalvo's recollection of deliberately defecating in her cot long after she is toilet trained exposes an awkward situation where the sounds of her parents' lovemaking in the same room in which she and her sister sleep prematurely heightens her awareness of sexuality. It also reveals the extent of her parents' poverty—not only is there no privacy in the tiny apartment, but there is no bathtub or shower, so Louise's nighttime release merely increases the work that her mother performs in the cold-water fourth-floor walk-up in which exhaustion rules her days.

For Louise, the library becomes an inviting space of safety and order, which she continues to inhabit during her adolescence when she chooses to perform transgressive sexual acts so in contrast to her parents' stifled

moans and the rigid gender expectations placed on 1950s girls. Not one
to pass up a chance at dismantling the work/life binary, Louise describes
having sex with Carmine in the library stacks, appropriating the stock
male line by saying to her boyfriend, "But I can't wait" (154). In Mrs.
Purdy's high school English class, Louise further solidifies the connection between sexual and textual desire by offering an expert interpretation of Shakespearean sonnet 87, "Farewell! Thou art too dear for my
possessing." Louise marks this classroom recollection as a pivotal moment in her development as an aspiring intellectual whose personal experiences enhance her literary skills and cannot be divorced from her life
in literature:

> In this moment, my hidden life of love and sex counts for some-
> thing academically. It is transformed into something valuable
> beyond itself. Something I can draw upon to understand litera-
> ture. I can understand my life and transform its meaning
> because of what Shakespeare says; but I can understand Shake-
> speare better because of my life. And this will be true of every-
> thing I read. (185)

While DeSalvo's sexual relationships ultimately remain fixed within a
heterosexual female identity—including marriage to an Italian American man and motherhood that follows—she nonetheless knowingly
challenges a gender system that makes unspeakable female desire, expanding the boundaries of what can be spoken about by an Italian American woman in relation to her family of origin and to her individual
development. Rather brusque and dismissive about the short-lived sexual experience with a girlhood friend, Louise shifts her affections to boys
after the ninth grade because she felt "safer" with them because they
were "more predictable, more controllable" (143). Since girl-girl couples
were not unusual occurrences during Louise's adolescence, her movement toward strictly male/female coupling is indicative of the disciplinary power of heterosexuality itself and DeSalvo's subscription rather
than resistance to it.

Mary Cappello's *Night Bloom* is less a revisionary swerve from
Vertigo and more a reiterative teasing out the nuances of DeSalvo's topics, including Depression-era poverty, depressive mothers, prodigy
daughters, family genealogies, and sexual appetite. DeSalvo writes
frankly of her father's rage, her family's financial troubles, and her
mother's life of constant housework, her fear of the outside world,
and her thwarted literary ambitions. With agility, DeSalvo places her

childhood upbringing within the context of World War II, establishing a persuasive linkage between the experience of war and the battle she wages inside her father's house. Like her contemporaries—Diane Di Prima, Helen Barolini, Dorothy Calvetti Bryant, and Josephine Gattuso Hendin—Louise DeSalvo exposes the keenly felt shame of immigrant parents and children during World War II, countenanced and exacerbated by American culture when Italy became an enemy nation and an entire generation of Italians lived under suspicion in the United States.[10] Despite the fact that her father's educational plans were also stymied, DeSalvo recognizes, despite her paternal animosity, the gift of engagement with life that he bequeaths her. DeSalvo poignantly summarizes her parents' differences by writing, "My father was alive. My mother was afraid" (43). Mary Cappello might claim the opposite sentiment of her own parents.

Mary Cappello signals Louise DeSalvo in the very first line of her prologue to *Night Bloom*: "I'm four years old in 1964" (xiii), transparently mimicking the first line of her precursor's prologue: "It is 1956, and I am thirteen years old" (*Vertigo* xiii). In both introductions, the writers make references to rage, whether it is DeSalvo's infuriating arguments with her father or Cappello's early mastery of the word "violence." Cappello immediately intellectualizes family conflict while DeSalvo bluntly claims a working-class sensibility in tone and action, landing through sheer frankness a solid blow to her reader's solar plexus. Rather than paralyzing the reader with verbal gymnastics, DeSalvo's outspoken candor establishes an intimacy between author and reader, promising control and creativity through the process of writing.

Both DeSalvo and Cappello refuse to accept patriarchal anger as a means of controlling the family, but as children they lack the means by which to cope with their father's anger and must develop strategies— verbal and written—to protect themselves. Midway through her memoir, Cappello makes a direct reference to her precursor's work, aptly describing *Vertigo* as "groundbreaking" (125) in its insistence on breaking the silence about the suicidal depression of women in DeSalvo's family. DeSalvo ironically does Cappello a better turn in her back-cover blurb of *Night Bloom*, employing pugilistic diction in her comment, "I was knocked out by her original voice." Cappello furthers a connection to her literary foremother by writing in her acknowledgment page of DeSalvo's generosity in encouraging the writing of her own book, a gesture repudiated by Harold Bloom as the activities of weaker writers. Both writers remain firmly loyal to their stylistic strengths while simultaneously stroking each other's literary egos. DeSalvo remains true to her straightforward, colloquial prose style and Cappello maintains her intellectualism and poetic meanderings. If Cappello achieves a Bloomian kenosis, a movement toward a discontinuity with her literary precursor, then it is through her fusion of theory and memoir.

Unlike DeSalvo's *Vertigo*, Cappello's *Night Bloom* is insistently anti-confessional. Cappello refuses to submit her story to a confessional mode that solely focuses on sexual identity. Paralleling lesbian precursors of Italian America—particularly in the fictional works of Dodici Azpadu and Rachel Guido deVries—Cappello writes against the grain of typical coming-out stories, a genre of writing that conventionalizes lesbian identity. Rather, Cappello merges scholarly and poetic voices, uniting traditionally separated genres. Employing a fusion of postmodern feminism and queer theory allows Cappello to challenge monolithic models of sexuality, arguing à la Judith Butler, that such a category as heterosexuality for example is regulated through constant reiterations of sexual norms that enforce a heterosexual imperative that is nonetheless a social construct and not a biological determinant (Butler 367, 369).[11] Cappello's memoir constructs sexuality along the lines of family genealogy, identifying her lesbianism *within* family personalities, modeling her development on their nonconventional habits of mind and heart. Paradoxically, Cappello's lesbianism is less a dis-identification from her family of origin than is DeSalvo's resistance to her family in her refusal to abide by normative standards of gender behavior.

Throughout *Night Bloom*, Mary Cappello swerves away from the direct and accessible style of Louise DeSalvo, favoring a narrative style that is complex and theoretically driven. Her thematic focus in contrast parallels DeSalvo's, inviting comparison. Both DeSalvo and Cappello write nonlinear narratives, allowing them freedom to traverse past and present simultaneously, revealing the unordered reality of everyday living. DeSalvo describes her memoir as an "unlikely narrative," because she happily failed to fulfill the expectations of her class and gender. A generation later, Mary Cappello is less unlikely than her precursor to have gone to college, despite working-class antecedents. Rather, Cappello offers an interpretation of her unlikely story by connecting it to her unconventional sexual orientation: "I am reluctant to work with conventional narrative because my life, I, did not conform to the narrative meant for me" (55).[12] Cappello feels little need to reiterate that normative heterosexuality (marriage and monogamy) was presumed by her family, perhaps because it was—and perhaps because it wasn't.

Cappello's family of origin provided her with sufficient examples of unconventional narratives, beginning with her maternal great-grandparents. Cappello extends her genealogy by engaging in the activity of story telling through oral traditions passed from one generation to the next. In this way, Cappello suggests artistic antecedents through lived experience; the mysterious tale of her great-grandparents is a puzzle in which different pieces of their story are told by several people, including Rosemary Cappello, who becomes, along with Mary's maternal grandfather, one of the author's most formative storytelling mentors.

Cappello begins *Night Bloom* with the oral tales that emerged from her maternal great-grandfather's migration to America. Multiple versions of the story abound, but a complete narrative remains illusive. In response, Cappello creates a collage-like story concerning her maternal great-grandparents based on shards of information gleaned from various family members, including her mother. A landscaper and fixer of furnaces, Antonio Petracca was also a master gardener whose story—the master narrative—remains shrouded in mystery until Mary Cappello arranges the various pieces and names the unspeakable—a tale of patriarchal prerogative as injurious as Rosa Cassettari's first marriage in *Rosa: The Life of an Italian Immigrant*. Mary initially offers a tale which reads like one of Jerre Mangione's folk stories from *Mount Allegro*, including, predictably, acts of infidelity, sexually transmitted disease—"that unspeakable scourge . . . syphilis"—and exile from Antonio's birthplace (*Night Bloom* 11). As lesbian autobiographer, Mary is also an ethnic daughter, and, as such, she topples the notion of not naming the unspeakable, a gesture of silence employed by many ethnic groups who guard stories and therefore protect what Julia Watson calls the "old culture's hegemony" (393).[13]

In telling the story of separate migrations for great-grandfather and great-grandmother, Cappello intervenes and examines the underlying effects of a sixteen-year separation after which Mary's great-grandmother made the journey to America even though her husband only sent for his remaining son, John. Mary Cappello learns from her mother—who hears only fragments of the story from her mother in Italian, the forbidden tongue—not the full, or real, or true story, but one clear strand: "All that my mother could tell me for sure was that my grandfather was forever estranged from his father, who after all had abandoned him and his mother in more ways than one" (8).

And it is this estrangement that organizes the narrative movement of Cappello's *Night Bloom*, for it examines how, in the prototypical immigrant narrative, the great-grandmother and her grandson withstand the pain of migration and its traumatic effects: "I like to think of my grandfather's survival of infancy and childhood as a testament to my great-grandmother's decision to cease to live in and through her husband and his passions, the beginning of my grandfather's life as an act of her will" (11). Through her own desire to de-center authorial control and thereby transform traditional ideas about narrative authority, Mary Cappello places her grandfather's and mother's stories alongside hers, destabilizing hierarchical notions of family over selfhood.[14] Cappello then introduces her maternal grandfather, John Petracca, in Part One of her memoir. A cobbler by trade, John arrived in the United States in 1916, and suffered as an adult under "the shadow of the Depression era and the trauma of impoverishment from which he never fully recovered" (25). In an attempt to link her story to his, Cappello incorporates her grandfather's journal entries (translated from the Italian), his daily acts of survival written on the materials of his shoe trade—the tabs used to mark down the repair job to be done—and the hopeless feeling of powerlessness when struggling to support his suffering family. On a frigid February in 1941, Petracca writes "to see my family in such dire need and me, tied to the star of torture, impotent to procure what is of absolute need makes me despair" (46). Despite a life of pain and loss, Cappello's grandfather chooses "forgiveness and the discipline of daily, concerted plying of a trade," forms of psychic survival to counter unrelieved impoverishment (35).

Like him, Cappello's own personal development embraces the practical acts of daily living and the aesthetic goal of rendering memory beautiful. Absorbing her grandfather's ethos and aesthetic activity of journal writing, Cappello creates a literary collage by uniting the voices of three generations of writers—grandfather (John Petracca), mother (Rosemary Petracca Cappello), and daughter (Mary Cappello). Such a structure emulates the forms that many immigrant novels take, organized as they are by generations. Like a third-generation daughter, Mary redeems not only the immigrant ancestors, but also those represented by the second generation, specifically Cappello's mother, who inherited "the pain or deformation caused by the material or laboring conditions" of her ancestors (43). Including excerpts and poems from her mother's journals, Mary Cappello reverses the traditional act of sloughing off the parental generation. By doing this, Cappello examines her mother's indigent background, revisiting and extending DeSalvo's mother-daughter portrayal through analysis and self-identification. Attributing her mother's avid letter-writing to a strategy she adopts to cope with an untenable marriage, Mary Cappello explains that this creative medium must "contain unspeakable truths and inappropriate yearnings other narrative options seem unable to admit" (73). Maintaining a fluid consanguinity to her immigrant forbears, Mary explains that letter writing links the generations, along with the "pathological sense of loss (in the form of depression) and fear (in the form of phobia) that characterizes my ethnic heritage: the manifest calls whose response was the letter" (73). Embracing all three generations, Mary legitimizes their "inappropriate" sounds: "call it the noise of my grandfather's desire to make a living crafting shoes, of my mother's desire to be accounted for as a woman, of my desire to love other women, of our collective desire to be writers in an American culture that stifles the imagination of difference and refuses artistic practice as a place around which the mind and heart might rally" (73).

Her father's daughter, Rosemary Cappello's voice echoes an unchanged familial pattern of joblessness, minimum wage and ill health. Inheriting the memory of her mother's pain, Mary Cappello asserts "Poverty afflicts, first and foremost, a person's body" (44). Reiterating DeSalvo's declaration that her mother was afraid, Cappello, an able detective herself, discovers in her grandfather's journals and in the annals of psychology the language of her mother's fear: "I see how living with the threat of losing one's heat, water, electricity, and not having enough food to eat can easily engender states of terror" (127). Unlike DeSalvo, who strives mightily during her development to disengage from her mother, Cappello seeks no disconnection from hers. Rather, Cappello recognizes the force of maternal inheritance, employing her critical skills to understand her mother's fear. While DeSalvo's scholarly work on Virginia Woolf leads her to understand herself as a woman and critic, Cappello's work as a critic helps her to empathize with her mother's phobias—particularly agoraphobia—when Mary was a child. For DeSalvo, suffering from illness frightens her into thinking that she is being forced to live her mother's life. For Cappello, chest pains are her body's way of teaching her to identify with the suffering of her family. Neither DeSalvo nor Cappello is willing to succumb to writing a traditional narrative that reinforces a false suggestion that subsequent generations improve on the past. But Cappello extends DeSalvo's memoir by composing a multivoiced narrative in which three generations inhabit the same spatial dimensions within a book insistently focused on the vexed relationship between artistic imagination and marginal status.

Alongside recurring references to the journal and the rosary—forms of linkage and meditation that dramatized the losses her family sustained—Cappello examines the garden as a central locus of her family legacy (225).

Each desired object demonstrates for Cappello "marks of something sighted, something sung when voicelessness threatened, instances of re-making in light of traumatic unmakings of their authors' worlds" (225). Time and space merge in Cappello's memory through the most important image in *Night Bloom*—the garden—as ethnic daughter embraces the generations through the plants her family tended. The principal domicile of men from both maternal and paternal sides of Cappello's family, the garden becomes a place of sanctuary and grace for them—from maternal great-grandfather Petracca to Mary's father, Joe Cappello. Joe's physical abuse of Mary's two brothers is juxtaposed to his love of gardening—learned from his wife's family—transmuting his angry body into a "perfectly shaped letter 'C,' . . . no longer himself but a form of benediction" (97). Through observing her father's patient work in the garden, Mary learns to recognize his intelligence and sensitivity, despite suffering from childhood poverty in the Sicilian section of South Philadelphia with nary a flower in sight. Like DeSalvo's father, Cappello's father's education was thwarted, but he learns to cultivate all manner of interesting plants and shrubs by following the example of his wife's father and family. Through Rosemary's influence in playing a central role in creating the garden, Joe becomes a wonderful gardener and his autobiographer daughter, Mary, inventively interprets the specialties of the garden through an Italian American imaginary, uniting both sides of her family.

The planting of lunaria—"'satin flower', 'moon wort', 'silver shilling,' or 'St. Peter's pence'"—becomes her father's most experimental gardening success (99). Mary waxes metaphorical after describing the practical gift-giving her father performs in sharing lunaria with city-dwelling family members, comparing the shape of the plant to the Host, to glass eyes, and to a patch of ice, each resonating with a specific memory of her Italian American family. Despite her anticonfessional and anti-Catholic positions, Cappello admits that even though she has left its precepts behind, Catholicism continues to assert itself as "the major tableau of my desiring. . . . It has left its indelible mark, and on some level I will never fully own the power and magic of its traces" (151). This marking, which suggests a cultural connection to a specific iconography and discourse that is Catholic, continues to inform Mary's mental habits, so much so that the thought of lunaria first recalls the Holy Communion, "[p]aper-thin monument to Christ's body" (107). Cappello's ruminations on glass eyes reveal a distinctly Italian Catholic hue, with prayers to special saints, such as Santa Lucia, the patron saint of eyesight. In trying to understand the origin of her father's fearful nature, Cappello recalls folkloric Mezzogiorno culture, which includes a belief in *il malocchio*, the evil eye, reinforcing a fatalistic attitude toward malevolent outside forces, including the seemingly innocuous activity of looking at someone that can strike without provocation.[15] Refusing to live in a world painted by her father's fears (112), Cappello instead overidentifies with the uncrossable patch of ice, which represents her mother's wintertime fears. Watching her mother's paralysis before a patch of ice, Cappello identifies more fully with her mother's fear than with her father's attempt to make her mother laugh. She concludes by explaining, "I must always be aware, and especially when I might be having fun, especially if I were laughing, that my mother could be in pain" (115).

In interpreting her family genealogy, Cappello joins maternal and paternal sides, employing Catholic iconography to connect her grandfather's cactus—called euphorbia—with her father's silver flower, lunaria:

> I notice a connection between the euphorbia and lunaria, and thus between the Sicilian and Neapolitan influences in my life: both plants can be said to yield the perfume of religious dogma— lunaria is a member of the Cruciferae family, meaning crosslike or bearing a cross, and euphorbia, we will recall, invokes a crucifixion. Euphorbia, for me, is a much harder text than lunaria to read. It's not so much a story as a symbol, and a symbol of Italian American immigrant suffering at that . . . the cross described in my immigrant grandfather's journals. He writes, "Pirandello was right in saying: and I quote, 'In life every man wears a mask.' The mask, however, is like the cross: no matter how light it might be, its weight in the end is unbearable." (119–120)

Cappello's reiteration of the iconic cross allows her to make cultural contact with *the* paternal literary forbear: Pietro di Donato, whose *Christ in Concrete* is constructed around scenes of crucifixions—fact and symbol of Italian American immigrant suffering. Cappello's version of speaking in tongues, while less damning and dramatic than di Donato's linguistic tour de force, is no less ventriloquial. The memoirist moves beyond Catholic iconography through a final recursion to her mother's own brand of gardening, which ritualizes community through the night-blooming cereus plant. Doing this allows Cappello to replace the fatalistic fears epitomized by the malocchio with her mother's passion for the magical night-blooming flower that requires one to *look* and not fear "being alive as it lived and died before our own eyes" (252). Replacing old-world imagery with its fears and silences, Cappello offers an example of a new-world Italian American mother, who instills artistic vitality in her children: "With the same conviction that most Italian mamas said to their children '*Mangia! Mangia!*' (Eat! Eat!), my mother told me in English to '*look.*' She was always commanding me thus, with exuberance, and especially before flowers and paintings. . . . One must always retain the capacity to be astonished" (252).

True to her investigative and postmodern sensibilities, Mary Cappello designates a new category for her beloved mother that will remain neither unspoken nor entirely invisible. The flower of the cereus is transgressive; as Cappello puts it, "it's queer. In Freudian terms, it's polymorphously perverse. Undomesticated, it fails to grow in a containable direction" (*Night Bloom* 258). By "queering" her mother, Mary Cappello announces an unconventional sexuality that is nearer to the Italian American family than most would like to imagine. Simultaneously, Cappello echoes the concluding words of her literary mother, Louise DeSalvo, who also merges the "powerful totems" of her mother's kitchen items with her own, and, for the first time, accepts such a mingling with peace and hope (*Vertigo* 263). In contrast to masculine contestation, Mary Cappello, like several women writers, seeks mutuality in mother figures, a rewriting along the lines of a palimpsest rather than a literary theft.

Like Louise DeSalvo and Mary Cappello, Maria Mazziotti Gillan and Rose Romano revisit their original families in order to pay tribute and bear witness to the stories they tell. Their most effecting poems set the record straight on the history of Italian immigration to America in late nineteenth and early twentieth centuries. Like memoirists, Gillan and Romano return to the generation of their parents and grandparents in order to explore and recapture a period of history no longer in existence. At times commemorative and elegiac, such poems also engage in fundamental historical work by placing the ideas and behaviors of their immigrant families in a context-laden world in which certain rules governed their lives. Unwilling to whitewash the facts of their ancestors' insecure existence in America, Gillan and Romano take risks by stating unpopular facts about them, including commentary about how such insecurity produced Italian American insularity and a perceived inability to change. Both poets place their observations in the context of a historical period that produced such behavior in Italian Americans. Impassioned about Italian American cultural identity, Gillan and Romano concomitantly critique and celebrate past lives.

Maria Gillan is the founder and executive director of the Poetry Center at Passaic County Community College, the director of the Creative

Writing Program at State University of New York at Binghamton, and editor of the *The Paterson Literary Review*. With the publication in 1985 of Helen Barolini's *The Dream Book* and Emelise Aleandri's 1987 staging of "The Dream Book Revue" at the CUNY Graduate Center in New York, Maria Gillan's work and voice became known to a generation of younger poets of Italian American background.[16] Before she became a household name in Italian American poetry, Maria Gillan was publishing her work in journals, small presses, and as chapbooks, including the inaugural Chapbook #1 for Rose Romano's short-lived series from Malafemmina Press. The title of that chapbook—*Taking Back My Name*— is revelatory in at least two ways. Like many Italian American women of her generation and before (Josephine Hendin, Sandra M. Gilbert, Marianna Torgovnick, Dorothy Bryant, and, much earlier, Frances Winwar), Maria Gillan's surname obscures her Italian origins. In an effort to illuminate cultural identity, Maria began adding "Mazziotti" to her imprimatur in 1985, linguistically claiming Italian American culture as fundamental to her identity.[17] Gillan's gesture also reveals her connection to and commonality with contemporary women poets, who constitute a formidable literary movement influenced by feminism.

In her analysis of American women poets—particularly those poets writing in post-1960s America—Alicia Ostriker identifies several recurring motifs, which offer an interpretive lens by which to analyze both Gillan's and Romano's poems.[18] According to Ostriker, the central project of the women's poetry movement is the quest for "autonomous self-definition." Ostriker goes on to explain that shaping that quest "is a heritage, external and internal, which opposes female autonomy" (58). Gillan in particular registers the condition of marginality not merely for herself, but for her people, which is inclusive of her family, her childhood Italian neighborhood in Paterson, New Jersey, and the larger community of the working class, particularly women, whose autonomy is circumscribed by gender and class limitations. Like Louise DeSalvo, Maria Gillan also affirms female experience rendered invisible by the larger culture, encoding an audience within her poems, making the personal in effect communal. Alicia Ostriker describes the poetic emphasis on the communal, and the poet's voice directed toward the audience as an "imperative of intimacy" (11).

Both Gillan and Romano extend their poems toward implied readers, thereby toppling traditional poetic hierarchies between feeling and intellect, life and art, writer and reader. As Ostriker notes, "academic distinctions between the self and what we ... call the 'persona' move to vanishing point" (12). Gillan and Romano are deeply uninterested in T.S. Eliot's "extinction of personality" as, Ostriker explains, "the mandatory twentieth-century initiation ritual" for poets (12), for they are engaged in making visible the fact that Italian Americans *exist* contrary to their own tendencies toward self-negation and subscription to an outmoded dependence on the cultural code of silence: omertà. Communal transaction with readers, part of contemporary women poets' "imperative of intimacy" has especial relevance for ethnically identified women poets such as Maria Gillan and Rose Romano. Their poems often move toward what I call a poetics of community, a recursion to oral traditions that are memorized and incantatory. Such poems function as speakerly texts in the way that Rosa Cassettari's tales are told to a receptive audience, who retain the story and are capable of repeating it themselves; as Walter Benjamin explains, "the cardinal point of the unaffected listener is to assure himself of the possibility of reproducing the story," sharing companionship with the storyteller (*Illuminations* 97, 100). Such texts then become "sacred, communal, popular, and inseparable from the matrix of life" as Ostriker explains of the poetry of Audre Lorde, Judy Grahn and Ntozake Shange, and, I might add, Maria Mazziotti Gillan and Rose Romano (204).

Along with the breakdown of boundaries between poet/reader and self/other, contemporary women poets often use a poetic style that is informal. For Gillan and Romano, who speak on behalf of their communities, the imperative of intimacy compels a more fluid interaction between poet and reader, eliminating the role of privileged separateness. Through the use of repetition, refrain, and rhetorical questioning, Gillan and Romano, like many women poets, speak on "behalf of a community which has given [them] substance as [they] give it a voice" (Ostriker 190). In her analysis of literary influence, Alicia Ostriker observes that contemporary women poets do not perceive themselves as artists who must supersede the precursor, "*pace* Harold Bloom, on the Oedipal model of killing." Rather, the model many women poets follow is that of the Demeter/Kore (Persephone) model of "returning and reviving": "a female muse functions as a giver of confidence and a representative of an 'alternative line to the dominant male canon'" (192). In Italian American women's poetry, Maria Gillan has become its literary foremother. Her modus operandi is fundamentally collaborative. Poets like Rose Romano have a demonstrated connection with Gillan in poetic style and editing projects such as Romano's Chapbook series and her anthology *La Bella Figura*, which features Gillan's most famous poem—"Public School No. 18: Paterson, New Jersey"—as its first epigraph.

Maria Gillan's anthem song of Italian America, "Public School No. 18," is perhaps the most widely reprinted poem by an Italian American woman.[19] In it, Gillan recalls the shame foisted on her as a child in 1940s America where anti-immigrant, anti-Italian and anti-Catholic sentiments were strong in currency. Of her Anglo-American teachers, Gillan writes: "Without words, they tell me/to be ashamed./I am./I deny that booted country/even from myself,/want to be still/and untouchable/as these women/who teach me to hate myself" (*Where I Come From* 12–13). Throughout the poem, Gillan employs the language of criminality to emphasize the most egregious stereotype assumed about Italian Americans—that they are criminals and involved with the Mafia.[20] Words as seemingly devoid of ethnic association as "evidence" and "untouchable" and "deny" reverberate with specific meaning when attached to Italian Americans as Gillan knows: "the evidence is stacked against me"; "I deny that booted country"; and "[I] want to be still/and untouchable." When these lines are used to describe a child's experience in grammar school, the damage is inestimable. By virtue of her appearance, her name and first language, the school girl Maria is treated like a criminal—an outsider, an untouchable, an other. As Stephen Paul Miller remarks, "To be Italian, her teachers teach her, is to be marked as less than existing. Her 'country' is hence 'booted'" (58). As a child, Maria learns to wear her invisibility out of shame and as a form of self-protection.

In adulthood, shame turns to rage when Gillan realizes the violence inflicted on the self from learning to loathe one's cultural background. Only the poet can renounce ethnic hatred and refuse to be defined by it: "Remember me, Ladies,/the silent one?/I have found my voice/and my rage will blow/your house down" (13). For Gillan, autonomous self-definition emerges from reconnecting with one's ethnicity, which includes the mother tongue—the dialectal variety, not the national tongue of Dante—and which embraces the mother country—not Italy in toto, but the small villages from whence her parents came—and, finally, the hyphenated status she was bequeathed in America.

For Maria Gillan, oppression doesn't reside within the walls of her family home; heritage is redeemed by the poet in adulthood through a confessional awareness of her own complicity—through shame—in the denial of her Italian parents. As she writes of her father in "Betrayals," the lead poem of her collection, *Where I Come From*, "How I betrayed you,/over and over, ashamed of your broken tongue,/how I laughed, savage and innocent,/at your mutilations" (7), Gillan wends her way back to the family both as a form of reparation and as a reconstitution of her Italian American family during the mid-twentieth century. Contrite and angry, Gillan declares: "I am proud of my mother,/dressed all in black,/proud of my father/with his broken tongue,/proud of the laughter/and noise of our house" ("Public School No. 18" 13).[21] Gillan's declaration of independence from the oppressive public space of the schoolroom—which represents mainstream America—occurs many years later and arouses fury in the poet, but Gillan turns more often in her poetry to a language of love to invalidate spurious and hateful notions of her ethnic heritage. Throughout many of her poems, Gillan demonstrates that the house of stereotyping is made of straw. Gillan in contrast builds a brick house and solidly celebrates Italian American family and community.

"Public School #18" fortunately appeared in *The Dream Book*, which gave it visibility well beyond the small press—Chantry—where it was originally published in Gillan's book of poems, *Winter Light*. It is not surprising to find that Rose Romano's first book of poetry is entitled *Vendetta*, which, like Gillan's poetry, explores the relationships between the poet and her Italian American culture. The term *gridare vendetta*, to cry out for retribution, is Romano's response to the traditionally Italian injunction to be quiet, orally codified by the term "omertà." Like Gillan, however, Romano voices her anger not nearly so much at her Italian culture—with its self-deprecating silence—but at the larger culture that continues to define Italian Americans according to destructive stereotypes. Both Gillan and Romano portray Italian Americans in historically detailed ways, overturning reckless falsehoods conveniently harbored by mainstream America. Read in tandem, their poetry suggests collaboration rather than rivalry; Gillan functions as a precursor to Romano, but more as a "practical support" to the literary daughter's "own creativity rather than an object of awe" (Ostriker 192).

One of Gillan's most overtly political poems, "Columbus and the Road to Glory," was first published in the 1992 issue of *VIA* (*Voices in Italian Americana*) in commemoration of the quincentenary of the voyage of Columbus to the Americas. Three Italian American poets (Anne Paolucci, Joseph Tusiani, and Maria Gillan) and one Native American poet (E. Donald Two Rivers) were represented in the issue. Gillan's poem bears most resemblance in style and tone to Two Rivers' despite its careful defense of her father's celebration of Columbus during the October holiday. Both Gillan and Two Rivers accede to the Italian adulation of a flawed hero and the contradiction contained within the desire to canonize a renaissance explorer who did not found a new world (after landing in the Bahamas on his first ocean voyage), but rather one inhabited by "ancestors of the present native peoples" (Rivière 1). When placed in the context of her book of poems, *Where I Come From*, Gillan's Columbus poem achieves a gravitas as it is located alongside emphatic poems such as "Arturo" and "Growing up Italian," which recall mid-twentieth-century America. "Columbus and the Road to Glory" in particular refuses to ignore the history of Italian Americans during the first half of the twentieth century. The controversy surrounding the Columbian Quincentennial in 1992 was aimed at the belief of many that the "discovery" of America meant wholesale destruction of its native inhabitants. Celebrating Columbus Day—for Italian Americans in particular—was considered wrong-minded and condemned by those who subscribed to "political correctness," as Gillan states (83). Gillan's poem, however, is a historical corrective to basic ignorance about Italian Americans' relation to Columbus.

Immigrants from the booted country sought to recreate feelings of solidarity as Italians in America. As historians have explained, after the immigrant generation of the second Great Migration began to wane, Italians in America tried to reconcile the duality of being Italian American. One of the ways to achieve this reconciliation was through the celebration of Columbus, an icon for native-born Americans.[22] Along with the formation of the Sons of Italy, historians tell us, Columbus Day "served as the symbolic expression of this dual identity *par excellence*. By placing Italians at the very beginnings of American history through their surrogate ancestor, the anniversary of the 'discovery' of the New World served to legitimize their claims to Americanness at the same time that it allowed them to take pride in their Italianness" (Conzen et al., 28).

Gillan's poem follows along these lines, contextualizing the October event in terms of her father's life and the Italians in his Paterson community. Sharing the cultural significance of Columbus Day for her father's immigrant generation, Gillan explains that the holiday allowed him to "forget the laughter/of the Americans who spit at him/on the street, called him/'Dago, Guinea, Wop, Gangster,/Garlic Eater, Mafioso'" (82). On one special day, Gillan continues, Italians in America "could walk tall and be proud," refusing to be destroyed by memories that included the largely unknown fact that "the biggest mass lynching/in American history was of Italians" (83, 82).[23] The poet recognizes the social reasons underlying the need to cling to a tarnished hero, but she refuses to boycott the holiday because history continues to repeat itself through negative stereotyping of Italians in America.

Gillan concludes her poem in a forceful manner, casting aside the maternal injunction, "*Sta' zitta*, Don't make trouble!" Aware of the cultural belief of fare bella figura (the code of social behavior that governs an individual's public persona), Gillan nonetheless overturns the warning, "*non fare mala figura*" in favor of the American emphasis on self-revelation:

> but I say: Let us tell our mothers "*Sta' zitta,*"
> Let us tell them we don't care about *mala figura.*
> Let us put the pieces of Columbus back together,
> even if the cracks show, the imperfections.
>
> Let us pick up our flawed hero,
> march him through the streets of the city,
> the way we carried the statue
> of the Blessed Virgin at Festa.
> Let us forget our mother's orders,
> not to make trouble,
> not to call attention to ourselves,
> and in honor of my father and the men of the *Società*
> and in honor of my mother and the courage
> and pride she taught me,
> I say: No to being silent,
> No to calling us names
> No to giving up Columbus. (83–84)

Gillan unites sacred and secular by linking patron saint festivals, which paraded the statue of Mary or one of the saints through city streets, with the Columbus Day parade, suggesting the fluidity between sacred and secular in Italian thinking. The poet's use of the device of anaphora further testifies to the incantatory nature of Gillan's poetry, a ritual recitation as seductive as the Italian American emphasis on ceremony and procession. Stylistically echoing Walt Whitman, Gillan aligns herself to an American literary predecessor who regularly used anaphora as incantation as she celebrates the rarely experienced public autonomy of her father's generation.

Maria Gillan not only takes back her name, but she also invokes her country, not as a supplicant to a patron saint or a higher deity, but as a righteous poet who insists on social equality for her family: "Listen America,/this is my father, Arturo,/and I am his daughter, Maria./ Do not call me Marie" ("Arturo" 51). Having unlearned the self-hatred she adopted in an effort to acculturate American ways, Gillan sheds cultural invisibility, but the act of sloughing must be repeated in order to replace the layers of falsehoods that have accrued over the decades. Thus "Growing up Italian" parallels "Public School No. 18" and "Arturo" in its emphasis on reclaiming ethnic ties. Gillan reenacts this process of self-exploration which becomes both therapeutic and theatrical in its oral sound play:

> till one day, I guess I was forty by then,
> I woke up cursing
> all those who taught me
> to hate my dark, foreign self,
> and I said, "Here I am—
> with my olive-toned skin
> and my Italian parents,
> and my old poverty,
> real as a scar on my forehead," . . .
> and I celebrate myself
>   my Italian American self,
> rooted in this, my country, where
> all those black/brown/red/yellow
> olive-skinned people
> soon will raise their voices
> and sing this new anthem:
> Here I am
>   and I'm strong . . .
> and today, I take back my name
> and wave it in their faces
> like a bright, red flag. (56–57)

Employing an apostrophe to America in the quoted lines, Gillan proclaims a shared space with her country, directly repudiating the shame that paralyzed her for so long: "'Here I am—/with my olive-toned skin/and my Italian parents,/and my old poverty.'" That she discerns a racial distinction between old-world Italian origins and mainstream white hegemony accords accurately with the long-standing status of racial inbetweenness Italians endured in the new country. Describing her ethnic heritage in racially inflected terms, Gillan simultaneously demonstrates how cultural identity has been racialized in America for persons of color. Because whiteness had been redefined in her father's generation in an attempt to restrict immigration in the 1920s, incoming immigrant groups were disenfranchised through an exclusionary politics based on racial ideology. Italians were no exception, and Gillan makes note of this. As historian Matthew Frye Jacobson explains, "one might be both white *and* racially distinct from other whites" (6); by placing the descriptive "olive-skinned people" in its own line, Gillan clarifies this fact.

No longer ashamed of her cultural background, Gillan concludes "Growing up Italian" in a forceful manner, metaphorically waving her name "like a bright, red flag." For many contemporary women poets, including Gillan, revolutionary activity is demonstrated linguistically through the breakdown of boundaries between the poet and audience, through an elimination of hierarchy, and through diction itself (Ostriker, 168–178). Gillan's use of the color "red" for the flag illustrates this activity by implicitly alluding to the Red Scare of the 1920s which focused much of its fear (and hatred) on the nation's immigrants, including her Italian parents. The color of communism and, later, the left-wing Italian terrorist group of the 1970s—The Red Brigades, "red" evokes the poet's anger, previously latent and unexpressed. She's not taking it— defamation of her ethnic culture—anymore, and she takes back her name with the defiance and self-congratulation of the victorious warrior, flag in hand.

Rose Romano out-Gillans Gillan. She's the lesbian literary daughter whose poetry, sharing similar cultural terrain as Gillan, goes a step further in its anger, its use of oral features, and its explanatory style. Romano extends her audience to include some in the lesbian community of San Francisco where she lived in the 1990s, charging them with the same limited understanding of Italian Americans as the classroom teachers of Gillan's era. Founder and publisher of the journal devoted to Italian American women, Romano ran *La Bella Figura* from 1988 to 1992, culminating in her anthology, *La Bella Figura: A Choice*, published in 1993, and featuring Maria Gillan's poetry, alongside such poets as Anthony Valerio, Rina Ferrarelli, Maria Famá, and Antonio D'Alfonso. Romano inaugurated her series of chapbooks with Maria Mazziotti Gillan's *Taking Back My Name*, which not surprisingly begins with Gillan's "Growing up Italian." In seeking a female precursor in Gillan, Romano legitimized her own desire to write against the grain of mainstream poetry *and* unexamined ethnic nostalgia.

Like Maria Gillan, Rose Romano uses informal language and diminishes traditional distinctions between the self and the poetic persona. She's much too busy putting Italian Americans—including verboten lesbians—

on the literary map, and she's much too angry not to be incessantly
herself: "It's not easy being an angry poet/when you come from a cul-
ture/whose most profound statement of anger/is silence" ("Mutt Bitch,"
Vendetta 37). Romano's anger is less focused than her precursor on
her complicity in the dominant culture's denigration of Italian Americans
and more focused on breaking the historical silences regarding the griev-
ances her culture sustained. In addition, Romano complicates images of
her Italian American family structure through regular references to her
lesbian sexuality. Like Mary Cappello, Rose Romano merges Italian
American and lesbian family dynamics, suggesting mutuality through
the generations.

That Romano includes part of the San Francisco lesbian community
within mainstream culture in its disinterest in the cultural complexity of
Italian Americana suggests the pervasive invisibility of Italian Americans
even within other marginal groups. Romano challenges her segment of
the American lesbian community, which she feels is prescriptive in its
definition of otherness. As Romano revealingly explains, "what a lesbian
is depends to a great extent on where she fits in what is known as a 'hierarchy of pain.'. . . The lighter one's skin, the less respect one is entitled
to" ("Coming Out Olive" 161). Romano's fear is this: if she, as an Italian
American lesbian, is not allowed to name herself as "Olive,/neither
white/nor of color" ("Permission—Two Friends," *Vendetta* 33), she will
become the quintessential invisible woman, unrecognized by her culture
of heritage *and* the lesbian community: "not Madonna or puttana
enough,/. . . not light or dark enough" ("The Fly," *Vendetta* 40).

Claiming to be neither white nor of color, Romano explains that the
gay community in which she seeks connection isolates her: "either the
lesbian's view of the world is false or I don't exist" ("Coming Out Olive"
174). Such a fear compels Romano to reinvest with new meaning the
old proverbs of her culture: "Sicilians tell their children—/'A fly doesn't
enter a closed mouth.'/I'm standing now and I'm/telling the Sicilians,/the Italians,/and the Lesbians—/You can't spit a fly/out of a closed
mouth" ("The Fly," *Vendetta* 40). Romano insists here that, whether we
are Italians, Sicilians, or lesbians (or all three designations, which the
poet would claim), we cannot afford to be silent, thereby implicitly allowing others—the old culture and the new—to interpret and define our
behavior. As Julia Watson said of lesbian autobiography which is equally
true of Rose Romano's confessional poetry, "For the immigrant or multicultural daughter, naming the unspeakable is at once a transgressive act
that knowingly seeks to expose and speak the boundaries on which the

organization of cultural knowledge depends and a discursive strategy that, while unverifiable, allows a vital 'making sense' of her own multiple differences" (393). For Romano, the unspeakable has less to do with her sexual orientation than it has to do with her Italian culture, which she makes visible and audible in her poetry. Silence no longer works here (i.e., in America) Romano seems to be saying; speaking outside the confines of the family is fundamental to cultural survival.

· Falsely and narrowly defined throughout their history in America, Italian Americans must learn how to use language to revitalize and authorize their lives. Similar to Mary Cappello, Rose Romano attributes her sense of authorial power to her Neapolitan and Sicilian grandmothers, both familial and mythical. Romano embraces the power she feels in their constant nurturance. Rather than interpreting her grandmothers' household lives as a form of patriarchal oppression, Romano instead examines their domestic strength as fundamentally matriarchal: the Romano women are the heads of their households, a position that lesbians emulate in their own families. In "To Show Respect" (*rispetto* being a cardinal cultural code for southern Italians, especially between the classes), Romano implores readers to imagine and to remember the grandmothers, creatively connecting Italian American lesbians with their foremothers: "I watch my/grandmother/. . ./feel the thrill of knowing/someday I will be the grandmother,/sit at the head of the table, be my own/boss./. . . Imagine a room/full of Italian-American Lesbians,/ all of us our own bosses. Imagine and/remember" (*Vendetta* 24). Diminishing the differences between generations and sexual orientations, Romano expands the perimeters of what Julia Watson calls "cultural knowledge," and, like Cappello, she examines a sexual and cultural sensibility inhering within Italian American homes that provides an example for the lesbian granddaughter to emulate (393).

In an effort to provide fuller information on the cultural sensibilities of Italian Americans outside the home, Rose Romano also directly responds to the controversy surrounding Columbus in the 1990s. Romano's "The Family Dialect" functions as an explanatory and humorous analogue to Gillan's "Columbus and the Road to Glory." From her 1994 book, *The Wop Factor*, Romano's awareness of Gillan's work has made its mark on her poetry. As she does in several poems in *The Wop Factor*, Romano offers a corrective interpretation of Italian American history. In "The Family Dialect," Romano situates the poem in 1962, when she was a girl, and then spans thirty years, concluding in 1992, the quincentennial year of the voyage of Columbus. In contrast to the popular sentiment at women-only dances that labeled the voyager an oppressor, Romano candidly names the oppressor as those women within in her own lesbian community, accusing them of bandwagon jumping and po-litical correctness (*The Wop Factor* 15). These women, claims Romano, are blithely unaware "of the tortured logic of ignorance and/bigotry that made Columbus a hero/to Southern Italian/Sicilian-/Americans, tor-ture I bring to/bed with me every night" (*The Wop Factor* 15). Recalling Gillan's lines about her father's ethnic insecurity that compelled him and his generation into Columbus worship, Romano adds 'tortured logic" to the equation, suggesting both mental agony and circuitous movement, as Italians' path to Americanization met with repeated twists and turns.

To the poet's dismay, anti-Italian bigotry remained virulent in the 1990s, supplemented by a fundamental lack of interest by the lesbian community in Italian American history. Like Gillan, Romano explores the historiography of Columbus and his perpetual debunking, from the popularity of Leif Ericson in the 1960s to the misplaced pride of the 1990s when Romano is asked by Italian Americans to sign a petition to protest the October quincentennial celebrations. Romano indeed protests, but not in the expected manner. Instead, using interrogation and one of her favorite devices of repetition, anaphora, Romano echoes not only her literary foremother, Maria Gillan, but also America's poet, Walt Whitman: "Does it matter to anyone here that/Columbus was a Northerner at/a time when there was no Italy? . . . Does it matter to/any-one here that the overwhelming/majority of Italian-Americans are/Southerners and Sicilians?" (*The Wop Factor* 16–17)

Disgusted by those who refuse her didacticism—"They tell me not to explain things/in my poems"—Romano purposely reinforces the fact that she must often repeat herself even if her community is not listen-ing. "Does it matter/to anyone here that Italian-/Americans are so easy to shame [?]" (*The Wop Factor* 17). Like Maria Gillan, Rose Romano knows the cost of ethnic self-loathing, as she is the unfortunate recipi-ent of her parents' embarrassment over their dialect. Forced to speak English at home (in contrast to Gillan), Romano understands that relinquishing the family language was motivated by shame and self-censorship as spoken dialect was considered an inferior language in Italy and America.

Romano's final gesture in "The Family Dialect" is one of self-flagellation tempered by humor. As angry as she is, Romano is not with-out a wry sense of humor: "Does it matter/to anyone here that my best chance/of ethnic pride is to rip off my/skin and roll it in salt?/

Santa Rosalia, move over,/I'm coming to join you,/At least until the end/of the month" (*The Wop Factor* 18). Invoking her namesake, Rosalia, patron saint of Palermo, Sicily, Romano at the same time recalls the memory of her mother, who died when Romano was eight, but whose Sicilian ancestry she defended in childhood against her paternal, Neapolitan relatives.

Romano swerves away from Gillan in her ironic, and, at times, biting tone, but she regularly parallels her literary foremother in her invocation of traditional Italian American working-class families, whose language of love is intimately connected with food and the maternal. Taking Gillan a step further, Romano establishes a persuasive connection between culture and sexuality as she celebrates the connection between food and ethnicity in her belief that the love of food and the love of women are as natural and necessary as grandma: "I never knew where/her food ended and her body began—/. . . I think of lovers. Like/meatballs and ziti, . . ./—ritual words—/to make love,/. . . Everybody must know/that we eat. Until we have/a right to this place" ("That We Eat," *Vendetta* 26).

Love and anger coexist in Romano's poetry. She's not above taking on Maria Gillan's own mother, whose desire to be inconspicuous was a mark of her fear and ethnic shame. As though in belligerent response to Maria Gillan's mother, who utters the parental directive, "Sta' zitta!, Don't make trouble!" in "Columbus and the Road to Glory," Romano appropriates Italian cultural codes and places them alongside ethnic epithets, revising their meaning. A most compelling example of this occurs in the title poem "The Wop Factor." In it, Romano writes, "So I've been thinking . . ./maybe *la bella figura*/should be enhanced by the wop factor—/we want that extra weight—/. . . and when you slap us down/ we make noise" (*The Wop Factor* 24).

Making noise is Romano's antidote to Italian American acquiescence. Contrasting her people to other more visible—and revolutionary—ethnic groups in America, Romano offers her own form of linguistic battle, upping the ante from film depictions of Italian criminals breaking legs to bombing the theatres as a "call to action" against a century of media distortion of her ethnic group ("Breaking Legs," *The Wop Factor* 28). In defiance of her own will toward violence, however, Romano concludes "Breaking Legs" with a call to action through one of the basic features of women's contemporary poetry: autonomous self-definition. In a manner stylistically similar to Maria Gillan, Romano admits to being proud of her complexion, encouraging "Olives of the world [to] unite/and, just for us commari,/WOP—Women of Pasta,

But now I'm thinking that
if Italian-Americans had
a riot in the streets
people would think it was a festa
and ask us where's the food. (*The Wop Factor* 28)

Romano invokes the slogans of the early labor unions such as the IWW—International Workers of the World—whose organized strikes were lead by Italian radicals and intellectuals such as Arturo Giovannitti and Joseph Ettor. Recognizing strength in unity, Romano directly addresses her reader, engaging in a poetics of "communal transaction" between poet and audience (Ostriker 203). Such called-upon action, however, is undercut by Romano's own cognizance of the mainstream's reductive perception of Italian American culture due in part to the continued silence of this cultural group. That she concludes "Breaking Legs" with a humorous reference to la festa attests to Romano's recognition that Italian Americans are not taken seriously. Their cultural events such as the festa are stripped of religious and regional meanings, including the sine qua non of the festival, the procession, and its affirmation of sacred community membership.

In their poetry, Maria Mazziotti Gillan and Rose Romano place Italian Americans from past generations on the cultural map of America. Their talking and testifying exemplifies an oral theatricality that recalls Rosa Cassettari's life stories and Pietro di Donato's verbal gyrations.[24] Imagining the presence of an audience is a constitutive act for these poets, creating a habitable space for Italian American culture. Rose Romano and Maria Gillan also follow in the tradition of contemporary poets such as Audre Lorde, who has famously written: "for women, then, poetry is not a luxury. It is a vital necessity of our existence. . . . Poetry is the way we help give name to the nameless so it can be thought" (37). Expertly using language to give a name to the invisible history of Italian America, Gillan and Romano speak on behalf of communities that have suffered from social injustice, poverty, and loss of cultural traditions.

The literary relationship forged between earlier and more recent generations of writers attests to the increased visibility and external support that makes it possible for Louise DeSalvo and Maria Mazziotti Gillan to function as models for future writers. Literary influence that is mutually alluring can produce strong writers such as Mary Cappello and Rose Romano. Neither servile nor derivative in their writing, Cappello and Romano signal a connection to and not a dissociation from literary and genealogical ancestors. For these writers, appropriating the mother's tongue is an act of collaboration, not excision. Like their literary fore-mothers, Mary Cappello and Rose Romano make visible Italian American worlds through their autobiographical acts of speaking out. In turn, they have functioned as co-mentors to Louise DeSalvo and Maria Gillan, who have continued to enrich their focus on cultural identities through recent publications. DeSalvo's 2004 *Crazy in the Kitchen* might be said to revise and extend ideas introduced in her earlier memoir, *Vertigo*, and Gillan's 2002 *Italian Women in Black Dresses* continues, autobiographically, to detail her family life across the generations, with special focus on Italian mothers. For all four writers, their most radical act is returning to their original families, rooting out the secrets and silences that have too often thwarted their growth.

Despite archaic directives from family culture that prevent growth, U.S. writers of Italian America have steadily refused to heed such injunctions that would silence them, recognizing that such silences serve as an insidious form of cultural annihilation. To insure continuity of cultural identity, many writers, including those discussed above, approach the topic of death through storytelling, emphasizing that things change for Italian Americans, but do not necessarily end. For in the end, there are the stories, and stories of death sanction storytellers in ways that allow them to encompass and expand understandings of grief and loss. How Italian American writers tell stories of death is the focus of chapter 7.

7

Death/Morte

ༀ

What They Talk About
When They Talk About Death

Partire è un po' morire.
To leave is a little like dying.

—Italian proverb

Death . . . is the sanction of everything the storyteller can tell. He has
borrowed his authority from death.

—Walter Benjamin, *Illuminations*

That Italian Americans die in literature is as important as *how* they die.
Authors of Italian America are likely to agree with Maurice Blanchot,
who says that when we speak, we "are leaning on a tomb" (55). Italian
American writers frequently portray experiences of death, inconsolable
grief, and accompanying mourning rituals, especially in the early part of
the twentieth century, when Italian immigrants were subject to the
degradations of nativism, poverty, and untimely deaths. That Italians
in America suffered, died, and were mourned in the literature of
Italian America, illuminated not only their new-world status, but also,
and more importantly, their *humanity* through dying. As Blanchot
explains, "Death . . . raises existence to being, and it is within each one

of us . . . our most human quality; it is death only in the world—man only knows death because he is man, and he is only man because he is death in the process of becoming" (55). We will recall that Pietro di Donato applied the word "Christian" to mean "human," throughout *Christ in Concrete*. Di Donato's linguistic synecdoche transcends his desire to translate from the Italian to indicate the figure of *un povero cristiano*, a poor soul/beggar, and also, a figure of Christ. The author needs to hammer home the idea that his Italians are human, subject to an awareness of the hour of their death; his grieving Italian characters are equally human in their lamentations for the loss of the beloved.

Italian American literature is replete with portrayals of death and mourning. Many of the stories that are told about death and dying, mourning and bereavement rituals, reflect a modern-era sensibility toward such topics. In some works, a premodern sensibility toward dying pervades characterizations of death. The influences of Italian Catholicism (and its conventional belief in an afterlife), migratory status, regional provenience, and nostalgic recursions to a paradisiacal homeland illustrate a complex and ambivalent attitude many writers take toward topics of death and grief. Perhaps Italian American writers are having their cake and eating it, too. Hunger drove their ancestors from villages and small towns they never expected to leave. Mortality narratives are filled with portrayals of illness, death, and bereavement, endowing them with a fulsome authority that death gives these storyteller writers. In many of the works discussed in this chapter, continuity beyond death is emphasized through storytelling characters, who, in dying, underscore lessons in survival, moral value, and human commitment.

Italian Americans have been, like other writers, highly influenced by Western attitudes toward death. Portrayals of bereavement range from forms of madness to ritualized practices that contain grief. In nearly all of the narratives discussed in this chapter, continuities beyond death epitomize the desire to establish linkages that symbolize markers of continuation after a character's death. Only the "call of stories," to quote from Robert Coles's book of that title, can begin to satiate the need to tell the story of dying ancestors, and Italian American writers are filling that need. Through the incorporation of storytelling devices aimed at receptive listeners, writers of Italian America heed the call of stories to proclaim the voice of mortality for their ancestors, which is inclusive of death and continuity. As such, mortality narratives include personal experience stories, folktales retold in a modern context, folk wisdom offered to resist oppressions of poverty and silence, and appropriative uses of voice, which have in common emancipatory aims for the bereaved.

The large and growing body of literature on the subject of death and dying occurs simultaneously at a time in our history when the search for the fountain of youth has been found in endless middle-age and former death-sentence illnesses are treated medically, extending remission periods indefinitely. Much critical work on death by physicians (Kleinman, Coles), literary historians (Harrison, Cole) and social scientists (Ariès, De Martino, Frank) examines genres of literature, personal testimonials, and community mores to explore attitudinal changes toward death and the ways in which those left behind cope and mourn. Philippe Ariès's monumental *The Hour of Our Death* makes a formidable distinction in attitude toward death between primitive and modern societies. Ariès describes "tamed death" as "the oldest death there is," an ancient position which frightens moderns because of its closeness and familiarity to the dying person: "when we call this familiar death the tame death, we do not mean that it was once wild and that it was later domesticated. On the contrary, we mean that it has become wild today when it used to be tame" (*The Hour* 28).

According to Ariès, the premodern dying person first experienced a forewarning—through natural signs, or, more frequently, through inner conviction, and then went about approaching his end by assuming a recumbent position, expressing sorrow, forgetting the world, and receiving absolution from a priest in Christian societies (*The Hour* 6–18). "'Without haste or delay, but with a sense of proper timing,'" Christians and non-Christians alike died simply (Guitton; qtd. in Ariès, *Western Attitudes* 7). Until the nineteenth century, the dying person's acceptance of his premonition—'feeling his end approach'—was, as Ariès says, passed on "from age to age, unchanged, like a proverb" (*Western Attitudes* 6).

Nineteenth-century attitudes toward death—an era of *hysterical* mourning, according to Ariès, lasted no more than a century and a half, but paved the way for the seemingly contradictory model of death of the twentieth century, which Ariès calls "invisible death": "an extension of the affectivity of the nineteenth century. The last inspiration of this inventive affectivity was to protect the dying or the invalid from his own emotions by concealing the seriousness of his condition until the end. When the dying man discovered the pious game, he lent himself to it so as not to disappoint the other's solicitude. The dying man's relations with those around him were now determined by a respect for this loving lie" (*The Hour* 611–612; *Western Attitudes* 67).[1]

Like Ariès before her, Sandra M. Gilbert contemplates life's end in her encyclopedic *Death's Door: Modern Dying and the Ways We Grieve*, but adds a wrinkle to the accommodated death of the average, medieval thinker by recalling the idea of *timor mortis*: "our forebears felt a *timor* precisely of the rigors of *mortis*—the moment of mortality—rather than what followed it," which for moderns was the aftermath of death. Quoting another commentator, Gilbert adds that our modern fear of what follows death is also our preoccupation with "'death without an after-life'" (*Death's Door* 114–115). Alongside concerns regarding the existence (or not) of an afterlife, Gilbert also makes a distinction between two different ways of "*telling* death," represented by the antipodal words "expiration" and "termination" (*Death's Door* 106). Harboring spiritual overtones, the word "expiration" has roots in the Latin "*spiritus* (meaning breath) in which our concept of spirit originates[;] it means both 'to breathe out' and 'to breathe one's last' but also implies 'to breathe out the spirit or soul'" (*Death's Door* 107). Certainly the word "termination" (from the Latin for "end") lacks the power of transcendence, and, according to Gilbert, has become the modern definition of death, "the intransigent blankness of *terminations* that lead nowhere and promise nothing" (*Death's Door* 109).

The contrast between the expiring soul and the terminating body epitomizes the modern condition, the medicalization of dying, and the ongoing dialectic between faith and disbelief. Certainly the literature of Italian America is not unique in reflecting changing attitudes toward death, and, while Italian Americans were denizens of faith, their writers struggled to reconcile ideas about their Catholic religion with modern attitudes toward death and grieving, toward those dying and those mourning. The literature emerging from early twentieth-century Italian America tells stories of death that illuminate the vexed position of Italian immigrants in a country that used their bodies as labor, disrespected their culture, and denied their essential humanity. As if in response to the xenophobia of the new world, Italian American writers made sure their characters died. The deathbed scenes are employed to fascinate and stir pity, to incense and teach lessons. Such scenes also reinforce the Heideggerian stance toward mortality, that which made human beings human: "'Man dies constantly until the moment of his demise.' . . . [O]nly man dies. The animal perishes [because it] has death neither ahead of itself nor behind it'" (qtd. in Gilbert, *Death's Door* 127). Like their devotion to storytelling, folk and culinary traditions, writers of Italian America make dying an art, and, by turns, perform the pedagogical function of edifying an often indifferent and hostile public.

DEATHBED SCENES

> Dying
> Is an art, like everything else.
> I do it exceptionally well.
>
> —Sylvia Plath, "Lady Lazarus"

The visual image embodied in the descriptor "deathbed scene" is perhaps a misnomer, since death comes to Italian Americans at times outside the home and by occurrences that are frequently not natural. In or out of bed, Italian Americans are represented as dying because of the kinds of jobs they perform, which place them in dangerous and insalubrious environments. Representations of working Italians in the first part of the century dramatize death by "Job," to quote di Donato, and, in effect, examine how immigrant workers are inexorably killed by America. While he is not literally killed by the new country, the father in John Fante's *Wait Until Spring, Bandini* is one of the best early examples of the Italian immigrant myth of assimilation through a bitter and a largely unsuccessful struggle to "make" America, fare l'America. Despite an aesthetic devotion toward his masonry work, Svevo Bandini's primary desire to feed his family is upset by harsh Colorado winters, leaving him underemployed and subject to the hostility of native-born merchants, whose disdain alienates immigrant workers from community support.[2] Bandini's story is paradigmatic of the immigrant worker who, if not destroyed by America, then becomes a destructive agent himself within the perimeters of the Italian American family, unable completely to sustain the prerogative of patriarchal dominance or to attain a secure foothold on American soil. While no physical death occurs for Svevo, who reunites in springtime with the family he deserted in winter, the novel's final word "snowflake"—literalizes the family's future of poverty.

Work deaths symbolize immigrants' inability either "to make" America or to embrace "homemaking myths" about the new world that immigrants created to establish credibility about themselves as Americans.[3] From Garibaldi Lapolla's 1935 *The Grand Gennaro* to Josephine Gattuso Hendin's 1988 *The Right Thing to Do*, death by work, which is metonymically associated with America, represents one of the most persistent narratives within the Italian American oeuvre. The death stories told in many of these works include one or more of the following: "deathbed" scenes that are by turns grotesque and/or nostalgic; wounded storytellers overwhelmed by their dying; spiritual crises emerging from the loss of or ambivalence toward a traditional God; reversal of the canonical story of biblical Job, whose wealth and family are restored; repetition of folkloric stories that function as a form of resistance to American culture; and re-union fantasies in death that are told by the dying and internalized by listeners. In his analysis of illness narratives, Arthur Frank examines the social nature of suffering, explaining that ill people tell "uniquely personal stories, but they neither make up these stories by themselves, nor do they tell them only to themselves. Bodies and selves are . . . culturally elaborated" (170). Telling stories of death through the perspective of those dying is an attempt to remake the body-self through a "self-story" that is a form of "resistance" (Frank 170). The culturally elaborated story of immigration to America is written on the bodies of Italian American workers. Their authors, with fascinating differences, tell a similar tale.

The Grand Guignol of all death scenes is not featured in the canonized *Christ in Concrete* but its lesser-known predecessor by four years, *The Grand Gennaro* by Garibaldi M. Lapolla, published in 1935. Taking a page from the rags-to- riches stories of Horatio Alger and George Randolph Chester (whose 1908 *Get-Rich-Quick Wallingford* featured wily partners who made fortunes in finance), Lapolla subverts and parodies those optimistic tales through the protagonist Gennaro Accuci, the story of an immigrant *cafone*—by his own admission—who is destroyed after twenty years of ruthless striving for entrepreneurial success as East Harlem's king of the rag and metal industry. Thomas Ferraro notes that Lapolla's narrative intention is quite transparent by his use of the "witty literalization of the rags-to-riches metaphor . . . a ragpicker who pulls himself up by the bootstraps" ("Italian-American Literature" 278). Gennaro's grotesque death parodies this narrative scenario.

Lapolla carves out a slice of the East Harlem Italian colony in the 1890s before the heaviest migration of Italians to America and before the development of labor unions to protect workers. Through violent shrewdness, Gennaro succeeds in "making America," which translates to a story about "a nobody, a mere clodhopper, a good-for-nothing on the other side [who] had contrived by hook or crook in this new, strange country, . . . to amass enough money to strut about and proclaim himself the equal of those who had been his superiors in the old country" (5). What price for fare l'America? The grotesque form of Gennaro's death. The term grotesque not only suggests distortion, but also possesses qualities of the incongruous or unnatural. With regard to grotesque characters, Lapolla also may have taken a page from Sherwood Anderson's *Winesburg, Ohio* (1919), whose subtitle *The Book of the Grotesque*, offered a unifying conception of his characters that sheds light on Lapolla's protagonist: "It was the truths that made the people grotesques. . . . [T]he moment one of the people took one of the truths to himself, called it his truth, and tried to live by it, he became a grotesque and the truth he embraced became a falsehood" (Anderson 24). Gennaro's grotesque "truth," fare l'America by hook or crook, becomes an idée fixe and extends into every aspect of his life, making violence an inevitable part of his business and personal conduct. Through sheer intimidation and physical violence, Gennaro forced his boyhood friend, Rocco Pagliamini, to forfeit his flourishing junk business, which Gennaro appropriated, thereafter amassing a fortune. On behalf of the immigrant Rocco, Rose Green contends that "to the Italian, then, being an American was being like Gennaro, who drove a bargain at the end of a knife" (75).

Telling a cautionary tale, Lapolla's story of an Italian clodhopper making America is fraught with conflict and surrounded by ugliness. Hoisted by his own petard, as it were, Gennaro is later murdered by his childhood friend, Rocco, who literalizes for the reader a deserving fate for his foe: death by *hook* for the crook. Rocco digs a hooked spike into Gennaro's neck, watching him bleed out before dumping the dead body in the rag bin (363–364). Gennaro's ending is grotesque in yet another sense of that term as it is defined by modern critics who consider the grotesque also a "distrust of any cosmic order, and frustration at humankind's lot in the universe" (Harmon and Holman 240). *The Grand Gennaro* may very well be Lapolla's portrayal of the dangers of impatient assimilation for Italian Americans and in this way the novel parallels Guido D'Agostino's *Olives on the Apple Tree*, though the latter novel is less graphic and informed by an Italian ethos in the guise of the peasant intellectual, Marco. Gennaro's unnatural death is followed by "the most elaborate funeral in the history of Little Italy" (364). Such pageantry anticipates Mario Puzo's *The Godfather*, a novel that also critiques American capitalism and renders the death of its Italian American criminals as religious procession.

Gennaro's "deathbed" scene displays a complete lack of personal reflection regarding the losses he sustained by his migration to America. Fundamentally disconnected from spiritual matters, Gennaro experiences no epiphany or revelation about his life or at his untimely death. Lapolla makes no nostalgic reference to the homeland that did not value the peasants it starved. That the author emigrated with his parents in 1888 at the age of two from Basilicata, one of southern Italy's poorest regions, may have informed his refusal to pay homage to it. *The Grand*

Gennaro is utterly unsentimental in its depiction of end-of-century Italian Harlem and equally unsparing in its portrayal of the brutal costs incurred by its title character in his pursuit of the Italian immigrant version of the American dream: fare America.

In his stalwart focus on individual success, Gennaro Accuci's achievement of "grandness" is ultimately as hollow and false as another entrepreneur whose isolation becomes the essential element of his god-like sufficiency: Jay Gatsby. Gatsby's platonic conception of himself is no less grotesque than is Gennaro's violent compulsion to reign over the Italian American colony he never leaves. Fitzgerald and Lapolla offer not tragic but ignominious deaths for their American dream-seeking characters. The death from which Gennaro suffers is ultimately equated with the trash he came to own as the Rag King of Harlem. Deserved or not, Gennaro's death reflects the work he did in the new country. As in his homeland, the Italian immigrant in America is treated as less than human.

A deathbed scene ostensibly similar in its unnatural and violent form but decidedly different in tone from *The Grand Gennaro* is presented in Pietro di Donato's *Christ in Concrete* with a graphic description of Geremio's live burial in concrete at a building site that collapses in New York City. Unlike Lapolla's portrayal of Gennaro's unnatural death, di Donato suffuses the scene of Geremio's death with religious symbolism in order to begin his critique of Catholicism and to revise the myth of Christianity.[4] Inheriting from Catholicism the story of suffering and martyrdom, the immigrant Geremio remains wedded to the belief that God will provide, and that the story of salvation includes him, despite his realization that the building contractors are risking the lives of immigrant laborers for profit. As he suffocates underneath the pouring concrete, the death story Geremio tells himself evinces a premodern sensibility toward death, and, paradoxically, despite agonizing pain, Geremio ultimately experiences what Philippe Ariès calls "tame death."

Through di Donato's repeated references to literal dreaming and dreamy imagining the day before the accident, Geremio is forewarned of imminent death, experiencing as his premodern precursors an inner conviction of the hour of his death. Clearly premonitory is the fact that the building collapses on Good Friday, the Friday before Easter, observed by Christians in commemoration of the crucifixion of Christ. As horrifying and unthinkable as suffocation must be, Geremio *expires* rather than *terminates*, allowing for the spiritual overtones anchored in the word "expiration." Breathing his last and breathing out his spirit/soul, Geremio's last words are "cringingly and breathlessly" sung to Jesus Christ: "Jesu my Lord my God my all Jesu my Lord my God my all Jesu my Lord my God my all Jesu my Lord my God my all" (18). Incantatory in its effect, Geremio's final invocation to Christ functions as a ritual recitation that has its roots in pre-Christian magic; like a verbal charm, this conventionalized utterance also reinforces Geremio's Christian belief in transcendence and the existence of an afterlife.

By the middle of chapter 2 of *Christ in Concrete* (the equivalent of twelve pages in the original Bobbs-Merrill edition), Geremio is dead. Di Donato rejects the story of Christian martyrdom in order for the next generation—represented by firstborn Paul—to survive American forces of capitalism bent on destroying its labor pool embodied by immigrant workers. At the same time, the author emphasizes the continuity beyond death for the deceased and his grieving family. Di Donato does this by *framing* the novel—represented by the Geremio and Annunziata sections—around the Christian myth of suffering and salvation in order to examine the difficulty of relinquishing such a narrative, especially for first-generation immigrant Italians. That Annunziata's death at the novel's conclusion functions as a mirror image of her husband's untimely death is clearly deliberate on di Donato's part, rhetorically echoing the same recitative Christian prayers and alluding to the dance of the tarantella, which emphasizes the bite of the poisonous spider. Annunziata's bereavement will be further discussed in the second section of this chapter. Suffice it to say here that her grief is represented by her body in pain, which allows her to share her condition in memory of her deceased husband's death. Annunziata becomes, in Arthur Frank's words, a "dyadic body," immersed in suffering that is both individual and shared (35–36). The story she tells to her children at the end of her life is the medium she uses to reinforce the importance of "shared corporeality" (Frank 35), which ultimately privileges the Christian story of suffering unto others.

Despite a fatal illness contracted by treacherous working conditions, Pietro Dalli of Mari Tomasi's *Like Lesser Gods*, unlike his literary predecessors discussed above, is afforded the luxury of time as he accepts the household sort of tame death in which the dying person, "feeling his end approach," prepared for death (Ariès, *Western Attitudes* 6, 7). Like his literary forbears, Pietro's body is killed by the work he performs in America as an immigrant stone cutter who contracts tuberculo silicosis from inhaling silica-laden particles from working on granite in closed sheds. Tomasi's portrayal of Pietro's death from what was popularly referred to as "Stonecutters' TB" is spiritually resonant.[5] As Susan Sontag explains, the disease of tuberculosis possesses a mythology of soulfulness, "the dying tubercular is pictured as made more beautiful and more soulful" (*Illness as Metaphor* 17). Consumption traditionally develops because of poverty and deprivation, but a change in environment, is said to slow down the inevitable death. That tuberculosis is a disease of one organ—the lungs—which are located in the upper part of the body, Sontag continues, spiritualizes the illness and the body inhabiting it—as it does for Pietro Dalli of *Like Lesser Gods* (*Illness as Metaphor* 11, 14).

Tomasi debunks the punitive notion emerging from Christianity that a disease afflicting a person expresses moral character, yet she does suggest through her portrayal of illness that Pietro's disease dramatizes intense desire just as Sontag describes TB as a disease that is seen as "the vehicle of excess feeling" (*Illness as Metaphor* 45). Pietro is that man of tubercular character: "sensitive, creative, a being apart" to use Sontag's description—an artist as it were: a man whose artistic devotion to his carving work would likely kill him, but would also immortalize him as he, like a lesser god, memorializes others through carving tombstones.[6]

Tomasi's story of illness and death follows a predictable narrative trajectory, especially for tuberculars of the Christian variety: expanded consciousness and beatification by resignation, once Pietro accepts his status as an ill and dying body. Pietro achieves narrative distinctiveness not as a stonecutter but as a stonecutter who is ill and dying, accepting (without criticism) the artisanal vocation that killed him. Unlike Lapolla's Gennaro and di Donato's Geremio, Pietro's dying is arguably neither accidental nor unnatural. Like other tuberculars in his community, Pietro's body is ultimately confined, and of necessity, he is taken out of his daily routine, preparing him not only to experience what Sontag calls a "psychic voyage" to the other world but also to make literal through the construction of the sanatorium the bureaucratic response to physical illness emerging from advancing capitalism (Sontag, *Illness as Metaphor* 36).

The *via dolorosa* scene in which Pietro enters the world of the patient by sadly walking with his wife and daughter to the local sanatorium and the actual deathbed scene that reveals his final thoughts allows Tomasi to interpret dying within a Christian framework at the same time that she underestimates the toll that the granite industry had taken on a generation of immigrant men. In the context of familiar stories, Arthur Frank explains, dying is "not a loss of the old map and destination" [but rather an acceptance of] "where the map always led" (162). The story that Tomasi tells with the death of Pietro Dalli is the story of the Passion.

Using passive voice to suggest Pietro's increasing detachment from the world, Tomasi begins her Italian American version of the Passion with a reference to the Dallis' twenty-five-year marriage: "the anniversary dinner was eaten" (219) and ends with Pietro's deathbed plea of the "old world *paesani*, '*Gesù, Giuseppe e Maria!*'" (257). On his deathbed, Pietro eagerly awaits his dying, recognizing the necessity of the "great and final moment of release" and impatient with second-generation doctor, Gino Tosti, whose own father's untimely death from lung disease influenced his career in medicine (256). Refusing medical colonization of his body, Pietro nonetheless "suffers" the "tireless hands" of Gino, delaying his desire to die (257). Pietro has always accepted what Arthur Frank calls the "contingency" of the body, and the fact that "breakdown is built into it" (49). As such, Pietro perceives his own body-self as a "communicative body," associated with contingency and seeing "reflections of his own suffering in the bodies of others" (Frank 49). Pietro witnesses with pain "the grief-ravaged faces around him that tore at his heart" (Tomasi, *Like Lesser Gods* 256).

Once the faces around him blur, Pietro remembers his Italian homeland and in doing so fulfills the literal definition of nostalgia: the condition of being homesick. From the Greek, *nostos*, the etymological meaning of nostalgia is a return home, suggesting here that Tomasi's vision of life after expiration lies in the homeland. Superimposed on this image is the culturally elaborated story of Pietro's body-self made in America and reflecting the work that defined him: carving. Pietro's final thought returns him to his unfinished work, described in younger years as his little masterpiece. Before he dies, Pietro imagines "guiding the steel into the pattern of a slender cross" (257). The image of the cross recalls Christ's Passion, the Christian exemplar of suffering and martyrdom. But the reference is also Tomasi's homage to first-generation Italian American immigrant workers. Like illness, Tomasi contends, being an immigrant in America is learning to live with lost control. *How* one does that is important to witness; thus Tomasi's deathbed story of one Italian American immigrant is also a revision of the story of Job, demonstrating how to bear suffering and stigma in the new world with dignity and forgiveness.

Dorothy Bryant and Josephine Gattuso Hendin portray deaths as graphic and brutal as their early twentieth-century precursors, but their dying father figures do not go gently into that good night. Tame death has been replaced by modern dying. Earmarks of modern dying in Bryant's *Miss Giardino* (1978) and Hendin's *The Right Thing to Do* (1988) include loss of faith in a traditional God, the absence of an extended community to function as an entourage in public mourning processions, and, in the case of Hendin's *The Right Thing to Do*, the introduction of modern medical practices that protract life but do not save it. Traditional features typical of premodern deaths are included in both novels as well through representations of deathbed talks between dying fathers and their daughters. Philippe Ariès explains that in the nineteenth century, the disappearance of "pious clauses from the will had increased the importance of the final dialogue: the last farewells, the last words of counsel, whether in public or private" (*The Hour* 363). In the twentieth century, no such fond farewell is guaranteed.

Bryant and Hendin demonstrate that the loss of piety or the influences of medical consultation do not interfere with the private exchange occurring between dying fathers and their witnessing daughters. Equally premodern in both texts is an ensuing deathbed pardon, an old-world gesture that the dying bestowed upon lamenting bedside companions (Ariès, *Western Attitudes* 9). With enormous difficulty, the daughters in Bryant's and Hendin's novels accept fatherly pardons, simultaneously recognizing that such pardoning cuts both ways, but it also releases these daughters from punitive scripts that would otherwise continue to imprison them. Through storytelling, each dying father also devises a way to have a measure of success with his daughter, already having taught her about the hard knocks of behavioral aggression that she will undoubtedly meet in her future outside the family home. Both daughters internalize the determination of their fathers, but must learn how, through struggle and error, to transfer negative aggression to other creative goals.

Like the early twentieth-century novels, *Miss Giardino* and *The Right Thing to Do* feature illness as culturally representative of American society's treatment of immigrants, particularly the immigrant working men on the front lines of employment with few resources for protection. This situation is especially true of Anna Giardino's father, who suffers from lung disease contracted from mine work and whose illness is represented as neither increasing his soulfulness nor enhancing his consciousness. Stripped of all romantic or metaphoric implication, lung disease suffocates its victim; Anna describes herself as "thriving in the air that strangles" her father (*Miss Giardino* 13). While Gina Giardello's father of *The Right Thing to Do* never engages in the manual labor that threatened and killed so many of his literary precursors, his bodily suffering is chronic and, recast as disease—in his case, diabetes—"something essential to the experience of chronic illness is lost" (Kleinman 6).[7] The illnesses of both men—recast as disease or not—inexorably shape how each lives with lost control in a society that did not afford them much control to begin with.

The fathers' illnesses in both novels tell a similar story about cultural trauma, about immigrant men who did not "make America" and contemptuously rejected American ways. Their ill bodies condition the way they communicate with their daughters. Their stories are *literally* embodied, shaped by their specific illnesses. The "narrative wreckage" that emerges from their bodies in pain is a story told under conditions of "fatigue [and] uncertainty" (Frank 54). Both fathers suffer serious and fatal illnesses, using storytelling as "repair work on the wreck," which cannot possibly mend their bodies or extend their futures, but, like expectations for conventional narrative, can set in place a foreseeable future for their daughters, whose young adulthood has not been marred by the shipwreck of illness (Frank 54–55).

On their deathbeds, each father attempts to teach his daughter something about herself, but *in relation to him*. However, unlike the dying body-self in dyadic exchange with others, recognizing a "community of pain" to use Frank's description again (36), the dying fathers of Bryant's and Hendin's novels are clearly "dominating" bodies and they communicate their stories without entirely relinquishing their desire to control their daughters.[8] The dominating body "defines itself in *force*," assuming "the *contingency* of disease but never accept[ing] it" (Frank 46–47). Bryant's "Papa" and Hendin's "Nino" are dying men who are loath to lay down their sword. Their resistance is remarkable in the way they refuse to assimilate the oppressions of American culture. The defining feature in their personalities is anger, which does not abate as they become more ill. Given the fact that many Italian immigrant women and children had to share the problem of male authoritarianism, the patriarchal father figures of Bryant's and Hendin's texts possess dominating bodies that use aggression against their families *as they are dying*.

Both Anna Giardino and Gina Giardello have absorbed their father's displaced rage, but they have used it to counter their own vulnerability and to construct some armor for themselves. Only outside the father's grasp can Anna and Gina achieve a fuller selfhood; thus higher education and separation from home help each gain self-knowledge. Returning home to the deathbed prepares Anna and Gina to accept responsibilities to their families no longer solely dominated by destructive patriarchal behavior. Due to their father's patriarchal aggression, both Anna and Gina have become accustomed to dealing with hostility, which hardens them but also enables them to withstand behavioral aggression in mainstream culture. Bryant and Hendin deepen an understanding of these immigrant fathers, suggesting that their cruelties, while not acceptable, are saturated with their own disillusionment in America.

Having suffered from a supposed mugging that leaves her without memory of the incident, Anna Giardino struggles to reconstruct her life, beginning with the earliest memories that haunt her: her violent family household. Bryant rhetorically aligns Anna Giardino with death by having her wake in a hospital, lying like a "dead body, arranged" (*Miss Giardino* 1), and by inserting a newspaper article on "former English teacher Miss A. Giardino, 68," which reads like an obituary (*Miss Giardino* 23). In order to heal herself, Anna remembers her father's deathbed revelation, which will function as a foundational pedagogical lesson that she still must absorb, so that she does *not* die "in the same despair as her father, without even his hope of a new generation to benefit from his sacrifice" (*Miss Giardino* 146).

Bearing the "ascetic face of a saint" Papa lies dying and calls for Anna to perform the ritual vigil with him; while his fury his spent, he nonetheless insists on Anna's presence: "he wants me, only me. I must stay beside him so that when he opens his eyes he sees me" (*Miss Giardino* 17). The word "vigil" comes from the Old French to mean "devotional watching" and, originally, from the Latin to mean "wakefulness," or "alert;" the college graduate Anna vigilantly performs both tasks as she stays with her father as he dies. Papa's final words to Anna echo past cruelties, but illustrate his recognition that, of all his children, Anna bears most resemblance to her father in her struggle to survive *him*: "'The American,' he whispers.... 'Smart.'... 'You know,' he says with just a shadow of the old cruel irony, 'you ... are like ... me ... or you could ... never done it'" (*Miss Giardino* 18).

Anna's ability to survive the baneful aspects of her father's anger and disillusionment comes at a high price; nonetheless, her father's failed immigration story prepares Anna to recover her memory and to reclaim a working-class history reflected in her own feelings of powerlessness within the educational system: "And how had she differed from her father? ... He had a vision of a better life and had strained himself to the utmost to go after it. So had she. He had been used and abused by the forces in which he had put all his hope. So had she. ... She had learned to understand him by becoming him" (*Miss Giardino* 146). Anna's father, however embittered, paradoxically turns his illness narrative into a story that will ultimately help to heal his daughter. The potency of his narrative is embodied in Anna's recovery of memory, voice, and purpose as she affirms her life's trajectory in older age.

On the threshold of autonomous adulthood, Gina Giardello returns to the "place of old humiliations and failures" in order to visit her dying father in *The Right Thing to Do* (106). Despite being immobile and weak, Nino Giardello refuses surrender of his body to the contingencies of disease, managing to affirm an authoritative voice through storytelling that fascinates his daughter. Living in the United States for half a century has not changed Nino's devotion to *lu vecchiu vita* (the old way)—loyalty to family *sopra a tutto* (above all), and submission to male authority. Nonetheless, the way Nino retells a folkloric story from his boyhood in Sicily reflects a modernist recognition of historical discontinuity, multiple endings, and lack of closure. Functioning much like the cantastorie (history singer) of his Sicilian village, Nino draws on a narrative tradition that uses stories as moral exempla to convey a didactic lesson. His "memories" are calculated and deceptively simple like folktales; he has clearly imbibed the tradition of gifted tale-telling, understanding that stories are made more captivating through enhancement.

On his deathbed, Nino tells Gina a cautionary tale: he creates a childhood memory of his homeland village in which the community's decision to do the right thing is blurred by emotional attachments. The story recounts a dying daughter's request to be buried with her beloved father. Refusing to offer Gina one version of the story, Nino offers several instead, illustrating that uncertainty characterizes the Sicilian community's confusion over having done right by honoring the daughter's request since they disturbed her father's remains. By offering his own opinion at the end of the tale, Nino extends the perimeters of an old-world story into the new world by contending that the villagers should have buried the child alone.

Hendin suggests that Nino's conclusion to the story is also uncertain since he remains unable to relinquish his need to control his daughter's future. Nonetheless, Nino signals to Gina his realization that a child's autonomy is necessary for it to discover "its own road back to where it belongs" (190). As storytellers understand, one of the central themes of folktales is liberation, but such freedom can only be attained if at the same time we "liberate other people" (Calvino xix), a quality Rosa Cassettari conveyed so ably as she sought freedom from the enforced surveillance of her body by the institutions of family and Church. While Gina Giardello enjoys freedoms unimaginable to Rosa at the same age, she is nonetheless subject to the policing of her own body by a father who made "wreckage . . . with his words and his cane" (*The Right Thing to Do* 76).

Nino neither entirely releases his daughter nor requires her unquestioning submission. Rather, he conveys both his knowledge that she is like him and his fear that she will suffer because of that. Like Anna Giardino, Gina Giardello suffers early in life from excessive paternal domination, experiencing the dying father as a jail warden whose dominating body enthralls its prisoner. While both daughters are penalized by their fathers for rejecting outmoded Italian norms, they experience release through their deaths. Having internalized a kind of Foucauldian panopticism, Anna and Gina struggle to define themselves as acting subjects not in defiance of their surveilling fathers but in preparation for a world outside the parochialism of their Italian American family culture, but a world conditioned by similar forms of behavioral aggression, especially toward women. Wounded but not destroyed by the death of the father, Anna and Gina are poised to construct hyphenated Italian American identities inflected but not paralyzed by italianità.

Widows' Lamentations

> Let me go! Let me escape! This role I do not wish to play!
>
> —Annunziata, *Christ in Concrete*

In *Death's Door*, a young Sandra Gilbert incredulously questioned her mother's response to her father's untimely death, wondering "Why did she emphasize herself that way? . . . Why did she keep reiterating the fate of the *I* who was doing the lamenting rather than the sorrowful end of the *he* who was the subject of the lamentation?" (22). When Gilbert's own husband died a quarter of a century later, she replaced the alienation she felt from her mother's grief with a deeper historical understanding of widowhood, acknowledging instead the "reality of death for the one who has lost the *other* and in particular for the woman who has lost a man" (24).[9] Referring to the *Oxford English Dictionary*, Gilbert examines the Indo-European meaning of widow: "'to be empty, to be separated,' to be 'divided,' 'destitute,' or 'lacking,'" the etymology implying that "Death has entered the widow, . . . and she has entered death, for she is filled with vacancy and has dissolved into a void, a state or non-being that is akin to, if not part of, the state into which the dead person has journeyed, fallen, or been drawn" (*Death's Door* 24–25). Acquiring status only through marriage, a woman's loss traditionally has been interpreted as emptiness. As Gilbert explains, "society . . . asserts the widow's emptiness and not the widow herself" (27).[10]

   Plenty of widows from Italian American literature, despite a family structure that honors the paterfamilias above all, refuse nullification for practical and existential reasons. Widows such as Carmela of *The Grand Gennaro*, Lucia Santa of *The Fortunate Pilgrim*, Fortuna of *The Weak and the Strong*, Laura of *The Right Thing to Do*, Sarah of *Paper Fish*, and Maria of *Like Lesser Gods* (to name only a few) do not submit to the societal definition of widow as doomed persona non grata, her existence as a person ceaselessly suspended. Indeed, like Rose Romano's grandmother, who sits at the "head of the table," widowhood often symbolizes in Italian America a marker of continuity through matriarchal autonomy ("To Show Respect," *Vendetta* 24).

Unrelieved grief can also cause extreme psychic crisis; spousal loss is but one form this grief takes in Italian American literature. The widow taking center stage such as Annunziata of *Christ in Concrete* is an example from the tradition of lamentation. Expressing grief as a form of power, not emptiness, is the activity that "unnerves the world, not just her rage and grief, but the sudden, mysteriously privileged access to the other world" (Gilbert, *Death's Door* 30). The grief-stricken behavior of Italian American women emerges from a personal genre of lamentation—as opposed to literary examples of much "masculine grief-work," which traditionally tend to be "highly structured, eloquently styled, and clearly resolved modes (the public eulogy, the pastoral elegy" (Gilbert, *Death's Door* 31).[11] Unlike the formality found in funeral rites, lamentation is "intimate, private, oral, and informal" (Gilbert, *Death's Door* 33), often reflecting, what Benedetto Croce explains, a "kind of madness" in the wake of a loved one's death (qtd. in Harrison, *The Dominion* 55).

Christ in Concrete and *Like Lesser Gods* represent antipodal responses to widowhood. Di Donato and Tomasi present bereaved widows as different from each other as south Italy is from north Italy, as different as Manhattan is from Montpelier. Annunziata's grief is primal and self-destructive; Maria's grief is stoical and ritualized.[12] The madness from which Annunziata suffers dangerously parallels the now rare Indian practice of sati, in which self-immolation becomes Annunziata's narrative course, resulting in death, which emerges from unmediated grief. While clearly several years intervene before Annunziata gives up the ghost (she bears her eighth child shortly after her husband's death), di Donato writes her grief narrative as a timeless present, making it feel as though only days have passed. Unable to separate herself from her desire to be with her dead husband, Annunziata experiences guilt, as Benedetto Croce explains, "for living[;] it seems that we are stealing something that doesn't belong to us, we would like to die with our dead" (qtd. in Harrison, *The Dominion* 55). While such a desire may be considered insane and self-destructive, the impulse is not as unusual as one might think. As a recent grieving mother explained, "'I didn't want to *make* myself dead—I just wanted to be dead with Claire [her daughter]. I raged at the injustice of the fact that though she had needed me to give birth to her, she didn't need me to die with her'" (Schnell; qtd. in Gilbert, *Death's Door* 3). As Sandra Gilbert admits herself, she was not unusual in yearning to "enter an open doorway into death and *be* dead with someone much loved" (*Death's Door* 3). Annunziata knocks on death's door throughout *Christ in Concrete*.

Unlike her widowed sisters of other Italian American texts, Annunziata refuses to separate herself from the deceased, "opening up . . . distance [in an] attempt to make the dead die within rather than die with the dead" (Harrison, *The Dominion* 65). She rejects the idea of performing the role of widow, a formalized gesture that would insure some distance from her grief. Despite the community rituals accompanying the death of Geremio, Annunziata numbly maintains her impossible desire to be dead with her beloved spouse; she distances herself from others, and refuses to be governed by rule-bound performances of ceremony and shared norms of grief.[13] Benedetto Croce explains that "by expressing grief, in the various forms of celebration or cult of the dead, one overcomes heartbreak, rendering it objective" (qtd. in Harrison, *The Dominion* 56). Annunziata countenances no such separation. Her resistance is breathtaking.

On her deathbed at the novel's end, Annunziata, fully committed to the world of the dead, violently responds to her son Paul's rejection of the Christian story of salvation. She issues a lamentation that rejects all manner of distance when she catches her son by the throat "with a heart-ripping cry and thrust[s] him to the wall beating his face hysterically and screaming, 'Out! Out! The Lord's Paul is no more! Out! Ah Jesu [Gesù] give me the strength! My sainted son is Dead! Dead! Ahh dead!'" (231) Annunziata's verbal denunciation may seem theatrical or operatic, but it is not performed or externalized; it is an innermost, natural expression, and that is what makes it and her so dangerous.

To Paul and her brood of watching children, Annunziata's final deathbed words are "crooned" rather than spoken, recalling the incantatory chant uttered by Geremio in his final moments. Like the premodern penitent, Annunziata forgives Paul for renouncing *her* faith in the story of salvation; having forgotten the world, she awaits her desired death. According to Harrison, ancient and modern theorists speculated that the "human voice sang before it spoke," referring to Giambattista Vico's belief that "grief and joy [are] equally plausible candidates for the overwhelming passion that first moved the tongue to sing" (*The*

Dominion 62, 63). A cross between lullaby and lament, Annunziata's final song-like humming to her children attempts—impossibly—to soothe as she recedes further from consciousness.

By submitting to mournful and never-ending remembrance of her beloved husband, Annunziata never contains her grief. This grieving widow of Italian America refuses the obligation—as a mother, as a provider, as a human—to cope with her mortality by recognizing, as Harrison explains, "its kinship with others and to turn this kinship in death into a shared language"—into story, I might add (*The Dominion* 71). Unable to overcome the "persistent, contagious, and insane desire to die with the dead," Annunziata refuses to live as a dying person *without* the beloved (Harrison, *The Dominion* 70). It is her greatest—and arguably Italian American literature's greatest—transgression: against mortality, against living in the world, against living in America, against partaking in the formal protocols of grief-work amply embodied in Italian ceremonial practices and grief rites. Annunziata's grief remains, as Harrison explains, "locked in aphasia" (*The Dominion* 71), and her status in America as an Abruzzian immigrant woman only exacerbates her linguistic and cultural desolation. Nothing could be more different than Maria Dalli's widowed response to her husband's death in *Like Lesser Gods*.

In a final flicker of earthly humor, Pietro Dalli reverses the traditional deathbed vigil made by mourners by proudly observing his wife's dry-eyed face, which is "an inscrutable mask. . . . As strong as unflinching as granite she was" (256). Maria Dalli's love for her husband is no less intense than Annunziata's: what could be said for one applies to the other as they love their husbands "more than anything and anyone in the whole world, better than these her children who were woven of her own flesh, blood, and bone" (Tomasi, *Like Lesser Gods* 262). Both widows believe in a traditional God and a conventional Catholic afterlife that reunites what death has separated. They both take comfort in a vision of death as expiration rather than termination.

Unlike Annunziata, however, Maria is afforded the experience of sharing the illness narrative that her husband has time to embody and retell before his death. In this sense, Maria partakes in her husband's journey through agony to atonement. This quest narrative, Arthur Frank explains, using the narrative structure of the journey outlined by Joseph Campbell in his classic *The Hero with a Thousand Faces*, allows the ill person to realize "a sense of purpose, the idea that illness has been a journey" (117). In *Like Lesser Gods*, the truth learned about Pietro's illness is not prophetic, nor, in Tomasi's mind, demanding of social action, a course more likely taken by the radical di Donato. Pietro's illness story may have begun later in life than it did for his other sculpting paesani, but it was always a narrative in the making. Maria's futile attempt in her younger years to safeguard the health of her husband by destroying his work at the sheds does little to deter her husband's sense of purpose, which is only completed through suffering.

After his death, Maria submits to the formal protocols of grieving, allowing herself to achieve a reconciliation albeit tinged with bitterness over her husband's refusal to do any other work. She is one of the fortunate widows in the stonecutting community, married to her husband for twenty-five years and losing him to tuberculosis after her children are adults. Only with grim determination does Maria acquiesce to the Christian belief, "that death meant but a short separation and that some day she would join him in the unknown world he had reached before her" (*Like Lesser Gods* 262). Like di Donato, Tomasi distinguishes her immigrant Italian workers by drawing a connection between them and the story of the Passion. Just as Pietro plods to his Calvary symbolized by the hillside TB sanatorium, Maria accepts her husband's role as Christ-like, even confusing the words of Jesus with her husband's: "[S]he had almost forgot that it was Christ and not Pietro, who had said '*Let not your heart be troubled . . . and if I go and prepare a place for you . . . I will take you to Myself; that where I am, there you also may be*'" (*Like Lesser Gods* 262).

Maria has been atoning for her own "criminal act" for nearly two decades (*Like Lesser Gods* 262), stealthily having entered the closed sheds in order to vandalize her husband's nearly completed rococo cross. If indeed Maria makes a connection between Jesus and her husband, then she performs the role of grieving widow after Pietro dies in order to rewrite a script that she has been unwilling to read—that, in trying to destroy her husband's work, she was also potentially destroying his creative link to God. Since she comes to accept the spiritual implications of her husband's life work—in which working the stone and serving as God's instrument are one and the same—Maria must also ponder the unthinkable: that she attempted to kill him/Christ, too. Honoring her husband's work after his death allows Maria to attain the necessary distance needed to rectify a wrong she feels she committed in destroying his "little masterpiece" (*Like Lesser Gods* 264). Given the opportunity to atone, in her words, for "the crime" she committed so long ago, Maria chooses Pietro's original design for his tombstone to be worked by the hand of his partner, the artist Ronato. Making this choice on behalf of her husband affords Maria a powerful moment of communion with the dead, "experiencing a strange sensation, as if her husband were here with her and knowing, at last, that she, his wife, had been guilty of the crime. . . . [T]his decision, more than time itself, healed her of the bitterness she had felt for granite, and helped her to see that stone, beautiful and lasting, was worthy of being claimed as a lifework for Pietro and for any man" (*Like Lesser Gods* 266). That she also accepts the excessive intricacy of Pietro's rococo design over Ronato's classical "masterpiece of beauty" (264) suggests Maria's acceptance of her husband's creative autonomy. Maria's choice to memorialize her husband through his design allows her to ritualize his passing and mourn her separation from him through this objective symbolization. Unlike Annunziata, Maria will live into old age.

Traditional widowhood is replaced by women who mourn the dying beloved in the postmodern novels by Dorothy Bryant (*A Day in San Francisco*) and Carole Maso (*The Art Lover*). Desperately longing to support the ill person they love, the surviving protagonists of each novel take part in excruciating plots in which restitution is as unimaginable as watching the untimely deaths of young men. Alongside their emphatic witnessing is their realization that the loved one also suffers from a disease that in its early years affected mostly gay men—AIDS. Although Bryant and Maso characterize their grieving female characters as widows, literally speaking, neither has lost a spouse. Their close relationship with the beloved, their witnessing the ill person living vulnerably, and their intimate expressions of grief (in the form of lamentation rather than funeral rite) make them widows nonetheless. Like Sandra Gilbert's mother who exclaimed "'*I* wasn't ready.' '*I'm* a widow,'" these widowed women use testimony to tell incomplete stories of grief, illness, and death (*Death's Door* 22).

A Day in San Francisco (1982), Dorothy Bryant's seventh novel, takes place during the 1980 Gay Freedom Day Parade after the tragic assassinations two years before of George Moscone, mayor of San Francisco, and Harvey Milk, board supervisor.[14] Bryant deliberately chose this day to frame her novel in order to dramatize the fragility of freedom gained by gay liberation. Bryant situates her female protagonist inside a highly charged political atmosphere and within a kind of chaos narrative in which she struggles to name the illness affecting her gay son, Frank Lontana, who understands his ill body as inconvenience rather than as terminal or stigmatized. Even though HIV infection was not yet identified in 1980 as the virus that causes AIDS, Bryant forcefully interrupts the narrative to insert sexually explicit gay advertisements from the Castro District alongside equally cautionary pamphlets on sexually transmitted diseases such as herpes, syphilis, and gay bowel syndrome.

Interrupting her text with incessant and contradictory information on sexual behavior, Bryant mimics the disorder that is occurring for Frank as he experiences the constraints associated with his unnamed illness. The novel is willfully distracting and interruptive, with insertions of overwhelming information as though in response not merely to Frank's early stages of illness, but to the community's "culturally marked illness," as Arthur Kleinman explains, which includes "the . . . loss of body- and self-image, the stigma of self-earned illness, discrimination against homosexuals, and so forth. . . . That exoskeleton is a carapace of . . . a dominant societal symbol that, once applied to a person, spoils radically that individual's identity, and is not easily removed" (22). The title of Bryant's novel, *A Day in San Francisco*, though scrambled, is deliberately acronymous, associating Frank not only with the hospitable place of gay sexuality (San Francisco), but also with the inhospitable illness that will require his exile from normalcy (AIDS). That the Castro Street District where Frank rents a room is enveloped in fog is more than an atmospheric commonplace of San Francisco. The space becomes a metaphorical place of vagueness and obscurity for Clara, who will not achieve clarity with her son by the novel's end. For Frank, rented space on Castro Street is a form of gay campanilismo, an insulation that is both liberating and dangerous.

Frank Lontana rejects the very stigma of the diseased body, refusing to recast his illness as a disease, as an "it," a disorder that achieves a "particular nomenclature and taxonomy," stripping him of personal subjectivity (Kleinman 6). Early in its history, HIV infection was referred to as the gay plague, and, once named as AIDS, was understood in a premodern way, as "a disease incurred by people both as individuals and as members of a 'risk' group—that neutral-sounding, bureaucratic category which also revives the archaic idea of a tainted community that illness has judged" (Sontag, *AIDS and Its Metaphors* 46). Bryant inserts advertisements promoting promiscuous sexual practices which also flank the pages of Frank's published interview with a virulently antigay spokesman, both discourses visually existing side by side, reinforcing the profoundly polarized views of the city and ultimately foreshadowing the dissension between mother and son.

As Clara Lontana copes with what she intuits will not be a restitution narrative for her son, but rather a series of life-depleting illnesses that will eventually kill him, she uses storytelling to gain a tenuous measure of security. A professor of history, Clara Lontana's scholarship has focused on centralizing minority experience—specifically working-class and immigrant women's lives—to examine their initiation into a metropolitan and consumer society. When invited to give a lecture at one of the successful independent women's book stores in the newly gentrified Mission District of her childhood, Clara Lontana uneasily returns to that changed neighborhood, haunted by Depression memories and by her parents' joyless lives. The lecture Clara gives at Old Wives' Tales reflects a guarded capacity to analyze the political and personal motivations informing the behavior of Dan White, former city supervisor, who assassinated George Moscone and Harvey Milk. Expertly connecting her experience of the mediocre, inefficient (and often corrupt) men of the forties and fifties to the same kind of men of the seventies, who created a Dan White, a "living embodiment of . . . casually voiced pride in stupidity, cruelty, and fear," and whose antigay rhetoric and "anti-intellectual obscenities" were the reincarnation of the same "enemies" that questioned her capacity to teach because she was a mother, Clara adeptly makes moving connections between her gendered situation and her son's sexuality (*A Day* 47, 49, 53).

An Italian American intellectual *woman* of the 1940s and 1950s, Clara positions herself as a misfit, as a "thinly disguised alien, living in constant fear of exposure to ridicule and hatred," establishing an equally credible connection between her past situation and her son's present life (*A Day* 46). Winning the audience over with her deft analogical reasoning underwritten by autobiographical commentary, Clara Lontana might have left the book store with her old wives' tale in tact. But the questions following her talk—about her divorce, her son's coming out, her brand of Catholicism—dismantle the tidy narrative, leaving Clara questioning her own honesty. Unable adequately to articulate to the bookstore audience that severing herself from "her family's expectations" was as unacceptable to them as is her son's rejection of his mother's ideas about monogamy, Clara nonetheless reveals to the reader her own carefully repressed feelings about her son's sexuality *and* his risky sexual behavior (*A Day* 59). It is a story she cannot tell.

Clara Lontana's surname suggests that she has studiously distanced herself from her own deepest feelings about being a mother of a son whose sexual practices are literally killing him. In his discussion of the Latinate origins of Italian words, Robert Pogue Harrison includes "*lontano*" in this list of words that "reverberate in deep recesses of cultural memory" (*The Dominion* 73), and, along with words such as "*antico*" and "*oscuro*," lontano recalls an old, dark world for Clara that unearths her immigrant past, her parents' sacrificial lives, and her necessary rebellion from the exhausting conformities of heterosexual marriage and motherhood. As cleverly as she may be able to theorize about the connections between herself and her son, Clara cannot resolve her feelings about his sexual practices, making her incapable of hearing what may be described as the early drafts of Frank's illness narrative. In this sense, Clara experiences what Shoshana Felman, describes as "events in excess of our frames of reference" (qtd. in Gilbert, *Death's Door* 98).

When Clara finally gets to Frank's rented room, she is witness to the personal shock of seeing *less* of him, his thin, long face "Goyaesque," jaundiced with hepatitis. The absurdity of speaking at all is made apparent when Clara realizes that she has suspended her usual salutation with a nod, unable to "think of an answer. It was as if someone had greeted her in a foreign language, or one entirely inappropriate to the occasion, like praising her dress in the midst of a fire" (*A Day* 118, 119). In order to protect herself from the realization that she is witnessing her son as mortally ill, Clara resorts to form, mimicking not only her mother's furious dedication to cleaning but also Clara's own professorial devotion to argumentation.

In the penultimate section of *A Day in San Francisco*, Bryant separates mother and son visually by italicizing only Clara's comments and dropping quotation marks altogether. The story that Frank wants to tell his mother—but is prevented mostly—is the story of temporary illness, but a story nonetheless that he is struggling to gain some measure of sovereignty over, since *how* he is suffering far exceeds a full recovery. That he cannot fully accept his position of an embodied teller of his illness narrative might partially account for Clara's inability to receive his testimony of pain. Thus, Clara's concern revolves around interrogating her son's judgment—"How did you end up in this place?" and "[Y]ou think you can be with people who do these things and not be affected?"—rather than receiving his testimony empathically, being *with* him rather than *at* him (*A Day* 124, 128). Both are overwhelmed by the extremity of Frank's illness; both make mistakes verbally and resort to argumentative speech more reflective of dominating bodies that displace rage against contingency on other people as Arthur Frank has explained (47).

At the root of overwhelmed *memory*, Shoshana Felman finds in the activity of testimony a "*body* that is overwhelmed" (qtd. in Frank 139). Both mother and son experience "the body . . . in excess of any language that testimony can speak" (Frank 140). Not surprisingly, Clara drops down to her knees, feeling a "silent earthquake" at the center of her body after Frank unsteadily leaves the room to shower (*A Day* 123). She feels the excess of what can be spoken in her body, but, once submitting to the exigencies of her body after being summarily dismissed by her son, Clara inchoately experiences an "other-relatedness" when she unknowingly places her body within a community of pain as she walks the night streets of the Castro District. At the same time, as Elaine Scarry has noted, "whatever pain achieves, it achieves in part through its unsharability, and it ensures this unsharability through its resistance to language" (4).

In the final chapter of *A Day in San Francisco*, Bryant has Clara deliberately revert to, what Scarry calls, "a state anterior to language, to the sounds and cries a human being makes before language is learned" (4) producing "grating sobs," "blurring" sounds, and "strange singing" (*A Day* 143). As though already experiencing an unutterable death, Clara's body reacts in a stammering fashion, which is consistent with "overwhelming trauma" (Harrison, *The Dominion* 63), the blockage a response to the impossibility of rendering an account of illness with a voice that "calls out to the dead without response, that seeks to say what can no longer be heard, and that turns into itself only to prolong and articulate its call in words of grief" (Harrison, *The Dominion* 65).

In the final scene, Clara plods "mechanically forward, carrying her heavy, stiff body," as though it were a corpse itself (*A Day* 143). According to Harrison, "humans find their voice in the presence of a corpse" (*The Dominion* 65), which Clara discovers as she weeps uncontrollably on the dark streets of the Castro District, muttering words for the first time, and thereby vocalizing her loss as though she were already a widow. Clara utters continuously, "my son, my son," a lament encouraging grief within the personal genre of lamentation. Dialogue tags bracket Clara's words, "my son, my son," as though establishing personal communication with the absent though ubiquitous son. Despite her anticlerical stance toward the Catholic Church, Clara nonetheless places her story of Frank next to the Christian scenes of the life of Mary, represented by medieval and Renaissance artists. Her full incorporation into the scene of the dolorous Mary and the iconography of the pietà will require Clara to perform a task she has up to this point failed to do: *touch* her diseased son. Just as she is unable to listen to his story, allowing him an agency through suffering, Clara is unable, for all her professorial aplomb, to learn from her son a "pedagogy of suffering" that will enable her to share his suffering as a dyadic body (Frank 145).

Carole Maso's second novel, *The Art Lover* (1990), examines bodies in contact with each other. Shifting between fiction and autobiography, Maso's novel is dedicated to her friend, Gary Falk, who died in 1986 of AIDS. His death created a wild impatience in Maso that intensified her conviction "to living, working—loving with a new recklessness, abandon, urgent, urgent. Gary who taught me to do everything, to be everything, to want, to have, to try everything—to not be afraid anymore" (*Break Every Rule* 9–10). This vibrancy in Carole Maso and her fictionalized narrator, Caroline, is clearly in contrast to Bryant's Clara Lontana, whose body is bereft of energy by the conclusion of *A Day in San Francisco*. As Bryant before her, Maso examines the life of the ill—unpredictable, interrupted, and uncontrolled—bearing witness to the agony of the AIDS crisis in the late twentieth century. Like literary predecessors Pietro di Donato and Mari Tomasi, Maso retells the Christian story of salvation, albeit in a nonlinear, postmodern manner, dissenting from dominant family narratives so popular in earlier Italian American literature.

Using multiple forms of storytelling, Carole Maso explores bodies in pain, particularly focusing on contact between the ill body immersed in suffering alongside a witnessing listener, both of whom manage to maintain desire in the process of what Elaine Scarry calls "unmaking the world" (*The Body in Pain* 19). The narrator, Caroline, while admitting that she is "sick of [herself] trying to give shape to all this sorrow, all this rage, all this loss—and failing" (*The Art Lover* 148), struggles to maintain the intellectual vigor required of the artist to remake the world through storytelling. She feels "the toll that suffering takes" as she witnesses her friend's Steven's bouts of life-depleting illnesses (*The Art Lover* 149). Together, narrator and dying beloved collaborate as wounded storytellers, "fighting for our lives . . . speaking for our lives," refusing demonization of the AIDS illness, entirely erasing from their conversation any reference to illness as punishment or self-earned, God's judgment on a tainted community (*The Art Lover* 164).

Like Clara Lontana of San Francisco, New Yorker Caroline observes that Greenwich Village has become a "whole neighborhood dying," and, during the period of the nineteen eighties, the "city of AIDS" (*The Art Lover* 48, 41). Carole Maso embraces desire, admitting that she "didn't think living could ever be this dangerous," ruefully discerning between imagining dying for "that freedom, that pleasure," as opposed to actually dying for "this life of desire" (*The Art Lover* 197, 156). In contrast to Clara's pragmatic rejection of her son's "multiple sex contacts—yes, hundreds" (*A Day* 132), Caroline embraces her friend's "life of desire," memorializing the corporeal body in love with "blood moving . . . hair and sweat and highway . . . dark and light" (*The Art Lover* 156). *The Art Lover* functions as an in memoriam to desire itself, to Maso's recognition that fundamentally desire is always about wanting more. The narrator's constructive impulse throughout the novel is to submit the body's desire to language that not only contains it, but also celebrates it. The dying person never lacks desire, never falls out of love with himself.

The Art Lover is an example of incorporation, that is, a demonstration of how Maso incorporates the death of her friend Gary (fictionalized as Steven) into a multidimensional text revolving around multiple stories about loss and suffering. The fictionalized stories feature nuclear families whose lives are disrupted by conditions of modern life. Maso dismantles dominant narrative patterns characterized by the traditional nuclear family by showing how they are fraught by mental illness, father abandonment, and personal alienation. Creating nontraditional but commonplace family stories that parallel rather than contrast the narrative of gay desire and male-female friendship, Maso thus delegitimizes any one primary or quintessential family story. Choosing to fictionalize dominant heterosexual romance, marriage, and motherhood as subject to long-term suffering and grief allows Maso to incorporate the story of friendship between homosexuals alongside rather than apart from other family narratives.

In doing so, Maso's narrator also assumes traditional roles such as mother, sister, and lover in response to the dying. Carole Maso and her fictionalized narrator, Caroline, likewise experience the deep-boned grief of the widow, but necessarily *outside* the perimeters of patriarchy, allowing them access to the other world without succumbing to the doom of desperation. Throughout the entire novel, Maso struggles to comprehend the fact that her best friend died young from an incurable disease: "I can't believe this happened to *you*" (emphasis added; *The Art Lover* 206), Carole writes in contrast to the conventional widow's response: "*I wasn't ready. I'm a widow*" (Gilbert, *Death's Door* 22). At the same time, the observing witness knows that the wounded storyteller uses narrative as much for himself as for her: "Probably he will hurt me more than I can possibly imagine. Certainly we will never be the same again" (*The Art Lover* 237). Together, they are learning to be together with stories, turning illness into a potent story about what Arthur Frank calls "other-relatedness," "this other *has to do with me, as I with it*" (Frank 35). As a result, the grieving narrator of *The Art Lover* claims a filial relationship with the beloved that transcends their time on earth together: "I will not leave his side. I will stay with him through whatever is to come. Of this I am sure. I will love him even more than I do now. He is my brother, and looking at him and knowing all of this, I realize that it is as perfect a moment on earth as I can expect" (*The Art Lover* 238).

Throughout the novel, whether functioning as fictional narrator or autobiographer, Maso focuses on the absent presence, discovering through the act of writing itself how to cope with her own mortality while mourning the death of the loved one. Placing loss within other contexts—astronomical, historical, and biblical—Maso enlarges the narrator's personal grief, which enables her to convert narratives of chaos—which are fundamentally antinarratives—to narratives of restoration, despite feelings of incredulity and powerlessness. Unlike Annunziata of *Christ in Concrete*, Carole/Caroline does not want to die with the beloved other, Gary/Steven. Through literature and art, the grieving Carole achieves life-sustaining distance by "making the dead die within rather than die with the dead" (Harrison, *The Dominion* 65). *The Art Lover* explores the creativity involved in finding such contexts for mourning. Inserting mini vignettes on the suffering, death, and afterlife of Jesus Christ, for example, Maso explores the spiritual dimensionality of grief and loss, transcending ideas about linearity and historical chronology. The story of Christ's Passion in Maso's hands is not confined by the usual order of events, a series of scenes told in a chronological and topographical order. Maso instead recalls bits and pieces of the Passion history, enhancing biblical account(s) with visual representations of Jesus Christ before and after his death, including references and details of Giotto's *Noli Me Tangere* and da Vinci's *The Last Supper*.

Christ appears in *The Art Lover* as art critic, as reciter of poetry, as guider of Catholic souls, as converser with Caroline, and, as a desiring man who wants to live beyond age thirty-three. Employing a form of prosopopoeia, Maso gives voice to the dead Jesus perhaps to suggest his resurrection, but more forcefully to demonstrate his profound understanding of the paradoxical nature of human grief. In his interpretation of Giotto's *Noli Me Tangere*, which depicts Christ's appearance to Mary Magdalene after his resurrection, Christ recognizes the artist's desire to formalize human grief by submitting it to ritualized lament as opposed to the primal desire to die with the dead. Appropriately titled "Jesus and the Lamentation" Jesus identifies Mary Magdalene as his mother, recognizing her role in the story of salvation as she provided for his needs, assisted at his crucifixion and burial, and discovered the empty tomb. Jesus then appears to the weeping Mary outside near the tomb and enjoins her not to cling to him, but to announce his resurrection to the brethren (John 20:11–18). In his evaluation of the artist's representation, Jesus explains: "Giotto sets off the frozen grief of the human mourning against the frantic movement of the weeping angels among the clouds, as if the figures on the ground are restrained by their collective duty to maintain the stability of the composition" (Maso, *The Art Lover* 111).

As if in response to that duty, Maso resumes the other fictional family narratives after writing of the death of Steven in "Winter" and Gary in "More Winter," lamenting her loss like Mary of Magdala, grateful for having ministered to their dying. Unable to believe entirely in the doctrine of resurrection, Caroline cannot answer Steven's question about the existence of God, but she feels the "dream of resurrection" breaking in her heart (*The Art Lover* 163). Concluding *The Art Lover* significantly in spring, Maso interprets the idea of resurrection in a distinctly corporeal manner. Plucking a strand from her fictional narrative about Caroline's brother Grey, who makes his living as an art restorer, Maso imagines and complicates the narrative of restoration for all her characters, including Jesus Christ, whose face has nearly vanished from da Vinci's *The Last Supper*. In their responses to the restoration of Christ's face, the fictionalized characters on Maso's pallet respond with various degrees of belief in the afterlife, but Caroline remains all possibility, grateful only for "having such a dream. I'm so high up, standing on the scaffold with Max and Mom, Grey and David. With Steven . . . I guess I'm still hoping we might rise. Or maybe, just perhaps, holding hands here through this final section, we've already risen" (*The Art Lover* 229).

Along with the other writers in this chapter, Carole Maso is telling stories about death. To do so, as Maso knows, is "always to get it wrong" (*The Art Lover* 199). In the autobiographical interlude of *The Art Lover*, Maso tells Gary that writing it down is getting it wrong, but "here, wanting you back, it's the closest I can get to heaven—where I like to picture you" (199). Sandra Gilbert references philosopher Michel de Certeau, adding that the dead are both "the subjects and *shapers* of narrative. For death is the end of all story as well as the mysterious blank out of which story starts and against which it sets itself while at the same time it is what is 'impossible to tell'" (*Death's Door* 97–98). In other words, even if it is written wrong (and it will be wrong), writing about the dead must be done. Mourning the loss of the loved one and learning how to live as a dying creature are painful human requirements. Similar to the genre of tragedy, mourning rituals, Susan Letzler Cole explains, are performances of "ambivalence on behalf of an absent presence" (1). For Carole Maso and the mourners represented in Italian American literature, the paradox of grieving comprises the desire to "sustain relationships with the (beloved) dead; at the same time, paradoxically, to collaborate in bringing these relationships to an end" (Cole 6). In each goodbye, there is a little death.

NARRATIVE DEATH

> We know we will die. This is our saving grace in a sense. No animal knows this but us. . . . It is our special sadness, this knowledge, and therefore a richness, a sanctification.
>
> —Don DeLillo, *The Names*

> Death of course is precocious: it always comes too soon; it always knows more than we do.
>
> —Mary Cappello, *Awkward: A Detour*

Textual endings, Robert Scholes writes, are a "kind of death," and readers of narrative resist concluding their engagement with a book because of the inevitability of it ending—"and the more pleasure the book is giving us the more strongly we feel this—we don't want it to end. We want it go on forever. But books, like lives, do not go on forever" (18, 19). The writers discussed in this chapter swerve away from narrating death as a final gesture or denouement in their conclusions; with the exception of Pietro di Donato's *Christ in Concrete* and, arguably, Carole Maso's *The Art Lover*, writers of Italian America resist this form of traditional narrative closure. The authors, like their dying loved ones, have borrowed their authority from death, to quote from Walter Benjamin, but they have not chosen to end their stories with this form of closure, perhaps recognizing that death always knows more than they do. Resisting the tendency to conclude their narratives with an authoritative portrayal of death, the writers featured here and in Italian American literature generally shift toward more open endings, rejecting not only the closure that death guarantees, but also suggesting their staying power as immigrant Italians to the new world, as Italian Americans, and as authors living and writing in America.

The kinds of endings readers of Italian American literature experience are more in sync with reprisals in the musical sense of that word than conclusions, perhaps a deliberate return on the part of authors to recall the oral traditions of their ancestors. Open-ended narratives attract attention not for their evasion of traditional closure, but for their desire to inscribe tendencies in contrast to conventional linear time and unified endings. Lack of closure allows authors of Italian America to assert equal familiarity with oral traditions stemming from ancestral stories and with technically innovative narrative traditions, beginning in the late nineteenth-century with European and American novels. Open-ended narratives illuminate the tendency in Italian American works to reprise, or, to return to an earlier story time and theme, and, closely related, to anticipate a different narrative future in which characters are verging on a threshold, a new beginning, an onset at the narrative's end. Reprisals and anticipation are at times simultaneously enacted, and, while those processes of closure may seem contradictory, Wallace Martin argues that narrative plots are infected by contradiction: "the use of both 'tieing up' and 'unraveling' to describe endings is not an accidental looseness of usage but an inherent undecidability in language and thought. . . . The dialectic of desire and satisfaction cannot be stopped" (85).

As though in response to the impossibility of achieving narrative fulfillment through the plot's conclusion, authors of Italian America reveal the dialectic of desire and satisfaction in their endings. From Rosa Cassettari's as-told-to autobiography of immigrant life to Tony Ardizzone's portrayal of folkloric communities in his novel, *In the Garden of Papa Santuzzu*, the desire to begin the story again determines how endings are told and written. Rosa Cassettari certainly continued her storytelling adventures in Chicago after Marie Hall Ets interviewed her in the early part of the twentieth century. Yet Marie's desire to see Rosa's story in print continued well past Rosa's lifetime. In collaboration with several influential voices who shepherded the work into print, Ets succeeded after a long hiatus in seeing the story of Rosa's life (with Marie's authorial imprimatur) published in 1970. Satisfaction achieved? Rosa's final words expose unfinished business in her beloved homeland as she desires to return to Italia equipped with the imperial English language. Such desire is less nostalgic than didactic, for Rosa refuses to be demeaned any longer by the religious authorities of her embattled youth. But she never returns, so the story must be retold. Hope remains unfulfilled.

Contemporary writers John Fante and Mari Tomasi conclude their respective novels, *Wait Until Spring, Bandini* and *Like Lesser Gods* in an open-ended manner by suggesting that their stories will continue, despite the sorrow of abandonment and loss. Fante uses ellipses marks after his concluding word, "snowflake," thereby inviting the reader to fill in the space, and speculate on a narrative with which he or she is familiar: the impoverished lives of the Bandini family and the objective correlative of that destitution: the cold, unyielding terrain of the Coloradan landscape. Their sad story will begin again. Beginning and ending in medias res, Tomasi continues the story of Granitetown after Pietro's death, resisting the desire to authorize herself as grim reaper for the elder statesman of that community: Mister Tiff. With a self-referential wink to the activity of narrating an ending, Tomasi writes: "[Mister Tiff] reflected that if he were a character in a book the author might seize upon this moment to bring his aging life to an end. But blood, not ink, flowed from his heart" (288). Rather than functioning merely as a denouement, Tomasi's final chapter functions more like an "after-history" common to epilogues, in which "loose ends" are allowed to drift into the future, serving to "graft the novel, which when read is apart from life, back onto the real time of history, joining it and the reader to our world" (Martin 84). Tomasi thus offers her readers a "story in the company of the storyteller," establishing companionship between teller, tale, and listener (Benjamin 100).

Tina De Rosa and Tony Ardizzone elude traditional closure, recall oral Italian storytelling traditions, and graft narrative time onto historical time. Grandparental figures loom in their conclusions as present speakers, not as lost loved ones. On the final page of *Paper Fish*, Carmolina reminds her Grandma that "nothing goes away;" De Rosa uses an epilogue in her conclusion as a framing device to bracket the community lives of Italian Americans in a continuous present, aware that the real time of history has vanquished the Little Italy of her youth. De Rosa emphasizes narrative and historical continuity that is underscored by naming, linking four generations, from Great-grandmother Carmella to her great-granddaughter, Carmolina, who has internalized the determination and creativity necessary for her future role as storyteller.

Similar to De Rosa, Ardizzone also frames his tale with the voice of Rosa Dolci, wife of Salvatore, the third son of Papa Santuzzu, but also the cantastorie of the Santuzzu extended family. Rosa retells the stories of her ancestors to her grandchildren while they are visiting Sicilia, permitting Ardizzone to reach beyond Little Italies and to historicize "the land that time forgot" (337). In passing the story on to her grandchildren, Rosa simultaneously relives and lives past the past, confessing her never-ending sorrow over abandoning Santuzzu for the new world: "we left him, alone to die" (335). Rosa Dolci's sorrow, like her historical predecessor, Rosa Cassettari, is sweetened by the storyteller's ability to "give voice to our true songs and stories" (Ardizzone, *In the Garden* 339).

Sorrow pervades the narratives of Mario Puzo's *The Fortunate Pilgrim*, Dorothy Bryant's *Miss Giardino* and Josephine Gattuso Hendin's *The Right Thing to Do*, but narrative anticipation controls the conclusions of their respective works. In each narrative ending, the female protagonists are poised on a threshold, symbolizing a moment of transition and an illumination of the opposing demands of separate worlds. Despite their different circumstances, these women are not lighting out "for the Territory ahead of the rest," as Huckleberry amiably expressed at the conclusion of his episodic journey (Twain, *Huckleberry Finn* 245). Rather, their point of beginning occurs at narrative conclusions inflected by a world of childhood mourning and adult independence.

Self-reflexively ushering in "the happy end to this story," Puzo's concluding chapter of *The Fortunate Pilgrim* examines Lucia Santa's difficult leave-taking of her Tenth Avenue tenement of forty years for a tree-lined street on Long Island. Paralyzed by the moment of transition, Lucia Santa, instead of moving toward the door, sits "on the backless kitchen chair" and weeps (279, 280). Lucia Santa's sorrowful past has developed in her a threshold of pain in excess of anything she could have imagined. To commemorate requires that she sit on a backless chair, the literalization of her impoverishment, the symbol of the support she was compelled to find within herself. But she gets up and goes. The story begins again. Like Lucia Santa, Anna Giardino leaves her home of decades on Phoenix Street for greener emotional pastures. Bryant employs the metaphor of the phoenix to describe Anna's reinvention after suffering a traumatic childhood and prolonged psychological aftereffects in adulthood. Crossing the threshold into a healthier life, the sixty-eight-year-old Anna is emotionally reborn, embracing a freedom in contrast to the one she sought in becoming a financially autonomous professional woman. Reconstructing her private life ultimately gives Anna the freedom to embrace without fear her mother's spirituality. Proclaiming "angel wings!" in the conclusion, Anna Giardino moves past the painful scenario of her immigrant past and toward a future filled, at last, with hope.

Equally hopeful is Gina Giardello's threshold experience at the conclusion of Hendin's *The Right Thing to Do*. A young woman, Gina is poised to test the implications of her hard-won independence. Unlike Santa Lucia and Anna whose age influences (but does not undermine) the anticipatory nature of their narrative conclusions, Gina's youthfulness places her at the juncture between old-world demands and new-world lures. That she, unlike the older women, is outdoors at night, walking toward New York City, attests to her desire and recognition that the city will enable her expression of individualism unknown to her fictional sisters. Unwilling, however, to eschew familial responsibility, Gina's age nonetheless affords her the luxury of putting that issue on the back burner, uttering at the conclusion a future promise to her deceased father, "'someday I'll write you a letter.' But it was the bridge arching, the white wind soaring, the chilling purity that made the night right" (211). The right thing for Gina is the pleasure of urban mobility—anticipation—

with the promise of family reconnection on her own terms and in her own time. Clearly, Gina aims to carry the voices of her heritage with her into her future.

Portraying suffering, death, and mourning in an effort to make certain that Italians in America were perceived if not accepted as more than expendable laborers, metonymically reduced body parts, authors performed an inestimable pedagogical service in fleshing out hearts and souls. The topic of death gave writers permission to insist on the profoundly human nature of their grief-stricken characters, aligning them more centrally within the American family. The folk materials offered by storytelling characters to their families and communities are lessons in survival and lessons for the future, reinforcing the fact that relationships change but do not end after death. For good and bad, these stories are internalized by the next generation—"the voices we carry within us"— as Maria Gillan writes (*Where I Come From* 69). U.S. writers of Italian America examine how you carry your ethnic history with you, not always as a burden, but often in useful and unanticipated ways. Mary Cappello interprets the craft of rosary making as a way for her grieving Aunt Josephine to devise a "poetics of loss, a way of confronting emptiness" (*Night Bloom* 229). "Sensual as a nipple," a rosary bead reattaches one to a palpable sense of "something held," and it reconnects Mary not only to her Aunt but also to a "homespun theory" of the Catholic Church, which she finds more amenable (*Night Bloom* 230). Usefully, Cappello converts the family handicraft of rosary making to a communal legacy that insures a more sustained relationship to her family, connecting them like a cord, like beads on a string: "Rather than saying the rosary, my family should have gone for walks hand in hand. We should have walked and walked" (*Night Bloom* 241).

Used as a source of strength, the ethnic history and stories of Italian America teach important lessons about survival and human commitment. Like Persephone returning, writers of Italian America portray death as a story of continuity, a story about how things change, but don't end. For all his distancing measures to separate himself from his cultural history, Nick Shay of Don DeLillo's *Underworld* lives with "ten thousand uprooted tales" that he claims his teacher in the Bronx, Albert Bronzini, inherited (472). After his mother dies, Nick emphasizes the ineluctability of family ties, the quality of continuity of life after loss: "When my mother died I felt expanded, slowly, durably, over time. I felt suffused with her truth, spread through, as with water, color or light. I thought she'd entered the deepest place I could provide, the animating entity, the thing, if anything, that will survive my own last breath, and she makes me larger, she amplifies my sense of what it is to be human. She is part of me now, total and consoling. And it is not sadness to acknowledge that she had to die before I could know her fully. It is only a statement of the power of what comes after" (804).

U.S. writers of Italian America continue to tell stories of the power of what comes after. Valuing the significance of folkloric voices, writers innovatively examine how the folk wisdom of their culture enables new voices as they resist oppressions of silence and misunderstanding. The concluding chapter examines how Italian American writers managed throughout the twentieth century to keep ancestral stories available for future storytelling generations.

8

Revival/Risorgimento

⟡

Stories Continue

SHAPING U.S. ITALIAN AMERICAN WRITING

Chi va piano, va sano e va lontano.
One who goes slowly, goes soundly, goes far.

—Italian proverb

The storyteller joins the ranks of the teachers and sages. . . . The storyteller is the figure in which the righteous man encounters himself.

—Walter Benjamin, *Illuminations*

REVIVAL, ITALIAN AMERICAN STYLE

From the voices of justice to the voices of mortality, Italian Americans have adapted folk materials from their ancestors' *paesi* to create artful narratives that resist oppressions of silence, overlaying them with individual and communal uses of voice. The English word "revival," the first part of this concluding chapter's title, with its emphasis on restoration and reintroduction, suggests the usefulness of retrieval in an effort to restore to vitality *and* to restore to general use and acceptance (*OED* 2531). Its Italian quasi-equivalent, "risorgimento," functions to ballast the

211

activity of retrieval, and yet its meaning carries a more weighty significance. The revolutionary movement known as il Risorgimento began in early nineteenth-century Italy and led to the proclamation of the Kingdom of Italy (1861) and its partial unification (1871), establishing northern Italian governmental control of all regions. Despite Garibaldi's successful defeat of the Bourbon forces by way of Sicily, southern Italians in particular felt the sting of being "conquered" by their own country— the Piedmontese government, which was as foreign to those in the Mezzogiorno as the idea of nationalism itself as many "had never encountered the term *Italia* before" (Duggan 135, 130).

Of the many rebellions that erupted after unification, including local strikes by farm and sulfur workers in Sicily, popularly known as the *Fasci siciliani*, aimed to "mobilise the peasants and improve their pay," which was crushed by the Crispi government (Duggan 167), no rebellion was fiercer than leaving their old villages in a new nation that ignored their economic needs. In the peak years of their migration—1880–1910— Italians left a country that did not exist as a nation for them *until* they left it en masse. Their emigration from their homeland was an uprising that comprised "the final and most emphatic protest of all—the mass exodus of millions of Italians in forthcoming generations who were no longer able to tolerate the economic and political inequities decreed by the new government in the name of progress and social justice" (Mangione and Morreale 61). While the Italian migration was part of a changing global economy that enabled emigrants from many countries to leave, migration effectively allowed disenfranchised Italian rural workers and artisans to use mobility as an act of resistance against a newly unified Italy. In America, immigrants became Italian. In America, Italian Americans became European. Writers of Italian America empathized deeply with the stories they heard from parents, extended families, and communities, incorporating voices of folk wisdom and individualism into a multivocal canon that reflects and enhances U.S. multiethnic writing, part and parcel of the verbal productions of U.S. writers.

One of the central ways Italian American works have been revitalized is through the intertwining activities of book reprinting and classroom teaching. Susan VanZanten Gallagher explains that a critical perspective that highlights the way "social, ethnic, and gender positions construct aesthetic and cultural value" helps to reinforce the preeminence of *how* one reads, opening up further discussion regarding the material conditions in place that make it possible to read works and adopt them for teaching on syllabi (55). If we accept Gallagher's assertion that "pedagogy often begins the canonical process rather than existing only as a product of that process" (66), then we might better appreciate the inseparable nexus of manuscript publishing, personal advocacy, word-of-mouth sponsorship, prescient publishers, scholarly critiques, conference panels, book exhibits, and, not the least—syllabi inclusion.[1] When all is said and done, the classroom and the syllabus insure the reinforcement of a book *maintaining* visibility and, whether or not it is taught to students as noncanonical, it is received, as Jeffrey Insko explains, by students as canonical (346), echoing John Guillory's explanation that individual works "confront their receptors first as canonical, as cultural capital" (56). The 1996 republication of Tina De Rosa's *Paper Fish* is a vivid example of the intimate connection between the pedagogical and the canonical.

In 1980, with a press run of only one thousand copies, the Wine Press published its one and only novel: Tina De Rosa's *Paper Fish*. The book's publication was made possible, in part, by grants from the National Endowment for the Arts and the Illinois Arts Council, to whom the publisher gratefully acknowledged on the copyright page of the first edition. What material conditions and fortuitous events led to this novel's eventual republication by the Feminist Press sixteen years after it was first published, helping to insure its continual visibility into the future? An "underground phenomenon," to borrow from Mary Helen Washington's description of the devotees of *Their Eyes Were Watching God* ("Foreword" x), took place that kept alive De Rosa's virtually unknown novel until it acquired an institutional support system that marks it as one of the earliest canonized books in Italian America.

The "Risorgimento" began in Chicago, De Rosa's hometown. Before the literature of Italian America had any visibility as a field of inquiry or a discipline of specialization, Fred Gardaphé, then a professor at Columbia College in Chicago, initiated the process of recovery on behalf of Tina De Rosa's novel. The first critic to write about *Paper Fish*, Gardaphé reflects the importance of word of mouth and personal advocacy on behalf of the undiscovered work: "I gave a copy to every major literary figure I could find. I must have photocopied it [*Paper Fish*] 100 times. I met publishers and I sent them copies, and they all said it was 'too literary for our press'" (Gardaphé; qtd. in Lauerman 3). Undeterred and unconvinced, Gardaphé introduced the book to Florence Howe, then director of the Feminist Press, whom he auspiciously met at a working-class studies conference. A publishing house based at the City University of New York, the Feminist Press reclaims the works of women, especially working-class writers, and keeps their books in print.

Florence Howe's response to Tina De Rosa's *Paper Fish* echoes another small publishing house in Seattle committed to women writers, Seal Press, and publisher Faith Conlon's exuberant response to the African writer's, Tsitsi Dangarembga's *Nervous Conditions*, a few years earlier (Gallagher 58). Howe relates: "I read it the first night I got it from Fred and gave it to somebody else in the office who read it the second night. . . . We were so bowled over that we sent it to Louise DeSalvo, an Italian American writer who could not believe she didn't know about it. She gave us a quote [blurb] [(for the book jacket)], calling it 'the best Italian-American novel by a woman in this century.' Most of the other people we sent it to or discussed it with said that they knew about it, that they had photocopies" (qtd. in Lauerman, 3).

Louise DeSalvo's superlative praise for *Paper Fish* on its front cover was indeed a gesture of canonization. That the activity of reclamation on behalf of De Rosa's novel gained momentum initially through word-of-mouth attests to the commitment of those scholars and writers who refused to stop talking about *Paper Fish*, perhaps also testimonial to a culture whose oral traditions continue to influence their way of being in the world. When De Rosa first published *Paper Fish*, she also wrote an essay for the now-defunct magazine, *Attenzione*, titled "An Italian-American Woman SPEAKS OUT," proclaiming the preeminence of her voice inflected by her cultural background: "full of color, loud music, loud voices" (38).

Initiating the process of canonization for Italian American women writers, Helen Barolini included a selection from *Paper Fish* in her self-described literary manifesto, *The Dream Book: An Anthology of Writings by Italian American Women*, first published in 1985, five years after the publication of De Rosa's novel. Intending to establish "once and for all, that we exist, we are writers, we are part of the national literature" (qtd. in Ahearn 47), Barolini unlocked the historical and social constraints that limited perceptions of the contributions of Italian American women, not the least of which were the literary hegemonies and oversights of the American publishing world. Barolini's understandable desire to establish "once and for all" that such writers exist belies the malleable and mercurial nature of canons themselves.[2] What Barolini's anthology and Florence Howe's advocacy began was the reintroduction of a work's presumed worthiness to be read, to be taken seriously. The canonical process continued with what Henry Louis Gates describes as a "second-order reflection upon those primary texts that define a tradition and its canon" ("Criticism in the Jungle" 8) with critics such as Fred

Gardaphé and Edvige Giunta leading the way. Giunta's Afterword to the republication of *Paper Fish* reinstated the rich, material specificity of De Rosa's novel: the complication of cross-cultural identities, the idealization and mythologizing of community, and the intersection between immigrant memory and working-class history.[3]

Second-order reflections have potential to enlarge the discursive power of previously noncanonical writers through critical engagement in multiple forums, including the creation of the Italian American Discussion group at the Modern Language Association, which had its inaugural session in the 1998 December convention in San Francisco.[4] In addition, classroom teaching instrumentally assures the ongoing process of canon production, and republication of previously invisible works assures continual reintroduction of them on the syllabus. The concurrent development of Italian American Studies Programs within the academy lends legitimacy to the enterprise of retrieval not only of literature but also of the complicated history of subaltern cultures.[5]

The extended example of *Paper Fish*'s resurrection within the academy reflects the emphasis placed on the cultural worth of certain literatures and specific texts. Thus it is not surprising that arguably the most visible work by an Italian American woman writer emerges out of high modernism with an affinity to that avatar of such writing, Virginia Woolf. That Tina De Rosa's *Paper Fish* was my initial choice of text to interpret through the lens of modernism but within the realm of a realist story reflected in the late 1980s my cognizance of academic critical discourse that values high-literary reading practices and my desire to reinstate the value of ethnic realism that functions, as Rita Felski writes, as a "vital part of oppositional discourse" to postmodern and highbrow modernist literary canons (qtd. in Rimstead 183).

Tina De Rosa's literary experimentalism meets with historical realism in *Paper Fish*, producing, as Josephine Hendin writes, "innovative forms [that] juxtapose social realism with inventive symbolism and language" ("Social Constructions and Aesthetic Achievements" 18). That is but one interpretive lens through which to read *Paper Fish*, and my inclusion of the term "historical realism" may be greeted with skepticism when one observes De Rosa's tendencies toward ethnic chauvinism regarding her representation of the Italian community. A counterreading insists on De Rosa's resistance to hegemonic American culture, her carving out a space of containment, honoring an invisible and silenced people, their neighborhood destroyed. Readers cannot leave the text without hearing their poetic and accented voices.

Groundbreaking work published on ethnic writers in fact began with theorizing vernacular and oral traditions, narrative and language, folklore and myth, genre and gender, producing a multiplicity of meanings that do not emphasize or value one original truth. The publication of Jerre Mangione's *Mount Allegro* preceded by several decades the secondary discourse that followed, but this memoir's devotion to oral traditions makes it optimum for such analysis. In yet another reprinting of Mangione's memoir, *Mount Allegro* recently earned the debatable distinction of a "minor classic of American literature," and was bestowed the New Critical compliment of "high level of artistry," code words—along with "minor classic"—that potentially anchor ethnic works tenuously and unequally within traditional literary discourse (Nassar, "Foreword" ix). Possessing formal qualities of its own that merit discussion, *Mount Allegro* continues to resist being minoritized aesthetically or linguistically, simultaneously embracing storytelling traditions of ordinary folk and narrative sophistication in style and tone.

If we look again at Jerre Mangione's generically slippery work of autobiographical fiction/memoir/oral history/communal biography, the style of writing that is elaborated by multiple voices and subdued by folktale morality, we will hear a ventriloquial voice—hybridic, some theorists may prefer—that could have only been produced in early twentieth-century America by immigrants incorporating dialectal Sicilian and various levels of English.[6] A rudimentary impulse insists on reading Mangione's memoir back through vernacular traditions, but also forward, into an analysis of the "cultural work" (to use Jane Tompkins's felicitous phrase) Mangione performed by writing such a book. As Robert Scholes reminds us, "reading has two faces," which includes both backward and forward movements (7, 8). Whether or not engaged in semiotics, as critics of literature, applying dialectical approaches to interpretation enable complex cultural critiques of emergent literatures, including works of Italian America.

Ensuring a body of published texts continues to inform the process of revitalization for literary Italian America. Despite the ominous fact that book culture itself seems to have receded in the millennium,[7] a book still signifies a "'manifest discourse' . . . more so than tattered photocopies of journal articles," or novels, I might add (Luke and Gore 2). The poststructuralist agenda which rejects foundational truths necessarily puts into question fixed ideas about the individual, but just as feminine subjectivity remains central to feminist theories, historically laden cultural subjectivity continues to be part of a critical discourse on literary texts with ethnicity as an underlying focus. As bell hooks points out, "It's easy to give up identity, when you've got one" (qtd. in Luke and Gore 6). Similar to feminist theoretical projects, ethnic literary discourses are often loath to abandon the subject. If we keep in mind Antonio Gramsci's idea of hegemonic subjects, we might be able to appreciate the cultural work Italian American texts perform in creating counterhegemonies within their writings, calling for a "sustained probing of the text's various positionings via hegemonic ideologies" (Palumbo-Liu 22 n. 4).

Counterreadings are interventionist in purpose: they map out, as David Palumbo-Liu explains, "possible spaces of resistance" (2). Remaining alert to the ways that critical attention to ethnic literature can be contained and co-opted by "discourses that ultimately defer to mono-cultural prescriptions of 'aesthetic value'" thereby managing and neutralizing textual conflict and tension (Palumbo-Liu 6, 12), scholars must fruitfully theorize oppositional readings that articulate counterhegemonic textual practices. Such work (articulated within the ethnic text and discussed within the academy) is an act of resistance (on the part of authors and their interlocutors) and a probative decision to raise consciousness on the part of new readers.

Institutionalization of a developing canon within Italian American letters must be met with a vigilant eye for its inheritors. David Palumbo-Liu explains that "[u]pon being brought in from the margins, [minority discourse] . . . loses its latitude as a counterdiscourse and its ability to designate a shifting open space outside the hegemonic" (17). Or, as Toni Morrison puts it, "There must be a way to enhance canon readings without enshrining them" ("The Afro-American Presence" 205). The analysis of Italian American literature within the academy faces a similar challenge of being subsumed under the rubric of "homogenized difference," and managed in such a way as to erase, or at least, neutralize conflict (Palumbo-Liu 5). Imagine a world of Mister Tiffs easing tensions, mending fissures, and smoothing the ground of a rough-hewn cultural history. That the study of Italian America is presently sequestered at my university within a "European Language" Department, given "minor" status, its literature ignored as a category of both "American" and "multiethnic" literature from the perspective of the "English" Department, confused and sometimes merged with "Italian" literature, or taught as an add-on in American literature courses, both threatens and dilutes its cultural vitality *and* inspires broader conceptions of U.S. writing that is culturally resonant and invitingly comparative.[8]

A case history from the annals of American literature reveals the changing currents of historical and political life that made visible cultural productions by second-generation Italian Americans. In the first half of the twentieth century, the late nineteen thirties were the most literary of times for Italian Americans, and might have potentially insured their fuller inclusion within the national literature. Their literary visibility occurred during a historical juncture that valued—at least temporarily—the voices of working-class writers from various ethnic groups before processes were set in motion that silenced them for the next half century.

LITERARY ITALIAN AMERICA:
A CASE STUDY FROM THE 1930S

In *Canons and Contexts*, Paul Lauter cites three influential factors responsible for the progressive elimination of black, white female, and all working-class writers from the American literary canon: "The professionalization of the teaching of literature, the development of an aesthetic theory that privileged certain texts, and the historiographic organization of the body of literature into conventional 'periods' and 'themes'" (27). The erasure of literary Italian America is due partly to these factors.

In the late 1970s and early 1980s Lauter surveyed the territory of "American literature" drawn after World War I, which produced "an essentially new, academic canon . . . [which] exerted an increasingly hegemonic force in American culture" (Lauter, *Canons and Contexts* 23). Around the same time, Jane Tompkins showed how editors of anthologies were "active shapers of the canon" (188), and judgments about literary values changed dramatically during the first sixty years of the twentieth century, that is, roughly from Fred Lewis Pattee's 1919 anthology, *Century Readings for a Course in American Literature* to Perry Miller et al.'s 1962 *Major Writers of America*, in which "the notion of who counted as a 'major writer' and even the concept of the 'major writer' had altered dramatically. Whereas Pattee's single volume, compiled at the close of World War I, contained hundreds of writers, Miller's much larger two-volume work, published at the close of the Cold War, contained only twenty-eight" (188). In 1919, Fred Lewis Pattee, one of the "earliest professors of American literature" included in *Century Readings* the works of Harriet Beecher Stowe, Mary Wilkins Freeman, Sarah Orne Jewett, Helen Hunt Jackson, Rose Terry Cooke and more. Less than twenty years later, Howard Mumford Jones and Ernest E. Leisy published *Major American Writers* (1935), which includes early American writers such as William Byrd and Philip Freneau, but no women at all, until "later additions included Dickinson to their canon" (Lauter, *Canons and Contexts* 25, 26).[9]

Many factors contributed to the exclusion of ethnically identified writers from anthologies and syllabi, not the least of which was the way the teaching of literature and reading choices shifted in the 1920s to academic professionals, who were mostly male and white: "professors, educators, critics, the arbiters of taste of the 1920s, were, for the most part, college-educated white men of Anglo-Saxon or northern European origins [and felt] a quickening demand for some power and control over their lives from Slavic, Jewish, Mediterranean, and Catholic immigrants from Europe, as well as black immigrants from the rural south" (Lauter, *Canons and Contexts* 28).[10] In their separate genealogies of American literary anthologies, both Lauter and Tompkins showcased the processes set in motion by editors themselves, who, in their untested acceptance of the inherent value of literary works, did not or refused to *recognize* "their own role in determining which are the truly great works" (Tompkins 188).

With this genealogical overview of the development of the academic canon, it would seem fairly impossible—given the majority of anthologists' aims—for Italian American literature to filter through, and, for the most part, such literature was not placed on reading lists in American universities.[11] The decade of the 1930s nonetheless experienced a literary reprieve of historical import, which validated immigrant and minority writing. As Jane Tompkins explains, despite the New Critical regulatory method of close reading, which focused narrowly on language and form, "*literary* judgments of value do not depend on literary considerations alone, since the notion of what is literary is defined by and nested within changing historical conditions" (195). The Depression was one such historical condition which shifted, at least momentarily, the literary landscape. As Tompkins clarifies, historical conditions

> are not external to the systems of valuation that they modify, but are themselves articulated within them. Thus for example, the economic conditions of the Depression that called attention to working class, immigrant, and minority experience, could have been seen and described as they were only from within a value system that already insisted on the importance of the common man and took seriously the sufferings of ordinary people. (195)

In terms of publication and visibility, arguably the most successful writers of Italian descent during the Depression era were John Fante,

Jerre Mangione, and Pietro di Donato, though each was progressively erased from literary and academic purview after World War II, due to equally influential historical conditions to which I will return.[12] These writers established vital connections to the American publishing world, achieved early success and support from powerful literary advocates, and called attention to immigrant struggles in their writing. They came of age at a time when other working-class writers—Agnes Smedley, Tillie Olsen, Mike Gold, and Meridel LeSueur—to name just a few, were also writing and seeing print. Having achieved a visible presence in American letters did not guarantee secondary critical discussion, which then benefited from canonical practices within the academy that kept such works in favor.

In his chapter, "Left Out: Three Italian American Writers of the 1930s," Fred Gardaphé poses three possibilities for the limited critical attention given to Fante, di Donato, and Mangione during a historical juncture when such writing was kept visible through anthologies and critical practice. Echoing Paul Lauter's earlier survey of the 1920s literary canon, Gardaphé attributes the following reasons for the exclusion of these writers from further consideration: historical periodization, interpretive theoretical models, and the religious orientation of these writers. The construction of historical categories excluded Italian American writers who published *late* in the 1930s, and more often in the 1940s, which, "contributed to their being left out, as evidenced by Warren French, who writes that '1939 and 1940 marked not only the end of an era in social and political history, but the end of a literary generation, especially in the creation of the social novel'" (Gardaphé, *Leaving* 55).[13] Not so for Italian American writers of the second generation, who were only beginning to mark the era with cultural productions inflected by *class* and *ethnic* considerations.

Second, one of the dominant critical approaches applied to examining Depression-era literature of the 1930s focused on Marxist criticism that "privileges class-conscious texts over those texts that emphasize ethnic, gender, or racial issues," which would seem perhaps to favor Italian American writers (Gardaphé, *Leaving* 55). Not so explains Gardaphé, for the established critics of the day considered the writings of a di Donato, for example (with his stated refusal to abide by literary prescriptions or efface class or ethnic identity), "neither politically charged nor stylistically innovative" (*Leaving* 57).[14] The linguistic innovation inscribed within *Christ in Concrete* demonstrates substantive artistry that connects di Donato to modernist writers of the early twentieth century. But given the rather traditional structures of many second-generation Italian

American narratives, inclusive of di Donato, it becomes excusable to overlook them, despite stylistic innovations that merge European oral traditions, including folktales, with developmental narratives. As Gardaphé explains, "All three writers wrote episodic bildungromans in the naturalist or realist tradition—more obviously influenced by Dreiser and Dostoyevsky than by Eliot and Joyce. Thus caught between the two dominant reading modes traditionally applied to texts of the period, their work falls through the critical cracks into an oblivion that would only be detected long after publication" (*Leaving* 57).[15]

Superadded to the constraints of periodization and the shifting attitudes these writers took toward communist party politics (except for Fante, whose characters deliberately dis-identify with working-class matters), Gardaphé's third claim focuses on the issue of religion. As discussed in chapter 2 on faith, traditional Italian American Catholicism was at odds with the more doctrinal form of institutionalized American Catholicism controlled by the Irish. As different as they were stylistically, Fante, di Donato, and Mangione were devoted philosophically to a brand of Catholicism at odds with a desire for American assimilation *and* in conflict with American Catholic traditions. Fante's portrayal of characters with abiding connections to an Italian Marianist Catholicism, di Donato's decision to conclude *Christ in Concrete* with a devotional rather than a revolutionary ending, and Mangione's cognizance that his virulently antifascist principles were not in conflict with his brand of Catholicism, served, according to Gardaphé, to impede their being documented by 1930s critical culture: "These three writers are but a few of the many unstudied voices who can reward a revisionist history of the 1930s from the perspective of Italian American ethnicity" (*Leaving* 65).

For all their publication successes, these writers did not reap the benefits of sustained secondary discourses or anthology inclusion (within the academy) until the latter part of the twentieth century. Initially receiving high praise from contemporary critics, Fante and Mangione in particular managed to get their other works published.[16] If the most lauded and most visible writers of 1930s Italian America, John Fante, Pietro di Donato, and Jerre Mangione, were underrecognized during an era that prioritized immigrant voices, then it's not hard to imagine less visible writers of Italian America doomed to a longer-term obscurity, which extended into the latter half of the twentieth century. Writers of Italian America did not experience a literary resurgence until the 1980s; unlike the 1930s example, however, attention continues to be paid to their literature in the millennium.

Studs Terkel proclaims in the preface to the republication of *Christ in Concrete*, "1939 was the year for me." It was certainly the year for di Donato and for the trio of Italian American writers whose work was acclaimed during the years 1938 to 1942, from Fante's critically acclaimed *Wait Until Spring, Bandini* to Mangione's best-seller *Mount Allegro*. Momentum typically rewards, but for Italian Americans nationwide, World War II intervened and erected a massive road-block that took more than one bricoleur to dismantle. Movements for social change in the 1960s spurred Italian Americans to make concerted efforts to restore visibility to their writers. The establishment of the American Italian Historical Association in 1967 partly enabled this process. Emphasizing "scientific research . . . in search of objective knowledge" (Cavaioli 1), this academic association initially reflected the same desire of the New Critics in postwar 1950s, who struggled to "establish literary language as a special mode of knowledge" (Tompkins 194), thereby promoting a kind of scientific rigor that was slow to develop interpretive frameworks for the study of literary Italian America. Primarily comprised of social scientists, the American Italian Historical Association was nonetheless willing to cross borders intellectually, convening in 1969 to discuss "The Italian American Novel," the publication year of Mario Puzo's bestselling *The Godfather*, to which I will later return.

Suffice it to say, fifty years after their mass migration, Italians in 1940s America were "the largest foreign-group in the United States" (DiStasi, "How World War II" 169), and "visibly moving toward the central currents of literary and cultural history" (Viscusi, *Buried Caesars* 95). Once Italy became an enemy nation, however, Italians in America (especially those who had not taken out their citizenship papers), were considered enemy aliens. According to Lawrence DiStasi, "with this designation came a series of blows . . . that frightened, fractured, dispersed, and silenced most Italian Americans for a generation" (170). Robert Viscusi examines the course of Pietro di Donato's literary career interwoven with this history, and, while his conclusions can be contested, his analysis of di Donato's engagement with immigrant memories is eminently persuasive:

World War II had discredited Fascism. The peace discredited Communism. After World War II, U.S. Italians wanted to forget their history of violent political expression because both the Fascist Right and the Communist Left had become positions for pariahs. During the 1950s and 1960s, as U.S. Italians set about forgetting their Italian languages and customs in favor of Anglo-American languages and customs, they also industriously went about forgetting their own past. . . . [D]i Donato was still there [in the 1960s], where other U.S. Italians had left him thirty years earlier: still Italian, still radical. (*Buried Caesars* 105)

Pietro di Donato's resistance to dominant discourse places his work alongside other ethnic texts that compel a probing of this work's oppositional perspective in contrast to dominant American beliefs. Nontraditional in all things—religious, political and literary—di Donato and his 1930s literary brothers, Fante and Mangione, managed in different ways to disrupt an idealist paradigm about Italian American family life and its patriarchal master narrative that insists on the supremacy of male authority and family cohesion.

In the 1930s when the majority of the second generation was assimilating into American society, their writers were puncturing the nostalgia that attends those who chose not to remember their ancestors' vexed history. Revisiting writers of the 1930s enables a critical conversation that actively resists cultural erasure. The material specificities that make writers of Italian America part of ethnic American literature include a resistance to the prevalent discourses about benevolent patriarchy and unaided bootstrapping mobility, triumphalist narratives in the Italian American imaginary that simplified complex images and active resistance regarding the difficult measures taken toward assimilation. Refusing to succumb to an uncritical allegiance to their story of diaspora, writers of the 1930s and beyond have explored the contradictory demands of assimilation and the acquisition of whiteness. Italian Americans may have been historically coded as racially distinct from other whites, but their literature in large part focuses on their European antecedents in their regular use of oral traditions and Italian cultural codes that marked their behavior.

Creating stories about linguistic loss, poverty and social justice, Italian Americans write narratives that function as a "minority revolt against Americanization."[17] Their narratives of resistance unflinchingly portray the responses to being colonized by a homeland that starved them and a new world that exploited them. Writers of Italian America developed compensatory narratives as measures of protection and beauty, barricading themselves from a chaos that inherently negates the possibility of remedy, progress, contentment—storytelling, itself. As Gregory S. Jay explains, much of the work of ethnic writers "tries to recover traditions rather than rebel against them," having experienced "the historic destruction of dominated (sub)cultures by privileged classes" ("The End" 23).

Such recovery eschews essentialism. Citing the work of Michael M. J. Fischer, Jay also argues that "ethnicity is less an essence than a constantly traversed borderland of differences," or, as Fischer puts it "'something reinvented and reinterpreted in each generation by each individual'" (qtd. in Jay "The End" 23). In contrast to depictions of harmonious Italian American life in media representations, writers of Italian America recognized that their process of recollection, as Jay explains, "does not entail a simple nostalgia or the dream of recreating a lost world: more painfully and complexly it involves a risky translation of recovered fragments into imagined futures by way of often hostile presents" ("The End" 23). Like other ethnic writers, Italian Americans have necessarily managed to distance themselves from the lives within the stories they have told, thereby inscribing mediation into their narratives, making storytelling itself possible.

TOWARD THE SHAPING OF U.S. WRITING BY ITALIAN AMERICANS

Those of us devoted to the ongoing recovery of Italian American writers from obscurity must recognize the necessity of assuming a "troubled, self-conscious relationship with sources and traditions" (Rinehart, "Feminist Theorizing" 73), especially because we are chin-deep involved in determining how this literature will be perceived, valued, and interpreted in the future. Introducing underrepresented texts to readers requires an awareness of the intersection between redefined modes of scholarship and pedagogy. It is not enough to exclaim that placing newly restored texts on a syllabus is an act of canon reformation, but one must also challenge the idea of those works as reinforcing eternal truths or as centralized sources of "cultural authority" (Alberti xvi). As Martha Cutter explains, "our own teaching practices will replicate the very structures of authority and domination which the [traditional] canon presents, the very structure we seek to escape" (127). For the study of U.S. writing of Italian America, intervention is needed from the beginning, so that the ideological underpinnings that produced a dominant, traditional canon are not reproduced in this burgeoning field. How might such work be done?

I am heartened by the revisionist work of the previously cited critics Gregory S. Jay and David Palumbo-Liu, who, along with others, have compelled a reconsideration of the study of U.S. writing from a transcendental core of values to a "multicultural and dialogical paradigm"

(Jay, "The End" 4) in order to practice a "critical" multiculturalism based on counterreadings that demonstrate "key elements [of] resistance to and subversion of dominant discourses" (Palumbo-Liu 22 n. 4). This work does not prevent the activity of close reading or the discussion of formal properties within Italian American literature. Rather, discussions should involve the application of several methods of reading, including, to wit, "the study of power, political uses of language, and orders of discourse'" (Cain; qtd. in Diffley 12 n. 10).

Deborah Madsen's discussion of American literature vis-à-vis a postcolonial paradigm also usefully enriches conceptions of what constitutes literary expression in America, accommodating "the contributions of such colonized peoples as Native Americans, Chicano/as, Afro-Hispanic and African American peoples" ("Beyond the Commonwealth" 2).[18] Seeking to create "an authentic postcolonial canon" Madsen includes the United States in her purview, examining a body of writing that, à la Ashcroft, Griffiths and Tiffin, explores "the experience of exile or dispossession or cultural erasure," and stylistic techniques used by such writers that include "the violation of Western principles of realism by use of allegory, magic realism, discontinuous narrative, irony, multiple languages, and so on" ("Beyond the Commonwealth" 5).

U.S. writers of Italian America reflect exilic status topically and stylistically, oft employing fragmented narrative structures and multiple languages. Such writing has meagerly benefited from traditional conceptions of American literature with its focus on nationalism and assimilating Anglo-Saxon virtues. But comparative methodology, a feature of postcolonialism, opens up a space for the verbal productions of Italian America, whose sense of place is influenced by historical domination in the homeland and literary dismissal in the new world. If we accept postcolonial study as just one of the avenues to take in the interpretation of Italian American writing, then we can participate in finding a way, as Jay puts it, "to read the texts produced by dominated peoples, . . . acknowledging their participation in narratives of resistance" ("The End" 21).[19] As discussed in chapter 1, for example, the voice of justice centrally influences the narrative focus of many Italian American writers, as they show how their cultural group actively and clandestinely resisted the laws and bureaucracies of the majority culture.

At the same time, the project of illuminating a recently identified field of U.S. writing by Italian Americans also exposes our own interpretive and pedagogical positions, in which "my own habits of omission and coercion are revealed, as well as my capacities for self-criticism and change"

(Rinehart, "Breaking Bad Habits" 29). Writers of Italian America have consistently produced works that go against the grain of traditional and indulgent stories that Italian Americans have told themselves about family, religion, racial identification, discrimination, and upward mobility. In order to create inventive ways for discussing and evaluating these works, we must simultaneously inspire communities of readers and "thinkers who listen and converse in new ways" (Rinehart, "Feminist Theorizing" 73). Borrowing from Antonio Gramsci's concept of hegemony, theorists of critical pedagogy examine the small "but potentially powerful spaces" as university classrooms, which have the capacity to become sites in which "organic intellectuals . . . elaborate a critical language to enable creative and critical consciousness among students" (Luke 27).

Replacing the term "theme" with its universalizing tendencies with the term "problematics" as Gregory Jay suggests "would put texts from different cultures within the U.S. into dialogue with one another."[20] Jay continues, "[U]nlike a theme, a problematic does not designate a moment in the history of the consciousness of a privileged subject. A problematic rather indicates an event in culture made up simultaneously of material conditions and conceptual forms that direct the possibilities of representation" ("The End" 22). Mediation supremely influences the cultural productions of Harriet Jacobs's slave narrative, *Incidents in the Life of a Slave Girl*, and Marie Hall Ets's as-told-to autobiography, *Rosa: The Life of an Italian Immigrant*. Placing these texts side-by-side in the classroom encourages a cross-cultural conversation about women whose external circumstances belie their ability to survive enormous odds. Only through the activity of telling their stories does each woman develop a historical self in eras that placed little value on them.

For both women, the painful acquisition of a personal voice is related to the act of creating public, historical selves. Such self-development violated historical and narrative paths that would keep such women imprisoned and silent. That Harriet Jacobs learned to read and write is not only a testimonial to her indomitable will, but also to the circumstances of her early childhood in slavery that still made the acquisition of literacy possible. Likewise, Rosa Cassettari learned in adulthood to speak in her adopted tongue, providing her the means to tell her stories to various audiences in Chicago, including the settlement houses, which, for all their built-in paternalism, made it possible for Rosa to become fluent in English. Part of textual analysis, then, would include a discussion about how these works were constructed, whom they were meant to persuade, and why their authors chose circumspection and indirection about certain matters they found personally repugnant and/or socially impossible to disclose. For both women, the "decision" to refer pseudonymously to themselves and the editorial supervision they received deeply influenced what they said and how they could say it. Genre influences of women's domestic fiction and slave narratives alongside abolitionism in antebellum America modified Jacobs's story just as generic features of the folktale and Marie Hall Ets's ordering of the narrative affected the written product of Rosa's orally told stories.

Pervading both documents are silences regarding matters of a sexual nature. Both prematurely sexualized, Jacobs and Cassettari dared to challenge nineteenth-century sexual mores in America and Italy, defying traditional ideology in radical ways. Jacobs and Cassettari refuse to sensationalize their illegitimate liaisons with men in their respective communities who provide them the means to escape sexual exploitation by a slave master in Harriet's case or a husband in Rosa's. Well aware of her grandmother's allegiance to the ideology of the cult of true womanhood, Harriet's status as a female slave denied her the capacity to fulfill it, simultaneously compelling her to advance an alternative sexual ideology that liberates as much as it anticipates future changes in sexual mores for all nineteenth-century women.

While the Italian cultural beliefs in fare bella figura (creating a beautiful public figure) and omertà have particular resonance for Italian women, Rosa does not always maintain them, especially after migrating to America, where, initially unable to speak English, she manages to obtain a divorce from a cruel spouse, marry the man whose friendship enabled her escape, and win a sense of freedom from her old-world destino. Although Jacobs and Cassettari may have come from different countries, their eventual escape to a freer land and their resilient attitudes about faith, womanhood, and domesticity unite them, offering forceful demonstrations of women living in America, seeking and redefining meanings of community.

Comparative perspectives place texts from different cultures like *Incidents* and *Rosa* into dialogue with one another, enlarging understandings of marginal histories and complicating analyses of how representation is modified and mediated. Discussing marginal subjectivity—particularly of women who find themselves thrice othered by race/ethnicity, gender, and foreignness—requires a search for new narrative models of emancipation, in contrast to traditional avenues of autonomy that would have further silenced if not killed these women. Doing this kind of textual analysis does not discard close reading practice, but rather involves examining the uses of power and the authors' resistance to generic structures that too easily domesticate rebellious voices. As Kathleen Diffley says, such practices "put the story back in history, the curse back in discourse, . . . [promoting a method that] makes the most of exegesis by acknowledging that its patterns begin outside the text" (11). The above comparison offers but one example of a useful way to continue the practice of reconstructing an American canon, reinforcing the fact that a multiethnic canon *is* American literature and Italian American works are part of it.

Exploring indigenous qualities within the works of Italian America often illuminate artistic strategies emerging from a complex cultural history. In striving to make such writing visible through creative scholarship and critical pedagogy, we also must be aware that minority discourse, as David Palumbo-Liu explains, "*once visible* as a represented and representative object, can indeed be stabilized and forced into a particular relationship with the hegemonic" (17). The linguistic analogy that Palumbo-Liu uses to illustrate the potential of dilution within ethnic writing is particularly apt for Italian America. He compares minority discourse to possessing the status of an idiom, that is,

> a linguistic code that circulates in a relatively private space. . . . As such, idioms have the weakness of being incomprehensible or only partially understandable outside their particular community of speakers. Nevertheless, this is also their strength, for they operate with relative autonomy from the ideological formations of the dominant linguistic code, and can thus comment upon the hegemonic—they are located in proximity but not engulfed by it. (17)

Like other ethnic writers, Italian Americans regularly insert into their writings Italian words, phrases, and other markers emerging from their dialects and cultural mores, sometimes though not always defining them rhetorically within the work or including such terms in a glossary.[21] Co-option occurs when an idiom is appropriated by the dominant code, which then increases its visibility but also dilutes its potency as a discursive practice within a minority discourse. The illustration that follows shows how a particular linguistic or cultural code has the potential to gain currency within dominant discourse but also then has potential to reduce its efficacy as ethnically coded linguistic armor.

What is the most famous—or infamous—idiom in Italian American parlance? The Oscar goes hands-down to Mario Puzo. Even though Puzo describes Don Corleone speaking "blandly" when he says "'I'll make him an offer he can't refuse'" (*The Godfather* 39), like Nora's slamming door, the sound reverberated round the world. Sounding a clear note in a 2007 interview with Gwen Ifill, Melba Pattillo Beals, one of the pioneer black students who entered Little Rock Central High School in September 1957, stated that revolutionary progress was made when segregated blacks shifted in attitude from "'Please, will you give us?' . . . [to] 'Hey, we're going to make you an offer that you can't refuse.'" In Beals's mouth, Puzo's idiom continues to pack a wallop, since its appropriation reflects a historical paradigm shift from hegemonic structures of institutionalized racism and segregation to a slow, but "inexorable" change in tone and action (Ifill, "Desegregation" 3).

Laudatory claims about *The Godfather* proliferated after its 1969 publication. Despite the novel's "middle-brow" status, it continued to appeal to academics nursed on high modernism, sufficing to demonstrate the enormous appeal of Puzo's mass-market, bestselling novel, the success of which catapulted its author into the national limelight: "*The Godfather* has done more to create a national consciousness of the Italian American experience than any work of fiction or nonfiction published before or since" (Gardaphé, *Italian Signs* 89). "*The Godfather* is a remarkable achievement. And it can lay claim to being the world's most typical novel, in part because of its vast popularity" (Torgovnick 114). "With the publication of *The Godfather* . . . Mario Puzo became the greatest multiethnic literary success in an American literary climate that had only begun to register such seismic changes in its critical mapping" (Messenger 51). "[T]he only two Italian American novels to have entered the ordinary syllabus of American literature advertise in their titles exactly the same impulse to divinity: *Christ in Concrete* and *The Godfather*" (Viscusi, *Buried Caesars* 148). "By century's end 'The Godfather' referred less to a book or film than to a modern secular mythology of Romanesque proportions and ancestry" (Ferraro, *Feeling Italian* 107).

Constructing a family myth, Mario Puzo willfully romanticized the godfather patriarch in order, as Rose Basile Green early stated, to sculpture an "ice-coated snowball and hurl it directly in the face of American duplicity" (335). But what gave Don Corleone's idiom its nearly inhumanly powerful punch was his "bland" delivery of that statement—"I'll make him an offer he can't refuse"—in effect, his performance of bella figura operating within a cultural milieu that cannot even be comprehended by other Italian American interlocutors, such as Johnny Fontane—a Frank Sinatra simulacrum—the character to whom the Don speaks. Yet, as Puzo clarified regarding the crooner-turned movie-star, Sinatra's northern Italian provenance is to a southern Italian "as alien as being an Englishman" (*The Godfather Papers* 46). Johnny Fontane gets the Hollywood part, but never gets Don Vito.

Puzo's famous idiom continues to enjoy a steady after life not only in literary and cinematic circles but also in ordinary conversation. Unanchored from its original moorings, however, Puzo's idiom has also been overused, caricatured, reduced, and changed in meaning. Though less seductive than viewing Francis Ford Coppola's film adaptations of *The Godfather*, an edifying reentry into the language of Puzo might occur in the classroom as the majority of university students have never read *The Godfather*. Reading Puzo's novel may very well be de-familiarizing for them, as it reflects a process that takes place when entering a text of epic proportion and melodramatic construction.

Like his literary forbears, Bernardino Ciambelli, Guido D'Agostino, Pietro di Donato, and John Fante before him, Mario Puzo offers a savvy critique of American capitalism, linking the Sicilian American family with capitalist immorality, mirror images of each other, albeit distorted. Arguably, Puzo's greatest ideological achievement was his ability to seduce readers into accepting the Corleone form of justice as reasonably virtuous in contrast to the faceless style of American corporatism. Though borrowing generously from early twentieth-century literary and cinematic traditions representing Italian American criminality, Puzo paved the way in the second half of the twentieth century for the creation of a character like Don DeLillo's filmmaker Frank Volterra of *The Names*, whose comment that "Italians have made the family an extremist group" (202), reverberates uneasily around the cottage industry that sprung up after *The Godfather*'s publication and Puzo's subsequent collaboration(s) with Coppola on the popular film adaptations. DeLillo's nomenclatural nod to Puzo—to Coppola, *anzi*—reflects an admiration for the earth-turning change *The Godfather* effected in popular culture, replacing the western American frontier with the urban immigrant enclave.

One of the earliest and most astute critics of *The Godfather*, Rose Basile Green, believed that the "Italian American novel" came of age with Puzo's bestseller. With its publication, Green confidently asserted that Puzo's verbal art would now be "evaluated on equal terms with other writers" (368). Aware of America's "psychic obsessions" with violence and criminality, Green stated the obvious by noting how Puzo's novel benefited from such obsessions, since Puzo dealt aggressively "with areas of Italian American experience to which the mass media have given national notoriety" (336). Green's interpretation of Puzo's novel as the story of America spurred subsequent critics to analyses both innovative and illuminating. Fred Gardaphé interprets the novel as a tale of reverse assimilation; Thomas Ferraro as the story of the fusion of kinship with capitalism. Pellegrino D'Acierno argues that the novel is a tale of seduction in which readers are entrapped by the network of godparenthood. Robert Viscusi discusses the novel as a tale of divided loyalties centralized in American ideology and Chris Messenger examines the bestseller as a popular narrative that performed a complete takeover in American fiction. Puzo's aim was to present a myth, portraying an enclosed world of Sicilian Americans protected by a familial system of *comparatico* under the auspices of the benevolent despot Don Vito, who fights, to his way of thinking, righteously against corrupt American institutions of business and government.

For twentieth-century Italian American readers, especially from the generation of World War II, *The Godfather* became their version, not of everybody's but certainly of their protest novel, painfully recalling the image of criminality associated with their cultural group since the nineteenth century. Anti-defamation groups decried the author's resurrection of the criminal element, and Puzo admitted to acquiescing to marketplace desires by using brutal themes specific to much contemporary fiction. In doing so, he coddled and assaulted readers. The "Italian American insider-hood" that Thomas Ferraro claims is invited by Puzo's text is deeply masculinist and misogynistic, compelling a resistance from readers for whom insider status is an invitation to the kinds of imprisonment and surveillance from which Harriet Jacobs and Rosa Cassettari suffered. Such essentialist notions may be seductive for men, with emphasis on *may*, but they are lethal for women, for the novel does not "make friends" as Ferraro exclaims, with women, Sicilian or American (*Feeling Italian* 115).

Was Rose Green prescient in her belief that with *The Godfather* Puzo joined the "general family," paving the way for an evaluation of his art on "equal terms" with that of other writers (368)? Green made that statement in 1974, only a few years after the novel's 1969 publication. One of the earliest advocates of the literary risorgimento of Italian America, Green believed that "those who control the machinery of critical support and sales distribution may eventually make an honest and empirical evaluation of all those Italian American novels that quietly and systematically have gone out of print" (368). Those critics I quoted above provide support for Green's optimism, since Puzo, along with other U.S. writers of Italian America, have had their works reprinted and evaluated by scholars who challenge monocultural prescriptions of aesthetic value, offering instead counterreadings that maintain possible spaces of resistance for Italian American texts. Thus, academic scholarship has largely been responsible for putting the linguistic code of Italian America back into its textual space(s), in multitudinous ways, allowing for the maintenance of cultural difference.

Linguistic codes inform Italian American writing, challenging the linguistic insularity of English language texts, in effect disturbing (and redistributing) the internal security of traditionally conceived canonical works. Despite its homage to high modernism, Tina De Rosa's *Paper Fish* refuses to be brought in "from the margins" as Palumbo-Liu puts it (17). The novel is insistently resistant. It refuses to explain itself, to locate itself geographically, or to make its language easy for readers. University students have told me they despair of reading *Paper Fish*—it's so verbally demanding, and so unrelentingly sad. It does not comfort them to hear me refer to other novels like Julia Savarese's *The Weak and the Strong*, Richard Wright's *Native Son*, or Toni Morrison's *The Bluest Eye*, for equally painful stories. That list is endless. I have to convince them otherwise: to bribe them with *Paper Fish*'s brevity; to tell them that the act of confronting "a text which is resistant, intangible and even difficult is what the process of teaching cultural difference is all about" (Gallagher 64).

Perhaps Tina De Rosa isn't an inviting sort of writer; maybe she doesn't want readers inside the enclosure of the Little Italy she mourns. Perhaps the price of entry for readers requires civility, respect, and patience, qualities of which students are increasingly in short supply, bombarded by the disturbance and noise of a media-driven age. As Martha Cutter explains, "Reading, as [Robert] Scholes argues, is not only a textual activity; it is a skill which helps students make sense of their environments and resist the continuing assaults of the manipulative structures of their worlds" (127). Those very structures of the world are what De Rosa laments as she witnesses the inexorable dismantlement of her childhood Little Italy. If one of the roles of reading literature is imaginative identification with a created world, then Tina De Rosa's *Paper Fish* is in fact an invitation to enter that space and mourn with her. Once inside, readers engage with the serious world of all serious books, because the real life of the book world is, as Toni Morrison says, "about creating and producing and distributing knowledge; about making it possible for the entitled as well as the dispossessed to experience one's own mind dancing with another's" ("The Dancing Mind" 16).

Read aloud, *Paper Fish* emerges as another kind of book: funny, warm, and hospitable. After Carmolina runs away from home, the neighborhood searches for her, from the skinny widows in black to the seed man pushing his green cart. De Rosa portrays the phenomenon of campanilismo as internally secure and externally threatened, for they have lost one of their own—and they will lose her and their neighborhood, soon and forever. While all the normal routines of the day take place, the neighbors search for and speak about Carmolina as they haggle for vegetables, pick rags, hear confession, blow the horn for seeds, calling out 'Peeee-staaaa-sheee-ooo' and 'Carrr-mo-leeee-naaaa' in one breath (*Paper Fish* 36). Such a scene begs for the attention that reading aloud gives it, legitimating the condition of orality in a work that is stylistically and structurally demanding as written text.

Alongside linguistic codes in ethnic texts that maintain cultural currency within a particular community, gestural codes also have the potential to comment upon the hegemonic. In her epilogue, Tina De Rosa incorporates an Italian gesture that functions to do just that: disparage a city and a metropolitan economy that treats working-class space as disposable. To that end, De Rosa offers the gesture in all its howling silence as one of the unabashedly angry moments in *Paper Fish*, and it emerges from the lived experience of immigrant Italians in Chicago, pushed into a second diaspora:

> "The city she run over you children and smash them flat, like this."
> Stephanzo rammed his hand into his crooked arm. "They call us
> wops. They say these streets have to go. Open you damn eyes."
> The two men faced each other in the dark street. The fire in
> their eyes burned, they did not see each other, then Giovanni
> felt his anger go soft.
> "You give *me* the arm, Stephanzo? *Me*?" (118)

At once an assertion of subjectivity and incredulity, Giovanni's question is the one De Rosa answers with *Paper Fish*, insisting on the integration of memory and desire. A practiced storyteller, De Rosa understands her skills as a writer are analogous to her craftsmen forbears, recognizing that "in genuine storytelling the hand plays a part which supports what is expressed in a hundred ways with its gestures trained by work" (Benjamin, *Illuminations* 108).

On the final page of *Paper Fish*, Carmolina her mouthpiece, De Rosa reminds her long-dispersed community that "nothing goes away," in opposition to the idiomatic gesture that delivers its potent blow to an American culture the author refuses to address or confront verbally, saving her beautiful language for her cultural community (121). Protest can emerge quietly, too, De Rosa seems to be saying, and her strategy of resistance is echoed by several writers of Italian America.

OUTSETTINGS

In her analysis of subaltern cultures, Deborah Madsen explains that through the "complex manipulation of language" native writers make the "attempt to speak and yet preserve their authenticity" ("Beyond the Commonwealth" 9). U.S. writers of Italian America, through their inventive use and recreation of vernacular expressions—verbal and gestural—continue to create resistant texts with indigenous qualities that are being mined. We who study the verbal art of Italian America have set out on a journey mapped by early pioneers of this field such as Olga Peragallo, Giovanni Schiavo, Rose Basile Green, and Rudolph Vecoli to name just a few. I end with the word "outsettings" because it suggests both a course of action and also a space that lives or lies in the open or outside an enclosure. Narratives of Italian America have been illuminated by scholarship that has enabled portals into analyses of these works.

Many of those scholars—veteran and newly minted—might be boldly described as Cornel West describes those scholars and artists associated with the new cultural politics of difference: "an energetic breed of New World *bricoleurs* with improvisational and flexible sensibilities" as "intellectual and political freedom-fighters with partisan passion, international perspectives, and, thank God, a sense of humor" (36). Like expert artisans, writers of Italian America coordinate "the soul, the eye and the hand," and have managed, as in Walter Benjamin's epigraph to this final chapter, to join the ranks of teachers and sages, discovering within their storytelling their righteous selves (Benjamin 108). As we continue to shape the field, resurgent voices of Italian America acquire value and significance as their histories, cultural backgrounds, and artistic strategies are clarified by creative scholarship able to meet this rich body of writing on its own, multilayered terms.

Notes

⌒

1. JUSTICE/GIUSTIZIA—PRIVATE JUSTICE AND THE FOLKLORIC COMMUNITY IN THE WORLD OF ITALIAN AMERICANS

1. In *The Golden Door*, Thomas Kessner describes the "ethnic grooves" carved by the early settlers and continued by Italian immigrants who retained their old-world subdivisions in the streets of lower Manhattan: "Mott Street between East Houston and Prince held the Napoletani; the opposite side of the street was reserved for the Basilicati [Lucani]. Around the corner the Siciliani settled Prince Street, while two blocks away the Calabresi lived on Mott between Broome and Grand. Mulberry Street was strictly Neapolitan, and Hester Street, running perpendicular to Mulberry, carried the local color of Apulia" (16).

2. Illiteracy rates were high in the Mezzogiorno and for poor people throughout Italy. In *Blood of My Blood*, Gambino offers these figures: "In 1901, a time when the total illiteracy rate of Italy was 38.30 percent, 62 percent of the Southern Italian men landing at Ellis Island were totally lacking the ability to read or write any 'recognized language or dialect,' as the record puts it, and 74 percent of the women were illiterate" (85).

3. Italian immigrants did not universally prevent the education of their children, though many considered the public school a threat that undercut the family's cultural authority and financial stability (represented by the children's pay envelope). See Dorothy Bryant's *Miss Giardino* for a representation of the importance of books, reading, and the English language to the development of second-generational characters.

4. I take this description from Micaela Di Leonardo's chapter on family models and kinship realities for California Italian Americans in *The Varieties of Ethnic Experience*. Reinforcing the fact that there is "no monolithic Italian *family* pattern," and that the intense regional solidarity

expressed as campanilismo is in reality far more complex, Di Leonardo explains that campanilismo is "a product of settlement patterns and ethnic mix. . . . [T]he developing California economy [may] help us to see beyond the vision . . . that Italian-American family culture creates an ambitionless, self-reproducing, urban working class" (93, 95).

5. In "Ethnicity and the Post-Modern Arts of Memory," Fischer describes narratives about ethnicity in terms similar to the authors under consideration: "It is a matter of finding a voice or a style that does not violate one's several components of identity. In part such a process of assuming an ethnic identity is an insistence on a pluralist, multidimensional, or multifaceted concept of self" (196). As Fischer suggests, a new identity is created when one becomes not Italian in America, but Italian American. As there is no role model for such a position, Italian Americans, like other ethnic writers, must discover and invent new ways to examine this development.

6. The definition given of "italianità" in *From the Margin: Writings in Italian Americana* fleshes out this evasive term: "italianità" includes "real and mythical images of the [home]land, the way of life, the values, and the cultural trappings of [the writers'] ancestors. . . . Language, food, a way of determining life's values, a familial structure, a sense of religion" (Tamburri et al. 6, 9).

7. In the preface to the reprinting of *Christ in Concrete*, Studs Terkel writes: "1939 was the year for me. Two of the most powerful American novels of our time were published in 1939. One was *The Grapes of Wrath* by John Steinbeck, the other was *Christ in Concrete* by a young bricklayer named Pietro di Donato. . . . Both novels portrayed the travails of working people faced with obstacles, battling overwhelming odds in their attempts to survive troubled times. In both cases the heroism of the non-celebrated was celebrated." For a recent analysis of di Donato's *Esquire* short story, "Christ in Concrete," originally available from the publisher as a book, see chapter 3 of Thomas Ferraro's *Feeling Italian: The Art of Ethnicity in America.*

8. For an analysis of *Christ in Concrete* as a rewriting of the Christ myth, see Fred Gardaphé's *Italian Signs, American Streets* (66–75). See also Patrizia Benolich's examination of di Donato's unbridled use of idiomatic spoken language in her chapter, "Once There Were Mountains" (20–75).

9. Di Donato's final novel, *American Gospels*, is in the process of being posthumously published. Excerpts from this book and a tribute to di Donato are included in *Voices in Italian Americana* 2.2 (Fall 1991): 1–76.

10. In her chapter "A Genuine Article," Heather McHugh explains that "the 'the' feels in such regards coercive; it sets up a noun as an afore-mentioned entity (and yet smacks of the unduplicated)" (88). That di Donato elides the definite article but capitalizes the subsequent noun reinforces how severely immigrants were dominated by their need to find and keep work. "Job" possesses the qualities of sacredness as does its preceding, though absent, definite article. The ubiquity of the word "Job" throughout di Donato's novel also emphasizes how work both supports and destroys the lives of immigrants.

11. As Rudolph Vecoli explains, "an aggressive anticlericalism became a powerful force in late nineteenth-century Italy as nationalist, liberal, so-cialist views prevailed. . . . The anticlericalism of the Italians scandalized the American Irish, who were distinguished by reverence and respect for their priests. . . . In their religion as in all else, the peasants [from the Mez-zogiorno] were intensely parochial and traditional" ("Prelates and Peas-ants" 222, 224). Di Donato also ascribes to Italian anticlericalism when he says "We Italians are really essentially pagans and realists" (von-Huene Greenberg 36). I examine in more detail the folkloric voices of faith from the point of view of women writers in chapter 2.

12. "Stone" is reprinted in Walter Biddle and Paul A. Eschholz's collection *The Literature of Vermont: A Sampler*.

13. In "The Italian Story in Vermont," Tomasi describes one resi-dential street in Barre as "*la strada delle vedove*"—the street of widows—indicating the high death toll from tuberculo-silicosis. With no state compensation or insurance, many women whose husbands had died early deaths skirted the Prohibition law and sold homemade wine, using "the profits to care for [their] children" (82, 81).

14. Robyn Young explains that "the center of the Barre anarchist movement was Luigi Galleani, an Italian who edited the anarchist paper, *Cronaca Sovversiva (Subversive Chronicle)*. . . . Anarchists and socialists shared the same goals: to overthrow capitalism, to abolish private property and to establish a class-free society" ("Barre's Anarchists" 3A). For exten-sive treatment of the anarchist movement in America, see Paul Avrich, *Sacco and Vanzetti: The Anarchist Background*.

15. In *Claiming a Tradition*, I examine how, in giving Michele Tif-fone the same first initials and surname syllabication as the author's, Mari Tomasi is able to maintain her own cultural authority regarding the stonecutting industry in Italy and America (30–31).

16. Long after he had left his Rochester community, Mangi-one learned the lengths to which immigrants went to prove they were

"a civilized and moral people, not criminals involved with the Mafia or the Black Hand, as the press would have the community believe. As evidence of their good character, the Sicilian community decided to enact the Passion Play [in 1908]. Included in the cast were milkmen, masons, ditchdiggers, shoemakers, bakers, tailors, factory hands, among them some of my relatives. . . . The next day came the big payoff: the same newspapers that had been headlining Sicilian crime on their front pages devoted the same kind of space to praising the Sicilian community for making such an impressive contribution to the city's cultural life" (*An Ethnic* 15–16).

17. For an analysis of scenes from the enclosed topology of *Mount Allegro*, see Boelhower's chapter "A New Version of the American Self," in his *Immigrant Autobiography in the United States* (179–230). In "Humor, Ethnicity, and Identity," John Lowe examines the way in which humor in *Mount Allegro* is used as a "corrective version" of the communal life of one's ethnic group.

18. In *Italian Folktales*, Italo Calvino writes that "the moral is always implicit in the folktale in the victory of simple virtues of the good characters and the punishment of the equally simple and absolutely perverse wrongdoers" (xxx).

19. In his preface to the reprinting of *The Fortunate Pilgrim*, Mario Puzo explains that his plans to make himself the hero were toppled when he discovered "that my mother turned out to be the hero of the book." Puzo's mother was also the model for Don Corleone, the Mafia chieftain of *The Godfather*: "Whenever the Godfather opened his mouth, in my own mind I heard the voice of my mother. I heard her wisdom, her ruthlessness, and her unconquerable love for her family and for life itself" (xi, xii). Describing those impoverished peasants as "illiterate Colombos," Puzo admitted that he belatedly recognized their invisible heroism: "they made it without tranquilizers, without sleeping pills, without psychiatrists, without even a dream" (*The Godfather Papers and Other Confessions* 17).

20. The most famous linkage made between food and violence in the Italian American canon actually occurs in the film adaptation of *The Godfather* in which Clemenza, after supervising the execution of turncoat Paulie Gatto, utters "Leave the gun, take the cannoli." For a brilliant analysis of this scene, see John Paul Russo's "The Hidden Godfather: Plenitude and Absence in Francis Ford Coppola's *Godfather I* and *II*." Sandra Gilbert, frustrated by the mythologizing of Italian American criminality, deliberately makes the same connection in her poem "Mafioso": "Frank Costello eating spaghetti in a cell/at San Quentin,/

Lucky Luciano mixing up a mess of/bullets and/calling for parmesan cheese,/Al Capone baking a sawed-off shotgun/into a huge lasagna—/Are you my uncles, my/only uncles?"

21. In his tribute to Mother Cabrini, Ardizzone inserts in *In the Garden of Papa Santuzzu* a folktale told by immigrant Italians to suggest her miraculous powers over institutionalized authorities. In 1960, Pietro di Donato published a biography of Cabrini called *Immigrant Saint*. See also Mary Louise Sullivan's biography, *Mother Cabrini: "Italian Immigrant of the Century."*

2. FAITH/FEDE—PLENTY TO CONFESS: WOMEN AND (ITALIAN) AMERICAN CATHOLICISM

1. Many scholars and writers of Italian America emphasize the contrast between genders regarding attitudes toward doctrinal Catholicism. For example, in her memoir *Were You Always an Italian?* Maria Laurino writes of her extended family: "These men played with faith, letting the women, the madonnas, be the standard-bearers of devotion, but never abandoned their religion. Men could be scoundrels . . . and of course be forgiven for their sins—as long as the women did the praying for them" (158). Laurino's words echo the famously final scene of Mario Puzo's *The Godfather*, in which the converted Catholic Kay Adams "said the necessary prayers for the soul of Michael Corleone" (443).

2. Robert Viscusi examines the political import of this concept of the extension of the Italian (American) family into the world at large in his analysis of Mario Cuomo's gubernatorial campaign: "When Cuomo campaigned for governor [of] New York State on the allegorical program that the government should work as a family does, the candidate spoke in the visionary political tradition that he shares with Italian writers of every age—Virgil, Dante, and di Donato, no less than many humbler talents. . . . Cuomo's vision generalizes intimate family relations in the Sunday Feast, placing around them the image of a vast patriarchal government that treats its citizens as children and its officials as parents" (*Buried Caesars* 130–131). This image also describes the official treatment of the Catholic Church hierarchy toward its congregants.

3. Citing the work of Gabriele De Rosa, Michael P. Carroll notes that "popular Catholicism in southern dioceses was shaped more by the *chiese ricettizie* (a type of local church in which a group of priests, all of whom had to be native to the area [administered] land held in common) more than anything else" (178).

4. Kerby Miller applies Antonio Gramsci's theory of cultural hegemony to analyze the migration of Irish Catholics to America and their assimilation into American culture. Along with integration into the Democratic Party, "Catholicism became the primary expression of Irish-American consciousness . . . Rome appointed more American bishops of Irish birth or descent, who imported thousands of priests and teaching nuns from Ireland. Soon [during the decades of the 1830s through the 1850s] American Catholicism was rapidly expanding its institutional infrastructure under a largely Irish hierarchy and clergy" (113).

5. Peter R. D'Agostino adds depth to what has been termed the "Italian problem" in the United States by attributing it to the phenomenon of the Roman Question, which

> persisted as a theological, cultural, and political rupture from 1848 until 1929, when the pope attained a small temporal sovereignty, the State of the Vatican City. . . . Catholics responded to the Risorgimento—the movement to unify Italy—and the concomitant loss of the Papal states, by creating . . . the ideology of the Roman Question, a constituent element of Catholic culture that, in the United States, generated boundaries separating Catholics from other Americans. . . . From 1880–1940, Catholics lamented immigrants' unwillingness to finance parishes, their lack of respect for clergy, aberrant devotional styles, vulnerability to Protestant proselytizing and radical politics, and veneration of Mary above Jesus. The ideology of the Roman question placed the blame for this "Italian Problem" on the doorstep of Liberal Italy. (3, 59)

6. In *Recollections of My Life as a Woman: The New York Years*, Diane di Prima also treats the shame and pain associated with being Italian during the World War II era. See especially the first five chapters, which focus on Diane's difficult relationship with her parents, who forbade their children from speaking Italian.

7. Gordon includes earlier published reviews and essays on Flannery O'Conner and Mary McCarthy in *Good Boys and Dead Girls*.

8. In her introduction to *The Dream Book*, Helen Barolini suggests that Italian American women writers might take as a model the inestimable Saint Catherine of Siena (1347–1380), the patroness of Italy and a Doctor of the Church, who "knew how to take on the men" (34). For an example closer to home, Sister Blandina Segale (1850–1941), a Sister of Charity who spent twenty years in frontier towns in the southwest (1872–1892), left an epistolary journal of her experiences serving with courage and determi-

nation the peoples of the southwest, Hispanic Catholics, and immigrant settlers. See her *At The End of the Santa Fe Trail*.

9. For an overview of the Second Vatican Council and the response of the American Catholic Church and its parishioners, see Jay P. Dolan's *In Search of An American Catholicism*, especially chapter 5: "An American Religion and a Roman Church, 1960–2001."

10. Gordon includes two essays specifically devoted to the issue of abortion in *Good Boys and Dead Girls*: "Abortion: How Do We Think About It?" and "Abortion: How Do We Really Choose?" 128–147.

11. Robert Orsi explains in "The Religious Boundaries of an Inbetween People: Street *Feste* and the Problem of the Dark-Skinned Other in Italian Harlem, 1920–1990," that feste also secured for Italians their boundaries against darker-skinned newcomers such as the Puerto Ricans, "who were too much like them for comfort [and the Italians incorporated the Puerto Ricans] into an overarching narrative that held them responsible for the demise of the community. . . . [T]he narrative was a theodicy, a story that endeavored to make sense of the great change, account for the decisions to leave, respond to the genuine sorrow people felt at the passing of a once thriving Italian world, and repair the fragmenting moral order" (337).

12. In *Alone of All Her Sex: The Myth and the Cult of the Virgin Mary*, Marina Warner explains that by the Middle Ages the Virgin had acquired "the lunar imagery previously applied to the Church": "As a sky goddess, Mary's colour is blue. . . . [A]s late as 1649, Francisco Pacheco in his *Art of Painting* still laid down that she should wear a blue cloak. Blue is the colour of space and light and eternity, of the sea and the sky" (258, 266).

13. Susan Caperna Lloyd examines bas-reliefs of Demeter (called the Santoni) and sees a small snake spiraled across her chest: "It formed a uroborus—the image of a snake feeding on its own tail. I remembered that Persephone's Latin name was Proserpina. Besides being a 'savior,' she was also known as First Serpent" (*No Pictures in My Grave* 116). De Rosa's descriptions of the powerful grandmother figure accord well with the agricultural goddesses of southern Italy and Sicily.

14. Personal conversation with the author. De Rosa has said, "Creation is close to priesthood. It's taking the ordinary and turning it into the extraordinary" ("An Interview" 23).

15. Recent works that involve a return to Italy as a central focus include Robert Ferro's *The Family of Max Desir*, Anna Monardo's *The Courtyard of Dreams*, Anne Calcagno's *Pray for Yourself and Other Stories*, Barbara Grizzuti Harrison's *Italian Days*, and Teresa Maggio's *The Stone Boudoir: Travels through the Hidden Villages of Sicily*. For an

analysis of the use of the mythological figure of Persephone in Italian American women's travel narratives, see Alison D. Goeller's "Persephone Goes Home: Italian American Women in Italy." Susan Caperna Lloyd also made a twenty-eight-minute documentary film of the Trapani procession in Sicily called *Processione: A Sicilian Easter.*

16. Before publishing her memoir *Night Bloom*, Cappello wrote an earlier—and more visceral—version of the topic of ethnicity and religion that was included in a book entitled *Fuori* (in Italian, meaning, "out," "outside"). This earlier essay, while less polished than the highly revised chapter in *Night Bloom*, is more probative and self-revealing, focusing intensively on the intersections between Cappello's Italian American family, the Catholic Church, and gay sexuality. I examine Cappello's *Night Bloom* more fully in chapter 6.

17. Mary Gordon, Leonardi's contemporary, writes in "More Catholic Than the Pope," "Anyone who has gone anywhere near Catholics in the past several years knows the dissatisfaction with the liturgy is enormous. The new Mass is piecemeal, tentative, on the whole a botched job" (*Good Boys and Dead Girls* 177). See also Nick Shay's comment when in Church with his elderly mother in Don DeLillo's *Underworld*: "And sometimes I sat with her through the mass in English, what a stark thing it was, without murmur or reverberation" (106).

3. STORY/RACCONTO—*UNA CHIACCHIERATA NEL PASSATO:* ROSA AND MARIE OF *ROSA: THE LIFE OF AN ITALIAN IMMIGRANT*

1. Born in North Greenfield, Wisconsin, in 1895, Marie Hall Ets became an author-illustrator of numerous children's books, from the 1935 *Mister Penny* to the 1974 *Jay Bird*. Ets won several awards for her writing and illustrations, including the New York Herald Award for *Oley, the Sea Monster* (1947), the Hans Christian Andersen honor for *Play with Me* (1956) and the Caldecott Medal in 1960 for her illustrations of *Nine Days to Christmas* (1959).

2. *Rosa*, 4. All citations are taken from the second edition of *Rosa: The Life of an Italian Immigrant* published by the University of Wisconsin Press in 1999.

3. When reading through the Marie Hall Ets Papers located at the Immigration History Research Center at the University of Minnesota, I noted that Ets originally had in mind a novel project, not mere transcription of Rosa's tales, though she ultimately transcribed the stories

from Rosa's point of view and voice. See also http://www.ihrc.umn.edu/research/vitrage/all/em/ihrc633.html.

4. Barbara Ciccarelli explains that one of the manuscript readers of *Rosa* recommended publication but required the elimination of parenthetical material—those asides or comments regularly made between Rosa and Marie—that Marie thought important enough to transcribe: "The comments in parentheses interrupt 'the' story because they suggest there is more than one story, one life being represented" (55).

5. In their introduction to *Women, Autobiography, Theory: A Reader*, Sidonie Smith and Julia Watson examine the complexity of collaborative texts, explaining that "in such texts issues of power, trust, and narrative authority become critical to the politics of collaboration. Such texts also require we acknowledge the importance of oral cultural forms and attend to the speakerly text, rather than remain preoccupied with the writerly effects of narrative" (28).

6. According to Elizabeth Mathias and Richard Raspa, "In the stables, women spun and embroidered, and men repaired rakes and other tools. Folk narratives developed in just such an atmosphere of communal work" (3).

7. "A revolving monument to infant abandonment, the wheel was both its central mechanism and guiding metaphor. It served as the point of transition, marking off the outside—with its uncontrolled sexuality, dangers, and passions—from the inside under firm institutional control. On the outside lay nature and sin, on the inside civilization and salvation. The wheel, in theory, ensured that the two worlds would not overlap, for only the baby could pass between them" (Kertzer 103).

8. For the publication history of the translation of *Rosa* into Italian, strengthening the connection that linked the Cuggionesi with their migration history and specifically with Rosa, see Ernesto Milani's "The Publication of the Translation of *Rosa: The Life of an Italian Immigrant*." In celebration of the book's publication in Italian, Rudolph Vecoli remarked: "'The translation was a collaborative project of some thirty Cuggionesi, a labor of love. Clearly Rosa has become the surrogate in the community's collective memory of the multitude of mothers, daughters, and sisters who left Cuggiono and other paesi for America'" (qtd. in Milani 230). Rosa would approve the collaborative nature informing the translation of her dialectically inflected English into Italian.

9. Mathias and Raspa interviewed Clementina Todesco, a brilliant storyteller originally from Faller, a mountain village in northern Italy and an Italian Alpine hamlet. Migration to America diminished Clementina's opportunities for tale-telling: "Once severed from the

community where tales were nurtured in a social matrix of shared work and play which had a focal time, evening, and place for human gathering, the stable, the old tale[-]telling did not survive" (8).

10. Sau-ling Cynthia Wong takes to task William Boelhower's model of immigrant autobiography (in *Immigrant Autobiography in the United States: Four Versions of the Italian American Self*) for "regarding immigrant autobiography as nothing less than a genotype of American autobiography." In her analysis of several Chinese immigrant autobiographies, an emphasis on what Boelhower calls the "dream anticipation" of America is absent: "'contact' with the 'utopian grammar' of America and its consequences [is] hardly portrayed, and cultural 'contrast' either not drawn or drawn more to enlighten Anglo readers than to map the protagonist's own 'Americanization.' Instead, the majority of the autobiography is devoted to the protagonist's preimmigration life in China." While Wong distinguishes between Chinese immigrants and the European immigrants "on whose autobiographies Boelhower builds his case" the as-told-to autobiography of Rosa often better parallels in focus the Chinese autobiographies that Wong analyzes (299, 304).

11. See Thomas Lee Philpott's chapter "Settlement House and Tenement House: 'With, Not For'" for a description of the reasons undergirding the development of settlement houses: "They took it for granted that the poor needed the help of emissaries from the ranks of education and privilege" (63).

12. Another immigrant autobiography that centralizes the settlement house as the focal point for the narrator's development is Hilda Polacheck's *I Came A Stranger: The Story of a Hull House Girl*. Betty Bergland describes this work as revelatory in "dimensions of immigrant/ethnic/Jewish/female life . . . centered in the spaces of the settlement house and the private home. . . . Hull House . . . provided a social space for exposure to visitors from all over the world; it provided a social space for meeting others [Hilda Polacheck's] age with shared interests; it offered a site in which debate and criticism of America was possible" (111–112). For both women, the settlement house was life altering, but in contrast to Rosa's focus on her premigration past, Hilda's stories are primarily set in America and feature her progression into a learned, middle-class culture.

13. Rosa's experience with the middle-class housekeeper draws attention to Rosa's working-class background, in which her body is exhausted and mistreated. For an earlier example of the heightened awareness of the body that emerges from class distinctions, see Anzia Yezierska's "Soap and Water."

4. LAND/TERRA—VILLAGE PEOPLE IN GUIDO D'AGOSTINO'S NOVELS

1. In the 1970s the Arno Press began to reprint works by and about Italian Americans in their collection called "The Italian American Experience." Besides reprinting Guido D'Agostino's novel *Olives on the Apple Tree*, Arno Press also published, among others, Pascal D'Angelo's *Son of Italy* (1924), Louis Forgione's *The River Between* (1928), Garibaldi Lapolla's *The Grand Gennaro* (1935), and Jo Pagano's *Golden Wedding* (1943). Jerre Mangione's *Mount Allegro* has managed to stay in print since it was first published in 1942. In fact fiction by Italian American writers made a splash on the national literary scene in the 1930s and 1940s, which I discuss further in chapter 8. In his 1946 article "Melting-Pot Literature," Carl Wittke lists several of the aforementioned authors, noting that "a new body of recent Italian-American novels" was making its way into American fiction (197).

2. Olga Peragallo's 1949 *Italian-American Authors and Their Contribution to American Literature* is a biographical compendium of fifty-nine writers of Italian American background. Hers was the first such book to gather together Italian Americans for literary purposes in the hopes that such a "biographical dissertation . . . might be useful to scholars" as Italian professor Giuseppe Prezzolini offered in his preface to her posthumously published book (ix). Rose Basile Green's 1974 *The Italian-American Novel: A Document of the Interaction of Two Cultures* widely expands on the efforts of Peragallo by examining the works of over sixty Italian American writers, demonstrating how they represented the national culture. Both Peragallo and Green began the process of canonization for Italian American writers. Their books, still invaluable, made possible the subsequent work of Helen Barolini, Robert Viscusi, Fred Gardaphé, and other scholars of Italian America.

3. I am thinking of the most well-known of early Italian American novels, *Christ in Concrete* and *Wait Until Spring, Bandini*, in which characters are engaged in precarious and peripheral outdoor work and, literally, cannot afford the luxury of enjoying the view. Arturo Bandini's first internal thought in *Wait Until Spring, Bandini* concerns the weather, which prevents him from doing much needed work: "Here was a disgusted man. . . . He hated the snow. He was a bricklayer, and the snow froze the mortar between the brick he laid" (11).

4. Like Rosa Cassettari, Jerre Mangione understood the fundamentally communal nature of the folktale. Told with humor and

wit, Mangione's folktales also reflect the communal strivings of the downtrodden.

5. D'Agostino is not the first Italian American writer to use the French culture as a distancing strategy. Luigi Ventura's 1885 *Peppino* was originally published in French, a language considered vastly superior to the dialects spoken by Italian immigrants. The educated Italian immigrant narrator, Mr. Fortuna of Ventura's novella, is able to establish a critical distance from the child laborer, Peppino, despite his affection for the boy. In a similar vein, through Chambord, D'Agostino is able to establish distance from the immigrant laborers, focusing instead on the romantic triangle that moves the plot forward in *Hills Beyond Manhattan*.

6. For historical information on the racial heritage of Italian Americans, see Matthew Frye Jacobson's *Whiteness of a Different Color: European Immigrants and the Alchemy of Race* and David Roediger's *Toward the Abolition of Whiteness: Essays on Race, Politics, and Working Class History*. See also Steven Belluscio's analysis of *Olives on the Apple Tree* as a male narrative of passing in *To Be Suddenly White: Literary Realism and Racial Passing*. Second-generation character, Emile Gardella, in *Olives* refuses to suffer for being the son of Italian immigrants, asserting the assimilative belief that his kids will grow up "'to think their ancestors came over on the Mayflower,'" to which his sister responds, reflecting current racial ideology, "'That'll be funny. Olive-skinned Yankees'" (133).

7. John Fante's boy protagonist, Arturo, in *Wait Until Spring, Bandini* suffers a similar form of shame as Emilio Gardella. They both absorb from the host culture a hatred of all things Italian. Donald Weber explains that the "immigrant experience can induce abject self-loathing, a debilitating state of consciousness that takes the dominant culture as a personal ideal, thus making the signs and expressions of one's local 'ethnic' affiliations shameful, in need of erasure" (70–71).

8. I am using the term "ethnic resilience" in Kerby Miller's sense of a culture maintaining its sense of ethnic identity: "ethnic resilience . . . stresses the persistence if not permanence of at least some important social patterns and beliefs that provide structure, continuity, and meaning in an alien and alienating New World" (97).

9. According to historian Christopher Duggan, "Mussolini's drive for conservative respectability was extraordinarily wide-ranging. He annulled the decrees sanctioning the peasant seizures of land after the war, to the particular delight of the southern *latifondisti* [large landowners]" (206).

10. During the period between 1880 and 1920 southern and eastern Europeans numbered "more than 27 million men, women, and children. In less than forty years they provided the bulk of the working force in the nation's key industries; by 1920 they accounted for two-thirds of the urban population, despite the fact that the large majority of them, particularly the Italians . . . had been farmers living in small villages" (Mangione, "A Double Life" 170).

11. In *O Pioneers!*, Alexandra offers a rather mystical response to her success in awakening a sleeping landscape: "The land did it. It had its little joke. It pretended to be poor because nobody knew how to work it right; and then, all at once, it worked itself. It woke up out of its sleep and stretched itself, and it was so big, so rich, that we suddenly found we were rich, just from sitting still" (69). Perhaps D'Agostino names his patriarchal figure in *The Barking of a Lonely Fox* "Alessandro" to pay homage to an earlier pioneer of enormous success, Alexandra Bergson of Cather's novel.

12. Although it is set in Sicily and not Sardinia, Giuseppe Tomasi di Lampedusa's 1958 *The Leopard* provides a portrait of landed society, which spans from 1860 to 1910. See also the 1963 Luchino Visconti film from the novel also titled *The Leopard*. During World War II, Guido D'Agostino worked for the Office of War Information in the radio division and helped to establish Radio Sardegna at Bortigali, Sardinia, before it was relocated to the city of Cagliari, Sardinia. "D'Agostino worked directly with five Italian officers and about 50 enlisted men who ran the station: 'I lived with the men, ate with them, slept with them, and obtained the technical equipment, scrounged for the food and the clothing for them' Guido recalls" (*Wayne Independent Interview*, November 20, 1983, n.p.). According to his nephew, Guido was profoundly affected by the devastation of the Nazis who "virtually just stripped the island of Sardinia, you know there was no food, no nothing. His job was to scrounge around for food and clothing and radio parts and other things that they needed to make the radio station work" (phone interview with Vince D'Agostino, October 18, 2005).

13. At the turn of the twentieth century, Italian immigrants in the South Village were highly represented in both skilled and unskilled work. According to Donald Tricarico,

In 1906 "67 percent of all factory jobs in the city were below Fourteenth Street" (Kessner, 1977: 50). The so-called "Venice of Industry" formed the eastern edge of the South Village Italian colony. The clothing industry was an especially important employer of Italian labor; in 1929 it still occupied 6,700,000 square feet of floor space in Village loft buildings (WPA, 1937). A 1905 sample of 4,169 Italian males living in the South Village and nearby east side Italian settlements found that 826 worked in the garment trades,—605 were tailors (Gutman, 1977: 529). A large number of Italian women were also employed in clothing production. Odencrantz found that roughly half of Italian women at a local settlement house were "making men's, women's and children's clothing" (1919: 38). The proximity of factories made it possible for mothers to take in work and supplement family income. (4)

14. By choosing to represent the historical era and the upper management of a distributive company, D'Agostino differs from another set of his contemporaries like Nelson Algren, Jack Dunphy, and Chester Himes who were chronicling the postwar city in transition. For a compelling discussion of how these writers critique the urban industrialism of the declining city, see Carlo Rotella's 1998 *October Cities: The Redevelopment of Urban Literature.*

15. Referenced by several characters, Joseph Petrosino functions as a kind of folk hero in the novel. At the turn of the twentieth century, Petrosino was one of the most famous Italians in America for warning President McKinley of potential assassination attempts. In the mostly Irish New York City police department, he headed a small, hand-picked unit of detectives of Italian descent who worked to ensure Italian immigrants were given fair treatment by investigating officers who fluently spoke the Italian language. Famous for his relentless and controversial pursuit of the New York's Black Hand mafia, he was murdered in Palermo in 1909. See Arrigo Petacco's 1974 biography entitled *Joe Petrosino* for more information on both the man and the New York City police department's treatment of Italian immigrants.

16. Mario Puzo's creation in *The Godfather* of Tom Hagen, the German-Irish orphan who eventually takes over as the *consigliere* (adviser) of the Corleone family parallels D'Agsotino's fictional Julian in that both men possess an outsider status that enlarges their understanding of the familial landscape in which they live and work.

17. See John Turturro's film *Mac* for an equally dramatic rendition of an auction scene between two men who hold opposing value systems. In Turturro's film, the newcomer Italian builder, Mac, opposes the Polish building contractor, who cuts corners and cares only about making money.

18. The land area called Fox Ledge still exists today and is owned by the great-nephew of Guido and Helene D'Agostino. Fox Ledge is known for its natural spring water bottled "at the source in northeastern Pennsylvania." For information on the business and a historical reference to D'Agostino's *The Barking of a Lonely Fox*, see www.foxledge.com. Guido D'Agostino's nephew, Vince, explained that one of his relatives began the business of "bottling the spring water. So they damned up the old . . . spring that Uncle [Guido] had and built a bigger cistern and pipes and stuff and started off small and by the time . . . Alfred had retired up here and had bought Uncle Guido's land a number of years before and then gave Guido and Helene life tenancy on it. You know it was their land to do with what they wanted to until their death" (phone interview with Vince D'Agostino, October 18, 2005). Guido D'Agostino's papers are collected at the American Heritage Center, University of Wyoming, including the typesetter's manuscript of *My Enemy, The World* and an unfinished novel about an Italian American artist/farmer entitled *Half the Journey*.

19. Included in the list that focuses on seven companies that have ranked highest, by average, from 2002 to 2007, for consistent innovation is Ernest & Julio Gallo (*Information Week* 1154 50, 52 S 17 2007). Established in 1933 in Modesto, California, Ernest and Julio Gallo winery has become a worldwide leader in grape growing and winemaking. See the E. & J Gallo Winery homepage for their environmental philosophy and "commitment to sustainability" http://jobs.gallo.com/World Class/Sustainability.asp. For a wide-ranging examination of Italian rural immigrants throughout the United States, see *Italian Immigrants in Rural and Small Town America*, edited by Rudolph J. Vecoli.

20. Micaela di Leonardo challenges misinformed analyses of Italian community culture, including Banfield's damaging *Moral Basis of a Backward Society* and its thesis that Italians were "immersed in family concerns and uncaring for the general welfare" and Gans's *Urban Villagers* and its thesis that Italians in America remain poor because "they (especially mothers) hold down their children and are present-oriented." (20).

5. History Singer/Cantastorie—Vernacular Voices in Paule Marshall's and Tina De Rosa's *Kunstlerromane*

1. Black Americans have suffered qualitatively harsher effects due to racism than Italian Americans. During the second great migration, Italian immigrants were racially coded and associated with nonwhites,

especially in 1891 New Orleans where "perceptions of racial distinctness became deadly," resulting in the lynching of eleven Sicilians and "carried out by the White League, a Reconstruction-era terror organization much like the better known Ku Klux Klan" (Jacobson 56–57; also see 58–62).

2. After Silla sells her husband's property in Barbados, an overt struggle between them for control ensues. Deighton then goes on a shopping spree, spending all the property money to purchase costly gifts for himself and each family member, after which Silla and the community shun him, eventuating in his leaving the family and joining the Father Peace Movement. After having him deported, Silla later learns that Deighton likely commits suicide by drowning on his way back to Barbados. For an analysis of the husband-wife conflict, see Denniston's *The Fiction of Paule Marshall*, chapter 2. For historical information on the importance of land ownership in Barbados, see George Gmelch and Sharon Bohn Gmelch's *The Parish Behind God's Back: The Changing Culture of Rural Barbados*. I am grateful to my former student, Carla Bryan, who examined the connections between the achievement of manhood in Barbadian culture to property ownership in "History, Property and Manhood in Crafting Paule Marshall's *Brown Girl, Brownstones*."

3. Marcus Lee Hansen's famous statement "what the son wishes to forget the grandson wishes to remember" (495) puts forth a second-generation dilution or degeneracy, which is questioned and complicated in both Marshall's and De Rosa's novels. For an analysis of Hansen's formulation of generations, see Werner Sollors, *Beyond Ethnicity*, chapter 7.

4. For an application of Hansen's thesis on generations to Paule Marshall's *Brown Girl, Brownstones*, see Heather Hathaway, *Caribbean Waves: Relocating Claude McKay and Paule Marshall*, chapter 4.

5. Heather Hathaway cites Barbadian writer George Lamming in the introduction to his autobiography, *In the Castle of My Skin*, to describe the collectivity of island communities. Lamming argues that Caribbean writers use a "method of narration where community and not person is the central character . . . [and] several centers of attention . . . work simultaneously and acquire their coherence from the collective character of the Village" (qtd. in *Caribbean Waves* 97).

6. In "Turbulence and Tenderness: Mothers, Daughters, and 'Othermothers' in Paule Marshall's *Brown Girl, Brownstones*," Rosalie Riegle Troester refers to those women in the community as "othermothers," who form and guide a young woman, thereby "relieving some of the pressure on the mother-daughter relationship" (13).

7. Though not unique to Italian culture, De Rosa describes the burden of being the child who is "the chosen one in the family, the one that will go on to do great things in your name. And Carmolina is already beginning [at a young age] to feel that role" ("Breaking the Silence" 239).

8. Paule Marshall expresses much of the same concern when composing her first novel, written at a fast pace: "I was so caught up in the need to get down on paper before it was lost the whole sense of a special kind of community, what I call Bajan (Barbadian) Brooklyn, because even as a child I sensed there was something special and powerful about it" ("Paule Marshall" n.p.).

9. De Rosa explains, "I never realized all the beauty that was there [in the old Taylor-Halsted Little Italy] until I started to write about it. In fact I never realize my own truth until I start putting it down on paper" ("An Interview" 23).

10. Marshall's first novel received excellent reviews upon initial publication. According to Heather Hathaway, the novel "was praised early on by literary critic Robert Bone [but] it was not until after the success of Marshall's second novel, *The Chosen Place, The Timeless People* (1969), combined with the attention given partly as a result of the developing feminist movement, that *Brown Girl, Brownstones* achieved widespread acclaim as an important coming-of-age tale of a young black woman. Its republication by the Feminist Press in 1981, appended by an important afterword by Mary Helen Washington which both interpreted and situated the novel within Marshall's œuvre, assured *Brown Girl, Brownstones* a secure position in African American and women's studies curricula" (169 n. 2). The republication of De Rosa's *Paper Fish*, with a well-researched afterword by Edvige Giunta, has assured its canonicity within *Italian* American letters and given the work a wide-ranging exposure because of the press's focus on working-class women writers. For an explanation of how the book came into the hands of then director Florence Howe, see "Lady in Waiting" by Connie Lauerman. Despite her eschewing all labels and casual dismissal of the very critics who resurrected her novel—"all the political stuff comes from the critics. . . . I'm just Tina and I'm just a writer"—the book would have remained an unknown and unread virtuoso work without the persistence of devoted scholars who fought for its republication.

11. In *Toward Wholeness in Paule Marshall's Fiction*, Joyce Pettis reminds us that in 1959, the publication year of *Brown Girl, Brownstones*, Rosa Parks set in motion the civil rights movement by refusing to relinquish her seat on a segregated bus in Montgomery, Alabama. In contrast to the burgeoning political activism, "the excavation of black literary

texts that had been forgotten, dismissed, or ignored remained in the future. The literary scholars and critics who would assume the work on a scale heretofore unexperienced in African-American writing were, in many cases, too young to envision what their careers would become. The women's movement and its offsprings of feminism and feminist literary criticism were amorphous shapes awaiting the definition that would follow in the wake of the civil rights movement" (9).

12. Barbara Christian explains that Toni Morrison's *The Bluest Eye* implausibly would later be considered a book for juveniles as well. She adds, "['T']he misrepresentation of both of these books seemed to do with an inability on the part of the publishing houses, journals, the literary establishment, to see the *Bildungsroman* of a black woman as having as much human and literary value as, say, D.H. Lawrence's *Sons and Lovers* or James Joyce's *Portrait of the Artist as a Young Man*" (107).

13. Jerre Mangione, then acting director of the Italian Studies Center at the University of Pennsylvania, wrote the back-cover commendation for the first edition of Tina De Rosa's novel: "*Paper Fish* is an outstanding literary event, a first novel that breaks through the barriers of conventional fiction to achieve a dazzling union of narrative and poetry. . . . Hers is a delightfully fresh voice, filled with ancient wisdom yet new and probing, miraculously translating the most ineffable nuances of human existence in a language that is consistently beautiful and vital."

14. In *The Fiction of Paule Marshall*, Dorothy Denniston cites Stuart Hall's description of the changing nature of cultural identity: "Cultural identities come from somewhere, have histories. But, like everything which is historical, they undergo constant transformation. . . . Far from being grounded in mere 'recovery' of the past, which is waiting to be found and which, when found, will secure our sense of ourselves into eternity, identities are the names we give to the different ways we are positioned by, and position ourselves within, the narratives of the past" (xiv).

15. For an examination of Paule Marshall's sea imagery and its connection to the black diaspora, see Gavin Jones's "'The Sea Ain' Got No Back Door': The Problems of Black Consciousness in Paule Marshall's *Brown Girl, Brownstones*."

16. Marshall writes, "They [her mother and her mother's friends] really didn't count in American society except as a source of cheap labor. But given the kind of women they were, they couldn't tolerate the fact of their invisibility, their powerlessness. And they fought back, using the only weapon at their command: the spoken word" ("From the Poets in the Kitchen" 630).

17. Humbert Nelli explains in *The Italians in Chicago* that on the Near West Side Italian district "in not one block of the entire area did Italians comprise the only ethnic group" (32). In her afterword to *Paper Fish*, Edvige Giunta cites Dominic Pacyga's essay on Chicago's ethnic neighborhoods, including the West Side, which, according to Pacyga, "was home to many ethnicities, including Irish, German, Mexican, Greek, Jewish, Polish, and Czech" (124). Despite the fact that a Mexican American family lives in the same apartment building as the Bellacasa family, there is no communication whatsoever between the different ethnic groups. Unlike Selina, who establishes relationships with the other tenants in the brownstone, including an Anglo-American mother-daughter couple, Carmolina is not represented as having any relationships outside her immediate family and paternal relatives. De Rosa's ethnic narrative of denial is a strategy she takes to endow her Italian American community with what Robert Orsi calls a "moral order": "This narrative is then mapped onto the landscape: it is safe here, our kind of people live there, we understand the codes in force here but not there. Conversation becomes cartography" ("The Religious Boundaries of an Inbetween People" 336).

18. Marshall's manipulation of time parallels De Rosa's. According to Dorothy Denniston, Marshall partakes in an African cultural concept of time, in which, "as a vehicle of measurement, time for many African peoples moves not in a linear fashion but in a cyclic continuum" (xviii).

19. In "My Father's Lesson," De Rosa credits her policeman father, who performed the lowest-rank work as a patrolman for twenty-four years, for teaching De Rosa how to do the work to become a writer. "I recognized that, ironically, I had inherited my father's position. He didn't expect his job, his paid employment, to make him happy. He didn't expect that the everyday realities of being a policeman could lift his spirits. Thus did he come home, seeking us, telling us stories, trying to forget. It is an amazing revelation to me, . . . to see, finally, what the writing *is*, to me, and to see, finally, that my father is the one who taught me how to do this" (15).

20. Nelli explains that "intermarriage with non-Italians had begun to take place at least by 1906. . . . Marriage with non-Italians extended beyond the West Side colony. . . . Weddings involving police officers reflected the tendency of the upwardly mobile men to marry outside the ethnic group" (196, 198).

21. For an analysis of the figure of the mater dolorosa in Italian American literature, see my "*Mater Dolorosa* No More? Mothers and Writers in the Italian American Literary Tradition."

22. De Rosa describes her experience of alienation in contrast to Hansen's generational paradigm that represents the third generation as assimilated and symbolically identifying with the immigrant/grandparental generation. Of her relation to her family, De Rosa writes, "When I was with the family, I knew where I belonged. But I was no longer with them. Not completely. Neither was I a part of the educated world I had entered. Not completely. I belonged nowhere, completely, anymore. . . . That is the inheritance, that is the curse, of being born into a world and into a family that wants you to enter another. You say partially goodbye to one, partially hello to another, some of the time you are silent, and if you feel a little bit crazy—and sometimes you do—then you write about it" ("An Italian-American Woman Speaks Out" 39).

23. Due to their painful family situations, neither Selina nor Carmolina is portrayed as a child, having assumed the mantle of adulthood prematurely. Marshall describes Selina's eyes as "set deep in the darkness of her face. They were not the eyes of a child. Something too old lurked in their centers" (*Brown Girl* 4).

24. For another poignant concluding city scene with a protagonist on the verge of artistic adulthood, see Josephine Hendin's *The Right Thing to Do*, discussed in chapter 7.

25. Using graphic images from war-ravaged Europe, De Rosa describes the destruction of the Taylor Street enclave in a similar manner: "When the city came and started knocking down the buildings of my old neighborhood, my father was very resistant. We were the last family to leave the block. As the buildings were being torn down, the city would mark a yellow X with paint on the next building to go and that's when I said to myself, 'I feel like I'm in Nazi Germany.' It was unspeakable sorrow" ("Breaking the Silence" 243).

6. PRECURSOR/PRECURSORE—MOTHER'S TONGUE: ITALIAN AMERICAN DAUGHTERS AND FEMALE PRECURSORS

1. That is not to say that di Donato did not consider his father a god. As Robert Viscusi writes, "the son's desire to recover the lost Italian father and godfather whose deaths are the turning points in the story . . . [a]nd the persistence of impossible desire [are] the theme[s] of di Donato's career, just as [they are] the force driving the language of *Christ in Concrete*" (*Buried Caesars* 101).

2. Unlike her male contemporary writers, Mari Tomasi remained unmarried, raising the conundrum for women who aspire to be artists

but make the choice to remain single in order to achieve that distinction, a decision male writers traditionally have not had to make. Unlike Fante and D'Agostino, Tomasi's publications were minimal.

3. Louise DeSalvo has supported the work of many writers, including Mary Cappello. Her front-cover commendation of Tina De Rosa's *Paper Fish* is a case in point. In collaboration with Edvige Giunta, DeSalvo edited an anthology of Italian American women writers, many of them poets, in *The Milk of Almonds: Italian American Women Writers on Food and Culture*. Maria Gillan has been instrumental in encouraging and publishing the work of Italian American poets in her position as editor of *The Paterson Literary Review*. Gillan has also coedited several multiethnic literary anthologies with her daughter, Jennifer Gillan. They include *Unsettling America: An Anthology of Contemporary Multicultural Poetry, Identity Lessons: Contemporary Writing about Learning to be American*, and *Growing Up Ethnic in America: Contemporary Fiction about Learning to be American*. With Jennifer Gillan and Edvige Giunta, Maria Gillan also edited an anthology of New Jersey Italian American writers called *Italian American Writers on New Jersey: An Anthology of Poetry and Prose*.

4. Many memoirs by Italian American women have followed DeSalvo's *Vertigo*. Some include: Flavia Alaya's *Under the Rose: A Confession* (1999), Maria Laurino's *Were You Always an Italian? Ancestors and Other Icons of Italian America* (2000), Beverly Donofrio's *Looking for Mary: Or, the Blessed Mother and Me* (2000), Carole Maso's *The Room Lit by Roses: A Journal of Pregnancy and Birth* (2000), Diane di Prima's *Recollections of My Life as a Woman: The New York Years* (2001), Susan Antonetta's *Body Toxic: An Environmental Memoir* (2001), Teresa Maggio's *The Stone Boudoir: Travels through the Hidden Villages of Sicily* (2002), Louise De-Salvo's *Crazy in the Kitchen: Food, Feuds, and Forgiveness in an Italian American Family* (2004), Kym Ragusa's *The Skin Between Us: A Memoir of Race, Beauty, and Belonging* (2006), Marisa Acocella Marchetto's *Cancer Vixen: A True Story* (2006), Mary Cappello's *Awkward: A Detour* (2007), and Jean Feraca's *I Hear Voices: A Memoir of Love, Death, and the Radio* (2007).

5. In the context of confessional feminist autobiography, *Vertigo* arrives late on the scene. Rita Felski offers an extensive list of such works from the 1970s and 1980s from the United States and Europe. Examples include Marie Cardinal's *The Words to Say It* (1975), Audre Lorde's *The Cancer Journals* (1980), and Ann Oakley's *Taking it Like a Woman* (1984). See Felski, "On Confession," 83.

6. Students both male and female have regularly admitted feeling as though DeSalvo's *Vertigo* speaks directly to them, enabling them to

feel an intimacy with the author and to validate their own feelings about parental relationships and growing up.

7. Several novels written by Italian American women portray domestic trauma and episodic violence. See Dorothy Bryant's *Miss Giardino*, Rita Ciresi's *Blue Italian*, Rachel Guido deVries's *Tender Warriors*, Josephine Gattuso Hendin's *The Right Thing to Do*, Carole Maso's *Ghost Dance*, Agnes Rossi's *The Quick: A Novella and Stories*, Julia Savarese's *The Weak and the Strong*, and Octavia Waldo's *A Cup of the Sun*.

8. See Louise DeSalvo's *Writing as a Way of Healing*.

9. The most notable critique of the institution of heterosexuality continues to be Adrienne Rich's "Compulsory Heterosexuality and Lesbian Existence." See also Judith Butler's *Bodies That Matter* for a complication of the categories of heterosexuality and homosexuality in her analysis of women's gendered homosexual bodies.

10. Feelings of shame and despair during World War II are explored in Diane di Prima's *Recollections of My Life as a Woman*, Helen Barolini's *Umbertina and Chiaroscuro: Essays of Identity*, and Dorothy Bryant's *Miss Giardino* and her essay in "Dorothy Bryant" in *Contemporary Authors Autobiography Series* 26.

11. In her analysis of the politics of gender in lesbian and heterosexual women's autobiographies, Julia Watson offers a useful overview of critiques of the system of gender formulated by such theorists as Teresa de Lauretis, Biddy Martin, and Judith Butler: "Gender has been a falsely stabilized category that acts to regulate and maintain heterosexuality as a fiction of great cultural power" (397). Throughout *Night Bloom*, Cappello subjects this fiction to the highest forms of scrutiny.

12. In an interview with Beacon Press when *Night Bloom* was first published, Mary Cappello describes her ideal writing as scholarly and poetic, two modes of writing considered antithetical to "an anti-intellectual culture such as ours." Such writing, Cappello explains, "enable[s] one another . . . [to make] possible a new voice in the space between." In her devotion to creating new voices within reconceived forms, Cappello comes closest to Carole Maso, whose postmodern works continually attempt to reinvent how narrative is conceived.

13. For an analysis of how the southern Italian culture has been used as an instrument of discipline by immigrants against their children, see Robert Orsi's "The Fault of Memory: 'Southern Italy' in the Imagination of Immigrants and the Lives of Their Children in Italian Harlem, 1920–1945."

14. At the conclusion of Toni Morrison's *Beloved*, Paul D. thinks "he wants to put his story next to hers," encouraging Sethe to embrace a subjectivity that includes a maternal voice but is not swallowed by it (273). In its construction, Morrison's novel parallels other works such as Cappello's that are assembled like collages, works told in bits and pieces from multiple voices. Consider also Maxine Hong Kingston's *The Woman Warrior*, Louise Erdrich's *Love Medicine*, and Carole Maso's *The Art Lover*. Ethnic literature abounds in such examples.

15. Investigating the evil eye belief, Lawrence DiStasi writes that "early in the life of anyone who belongs to a minority culture, there develops a quick sense of what one should or should not discuss on 'the outside.' What one has for dinner, what one's father thinks about church or white bread or the schools or the government, all these are unmentionable subjects for they run the risk of exposing one to public ridicule. During my childhood there was always one more of these, the unmentionable of unmentionables, *mal occhio*, or evil eye" (*Mal Occhio* 15).

16. Helen Barolini describes the responses of readers and writers to *The Dream Book* in "Reintroducing *The Dream Book*," in *Chiaroscuro*, and in the 2000 reprint of *The Dream Book*. Among others, Maria Gillan has been an influence on and a supporter of Rachel Guido deVries, Mary Russo Demetrick, Maria Famá, Denise Leto, Mary Ann Mannino, Vittoria Repetto, Mary Jo Bona, and Giana Patriarca.

17. Gillan writes, "In 1985, when Helen Barolini's *The Dream Book* ... came out, I saw my name, Maria Mazziotti Gillan spelled, out above my poem and saw it in a *New York Times* review where they quoted from it. I was, for the first time, incredibly proud of that name and all the lineage it embodied" ("Shame and Silence in My Work" 161; also see her "Why I Took Back My Name").

18. While she does not examine Italian American women poets through the lens of ethnicity, Alicia Ostriker does include commentary on Diane di Prima, Daniela Gioseffi, and Sandra M. Gilbert in her survey on women's poetry in America: *Stealing the Language: The Emergence of Women's Poetry in America*.

19. Besides appearing in Barolini's *The Dream Book*, Romano's *La Bella Figura: A Choice, and Taking Back My Name*, Gillan's "Public School #18," appears as the lead poem in *Sinister Wisdom* (#41), in a special issue devoted to Italian American lesbians. It has also appeared in Gillan's anthology, *Unsettling America*.

20. Sandra M. Gilbert's "Mafioso" is the best known and most reprinted mafia poem by an Italian American poet. Others include Felix

Stefanile's "A Review of the Film *Godfather VII*," Robert Viscusi's "Goons and Lagoons," Rina Ferrarelli's "Mafiosi," and Dona Luongo Stein's "Children of the Mafiosi."

21. Gillan emphasizes an emotional return to her Italian mothers by using the Demeter/Persephone model of revival in the same manner as many contemporary American women poets. In "Black Dresses," Gillan writes, "I dress now all in black like the old ladies/of my childhood" (*Italian Women in Black Dresses* 9).

22. Well before the large migration of Italians to America, native-born Americans revered Columbus. In 1828, Washington Irving published his scholarly but popular biography, *History of the Life and Voyages of Christopher Columbus*, which was hugely successful in America, serving to give the United States a hero it needed after the War of Independence. For a recent and balanced approach to Columbus that moves beyond conventional formulations of the explorer as either savior or villain see Ilan Stavan's *Imagining Columbus: The Literary Voyage*.

23. Richard Gambino's *Vendetta* boasts an unusually long subtitle: *A True Story of the Worst Lynching in America, the Mass Murder of Italian-Americans in New Orleans in 1891, the Vicious Motivations Behind It, and the Tragic Repercussions that Linger to This Day*. Also see Jerre Mangione and Ben Morreale's chapter "New Orleans—Wops, Crime, and Lynchings," in their *La Storia: Five Centuries of the Italian American Experience*.

24. I borrow this description from Geneva Smitherman's groundbreaking book on black dialect, *Talking and Testifying: The Language of Black America*.

7. DEATH/MORTE—WHAT THEY TALK ABOUT WHEN THEY TALK ABOUT DEATH

1. Ariès attributes this shift in attitude toward dying to three developments: industrialization, romanticism, and individualism: "Affectivity, formerly diffuse, was henceforth concentrated on a few rare beings whose disappearance could no longer be tolerated and caused a dramatic crisis: the death of the other. It was a revolution in feeling that was just as important to history as the related revolution in ideas, politics, industry, socioeconomic conditions, or demography" (*The Hour* 609). Ariès explains, "this exaggeration of mourning in the nineteenth century . . . means that survivors accepted the death of another person with greater difficulty than in the past. Henceforth, and this is a very important

change, the death which is feared is no longer so much the death of the self as the death of the other, *la mort de toi*, thy death" (*Western Attitudes* 68).

2. For further information on native-born American hostility toward Italians in Colorado, see Cooper; Collins; and Luconi.

3. In *Immigrant Minds, American Identities*, Orm Øverland examines characteristic homemaking myths of American ethnic groups of European origin and groups them into three main categories: "myths of foundation ('we were here first or at least as early as you were'), myths of blood sacrifice ('we fought and gave our lives for our chosen homeland'), and myths of ideological gifts or an ideological relationship ('the ideas we brought with us are American ideas')" (19).

4. For analyses of di Donato's critique of Catholicism, see Fred Gardaphé's introduction to the 1993 republication of *Christ in Concrete* and Robert Viscusi's *Buried Caesars and Other Secrets of Italian American Writing*.

5. For information on stonecutters' TB, see Tomasi's article "The Italian Story in Vermont," and her interview "White Walls and Quiet" in Tomasi and Richmond, *Men Against Granite* (162–166).

6. In her analysis of the myth of TB, Susan Sontag explains that the sensitive person contracts the disease, which "constitutes the next-to-last episode in the long career of the ancient idea of melancholy—which was the artist's disease, according to the theory of the four humours. The melancholy character—or the tubercular—was the superior one: sensitive, creative, a being apart." Shelley is said to have consoled Keats with the line: "this consumption is a disease particularly fond of people who write such good verses as you have done" (*Illness as Metaphor* 32).

7. Arthur Kleinman, M.D., makes useful distinctions between the terms "illness," "disease," and "sickness': "*Illness* refers to how the sick person and the members of the family or wider social network perceive, live with, and respond to symptoms and disability.... *[D]isease* is reconfigured *only* as an alternative in biological structure or functioning.... *[S]ickness* [is] the understanding of a disorder in its generic sense across a population in relation to macrosocial (economic, political, institutional) forces" (3–6).

8. Arthur Frank generates a typology of four ideal body types to examine illness narratives in *The Wounded Storyteller*: the disciplined body, the mirroring body, the dominating body, and the communicative body. He further explains that "Actual body selves represent distinctive mixtures of ideal types" and "How any individual responds to lost predictability is

woven into the dense fabric of how the other action problems of the body are managed" (29, 32).

9. Sandra Gilbert's husband was the victim of medical malpractice and suffered a postoperative death. See Gilbert's medical memoir, *Wrongful Death*, and elegiac poems in *Ghost Volcano*.

10. Gilbert also examines the nearly nonexistent Indian practice of *sati*, the practice of death-by-fire of Hindu widows or widow burning. Quoting anthropologist Lindsey Harlan, Gilbert writes, "'[W]hen a woman utters her sati vow, she places herself in the context of a vivid temporal fiction. Time is condensed, so that she becomes a *sahagamini*, "one who goes (*gamini*) together (*saha*) with one's husband"'" (*Death's Door* 29). For a subtle rendering of this practice in fiction, see Carol Shields's final novel, *Unless*.

11. Exceptions to the rule of traditional masculine responses to grief include Thomas Hardy's "wailing songs" in *Poems, 1912* that mourn the death of his wife and C. S. Lewis's classic bereavement text *A Grief Observed* (Gilbert, *Death's Door* 30). I might add here that the AIDS crisis in the 1980s and 1990s also produced harrowing responses to illness and grief, including Robert Boucheron's *Epitaphs for the Plague Dead*, Paul Monette's *Love Alone: 18 Elegies for Rog*, Michael Lassell's *Poems for Lost and Un-lost Boys*, Thom Gunn's *The Man With Night Sweats*, and *Brother to Brother: New Writings by Black Gay Men* (edited by Essex Hemphill).

12. As different, Maria Laurino might add, as Italian fashion designer Giorgio Armani and Gianni Versace, one born in "the genteel 'civic' north, the other from the rugged 'uncivic' south of Italy" (*Were You Always Italian?* 54). Laurino's description of southern-born Versace (from Reggio Calabria) aptly parallels di Donato's stylistic excess in *Christ in Concrete*: "Versace was surrounded by the tastes of southern Italy. It is the taste of poor and working-class people. . . . Bright Mediterranean colors, the earthy sensuality of peasants, the excessive pageantry of the religious south, and a baroque style that rejected simplicity as a metaphor for the Teutonic, northern way of life" (66).

13. In *The Dominion of the Dead*, Robert Pogue Harrison examines one of the most "probing books to date on the ancient forms of ritualized objectification" (56) by the Italian philosophical anthropologist Ernesto De Martino (in his comprehensive analysis of traditional Euro-Mediterranean mourning practices), *Morte e pianto rituale*. "For De Martino mourning rituals involve precisely such a separation, in the sense that their performative protocols get the griever to recommit him-

self or herself to the world of the living instead of dying (inwardly) with the dead" (170).

14. Bryant explained that publishing a book like *A Day in San Francisco* in 1982 was "an act of marketplace suicide with the audience I had built up" (personal communication with the author, April 22, 1997). See also Bryant's online book, *Literary Lynching: When Readers Censor Writers*, at http://www.holtuncensored.com/literary_lynching/ Chapter 7.html. For a useful overview of the post–World War II gay community in San Francisco, see John D'Emilio.

8. Revival/Risorgimento—Stories Continue: Shaping U.S. Italian American Writing

1. Susan Gallagher traces the canonical progress of a specific text: Tsitsi Dangarembga's novel, *Nervous Conditions* (1989), demonstrating the way in which "material conditions, accidental encounters, pragmatic needs, and ethical commitments all influence the formation of pedagogical canons" (66).

2. For further commentary on Barolini's trailblazing efforts to publish Italian American women writers, see Bona's "'But Is It Great?': The Question of the Canon for Italian American Women Writers" and Edvige Giunta's "Blending 'Literary' Discourses: Helen Barolini's Italian/ American Narratives."

3. See Edvige Giunta's "Afterword: 'A Song from the Ghetto'" in Tina De Rosa's *Paper Fish* and also Giunta's chapter 3 in *Writing with an Accent: Contemporary Italian American Women Authors*.

4. In their introduction to *The Politics of Literature*, Louis Kampf and Paul Lauter recall the high-handed tactics initially taken in 1968 by the premier organization, the Modern Language Association (MLA), in an effort to silence their demands to reconsider the practice of aestheticism in light of the Vietnam War and the repression of students and blacks. Thirty years later, in 1998, Josephine Gattuso Hendin chaired the first formal Discussion Session devoted to Italian American literature at the MLA. In a March 27, 1998, e-mail, she wrote to Fred Gardaphé, Anthony J. Tamburri, Mary Jo Bona, and Edvige Giunta the following: "I am looking forward to our session and applaud the efforts on all. What an achievement!" Not coincidentally, Sandra M. Gilbert was President of the MLA at the time when concerted efforts were made to establish wider institutional visibility for Italian American literary culture through affiliation with this organization. In 1991,

Anthony J. Tamburri assembled one of the earliest special sessions on Italian American literature and thereafter, with Gardaphé, initiated contact with Gilbert before she assumed the MLA presidency, introducing her to the viability of Italian American literature as a field of inquiry.

5. Fred Gardaphé offers a history of the first full-fledged Italian American Studies Program in the United States in "Creating a Program in Italian American Studies: The Case of SUNY at Stony Brook."

6. For a recent update on the genre conundrum regarding autobiographical writing, see Nancy K. Miller's "The Entangled Self: Genre Bondage in the Age of Memoir." For a generic analysis of *Mount Allegro* as "group-biography," see William Boelhower's *Immigrant Autobiography in the United States*.

7. As Gerald Graff cogently argued in the 1990s, "students [are] so alienated from traditional book culture that they cannot read the traditional selections at all" (94). According to an Associated Press-Ipsos poll released in 2007, "one in four adults read no books at all in the past year." For an analysis of how the Internet is dramatically reshaping literary studies, resulting in changes in reading practices, see Patricia Keefe Durso's "It's Just Beginning: Assessing the Impact of the Internet on U.S. Multiethnic Literature and the 'Canon.'"

8. In his reflection on the discourse of transnationalism and African American Studies, Mark Sanders examines the ways ethnic disciplines are limited by academic institutionalization. Largely U.S. focused, such disciplines produce scholars who are trained in "longer-standing disciplines and thus often specialize in fields that are nation-specific, that do not tend to be comparative, and that most frequently require the use of only one language, usually English" (813).

9. By Lauter's own admission, Judith Fetterley offered a useful corrective to his survey of the academic canon, finding evidence of exclusion much earlier than the 1920s (*Canons and Contexts* 22). See especially Fetterley's comment in *Provisions*: "By 1891 . . . it was possible for Houghton Mifflin to publish an anthology entitled 'Masterpieces of American Literature,' which predictably included no work by women writers" ("Introduction" 20).

10. In *Canon and Contexts*, Lauter continues: "Even women had renewed their demand for the vote, jobs, control over their bodies. The old elite and their allies moved on a variety of fronts, especially during and just after the First World War, to set the terms on which these demands would be accommodated. They repressed, in actions like the Prohibition Amendment and The Palmer Raids, the political and social, as well as

the cultural, institutions of immigrants and radicals" (*Canons and Contexts* 28). For an analysis of the scientific racism that informed the years bridging World War I with the mass migration of Italians to the Americas, see Donna Gabaccia's "Race, Nation, Hyphen: Italian Americans and American Multiculturalism in Comparative Perspective."

11. Guido D'Agostino's nephew, Vince D'Agostino, recalled his uncle discovering that his novel *Olives on the Apple Tree* was required reading in a New Jersey high school in the 1950s. A young man who pumped gas at the Jersey shore recognized the author and told him that he had read *Olives* for class (phone interview with Vincent D'Agostino, October 18, 2005).

12. An alternative list of writings by Italian Americans who produced books during and after the Depression include Garibaldi Lapolla's *The Grand Gennaro* (1935), Guido D'Agostino's *Olives on the Apple Tree* (1940), Mari Tomasi's *Deep Grow the Roots* (1940), Jo Pagano's *The Golden Wedding* (1943), Michael De Capite's *Maria* (1943), and George Panetta's *We Ride a White Donkey* (1944).

13. In *Leaving Little Italy*, Gardaphé offers an extended list of anthologies that excluded Italian American writers, from Granville Hicks's 1935 *Proletarian Literature* to Marcus Klein's 1981 *Foreigners*, which only briefly mentions Mangione's work on the WPA Writers Project (113 n. 3).

14. See "The Bricklayer as Bricoleur," Art Casciato's corrective to di Donato's contribution to the Third American Writer's Congress sponsored by the League of American Writers, the American Communist Party's leading cultural "front organization" (67).

15. In her 1993 examination of proletarian fiction, *Radical Representations*, Barbara Foley assured the continued exclusion of Italian America from her purview, focusing on only a dozen years, 1929–1941. In a chapter devoted to a subgenre of the classically bourgeois bildungsroman, which Foley labels the proletarian bildungsroman, the author examines protagonists who acquire "militant or revolutionary class consciousness," preventing discussion of how the category of ethnicity modifies that form of radicalism (327).

16. All three authors have recently experienced a literary resurgence within and outside of the academy. Of the three, John Fante has achieved what I'd call an international cult status that is not focused on his ethnicity but rather on his writing style, his Los Angeles locales, and his screenwriter connections to Hollywood. Fante enjoyed the advocacy of H. L. Mencken (see Moreau's *Fante/Mencken*), who fought to combat the literary hegemony of the Northeast, and James T. Farrell who championed

Wait Until Spring, Bandini as one of the few meritorious novels of the 1930s. The revival of interest in Fante's works began in the late 1970s–early 1980s with the longtime support of Fante's widow, Joyce, and the advocacy of John Martin of Black Sparrow Press, who reprinted all of Fante's previous novels. For an overview of Fante's literary resurgence in the United States and abroad, see Stephen Cooper's Fante biography, *Full of Life* and his introduction to his and David Fine's *John Fante: A Critical Gathering*; Richard Collins's preface to *John Fante: A Literary Portrait*; and Fred Gardaphé's "Evviva John Fante!" in *Dagoes Read*. In 2006, Teresa Fiore edited a special issue devoted to Fante in the bilingual journal *Quaderni Del '900* (6, 2006).

Jerre Mangione's *Mount Allegro* was described by Malcolm Cowley as having "more lives than any other book in our time" (qtd. in Gardaphé, *Leaving* 53). The press affiliated with Mangione's alma mater, Syracuse University, reprinted *Mount Allegro* in 1998 and the University of Pennsylvania Press reprinted *The Dream and the Deal* and *An Ethnic At Large* when Mangione was a professor of English and creative writing at the University of Pennsylvania (from 1961 to 1977). With writer Ben Morreale, Mangione published in 1992 the first full-length history of Italian America, *La Storia*, published by a large trade press, HarperCollins. The journal, *VIA*, dedicated a special issue (4.2, 1993) to Mangione to mark the fiftieth anniversary of the publication of *Mount Allegro*.

With the reprinting of Pietro di Donato's *Christ in Concrete* by a major trade press—Signet—the revival of this author was triggered in the 1990s primarily by Italian American scholars. The success of di Donato's 1939 novel launched him into a national limelight, earning him a celebrity status from which critics felt he never recovered. The journal *VIA* published a special tribute to di Donato in 1991 (2.2), which included excerpts of *Christ in Concrete*, *Three Circles of Light*, and *American Gospels*.

17. I am applying this phrase differently than John Higham, who used it to describe how immigrants reacted to the intense pressure of Americanization at the beginning of the twentieth century (254). See his *Strangers in the Land*, especially chapter 9, "Crusade for Americanization."

18. Taking a cue from Gilles Deleuze and Felix Guattari's critique of capitalism, Karen Piper warns against using the term "multiculturalism" to describe the diversity of cultures in the United States because it "places the non-Anglo subject in the impossible position of having to preserve difference without a land base or means of survival. . . . The *idea* of culture is resurrected, in all its difference, to keep in check any resistance to the material reality of the 'deterritorialized' landscape of capitalism"

(18). Piper states that the term "multiculturalism" is dangerous for two reasons: "first, it attempts to preserve cultures in a primordial state as objects for analysis; and second, it demands, conversely, that immigrants to the U.S. adapt to its market needs. . . . The U.S. is *not* a multicultural environment; it is a settler-invader territory that has taken property from the indigenous inhabitants and moulded it to the needs of global capitalism. The literature of the U.S., therefore, should be read as part of the global 'post-colonial canon' rather than as an internalized expression of multicultural difference (19).

19. See Patricia Yeager's "Editor's Column: The End of Postcolonial Theory?" for position papers on the continuation of postcolonialism as a useful paradigm in the geopolitical present.

20. In 2004, Anthony J. Tamburri created a Ph.D. seminar called "Problematics in Italian/American Culture" that prioritized secondary-source materials in an effort to analyze current issues that surround Italian American culture, including definitional categories of race, ethnicity, gender, and sexuality alongside such topics as the myth of origins, linguistic strategies, and organized crime.

21. For a discussion of the rhetorical work done by writers of Italian America, including the insertion of glossaries and defined terms, see JoAnne Ruvoli's dissertation-in-progress, *Framing Ethnicity: Storytelling in Italian American Novels.*

Bibliography

_ᗌꓯ

Abrahams, Roger D. Foreword. *Italian Folktales in America: The Verbal Art of an Immigrant Woman*. By Elizabeth Mathias and Richard Raspa. Detroit: Wayne State University Press, 1988. ix–xv.

Ahearn, Carol Bonomo. "Interview: Helen Barolini." *Fra Noi*. Sept. 1986: 47.

Alba, Richard D. *Italian Americans: Into the Twilight of Ethnicity*. Englewood Cliffs: Prentice, 1985.

Alberti, John. "Introduction: Reconstructing the Pedagogical Canon." *The Canon in the Classroom: The Pedagogical Implications of Canon Revision in American Literature*. Ed. John Alberti. New York: Garland, 1995. xi–xxx.

Anderson, Sherwood. *Winesburg, Ohio*. 1919. New York: Penguin, 1960.

Ardito, Linda. "Italian American Women and the Role of Religion." *Models and Images of Catholicism in Italian Americana: Academy and Society*. Ed. Joseph A. Varacalli et al. Stony Brook: Forum Italicum, 2004. 127–161.

Ardizzone, Tony. *In the Garden of Papa Santuzzu*. New York: Picador, 1999.

———. "Interview with Tony Ardizzone." By Cristina Bevilacqua. *Italian Americana* 19.2 (Summer 2001): 207–213.

Ariès, Philippe. *The Hour of Our Death*. New York: Knopf, 1981.

———. *Western Attitudes Toward Death*. Baltimore: Johns Hopkins University Press, 1974.

Ashcroft, Bill, Gareth Griffiths, and Helen Tiffin, eds. *The Empire Writes Back: Theory and Practice in Post-Colonial Literatures*. 1989. 2nd ed. New York: Routledge, 2002.

Avrich, Paul. *Sacco and Vanzetti: The Anarchist Background*. Princeton: Princeton University Press, 1991.

Baker, Aaron, and Juliann Vitullo. "Mysticism and the Household Saints of Everyday Life." *Voices in Italian Americana* 7.2 (1996): 55–68.

Barolini, Helen. "The Case of Mari Tomasi." *Italians and Irish in America*. Ed. Francis X. Femminella. Proc. of the Sixteenth Annual Conference of the American Italian Historical Association. Staten Island: American Italian Historical Association, 1985. 177–186.

———. *Chiaroscuro: Essays of Identity*. Madison: University of Wisconsin Press, 1999.

———. *The Dream Book: An Anthology of Writings by Italian American Women*. New York: Schocken, 1985. New York: Syracuse University Press, 2000.

———. Introductory Note. *Rosa: The Life of an Italian Immigrant*. By Marie Hall Ets. Madison: University of Wisconsin Press, 1999. xiii–xv.

Batinich, Mary Ellen Mancina. "The Interaction Between Italian Immigrant Women and The Chicago Commons Settlement House, 1909–1944." *The Italian Immigrant Woman in North America*. Proc. of the Tenth Annual Conference of the American Italian Historical Association. Ed. Betty Boyd Caroli, Robert F. Harney, and Lydio F. Tomasi. Toronto: Multicultural History Society, 1978. 154–167.

Belluscio, Steven J. *To Be Suddenly White: Literary Realism and Racial Passing*. Columbia: University of Missouri Press, 2006.

Benjamin, Walter. *Illuminations*. Ed. Hannah Arendt. New York: Schocken, 1969.

Benolich, Patrizia C. "Up Through the Concrete." Diss. State University of New York, Stony Brook, 2006.

Bergland, Betty. "Ideology, Ethnicity, and the Gendered Subject: Reading Immigrant Autobiographies." *Seeking Common Ground: Multidisciplinary Studies of Immigrant Women in the United States*. Ed. Donna Gabaccia. Westport: Greenwood, 1992. 101–121.

Bevilacqua, Winifred Farrant. "Rosa: The Life of an Italian Immigrant, The Oral History Memoir of a Working-Class Woman." *Italy and Italians in America: Rivista di studi anglo-americani* 3.4–5 (1984–1985): 545–555.

Birnbaum, Lucia Chiavola. *Black Madonnas: Feminism, Religion and Politics in Italy*. Boston: Northeastern University Press, 1993.

Blanchot, Maurice. *The Gaze of Orpheus and Other Literary Essays*. Barrytown: Station Hill, 1981.

Bloom, Harold. *The Anxiety of Influence: A Theory of Poetry*. New York: Oxford University Press, 1973.

Boelhower, William. *Immigrant Autobiography in the United States: Four Versions of the Italian American Self*. Verona: Essedue, 1982.

Bona, Mary Jo. "'But Is It Great?' The Question of the Canon for Italian American Women Writers." *Multiethnic Literature and Canon Debates*. Ed. Mary Jo Bona and Irma Maini. Albany: State University of New York Press, 2006. 85–110.

———. *Claiming a Tradition: Italian American Women Writers*. Carbondale: Southern Illinois University Press, 1999.

———. "*Mater Dolorosa* No More?: Mothers and Writers in the Italian American Literary Tradition." *Voices in Italian Americana* 7.2 (1996): 1–19. Rptd. *The Review of Italian American Studies*. Ed. Jerome Krase and Frank Sorrentino. Lanham: Lexington, 2000. 375–92.

———. Rev. of *Night Bloom*, by Mary Cappello. *Voices in Italian Americana* 11.1 (2000): 177–181.

———. Rev. of *Vendetta*, by Rose Romano and *Sinister Wisdom* 41. *Voices in Italian Americana* 2.1 (1991): 182–85.

———. Rev. of *Vertigo: A Memoir*, by Louise DeSalvo. *Footwork: Paterson Literary Review* 27 (1998): 391–93.

———. Rev. of *Where I Come From: New and Selected Poems*, by Maria Mazziotti Gillan. *Voices in Italian Americana* 7.2 (1999): 292–296.

Bona, Mary Jo, and Irma Maini, eds. "Introduction: Multiethnic Literature in the Millennium." *Multiethnic Literature and Canon Debates*. Albany: State University of New York Press, 2006. 1–20.

Bryan, Carla. "History, Property and Manhood in Crafting Paule Marshall's *Brown Girl, Brownstones*." Unpublished essay, 2007.

Bryant, Dorothy. *A Day in San Francisco*. Berkeley: Ata, 1982.

———. "Dorothy Bryant." *Contemporary Authors Autobiography Series* 26. Detroit: Gale Research, 1997. 47–63.

———. *Miss Giardino*. 1978. New York: Feminist, 1997.

Butler, Judith. "Introduction to *Bodies That Matter*." *Women, Autobiography, Theory: A Reader*. Ed. Sidonie Smith and Julia Watson. Madison: University of Wisconsin Press, 1998. 367–379.

Calvino, Italo. "Introduction: A Journey Through Folklore." *Italian Folktales*. 1956. Selected and retold by Italo Calvino. San Diego: Harcourt, 1985. xv–xxxii.

——— *Italian Folktales*. 1956. Trans. George Martin. San Diego: Harcourt, 1980.

Cappello, Mary. *Awkward: A Detour*. New York: Bellevue, 2007.

———. *Night Bloom*. Boston: Beacon, 1998.

———. "Nothing to Confess: A Lesbian in Italian America." *Fuori: Essays by Italian American Lesbians and Gays*. Ed. Anthony J. Tamburri. West Lafayette: Bordighera, 1996. 89–108.

Carroll, Michael P. "The Psychoanalytic Investigation of Italian Catholicism." *Models and Images of Catholicism in Italian Americana: Academy and Society*. Ed. Joseph A. Varacalli et al. Stony Brook: Forum Italicum, 2004, 177–194.

Casciato, Art. "The Bricklayer as Bricoleur: Pietro di Donato and the Cultural Politics of the Popular Front." *Voices in Italian Americana* 2.2 (1991): 67–76.

Cather, Willa. *O Pioneers!* Boston: Houghton Mifflin, 1913.

Cavaioli, Frank J. *The American Italian Historical Association at the Millennium*. Unpublished pamphlet.

Chodorow, Nancy. *The Reproduction of Mothering: Psychoanalysis and the Sociology of Gender*. Berkeley and Los Angeles: University of California Press, 1978.

Christian, Barbara. *Black Feminist Criticism: Perspectives on Black Women Writers*. New York: Pergamon, 1985.

Ciccarelli, Barbara. "An Introduction: *Rosa: The Life of an Italian Immigrant*." MA thesis. Miami University, 1995.

Cole, Susan Letzler. *The Absent One: Mourning Ritual, Tragedy, and the Performance of Ambivalence*. University Park: Pennsylvania State University Press, 1985.

Coles, Robert. *The Call of Stories: Teaching and the Moral Imagination*. Boston: Houghton Mifflin, 1989.

Collins, Richard. *John Fante: A Literary Portrait*. Toronto: Guernica, 2000.

Conzen, Kathleen Neils, et al. "The Invention of Ethnicity: A Perspective from the U.S.A." *Journal of American Ethnic History* 12.1 (Fall 1992): 3–41.

Cooper, Stephen. *Full of Life: A Biography of John Fante*. New York: North Point, 2000.

Cooper, Stephen, and David Fine, eds. *John Fante: A Critical Gathering*. Madison: Fairleigh Dickinson University Press, 1999.

Covello, Leonard. *The Social Background of the Italo-American School Child*. Diss. New York University, 1944. Leiden: Brill, 1967.

Cutter, Martha. "If It's Monday This Must Be Melville: A 'Canon, Anticanon' Approach to Redefining the American Literature

Survey." *The Canon in the Classroom: The Pedagogical Implications of Canon Revision in American Literature.* Ed. John Alberti. New York: Garland, 1995. 119–151.

D'Acierno, Pellegrino. "Cinema Paradiso: The Italian American Presence in American Cinema." *The Italian American Heritage: A Companion to Literature and Arts.* Ed. Pellegrino D'Acierno. New York: Garland, 1999. 563–690.

D'Agostino, Guido. *The Barking of a Lonely Fox.* New York: McGraw-Hill, 1952.

———. *Hills beyond Manhattan.* New York: Doubleday, 1942.

———. *My Enemy, The World.* New York: Dial, 1947.

———. *Olives on the Apple Tree.* New York: Doubleday, 1940. New York: Arno, 1975.

D'Agostino, Peter R. *Rome in America: Transnational Catholic Ideology from the Risorgimento to Fascism.* Chapel Hill: University of North Carolina Press, 2004.

D'Emilio, John. "Gay Politics and Community in San Francisco since World War II." *Hidden From History: Reclaiming the Gay and Lesbian Past.* Ed. Martin Duberman, Martha Vicinus and George Chauncey Jr. New York: Meridian, 1989. 456–473.

———. *Sexual Politics, Sexual Communities: The Making of a Homosexual Minority in the United States, 1940–1970.* Chicago: University of Chicago Press, 1983.

DeLamotte, Eugenia C. *Places of Silence, Journeys of Freedom: The Fiction of Paule Marshall.* Philadelphia: University of Pennsylvania Press, 1998.

DeLillo, Don. *The Names.* New York: Vintage, 1982.

———. *Underworld.* New York: Scribner, 1997.

De Martino, Ernesto. *Morte e pianto rituale: dal lamento funebre antico al pianto di Maria.* Turin: Bollati Boringhieri, 1975.

Demetrick, Mary Russo. *First Pressing.* Syracuse: Hale Mary, 1994.

Denniston, Dorothy Hamer. *The Fiction of Paule Marshall: Reconstructions of History, Culture, and Gender.* Knoxville: University of Tennessee Press, 1995.

De Rosa, Tina. "Breaking the Silence: An Interview with Tina De Rosa." By Lisa Meyer. *Adjusting Sites: New Essays in Italian American Studies.* Ed. William Boelhower and Rocco Pallone. Stony Brook: Forum Italicum, 1999. 221–243.

———. "An Interview with Tina De Rosa." By Fred Gardaphé. *Fra Noi* May 1985: 23.

———. "An Italian-American Woman Speaks Out." *Attenzione* May 1980: 38–39.

———. "Lady in Waiting." Interview by Connie Lauerman. *Chicago Tribune* Sept. 2, 1996, sec. 5: 1+.

———. "My Father's Lesson." *Fra Noi* Sept. 1986: 15.

———. *Paper Fish*. 1980. New York: Feminist, 1996.

DeSalvo, Louise. *Crazy in the Kitchen: Food, Feuds, and Forgiveness in an Italian American Family*. New York: Bloomsbury, 2004.

———. *Vertigo: A Memoir*. New York: Dutton, 1996.

———. *Writing as a Way of Healing: How Telling Our Stories Transforms Our Lives*. Boston: Beacon, 2000.

DeSalvo, Louise, and Edvige Giunta, eds. *The Milk of Almonds: Italian American Women Writers on Food and Culture*. New York: Feminist, 2002.

deVries, Rachel Guido. *How to Sing to a Dago*. Toronto: Guernica, 1996.

Di Donato, Pietro. *Christ in Concrete*. 1939. New York: Signet, 1993.

Diffley, Kathleen. "Reconstructing the American Canon: E Pluribus Unum?" *Midwest Modern Language Association*. 21.2 (1988): 1–15.

di Leonardo, Micaela. *The Varieties of Ethnic Experience: Kinship, Class, and Gender Among California Italian-Americans*. Ithaca: Cornell University Press, 1984.

Diner, Hasia, R. *Hungering for America: Italian, Irish, and Jewish Foodways in the Age of Migration*. Cambridge: Harvard University Press, 2001.

Di Prima, Diane. *Recollections of My Life as a Woman: The New York Years*. New York: Viking, 2001.

DiStasi, Lawrence. "How World War II Iced Italian American Culture." *Multi-America: Essays on Cultural Wars and Cultural Peace*. Ed. Ishmael Reed. New York: Penguin, 1997. 168–178.

———. *Mal Occhio: The Underside of Vision*. San Francisco: North Point, 1981.

Dolan, Jay P. *In Search of an American Catholicism: A History of Religion and Culture in Tension*. New York: Oxford University Press, 2002.

Duggan, Christopher. *A Concise History of Italy*. Cambridge: Cambridge University Press, 1994.

Durso, Patricia Keefe. "It's Just Beginning: Assessing the Impact of the Internet on U.S. Multiethnic Literature and the 'Canon.'" *Multiethnic Literature and Canon Debates*. Ed. Mary Jo Bona and Irma Maini. Albany: State University of New York Press, 2006. 197–218.

Esposito, Dawn. "The Italian Mother: The Wild Woman Within." *Screening Ethnicity: Cinematographic Representations of Italian Americans in the United States.* Ed. Anna Camaiti Hostert and Anthony Julian Tamburri. Boca Raton: Bordighera, 2002. 32–47.

Ets, Marie Hall. *Rosa: The Life of an Italian Immigrant.* 1970. Madison: University of Wisconsin Press, 1999.

———. *Rosa: vita di una emigrante italiana.* Trans. Francesca De Mattei et al. Ticino: Ecoistituto, 2003.

Famá, Maria. *Identification.* Philadelphia: Allora, 1996.

———. *Looking for Cover.* New York: Bordighera, 2007.

Fante, John. *Wait Until Spring, Bandini.* 1938. Santa Barbara: Black Sparrow, 1983.

Felski, Rita. "On Confession." *Women, Autobiography, Theory: A Reader.* Ed. Sidonie Smith and Julia Watson. Madison: University of Wisconsin Press, 1998. 83–95.

Ferraro, Thomas. *Ethnic Passages: Literary Immigrants in Twentieth-Century America.* Chicago: University of Chicago Press, 1993.

———. *Feeling Italian: The Art of Ethnicity in America.* New York: New York University Press, 2005.

———. "Italian-American Literature." *The Oxford Encyclopedia of American Literature.* Vol. 2. Ed. Jay Parini. New York: Oxford University Press, 2004. 275–284.

Fetterley, Judith, ed. Introduction. *Provisions: A Reader from 19th-Century American Women.* Bloomington: Indiana University Press, 1985. 1–40.

Fiore, Teresa. "Introduction: 'Fanteasticherie.'" *Quaderni del '900* 6 (2006): 7–16.

Fischer, Michael M. J. "Ethnicity and the Post-Modern Arts of Memory." *Writing Culture: The Poetics of Ethnography.* Ed. James Clifford and George E. Marcus. Berkeley and Los Angeles: University of California Press, 1986. 194–233.

Fitzgerald, E. G. Rev. of *The Barking of a Lonely Fox,* by Guido D'Agostino. *Saturday Review* 35:21 Jl 5 '52 170w. *Book Review Digest,* 1952: 222.

Foley, Barbara. *Radical Representations: Politics and Form in U.S. Proletarian Fiction, 1929–1941.* Durham: Duke University Press, 1993.

"Folk Tale." *Italian Americana* 17.1 (Winter 1999): 107–111.

Foucault, Michel. *The History of Sexuality. Volume I: An Introduction.* New York, Vantage, 1980.

Frank, Arthur W. *The Wounded Storyteller: Body, Illness, and Ethics.* Chicago: University of Chicago Press, 1995.

Friedman, Susan Stanford. "Women's Autobiographical Selves: Theory and Practice." *The Private Self: Theory and Practice of Women's Autobiographical Writings.* Ed. Shari Benstock. Chapel Hill: University of North Carolina Press, 1988. 34–62.

———. "Women's Autobiographical Selves: Theory and Practice." *Women, Autobiography, Theory: A Reader.* Ed. Sidonie Smith and Julia Watson. Madison: University of Wisconsin Press, 1998. 72–82.

Friedman-Kasaba, Kathie. *Memories of Migration: Gender, Ethnicity, and Work in the Lives of Jewish and Italian Women in New York, 1870–1924.* Albany: State University of New York Press, 1996.

Gabaccia, Donna. "Race, Nation, Hyphen: Italian-Americans and American Multiculturalism in Comparative Perspective." *Are Italians White? How Race is Made in America.* Ed. Jennifer Guglielmo and Salvatore Salerno. New York: Routledge, 2003. 44–59.

Gabaccia, Donna, ed. *Seeking Common Ground: Multidisciplinary Studies of Immigrant Women in the United States.* Westport: Greenwood, 1992.

Gallagher, Susan VanZanten. "Contingencies and Intersections: The Formation of Pedagogical Canons." *Pedagogy* 1.1 (2001): 53–67.

Gambino, Richard. *Blood of My Blood: The Dilemma of Italian-Americans.* 1974. Toronto: Guernica, 1996.

———. *Vendetta.* 1977. Toronto: Guernica, 1998.

Gannett, Lewis. Rev. of *Olives on the Apple Tree*, by Guido D'Agostino. *Boston Evening Transcript.* 9 N 5 '40 500w. *Book Review Digest*, 1940: 219.

Gardaphé, Fred. "Creating a Program in Italian American Studies: The Case of SUNY at Stony Brook." *Teaching Italian American Literature, Film, and Popular Culture.* Ed. Edvige Giunta and Kathleen McCormick. New York: Modern Language Association, 2010.

———. *Dagoes Read: Tradition and the Italian/American Writer.* Toronto: Guernica, 1996.

———. *From Wise Guys to Wise Men: The Gangster and Italian American Masculinities.* New York: Routledge, 2006.

———. "Italian American Novelists." *The Italian American Heritage.* Ed. Pellegrino D'Acierno. New York: Garland, 1999. 165–191.

———. *Italian Signs, American Streets: The Evolution of Italian American Narrative.* Durham: Duke University Press, 1996.

———. *Leaving Little Italy: Essaying Italian American Culture*. Albany: State University of New York Press, 2004.

Gates, Henry Louis, Jr. "Criticism in the Jungle." *Black Literature and Literary Theory*. Ed. Henry Louis Gates. New York: Methuen, 1984. 1–24.

——— *The Signifying Monkey: A Theory of African-American Literary Criticism*. New York: Oxford University Press, 1988.

Gilbert, Sandra M. *Death's Door: Modern Dying and the Ways We Grieve*. New York: Norton, 2006.

———. Foreword. "In the Stone Forests of Yearning." *Reconciling Catholicism and Feminism? Personal Reflections on Tradition and Change*. Ed. Sally Barr Ebest and Ron Ebest. Notre Dame: University of Notre Dame Press, xi–xix.

———. *Ghost Volcano*. New York: Norton, 1995.

———. "Mafioso." *In the Fourth World*. Tuscaloosa: University of Alabama Press, 1979.

———. *Wrongful Death: A Memoir*. New York: Norton, 1995.

Gilbert, Sandra M., and Susan Gubar. *The Madwoman in the Attic: The Woman Writer and the Nineteenth-Century Literary Imagination*. New Haven: Yale University Press, 1979.

Gillan, Jennifer, Maria Mazziotti Gillan, and Edvige Giunta, eds. *Italian American Writers on New Jersey: An Anthology of Poetry and Prose*. New Brunswick: Rutgers University Press, 2003.

Gillan, Maria Mazziotti. *All That Lies Between Us*. Toronto: Guernica, 2007.

———. *Flowers from the Tree of Night*. Brooklyn: Chantry, 1981.

———. *Italian Women in Black Dresses*. Toronto: Guernica, 2002.

———. "Public School No. 18, Paterson, New Jersey." *Where I Come From: Selected and New Poems*. Toronto: Guernica, 1995. 12–13.

———. "Shame and Silence in My Work." *Breaking Open: Reflections on Italian American Women's Writing*. Ed. Mary Ann Vigilante Mannino and Justin Vitiello. West Lafayette: Purdue University Press, 2003. 153–175.

———. *Taking Back My Name*. Chapbook 1. San Francisco: Malafemmina, 1991.

———. *Where I Come From: Selected and New Poems*. Toronto: Guernica, 1995.

———. "Why I Took Back My Name." *Voices in Italian Americana* 9.1 (1998): 31–33.

———. *Winter Light*. Midland Park: Chantry, 1985.

Giunta, Edvige. Afterword: "'A Song from the Ghetto.'" *Paper Fish*. By Tina De Rosa. New York: Feminist, 1996. 123–142.

———. "Blending 'Literary' Discourses: Helen Barolini's Italian/American Narratives." *Beyond the Margin: Readings in Italian Americana*. Ed. Paolo Giordano and Anthony J. Tamburri. Madison: Fairleigh Dickinson University Press, 1998. 114–130.

———. *Writing with an Accent: Contemporary Italian American Women Authors*. New York: Palgrave, 2002.

Giunta, Edvige, and Kathleen McCormick, eds. *Teaching Italian American Literature, Film, and Popular Culture*. New York: Modern Language Association, 2010.

Gmelch, George, and Sharon Bohn Gmelch. *The Parish Behind God's Back: The Changing Culture of Rural Barbados*. Ann Arbor: University of Michigan Press, 1997.

Goeller, Alison D. "Persephone Goes Home: Italian American Women in Italy." *MELUS* 28.3 (Fall 2003): 73–90.

Gordon, Mary. *Good Boys and Dead Girls: And Other Essays*. New York: Viking, 1991.

Graff, Gerald. *Beyond the Culture Wars: How Teaching the Conflicts Can Revitalize American Education*. New York: Norton, 1992.

Green, Rose Basile. *The Italian-American Novel: A Document of the Interaction of Two Cultures*. Rutherford: Fairleigh Dickinson University Press, 1974.

Guglielmo, Jennifer, and Salvatore Salerno, eds. *Are Italians White? How Race Is Made in America*. New York: Routledge, 2003.

Guillory, John. *Cultural Capital: The Problem of Literary Canon Formation*. Chicago: University of Chicago Press, 1993.

Hall, Stuart. "Gramsci's Relevance for the Study of Race and Ethnicity." *The Journal of Communication Inquiry* 10.2 (1986): 5–27.

Hansen, Marcus Lee. "The Third Generation in America." *Commentary* 14 (1952): 492–500.

Harmon, William, and C. Hugh Holman. *A Handbook to Literature*. 7th ed. Upper Saddle River: Prentice Hall, 1995.

Harrison, Robert Pogue. *The Dominion of the Dead*. Chicago: University of Chicago Press, 2003.

———. *Forests: The Shadow of Civilization*. Chicago: University of Chicago Press, 1992.

Hathaway, Heather. *Caribbean Waves: Relocating Claude McKay and Paule Marshall*. Bloomington: Indiana University Press, 1999.

Hauser, Marianne. "Exile's Conflicts." Rev. of *Hills beyond Manhattan*, by Guido D'Agostino. *New York Times* 18 Jan. 1942: BR 7.

Hendin, Josephine Gattuso. *The Right Thing to Do*. 1988. New York: Feminist, 1999.

———. "Social Constructions and Aesthetic Achievements: Italian American Writing as Ethnic Art." *MELUS* 28.3 (Fall 2003): 13–39.

Higham, John. *Strangers in the Land: Patterns of American Nativism, 1860–1925*. 1955. New Brunswick: Rutgers University Press, 2004.

Hirsch, Marianne. *The Mother/Daughter Plot: Narrative, Psychoanalysis, Feminism*. Bloomington: Indiana University Press, 1989.

Ifill, Gwen. "Desegregation Pioneers Reflect on Education Milestone." Transcript. *Online NewsHour*. 25 Sept. 2007. http://www.pbs.org.

Insko, Jeffrey. "Generational Canons." *Pedagogy: Critical Approaches to Teaching Literature, Language, Composition, and Culture* 3.3 (2003): 341–358.

Irving, Washington. *History of the Life and Voyages of Christopher Columbus*. 1828. New York: Putnam, 1863.

Jacobson, Matthew Frye. *Whiteness of a Different Color: European Immigrants and the Alchemy of Race*. Cambridge: Harvard University Press, 1998.

Japtok, Martin. "Paule Marshall's *Brown Girl, Brownstones*: Reconciling Ethnicity and Individualism." *African American Review* 32.2 (Summer 1998): 305–315.

Jay, Gregory S. *American Literature and the Canon Wars*. Ithaca: Cornell University Press, 1997.

———. "The End of 'American' Literature: Toward a Multicultural Practice." *The Canon in the Classroom: The Pedagogical Implications of Canon Revision in American Literature*. Ed. John Alberti. New York: Garland, 1995. 3–28.

Jaye, Michael C., and Ann Chalmers Watts, eds. *Literature and the Urban Experience: Essays on the City and Literature*. New Brunswick: Rutgers University Press, 1981.

Jirousek, Lori M. "Spectacle Ethnography and Immigrant Resistance: Sui Sin Far and Anzia Yezierska." *MELUS* 27.1 (Spring 2002): 25–52.

Jones, Gavin. "'The Sea Ain' Got No Back Door': The Problems of Black Consciousness in Paule Marshall's *Brown Girl, Brownstones*." *African American Review* 32.4 (Winter 1998): 597–606.

Juliani, Richard N. "The Interaction of Irish and Italians: From Conflict to Integration." *Italians and Irish in America.* Ed. Francis X. Femminella. Staten Island: The American Italian Historical Association, 1985. 27–34.

Kampf, Louis, and Paul Lauter, eds. Introduction. *The Politics of Literature: Dissenting Essays on the Teaching of English.* New York: Pantheon, 1972. 3–54.

Kertzer, David I. *Sacrificed for Honor: Infant Abandonment and the Politics of Reproductive Control.* Boston: Beacon, 1993.

Kessner, Thomas. *The Golden Door: Italian and Jewish Immigrant Mobility in New York City 1880–1915.* New York: Oxford University Press, 1977.

Kleinman Arthur, M.D. *The Illness Narratives: Suffering, Healing & the Human Condition.* New York, Basic, 1988.

La Gumina, Salvatore, ed. *WOP! A Documentary History of Anti-Italian Discrimination in the United States.* 1973. Toronto: Guernica, 1999.

Lang, Amy Schrager. *Prophetic Women: Anne Hutchinson and the Problem of Dissent in the Literature of New England.* Berkeley and Los Angeles: University of California Press, 1987.

Lapolla, Garibaldi M. *The Grand Gennaro.* 1935. Edited with an Introduction by Steven Belluscio. New Brunswick, NJ: Rutgers University Press, 2009.

Lauerman, Connie. "Lady in Waiting." Interview with Tina De Rosa. *Chicago Tribune* 2 Sept. 1996, sec. 5: 1+.

Laurino, Maria. *Were You Always an Italian? Ancestors and Other Icons of Italian America.* New York: Norton, 2000.

Lauter, Paul. *Canons and Contexts.* New York: Oxford University Press, 1991.

Lehan, Richard. *The City in Literature: An Intellectual and Cultural History.* Berkeley and Los Angeles: University of California Press, 1998.

Leonardi, Susan J. *And Then They Were Nuns.* Ann Arbor: Firebrand, 2003.

Levi, Carlo. *Christ Stopped at Eboli.* 1947. Trans. by Frances Frenaye. New York: Ferrar, 1963.

Lloyd, Susan Caperna. *No Pictures in My Grave: A Spiritual Journey in Sicily.* San Francisco: Mercury, 1992.

———. *Processione: A Sicilian Easter.* Dir. Susan Caperna Lloyd, 1989.

Lorde, Audre. "Poetry Is Not a Luxury." *Sister Outsider.* Trumansburg: Crossing, 1984. 36–39.

Lowe, John. "Humor, Ethnicity, and Identity in Jerre Mangione's *Storia.*" *Voices in Italian Americana* 4.2 (Fall 1993): 31–49.

Luconi, Stefano. "The Protean Ethnic Identities of John Fante's Italian-American Characters." *John Fante: A Critical Gathering*. Ed. Stephen Cooper and David Fine. Madison: Fairleigh Dickinson University Press, 1999. 54–64.

Luke, Carmen. "Feminist Politics in Radical Pedagogy." *Feminisms and Critical Pedagogy*. Ed. Carmen Luke and Jennifer Gore. New York: Routledge, 1992. 25–53.

Luke, Carmen, and Jennifer Gore, eds. Introduction. *Feminisms and Critical Pedagogy*. New York: Routledge. 1–14.

Madsen, Deborah, L. "Beyond the Commonwealth: Post-Colonialism and American Literature." *Post-Colonial Literatures: Expanding the Canon*. Ed. Deborah L. Madsen. London: Pluto, 1999. 1–13.

———, ed. *Post-Colonial Literatures: Expanding the Canon*. London: Pluto, 1999.

Makarushka, Irena. "Tracing the Other in *Household Saints*." *Literature and Theology*. 12.1 (March 1998): 82–92.

Mangione, Jerre. "A Double Life: The Fate of the Urban Ethnic." *Literature and the Urban Experience*. Ed. Michael C. Jaye and Ann Chalmers Watts. New Brunswick: Rutgers University Press, 1981. 169–183.

———. *An Ethnic at Large: A Memoir of America in the Thirties and Forties*. 1978. Philadelphia: University of Pennsylvania Press, 1983.

———. *Mount Allegro*. 1943. New York: Syracuse University Press, 1998.

Mangione, Jerre, and Ben Morreale. *La Storia: Five Centuries of the Italian American Experience*. New York: HarperCollins, 1992.

Marshall, Paule. *Brown Girl, Brownstones*. 1959. New York: Feminist, 1981.

———. "From the Poets in the Kitchen." *Callaloo* 24.2 (2001): 627–633.

———. "A *MELUS* Interview: Paule Marshall." By Joyce Pettis. *MELUS* 17.4 (Winter 1991–1992): 117–129.

———. "Paule Marshall." *Contemporary Authors Online*. Gale, 2001.

Martin, Biddy. "Lesbian Identity and Autobiographical Difference[s]." *Life/Lines: Theorizing Women's Autobiography*. Ed. Bella Brodzki and Celeste Schenck. Ithaca: Cornell University Press, 1988. 77–103.

Martin, Wallace. *Recent Theories of Narrative*. Ithaca: Cornell University Press, 1986.

Marx, Leo. "The Puzzle of Anti-Urbanism in Classic American Literature." *Literature and the Urban Experience*. Ed. Michael C. Jaye and Ann Chalmers Watts. New Brunswick: Rutgers University Press, 1981. 63–80.

Maso, Carole. *The Art Lover*. Hopewell: Ecco, 1990.

———. *Break Every Rule: Essays on Language, Longing, and Moments of Desire*. Washington, D.C: Counterpoint, 2000.

———. *The Room Lit by Roses: A Journal of Pregnancy and Birth*. Washington, D.C: Counterpoint, 2000.

Mathias, Elizabeth, and Richard Raspa. *Italian Folktales in America: The Verbal Art of an Immigrant Woman*. Detroit: Wayne State University Press, 1988.

McHugh, Heather. *Broken English: Poetry and Partiality*. Hanover: Wesleyan University Press, 1993.

Messenger, Chris. *The Godfather and American Culture: How the Corleones Became "Our Gang."* Albany: State University of New York Press, 2002.

Milani, Ernesto. "The Publication of the Translation of *Rosa: The Life of an Italian Immigrant.*" *Italian Americans and the Arts and Culture*. Selected Essays from the 36th Annual Conference of the American Italian Historical Association. Ed. Mary Jo Bona, Dawn Esposito and Anthony J. Tamburri. New York: American Italian Historical Association, 2007. 222–236.

Miller, Kerby A. "Class, Culture and Immigrant Group Identity in the United States: The Case of Irish-American Ethnicity." *Immigration Reconsidered: History, Sociology, and Politics*. Ed. Virginia Yans-McLaughlin. New York: Oxford University Press, 1990. 96–129.

Miller, Nancy K. "The Entangled Self: Genre Bondage in the Age of Memoir." *PMLA* 122.2 (March 2007): 537–548.

Miller, Stephen Paul. "Scrutinizing Maria Mazziotti Gillan's *Where I Come From.*" *Voices in Italian Americana* 10.1 (1999): 56–62.

Moreau, Michael, ed. *Fante/Mencken: John Fante and H.L. Mencken, A Personal Correspondence, 1930–1952*. Santa Rosa: Black Sparrow, 1989.

Morrison, Toni. *Beloved*. New York: Knopf, 1987.

———. "City Limits, Village Values: Concepts of the Neighborhood in Black Fiction." *Literature and the Urban Experience: Essays on the City and Literature*. Ed. Michael C. Jaye and Ann Chalmers Watts. New Brunswick: Rutgers University Press, 1981. 35–43.

———. "The Dancing Mind." Speech upon Acceptance of the National Book Foundation Medal for Distinguished Contribution to American Letters. 6 Nov. 1996. New York: Knopf, 1996.

———. "Unspeakable Things Unspoken: The Afro-American Presence in American Literature." *Modern Critical Views: Toni Morrison*. Ed. Harold Bloom. New York: Chelsea, 1990. 201–230.

Mulas. Franco. "A *MELUS* Interview: Jerre Mangione." *MELUS* 12.4 (Winter 1985): 73–87.

Nassar, Paul Eugene. Foreword. *Mount Allegro*. By Jerre Mangione. Syracuse: Syracuse University Press, 1998. ix–xiii.

Nelli, Humbert S. *The Italians in Chicago: 1880–1930, A Study in Ethnic Mobility*. New York: Oxford University Press, 1970.

Oates, Joyce Carol. "Imaginary Cities: America." *Literature and the Urban Experience*. Ed. Michael C. Jaye and Ann Chalmers Watts. New Brunswick: Rutgers University Press, 1981. 11–33.

Orsi, Robert Anthony. "The Fault of Memory: 'Southern Italy' in the Imagination of Immigrants and the Lives of Their Children in Italian Harlem, 1920–1945." *Journal of Family History* 15.2 (1990): 133–147.

———. *The Madonna of 115th Street: Faith and Community in Italian Harlem, 1880–1950*. New Haven: Yale University Press, 1985.

———. "The Religious Boundaries of an Inbetween People: Street *Feste* and the Problem of the Dark-Skinned Other in Italian Harlem, 1920–1990." *American Quarterly* 44.3 (1992): 313–347.

Orsini, Daniel. "Rehabilitating di Donato, a Phonocentric Novelist." *The Melting Pot and Beyond: Italian Americans in the Year 2000*. Ed. Jerome Krase and William Egelman. Proc. of the 18th Annual Conference of the American Italian Historical Association. Staten Island: American Italian Historical Association, 1987. 191–205.

Ostriker, Alicia Suskin. *Stealing the Language: The Emergence of Women's Poetry in America*. London: Women's, 1987.

Øverland, Orm. *Immigrant Minds, American Identities: Making the United States Home*. Urbana: University of Illinois Press, 2000.

Palumbo-Liu, David, ed. Introduction. *The Ethnic Canon: Histories, Institutions and Interventions*. Minneapolis: University of Minnesota Press, 1995. 1–27.

Peragallo, Olga. *Italian-American Authors and Their Contribution to American Literature*. New York: Vanni, 1949.

Petacco, Arrigo. *Joe Petrosino*. Trans. Charles Lam Markmann. New York: MacMillan, 1974.

Pettis, Joyce. *Toward Wholeness in Paule Marshall's Fiction*. Charlottesville: University Press of Virginia, 1995.

Philpott, Thomas Lee. *The Slum and the Ghetto: Neighborhood Deterioration and Middle-Class Reform, Chicago, 1880–1930*. New York: Oxford University Press, 1978.

Piper, Karen. "Post-Colonialism in the United States: Diversity or Hybridity?" *Post- Colonial Literatures: Expanding the Canon.* Ed. Deborah L. Madsen. London: Pluto, 1999. 14–28.

Pipino, Mary Frances. *"I Have Found My Voice": The Italian-American Women Writer.* New York: Peter Lang, 2000.

"Poll: 1 in 4 Adults Read No Books Last Year." *Associated Press.* 22 Aug. 2007. http://printthis.clickablility.com.

Prose, Francine. *Household Saints.* New York: Ivy, 1981.

Puzo, Mario. *The Fortunate Pilgrim.* 1964. New York: Ballantine, 1997.

———. *The Godfather.* New York: New American Library, 1969.

———. *The Godfather Papers and Other Confessions.* New York: Putnam, 1972.

Rev. of *Hills Beyond Manhattan*, by Guido D'Agostino. *New Republic* 106:214 F 9 '42 80 w. *Book Review Digest*, 1942: 180.

Rich, Adrienne. "Compulsory Heterosexuality and Lesbian Existence." *Blood, Bread, and Poetry: Selected Prose, 1979–1985.* New York: Norton, 1986. 23–75.

———. *Of Woman Born: Motherhood as Experience and Institution.* 1976. New York: Norton, 1986.

Riis, Jacob A. "Feast-Days in Little Italy." *Century Magazine* 58 (Aug. 1899): 491–499.

———. *How The Other Half Lives: Studies among the Tenements of New York.* 1890. New York: Dover, 1971.

Rimstead, Roxanne. "Between Theories and Anti-Theories: Moving toward Marginal Women's Subjectivities." *What We Hold in Common: An Introduction to Working-Class Studies.* Ed. Janet Zandy. New York: Feminist, 2001. 182–198.

Rinehart, Jane. "Breaking Bad Habits in Good Company: The Subversive Core of Excellent Teaching." With Mary Jo Bona and Cate Siejk. Unpublished keynote address. 8 Apr. 1999.

———. "Feminist Theorizing as a Conversation: The Connections between Thinking, Teaching and Political Action." *Women and Politics* 19.1 (1998): 59–89.

Rivière, Peter. *Christopher Columbus.* Phoenix Mill, UK: Sutton, 1998.

Roediger, David R. *Toward the Abolition of Whiteness: Essays on Race, Politics, and Working Class History.* London: Verso, 1994.

Romaine, Elaine. "you were always irish, god." *The Dream Book: An Anthology of Writings by Italian American Women.* Ed. Helen Barolini. New York: Schocken, 1985. 306.

Romano, Rose. "Coming Out Olive in the Lesbian Community." *Social Pluralism and Literary History: The Literature of the Italian Emigration*. Ed. Francesco Lorrigio. Toronto: Guernica, 1996. 161–175.

———, ed. *La Bella Figura: A Choice*. San Francisco: Malafemmina, 1993.

———. *Vendetta*. San Francisco: Malafemmina, 1990.

———. *The Wop Factor*. Brooklyn: Malafemmina, 1994.

Rosa, Alfred. "The Novels of Mari Tomasi." *Italian Americana* 2.1 (1975): 66–78.

Rotella, Carlo. *October Cities: The Redevelopment of Urban Literature*. Berkeley and Los Angeles: University of California Press, 1998.

Russo, John Paul. "DeLillo: Italian American Catholic Writer." *Altreitalie* 25 (luglio–dicembre 2002): 4–29.

———. "The Hidden Godfather: Plenitude and Absence in Francis Ford Coppola's *Godfather I* and *II*." *Support and Struggle: Italians and Italian Americans in a Comparative Perspective*. Ed. Joseph L. Tropea, James E. Miller, and Cheryl Beattie-Repetti. Proc. of the Seventeenth Annual Conference of the American Italian Historical Association. Staten Island: New York, 1986. 255–281.

Sanders, Mark A. "Brief Reflections on the Discourse of Transnationalism and African American Studies." Ethnic Studies in the Age of Transnationalism. *PMLA* 122.3 (May 2007): 812–814.

Savoca, Nancy, dir. *Household Saints*. 1993.

Scarry, Elaine. *The Body in Pain: The Making and Unmaking of the World*. New York: Oxford University Press, 1985.

Schneider, Jane. "Of Vigilance and Virgins: Honor, Shame and Access to Resources in Mediterranean Societies." *Ethnology* 10.1 (1971): 1–24.

Scholes, Robert. *Protocols of Reading*. New Haven: Yale University Press, 1989.

Sciorra, Joseph. "'We Go Where the Italians Live': Religious Processions as Ethnic and Territorial Markers in a Multi-ethnic Brooklyn Neighborhood." *Gods of the City: Religion and the American Urban Landscape*. Ed. Robert A. Orsi. Bloomington: Indiana University Press, 1999. 310–340.

Segale, Sister Blandina. *At The End of the Santa Fe Trail*. 1948. Albuquerque: University of New Mexico Press, 1999.

Shields, Carol. *Unless*. London: Fourth Estate, 2002.

Simmel, Georg. *On Individuality and Social Forms*. Ed. and intro. David N. Levine. Chicago: University of Chicago Press, 1971.

Sinister Wisdom 41. *Il viaggio delle donne*. Summer/Fall 1990.

Smith, Sidonie and Julia Watson. "Introduction: Situation Subjectivity in Women's Autobiographical Practices." *Women, Autobiography, Theory: A Reader*. Ed. Sidonie Smith and Julia Watson. Madison: University of Wisconsin Press, 1998. 3–52.

Smitherman, Geneva. *Talking and Testifying: The Language of Black America*. Boston: Houghton, 1977.

Sollors, Werner. *Beyond Ethnicity: Consent and Descent in American Culture*. New York: Oxford University Press, 1986.

Sontag, Susan. *AIDS and Its Metaphors*. New York: Farrar, 1988.

———. *Illness as Metaphor*. New York: Farrar, 1977.

Stavans, Ilan. *Imagining Columbus: The Literary Voyage*. New York: Palgrave, 2001.

Sullivan, Mary Louise. *Mother Cabrini: "Italian Immigrant of the Century."* New York: Center for Migration Studies. 1992.

Sylvester, Harry. Rev. of *Olives on the Apple Tree*, by Guido D'Agostino. *The Commonweal* 20 Dec. 1940.

Tamburri, Anthony. J. *A Semiotic of Ethnicity: In (Re)cognition of the Italian/American Writer*. Albany: State University of New York Press, 1998.

Tamburri, Anthony J., Paolo Giordano, and Fred L. Gardaphé, eds. *From the Margin: Writings in Italian Americana*. West Lafayette: Purdue University Press, 1991.

Taylor, Graham. *Chicago Commons through Forty Years*. Chicago: Cuneo,1936.

Teller, Walter Magnes. "Symbol of Security." Rev. of *The Barking of a Lonely Fox*, by Guido D'Agostino. *New York Times* 1 June 1952: BR 14.

Timpanelli, Gioia. "Stories and Storytelling, Italian and Italian American: A Storyteller's View." *The Italian American Heritage: A Companion to Literature and Arts*. Ed. Pellegrino D'Acierno. New York: Garland, 1999. 131–148.

Tomasi, Mari. "The Italian Story in Vermont." *Vermont History* 28 (1960): 73–87.

———. *Like Lesser Gods*. 1949. Shelburne: New England, 1988.

———. "Stone." *The Literature of Vermont: A Sampler*. Ed. Arthur W. Biddle and Paul A. Eschholz. Hanover: University Press of New England, 1973. 312–320.

Tomasi, Mari, and Roaldus Richmond. *Men Against Granite*. Ed. Alfred Rosa and Mark Wanner. Shelburne: New England, 2004.

Tomasi di Lampedusa, Giuseppe. *The Leopard*. 1958. Trans. Archibald Colquhoun. New York: Pantheon, 2007.

Tompkins, Jane. *Sensational Designs: The Cultural Work of American Fiction, 1790–1860*. New York: Oxford University Press, 1985.

Torgovnick, Marianna De Marco. *Crossing Ocean Parkway*. Chicago: University of Chicago Press, 1994.

Tricarico, Donald. *The Italians of Greenwich Village: The Social Structure and Transformation of an Ethnic Community*. Staten Island: Center for Migration Studies of New York, 1984.

Troester, Rosalie Riegle. "Turbulence and Tenderness: Mothers, Daughters, and 'Othermothers' in Paule Marshall's *Brown Girl, Brownstones*." *SAGE: A Scholarly Journal on Black Women* 1.2 (Fall 1984): 13–16.

Turner, Kay. "The Virgin of the Sorrows Procession: A Brooklyn Inversion." *Folklore Papers* 9 (1980): 1–26.

Twain, Mark. *Adventures of Huckleberry Finn*. 1884. Ed. Henry Nash Smith. Boston: Houghton Mifflin, 1958.

Ventura, Luigi Donato. "*Peppino*." *The Multilingual Anthology of American Literature: A Reader of Original Texts with English Translations*. Ed. Marc Shell and Werner Sollors. New York: New York University Press, 2000. 220–269.

VIA: Voices in Italian Americana: a literary and cultural review 3.2. 1992.

Vecoli, Rudolph J. "Are Italian Americans Just White Folks?" *Italian and Italian American Images in the Media*. Ed. Mary Jo Bona and Anthony J. Tamburri. Proc. of the 27th Annual Conference of the American Italian Historical Association. Staten Island: American Italian Historical Association, 1996. 3–17.

———. "Finding, and Losing, the Gems of Barre's Italian Immigrant Past: Anarchism, Silicosis, and a Slip of the Community Mind." *Times Argus* 26 Oct. 1989: 7+.

———. Foreword. *Rosa: The Life of an Italian Immigrant*. By Marie Hall Ets. Madison: University of Wisconsin Press, 1999. v–xi.

———, ed. *Italian Immigrants in Rural and Small Town America*. Essays from the 14th Annual Conference of the American Italian Historical Association. Staten Island, NY: The American Italian Historical Association, 1987.

———. "Prelates and Peasants: Italian Immigrants and the Catholic Church." *Journal of Social History* 2 (1969): 217–268.

Viscusi, Robert. *Buried Caesars and Other Secrets of Italian American Writing*. Albany: State University of New York Press, 2006.

———. "*De Vulgari Eloquentia*: An Approach to the Language of Italian American Fiction." *Yale Italian Studies* 1 (Winter 1981): 21–38.

von Huene-Greenberg, Dorothée. "A *MELUS* Interview: Pietro di Donato." *MELUS* 14.3–4 (1987): 33–52.

Waldo, Octavia. *A Cup of the Sun*. New York: Harcourt, 1961.

Warner, Marina. *Alone of all Her Sex: The Myth and the Cult of the Virgin Mary*. New York: Vintage, 1976.

Washington, Mary Helen. Afterword. *Brown Girl, Brownstones*. By Paule Marshall. New York: Feminist, 1981. 311–324.

———. Foreword. *Their Eyes Were Watching God*. By Zora Neale Hurston. New York: Harper, 1990. vii–xiv.

Watson, Julia. "Unspeakable Differences: The Politics of Gender in Lesbian and Heterosexual Women's Autobiographies." *Women, Autobiography, Theory: A Reader*. Ed. Sidonie Smith and Julia Watson. Madison: University of Wisconsin Press, 1998. 393–402.

Weber, Donald. "'Oh God, These Italians!' Shame and Self-Hatred in the Early Fiction of John Fante." *John Fante: A Critical Gathering*. Ed. Stephen Cooper and David Fine. Madison: Fairleigh Dickinson University Press, 1999. 65–76.

West, Cornel. "The New Cultural Politics of Difference." *Out There: Marginalization and Contemporary Cultures*. Ed. Russell Ferguson, Martha Gever, Trinh T. Minh-ha, and Cornel West. New York: New Museum, 1990. 19–36.

Williams, Phyllis H. *South Italian Folkways in Europe and America: A Handbook for Social Workers, Visiting Nurses, School Teachers, and Physicians*. New York: Russell, 1938.

Wittke, Carl. "Melting-Pot Literature." *College English* 7.4 (Jan. 1946): 189–197.

Wong, Sau-ling Cynthia. "Immigrant Autobiography: Some Questions of Definition and Approach." *Women, Autobiography, Theory: A Reader*. Ed. Sidonie Smith and Julia Watson. Madison: University of Wisconsin Press, 1998. 299–315.

Yeager, Patricia. "Editor's Column: The End of Postcolonial Theory? A Roundtable with Sunil Agnani, Fernando Coronil, Gaurav Desai, Mamadou Diouf, Simon Gikandi, Susie Tharu, and Jennifer Wenzel." *PMLA*. 122.3 (May 2007): 633–651.

Yezierska, Anzia. "Soap and Water." 1920. *Imagining America: Stories from the Promised Land*. Ed. Wesley Brown and Amy Ling. New York: Persea, 1991. 105–110.

Young, Robyn. "Barre's Anarchists." *Times Argus* 22 Sept. 1989: 3A+.

Index

family over individual, 115; belief in transplantation of immigrants through assimilation, 7; creation of representational characters by, 112; disconnect from family origins, 142; establishment of rural/urban dialectic by, 7, 96, 104; exploration of American emphasis on individualism, 98; giving voice to disenfranchised immigrants, 104; *Hills Beyond Manhattan,* 106–108; idea-driven narratives by, 97; inclusion of Italian cultural values in stories, 98; interest in fusion of Italian American identity with love of land, 103; *My Enemy, The World,* 95, 100, 108–113; *Olives on the Apple Tree,* 7, 96–98, 103–105, 108, 116, 181, 245*n1,* 263*n*11; portrayal of smaller enclaves of immigrants, 98; tie to skilled labor, 96–97; World War II experiences, 247*n12*

D'Agostino, Peter, 41, 240*n5*
D'Alfonso, Antonio, 167
Dangarembga, Tsitsi, 214
D'Angelo, Pascal, 45
A Day in San Francisco (Bryant), 195–199, 200
Death: acceptance of, 54; aftermath of, 178; attitudinal changes toward, 177; characterizations of, 176; continuities beyond, 176; deathbed scenes, 179–190; definition, 178; father-daughter relations in, 186–190; guilt for living, 191; humanity through, 175; invisible, 177; modern attitudes, 178; mourning and, 175, 176, 258*n1,* 260*n13*; narrative, 204–209; nostalgia and, 185; occupational causes, 179, 183, 184; portrayals of in Italian American literature, 176; premodern, 177, 186; relationships changing, 208; as result of indifferent business practice, 22; reunion fantasies in, 180; as story of continuity, 208;

talking about, 175–209; tame, 177, 182, 185; *via dolorosa* scenes, 184; widow's lamentations and, 190–203
Death's Door (Gilbert), 178, 190, 191, 198, 203
DeLamotte, Eugenia, 128, 133, 138
DeLillo, Don, 142, 204, 230
"DeLillo" (Russo), 40, 41
Denniston, Dorothy, 120, 121, 123, 127, 128, 134, 136, 252*n14,* 253*n18*
De Rosa, Gabriele, 41, 239*n3*
De Rosa, Tina, 7, 12, 119–140, 232, 251*n7,* 251*n9,* 254*n22*; adherence to Italian view of private justice by, 29; apprenticed by immigrants in storytelling, 125; "Breaking the Silence," 122; *campanilismo* and, 233; exploration of costs of transplantation for first-generation immigrants, 122; family precedence over legal system and, 28; focus on communities, 138; focus on Italian female power, 53, 54; identity constructions and, 123; importance of elders in teaching family generations, 30; interpretation of *festa,* 54; literary experimentalism of, 215; "My Father's Lesson," 30; *Paper Fish,* 29, 30, 53–56, 120, 206, 213, 214, 252*n13,* 255*n3*; on possession of authority, 54; reinforcement of private justice by, 28; representations of outside authority by, 31; resistance to hegemonic American culture, 215; use of processional ceremonies in stories, 51
DeSalvo, Louise, 8, 146, 147, 152, 159, 172, 173, 214, 255*n3*; acceptance of instability of family members, 149; addresses mental illness, 149; *Crazy in the Kitchen,* 173; creative revisionism of, 146; differing from school girl narratives of other Italian American writers, 147; nonlinear narrative style, 153; open discussion of sexuality by, 150, 151; references to rage, 152; regards family as fundamental